The Earth Brought Forth

A History of Minnesota Agriculture to 1885

By Merrill E. Jarchow

Minnesota Historical Society · St. Paul
1949

Copyright 1949 by the
MINNESOTA HISTORICAL SOCIETY
St. Paul

FOR MY MOTHER

An Appreciation

This book is one of the Centennial projects sponsored by the Committee on Agriculture for the Minnesota Territorial Centennial. May it not only live as a memorial to those who pioneered and builded throughout the past century of Minnesota's development, but also may it serve as a reminder of the fact that there still are builders and pioneers who will give of their time and efforts in the interest of the public good as manifest through the many civic leaders who have served on the hundreds of Centennial committees throughout this birthday year.

The publication of this book has been made possible by the generous contributions of several Minnesota concerns interested in Minnesota's agriculture. Their generous support merits the warmest admiration and appreciation. It is typical of the spirit through which this nation has grown and in which the hopes of the years ahead find strength.

The Agricultural Committee appreciates most deeply the contribution by Dr. Merrill Jarchow. Through his research and his authorship of this book he has given to those who follow the opportunity better to understand what has gone before. As we know where we have been and where we are going, we may know the better what to do.

J. O. CHRISTIANSON, *Chairman*
Committee on Agriculture for the
Minnesota Territorial Centennial

Foreword

To a sharp-eyed English observer the American Midwest seems to be at noon, and others describe it as having "come of age." Noontide and age mean maturity, a characteristic mark of which is the mood of retrospect and appraisal. No little impetus has been given to that mood, I think, by the centennials and other anniversaries celebrated of late in this American region. People are looking backward, around, and forward, and everybody senses the almost incredible change, the extraordinary metamorphosis, that time and circumstance have wrought.

There in the past, a wilderness unseen of white men — today the spacious cultivated garden of millions. There in the past, small and humble beginnings — today great achievement in things material and of the spirit. There in the past, hope surviving hardship and discomfort — today pioneer dreams come true.

Dr. Jarchow presents a major part of this modern metamorphosis — too often described only in general, if generous, phrase — in *The Earth Brought Forth,* and he does it in meticulous and fascinating detail.

His book is a major contribution not only to Minnesota in its Centennial year, but to national understanding of American agricultural history. Here, for a great American region, is the basic story of land and people, machines and crops. Here is the record of King Wheat and his temporarily obedient servants. And in these pages, that not wholly benevolent tyrant, after his brief day of glory, totters on his throne.

This book tells of public lands and their disposal, of experiments by ingenious farmers at society's roots, of harvests and markets, transportation, elevators and milling, malpractices and legal reforms, buildings and agricultural fairs, advancing mechanization, widening knowledge of farming — all fitted into a comprehensive narrative of a great far-reaching industry.

If the author had done nothing more than set forth in precise detail, as he has done, this catena of economic factors and forces, his contribution would be notable, but it achieves distinction through its underlying emphasis upon the people who built the farms of Minnesota — and their changing way of life.

The author never forgets that farmers are people — people living their lives, doing their work, meeting hardships, tasting achievement, dreaming dreams, knowing joy and sorrow. The farmer had a home — Dr. Jarchow takes us into it. The farmer played his part in the social and religious life of his community — Dr. Jarchow makes it vivid for us. The farmer had a wife — Dr. Jarchow introduces us to her. The farmer had children — Dr. Jarchow pictures them, even the barefoot boy, so often recalled only in nostalgic and romantic terms, but here remembered as being "next to hell" when he walked or ran across burned-over prairie or woods. And the farmer had a name — Dr. Jarchow presents us to Levi Countryman, Andrew Peterson, Ole Hedman, Martha Gilpatrick, and many another.

Behind these pages — see the footnotes that march by after the text — are farmers' diaries, letters, journals, ledgers, newspapers, magazines, recollections, and many other kinds of records which the author has combed over in his probing researches of many years. They testify to the integrity of the text. In clear, simple prose Dr. Jarchow shares with us the results of his patient and impressive scholarship on the farmer's saga. He has written a book of absorbing interest that deserves a wide audience in state and nation.

THEODORE C. BLEGEN

Preface

Agriculture was one of the principal pillars of Minnesota's territorial economy; it is a major segment of the state's economy today. Hence, it is only fitting that a large part of the Centennial activities should be focused upon and centered around the farmer, his interests and his way of life. The present volume is an attempt in a small way to commemorate the struggles, ordeals, sorrows, joys, and achievements of those pioneers who established Minnesota farming on a firm foundation and who adapted it to its own distinctive environment.

The story does not end, of course, with the period covered by this book. But the middle 1880's may be considered as the end of the formative period in the history of Minnesota agriculture. By that time specialized wheat farming — typical of a frontier area — was at an end in the older, southeastern section of the state, and diversified farming and dairying were well established. By the 1880's the major laws under which the farmer received his land had been enacted, and thousands of new farm homes, surrounded by substantial barns, sheds, corncribs, and granaries, had been erected. The early struggles of the Minnesota State Agricultural Society were over, and the state fair had found a permanent location. Railroad and grain marketing malpractices had been curbed to a large extent. Gasoline tractors, all-crop harvesters, hay balers, and corn-picking machines were still in the future, but the farmer had made great advances in mechanization. The Red River Valley had begun to pour its great wheat harvests into the granaries of the world. Minneapolis mills and St. Paul stockyards offered thriving and accessible markets, and railroads and a growing network of country roads reduced the transportation problem. A larger and denser population offered increasing social advantages. All was not sweetness and light by any means — witness the Grange movement of the 1870's and the Alliance movement of the 1880's — but the agriculture of the state had been placed on a sound footing by 1885 and its future course had been accurately charted.

Many persons have given generously of their time and counsel to make this study possible. Foremost should be mentioned Dean Theodore C. Blegen of the Graduate School of the University of Minnesota, who has served the author as a friend, teacher, adviser, and critic for nearly two decades. The staff of the Minnesota Historical Society, especially Mary W. Berthel, Bertha L. Heilbron, Lois M. Fawcett, Lucile M. Kane, and Willoughby M. Babcock have spared no effort to help. Only those who have participated in the production of a book can appreciate the author's debt to Mrs. Berthel, who edited the book and guided it through the press. Miss Heilbron has been of immeasurable service. Six of the chapters of the book appeared in modified form in *Minnesota History* under her careful editing, and some of the other chapters include items she unearthed. Dean Julius M. Nolte of the University of Minnesota Extension Division and director of the Minnesota Territorial Centennial, and J. O. Christianson, principal of the School of Agriculture at the University Farm and a member of the Centennial agricultural committee, first approached the author and suggested the writing of this book. Its publication has been made possible largely through the efforts of this committee. President Laurence M. Gould of Carleton College has been helpful and co-operative, as well as indulgent, and my colleague, Dr. Carlton C. Qualey, has given constant encouragement and advice. Another colleague, Professor Ralph L. Henry, gave the proofs the benefit of his long experience in the publication field. My former secretary, Marcia Cralle, merits special mention. She aided greatly by typing the rough draft of the manuscript and by keeping the office running smoothly, thereby saving the author time for research and writing. To all these people, and to others, I am sincerely grateful.

MERRILL E. JARCHOW

Northfield, Minnesota

Contents

A BIRD'S-EYE VIEW 3

A POWERFUL DETERMINANT 27

SETTLERS AND SPECULATORS 41

FREE LAND AND RAILROADS 61

THE FARMER'S HOME 80

RURAL SOCIAL LIFE 100

TOWARD MECHANIZATION 120

MECHANIZATION GAINS MOMENTUM 131

MECHANIZATION TAKES ON MODERN ASPECTS 148

WHEAT: KING OR TYRANT? 165

LIVESTOCK 188

THE BEGINNINGS OF DAIRYING 207

BIZARRE EXPERIMENTS AND SOUND AGRICULTURE 222

EARLY AGRICULTURAL SOCIETIES AND FAIRS 245

Illustrations

A PIONEER FARM	7
AN IMMIGRANT TRAIN IN A WESTERN TOWN	20
PHYSICAL FEATURES OF MINNESOTA	36
A COLONISTS' RECEPTION HOUSE	76
EDWARD B. DREW'S FARM IN WINONA COUNTY	98
A COUNTRY STORE AT FOUNTAIN	107
THRESHING WITH HORSEPOWER	128
A MCCORMICK SELF-RAKING REAPER	133
HARVESTING ON A DAKOTA COUNTY FARM	136
MOHAWK VALLEY STEEL CLIPPER PLOW	139
TWO-HORSE POWER THRESHER AND CLEANER	143
A DRILL IN OPERATION	145
STEEL-TOOTH SELF-DELIVERING HORSE HAY RAKE	147
AN ELWARD SELF-BINDING HARVESTER	150

A MARSH HARVESTER 152

ST. PAUL HARVESTER WORKS 159

FARM MACHINERY DEPOT AND FEED STORE AT ROCHESTER . . 162

A FLOUR MILL AT FILLMORE 168

A BONANZA FARM 177

BERKSHIRE BOAR "GEN. HANCOCK" 196

CHARLES A. DE GRAFF'S FARM IN WASECA COUNTY 198

PERCHERON NORMAN STALLION 201

SHORTHORN COW "BLUSH" 204

EARLY DAIRYING EQUIPMENT 209, 217, 218

A CHEESE FACTORY AT EYOTA 212

WILLIAM S. KING'S FARM IN MEEKER COUNTY 255

The Earth Brought Forth

A Bird's-eye View

Agriculture in the usual sense of the term did not exist in the region now known as Minnesota when the first federal census of agriculture was taken in 1840, although some small farming operations were carried on quite early at fur-trading posts, missionary stations, Indian agencies, and lumber camps. Probably the first agricultural locality to be settled was southern Washington County, and the first farmers were Joseph Haskell and James S. Norris, who settled on their claim near Afton in 1840. In the spring of that year, they turned three acres of sod in six days, and planted the ground to corn and potatoes. These three acres comprised the first farm north of Prairie du Chien. Haskell remained a bachelor in his cabin for ten years, baking his own bread on a barn shovel—a *new* shovel, according to his son—during much of the time; while Norris, in 1841, took up a new claim in Cottage Grove, and in 1845, he married Haskell's sister, Sophia Jane.[1]

Gradually more settlers came to the Cottage Grove region to open farms. One of the early comers was William R. Brown, who arrived in 1841 and kept a diary in 1845 and 1846 telling of his farming experiences. Most of this early farming was of the self-sufficient type, since markets and marketing facilities were lacking. Brown's wife made the soap for the family, as did most pioneer women, while Brown himself dressed the pork and pickled the beef for home use. A little produce, however, was sold. On February 26, 1846, Brown noted in his diary that he had sold one hundred bushels of oats at fifty cents a bushel at Fort Snelling, and, on March 2, 1846, that he had sold eggs in St. Paul at thirty-seven and a half cents a dozen. These early farmers, like later settlers, co-operated in building cabins, looking for lost livestock, exchanging seed, and harvesting crops. Interestingly enough, in addition to the ever-present corn, oats, and potatoes, a considerable variety of crops was grown, including wheat, barley, cabbages, onions, rutabagas, turnips, lettuce, beets, parsnips, tomatoes, and carrots.[2]

On June 1, 1849, the organization of Minnesota Territory was formally proclaimed. Concerning that time, a century ago, William W. Folwell has written: "Of rural settlement there was but a bare beginning, on the beautiful prairie lands abutting on Lake St. Croix in Washington County. With the exception of the trifling amount of produce from these farms and a few gardens and of wild game, the whole subsistence of the white population was brought up from below by steamboats." And the census taken to comply with provisions of the Minnesota organic act lends support to Folwell's statement, since it indicates that the number of persons living in the part of Minnesota where agriculture predominated was under four hundred. In fact, the entire population of Minnesota Territory, which included large parts of the Dakotas as well as the area of the present state, was listed as 4,780, undoubtedly a padded figure. The population within the boundaries of the present state was given as 3,740, of which 2,879 lived east of the Mississippi.[3]

The next census was that taken in 1850 by the federal government, which gave the population as of 1850 and agricultural statistics as of 1849. The population within the area of the later state was subsequently estimated to be 5,354, of which 2,271 or 42 per cent, lived in St. Paul, St. Anthony, and Stillwater. Farmers numbered 340, probably an exaggeration; 28,881 acres were in farms, though only 5,035 acres were improved; and farms totaled 157. Again, the number of farms given was undoubtedly too large. Washington County was listed as having 48 farms, Benton County 20, and Ramsey County 19. Outside of these counties, farming had only meager beginnings. The average farm in the territory contained about 238 acres, of which 40 were improved. The cash value of the farms amounted to $161,948, or $1,031 per farm. Oats, potatoes, corn, peas, and beans, in that order of importance, accounted for 95 per cent of all crops produced.[4]

Because of the dependence of the territory upon outside regions for foodstuffs, there was a great need for more farmers. Nearly every issue of the early newspapers printed inducements to farmers to come to Minnesota. The *Minnesota Pioneer* gave this assurance to prospective agriculturists: "*There is no danger of glutting the market.* Cultivate all the land you can, all of you, a hundred farmers where we now have one, and you will all be secure of high prices for years to come. It is doubtful whether agriculture will *ever* overtake the other interests of Minnesota." Between 1850 and 1857, the population of the entire territory increased by about 144,000. Settlement pushed north of St. Anthony up the Mississippi River as far as Gull Lake, while south of St. Paul the west bank of the river became lined with villages, and many farms were opened along the tributary streams flowing from the west. From the beginning of 1854, when the railroad from Chicago reached Rock Island, until August, 1857, settlers came to Minnesota at the rate of about 35,000 a year, and most of them turned to farming. Many of these newcomers were foreign born, attracted to the area by promises of a better life than the one they had led in Europe. At an earlier period, the first foreign elements to come to Minnesota were French half-breeds, Scotch, Irish, and Swiss from Canada; but, by the late 1850's, the largest foreign group was German, followed by Scandinavian, British, and French. All these groups made real and distinct contributions to the life and agriculture of the state.[5]

Many of these first settlers were extremely poor when they arrived in Minnesota. T. R. Stewart of Caledonia, for example, tells that after his father had paid his hotel bill and the freight on his goods from Massachusetts he had thirty-three dollars left. This was all he had to build a house and support a family of five for a year, until returns could be expected from his land. When William A. Budd came to Minnesota in 1856, he had twelve hundred dollars; but by the time he had obtained his cattle from Iowa, as well as his provisions and supplies for the first year, he had two dollars and a half left. The parents of Forest Henry at Chatfield had only ten dollars to live on during the winter of 1857–58. Mrs. Mary Jane Hill Anderson, telling of a land sale in 1855, said: "Nearly everyone had to borrow the money, for they had not raised enough crops to sell much." And Harriet Griswold at Cambridge wrote to her father in 1856 that "the land sale comes off next week, and I must run the risk of loosing [sic] my claim." These were probably typical cases.⁶

One of the better farms opened during this period was the Larpenteur farm on the road between St. Paul and St. Anthony. During the spring and summer of 1852, Auguste L. Larpenteur, with the help of two sons, sowed thirty acres of oats, twelve of corn, ten of potatoes, an acre of beans, half an acre of vines, a large field of wheat, and a large garden. He also raised swine, twelve calves, hundreds of chickens, guinea hens, and turkeys. His farm was opened in 1849, and he achieved much success with potatoes and spring wheat, although he could not always find a market for his wheat.⁷

The Minnesota commissioner of statistics, J. W. McClung, in 1860 estimated that it cost $795 to open a farm, including the price of implements, provisions, oxen, cows, a team and wagon, breaking about twenty acres, and building a house and fence. A family with from five hundred to a thousand dollars had to practice strict economy for several years. One of the first tasks confronting the settler was to build a cabin, and during its construction his family often lived with a kind neighbor. Another was to break a little land for a crop. Many settlers did not know how to break land, and many had the wrong kind of plow. Others had no horses nor oxen, and they had to hire the job done. Early writers and farmers suggested June and July as the best time to break new land, and recommended plowing to a depth of only two or three inches. The cost of breaking prairie generally was from two and one-half to three dollars an acre, while that of preparing tree and brush land was, of course, more. John Willoughby of Newport estimated that it cost five dollars an acre to clear and break his tree and brush lands. Often, however, the first crop more than paid for the cost of breaking the land. Potatoes, corn, or rutabagas were the usual crops sown on newly broken land, corn often being inserted in an opening made with an ax in the sod. By the following spring the land would be ready for a wheat crop.⁸

After building a cabin, breaking some land, and planting a few crops, the pioneer frequently had to turn his attention to the problem of fencing, since until the late 1870's livestock was allowed to run at large. It was thus a question of fencing crops. Most fences were made of wood, either chopped by the farmer himself or obtained from a sawmill in exchange for farm produce. The building of one of these worm, or rail, fences was no easy chore. According

A PIONEER FARM
[From the *Independent Farmer*, 1:5 (January 1, 1879).]

to T. R. Stewart, it required 6,720 rails, fourteen to the rod, to fence eighty acres, while the job of splitting the rails took one man about sixty-seven days. Further, it required 1,920 stakes and 960 blocks for the support of such a fence. The actual construction of the fence could be accomplished by one man in sixteen days, but one ox might knock down part of it in a single night.[9]

Compared even with the humblest Minnesota farms of today, the pioneer farms were usually crude and primitive. As Christopher C.

Andrews wrote of one farm: "The whole establishment, one would think who was accustomed to the eastern style of living, betrayed downright poverty. But let us stop a moment; this is the home of a pioneer. He has been industrious, and everything about him exhibits forethought. There is a cornfield all fenced in with tamarack poles. It is paved over with pumpkins (for pumpkins flourish wonderfully in Minnesota), and contains twenty acres of ripe corn, which, allowing thirty-five bushels to an acre, is worth . . . $630." And Andrews goes on to point out that his pioneer raised potatoes worth $150.[10]

Thus, in spite of dilapidated appearances, some pioneer farms made money. Mrs. Mary Jane Anderson wrote that after two years the home of her family was paid for, they owed nothing, and they could spend a little money as the crops were being raised. One thing that helped them, however, was a near-by cranberry marsh from which they gathered berries worth a dollar a bushel. Surely none of the average settlers amassed sudden wealth. Even the Anderson family lived in their original log cabin from 1854 to 1872, and they knew something of the darker side of pioneer farming. Indeed, it seems easier to find contemporary adverse criticisms of the state's agriculture in the middle 1850's than to find the reverse. Said one Faribault County settler, writing on April 4, 1857: "It appears that there are not ten farms in the county of ten acres of plowed land; that the people are all poor and that nobody is doing anything and no one wanting to do anything, but . . . all are contented and happy in the prospects of the future." In a similar vein, a St. Paul newspaper reported in 1858 that "farming in Minnesota now is nothing more than a multitude of heterogeneous and isolated experiments, blindly pursued at the risk and often at the loss of individual farmers . . . until the present year a very subordinate attention was paid to farming, the interest of the community being principally absorbed in projects of speculation." Markets often were poor and sometimes as far as thirty or forty miles from a farm; grasshoppers were destructive in some regions in 1856 and 1857; mosquitoes were numerous; plant diseases wrought some damage; and weather conditions were not always favorable.[11]

A BIRD'S-EYE VIEW

Undoubtedly there was much speculation in Minnesota, as elsewhere in the United States, between 1855 and 1857, and people were more interested in rising land values than in farming. As a result, provisions were scarce and prices were high to consumers, who included most settlers during their first year before they raised a crop. In the summer of 1857, flour was priced at from $6.50 to $7.50 a barrel; corn cost $2.00 a sack; oats were from $1.00 to $1.10 a bushel; potatoes were listed at $1.40 a bushel; butter commanded from $.35 to $.40 a pound; fresh pork sold for $.20 a pound; veal was nearly as high—from $.15 to $.20 a pound; and good hay was scarce at from $50 to $60 a ton. But the hardest times were still ahead! In the fall of 1857 a financial panic, precipitated largely by land speculation, reached Minnesota, where grasshoppers and prairie fires had already worked havoc. Numerous banks failed and "wildcat" money nearly drove all other out of circulation. Stories were told of farmers who, having sold cattle for bank notes, found that the banks had failed before they could get to town with the notes. City and county scrip was issued in places, but much trade was by barter. As a rather typical example, Timothy Chapman told of his father-in-law's failure to sell enough of his one thousand bushels of oats and wheat and about thirty acres of corn for the cash to pay his taxes. Some people actually lost their land, which was sold for taxes; many farmers had to go without groceries; and a general feeling of anxiety gripped the population.[12]

The panic, however, was not without a good side. It brought about an abrupt end of speculation in town lots and the return of such land to agriculture. Land values were put on a more solid foundation, and people began to realize that artificial rises in land values did not necessarily bring wealth. There was an exodus from towns to farms, while many farmers on improved land went farther west in the state. Between 1857 and 1860, the amount of cultivated land doubled and quadrupled in some counties; and by 1859 mortgage indebtedness had taken a sharp downward trend. According to the Minnesota commissioner of statistics, the mortgage debt in fifteen counties was $22,553 in 1854; a year later it was $150,014; in 1856 it rose to $1,176,905; a year later it totaled $1,787,158; in 1858 it reached the peak of $2,124,071; and in 1859 it dropped to $1,211,303. These statistics should be correlated with changes in population and the rise in the number of farms, but such information is not available. Nevertheless, the statistics are of some value in portraying a trend. Population in the fifteen counties in 1859 was undoubtedly greater than it was in 1857, and yet the mortgage indebtedness in 1857 was greater than it was in 1859. No new debts were contracted after 1857, and so the debt of 1858 was the result of the conversion into mortgages of all debts previously existing in other forms, and that of 1859 represented the renewal of matured mortgages. Thus, while Minnesota suffered many hardships as a result of the economic depression, the state was in a sounder condition at the end of the panic than it was before. People turned away from speculation to production and, while prosperity did not come to the great mass of farmers, Minnesota by 1859 not only could feed its population, but it also could export much farm produce. In the words of Edward V. Robinson: "The close of the decade 1850–1860 saw the new state an agricultural community solidly planted upon the soil."[13]

Developments during the 1850's can be traced through the census of 1860. At the end of the decade there were sixty-four counties in the state, and the total population was 172,023, compared with 5,354 in the same area in 1850. Settlement was most dense along the navigable portions of the Mississippi, St. Croix, and Minnesota rivers. Three towns, St. Paul, St. Anthony, and Minneapolis, each had a population of over 2,500, which would now class them as urban, and Stillwater had 2,380 inhabitants. The rural population, numbering 122,530, represented an increase of more than 3,100 per cent for the 1850's, a relative increase greater than that for the total population. The number of farms in 1859 was 17,999, a percentage increase of over 11,300, about three times as great as that for the total population. Land in farms totaled 2,711,968 acres; improved land in farms was 556,250 acres, a 10,900 per cent increase for the decade; and improved land per farm was slightly less than in 1849—30.9 acres as against 32 acres. Farms themselves were also smaller in 1859, averaging 151 acres, nearly an 18 per cent decrease since 1849. The value of farms—land and buildings—increased by more than 16,800 per cent to a total of $27,505,922, and the value of livestock grew to $3,642,841. By way of summary, and without marshaling further statistics, it should be noted that the number of farms, the total field crops, and the value of farm property during the 1850's each increased about three times as fast as did the total population—good evidence of the strides made by agriculture in spite of and, to some extent, because of the panic of 1857.[14]

During the 1860's the first agricultural periodical published in the state made its appearance. It was the *Minnesota Farmer and Gardener,* edited and published monthly at St. Paul from November, 1860, through April, 1862, by L. M. Ford. Ford was secretary of the Minnesota State Agricultural Society, an organization that played a prominent part in establishing the journal. Many valuable articles appeared in the publication during its existence, which was all too short. War, hard times, and lack of interest on the part of many farmers resulted in its untimely demise. In January, 1862, the editor complained that he did not have the farmers' support, and he pointed out that, while Minnesota farmers said they were too poor to subscribe to the *Farmer and Gardener,* several thousand of them took eastern agricultural papers. Not one in ten of the officers of the county agricultural societies took and paid for the magazine, although it was offered to them at fifty cents a year.

The second farm journal in Minnesota was the *Farmers' Union,* which appeared in August, 1867. Its editor was John H. Stevens, one of the prominent agriculturists of his day, who, according to his own testimony, cleared, above cost and expenses, three thousand dollars a year on the paper. The panic of 1873, however, brought the *Union* to an end the next year.[15]

The next venture was the *Minnesota Monthly,* issued in thirteen numbers during 1869 and 1870. Daniel A. Robertson, one of the state's leading agriculturists and an ardent Granger, was the editor. Hence, it is easy to understand how the *Monthly* was developed as "The Official Organ and Advocate of the Patrons of Husbandry, a Rural Order which is rapidly increasing in usefulness."

Two other periodicals of general agricultural interest were started in Minnesota before 1880—the *Minnesota Farmer,* begun in 1877, and the *Independent Farmer and Fireside Companion,* which first appeared on New Year's Day, 1879. Reference to the footnotes of the present volume will prove conclusively how valuable these old farm papers are to the student of agricultural history. As Everett Edwards has truly said, they contain "a vast treasure trove of data which historians have failed to exploit to full advantage.... The multitudinous subjects dealt with in agricultural periodicals constitute an integral part not only of agricultural, but of general economic, social, and, to a less extent, political history."[16]

One of the subjects which quite naturally filled many pages in the *Farmer and Gardener* was the effect of the Civil War on agriculture. In September, 1861, that periodical reported that some farmers were short of help and were compelled to pay high wages, but as a general thing there was no more inconvenience than usual. Very few harvest hands had turned soldiers as yet, while more and more farm machinery was being utilized, and immigrants, potential farm workers, were pouring into the state at the rate of fifteen thousand a year. But there is some evidence that the war did result in a certain labor shortage. In August, 1861, Oliver H. Kelley, of Grange fame, wrote: "I must lay the want of help to keep the weeds down to Jeff Davis." J. C. Mills, writing about Fillmore County, said that the war took able-bodied men, leaving invalids, old men, women, and children to operate the farms as best they could. And G. W. Allyn, in his reminiscences of Blue Earth County, told of the "women doing most of the farm work." It is probably correct to say, however, that the Civil War did not effect a serious labor shortage in the state.[17]

Minnesota's progress in agriculture between 1861 and 1865 was truly remarkable, but it is difficult to say whether it came because of the war or in spite of it. The production of wheat nearly doubled between 1860 and 1865, despite the Indian outbreak of 1862 and a severe drought in 1862 and 1863, and Minnesota agriculture became far more commercialized than it had been before 1860. Much new land was being taken up, some of it under the terms of the Homestead Act passed in 1862. In 1863, a total of 463,296 acres was claimed by settlers; in 1864, claims amounted to 665,750 acres, and in 1865, to

804,982. In postwar years this rate of increase was not maintained.[18]

One thing that the war did affect was the course of prices. In the winter of 1861, prices for farmers' produce of all kinds generally were very low. Wheat averaged about $.50 a bushel; butter ranged from $.06 to $.15 a pound; hay sold for from $2.00 to $4.50 a ton; eggs were around $.06 a dozen; poultry often could not be disposed of at any price; and hogs brought from $2.50 to $3.00 a hundredweight. Farmers were hopeful, however. They felt that the war, plus European demand, would cause a big rise in prices. But the rise did not come as soon as expected, and there was much disappointment in the state, which was admitted by the *Farmer and Gardener* in January, 1862: "All are sorely disappointed, and ourselves among the rest. What the prices will be another year, we shall not be in a hurry to decide." Farmers were advised to sell off their crops, even at the lower prices, and with the new year to resolve to keep out of debt by living in accordance with the times. The main reasons given for the low prices were the high freights from Chicago to the seaboard and the immense production of wheat. Chicago and Milwaukee on March 1, 1862, for example, had more than eight million bushels of grain in store.[19]

As the war progressed prices did begin to go up, largely as a result of paper money inflation. From 1861 on, gold and silver grew more scarce and finally disappeared. In July of that year the *Farmer and Gardener* reported that "they are paying gold for wheat, although the price is not so high as when currency or 'stump tail' was taken." Many western banks failed in the summer of 1861, and their money became worthless. Hence, the newspaper column containing a list of the banks of issue with the ever-changing value of their currency was read avidly. In November, 1862, George Biscoe of Cottage Grove wrote to his sister: "I find that I have bills on 19 different banks. Most of them are New England banks, a few New York, and one New Jersey. Only two or three of the Minnesota banks and those small ones. I told Eliza I ought to have a Bank note detector." During the last years of the war and for a year or so after it, if someone happened to have a dime or a quarter to exhibit a crowd soon gathered to see the curious relic. Greenbacks and state bank notes appear to have been the most common money used during the war. Minnesota was slow to take advantage of the National Banking Act of 1863, for only two national banks were chartered in the state before March, 1865.[20]

By July of 1863, the price of wheat was up to between $.75 and $.80 a bushel in St. Paul, oats were $.50 a bushel, flour sold for from $7.00 to $7.50 a barrel, and poultry brought $.10 a pound. In 1864, prices went even higher and, as a result, a St. Paul newspaper published an editorial headed, "Plant! Plant! Plant!" Farmers were enlightened about the national debt and told that it would swallow up a quarter of the assessed value of all property in the United States. Too many farmers in the state, it was said, contented themselves with holding 160 acres of land, stripping it of its timber, and living in expectation of a rise in real estate. Now they were urged to go to work, for "this calamitous war, either as the real or assumed cause, has swelled the prices of the commonest products till they almost rival in value the fabulous golden fruits of Hesperides. When wheat commands a ready, firm price of from 90¢ to $1.00 a bushel—oats 80¢—corn $1.15 to $1.20—potatoes 80¢ to 90¢, and when onions are considered cheap at $2.50 to $3.00 a bushel, certainly even the most avaricious cannot complain that farming in Minnesota does not pay." In July, 1864, Biscoe's wife wrote: "George has been to the store this evening and returning announced gold to be at 325. Is that not startling for those who live on their $500 a year? Common brown sugar is 30¢ per pound." And, in January, 1865, flour was more than $8.00 a barrel, wheat brought from $1.00 to $1.25 a bushel, corn sold for from $1.00 to $1.10, oats for $.75, eggs for $.30 a dozen, butter prices were from $.25 to $.30 a pound, tea cost from $1.50 to $2.00 a pound, and the price of beans was from $2.75 to $3.00 a bushel. But, as the war neared its end, prices came down somewhat. In March, 1865, Biscoe wrote: "I was very glad to learn this morning that the price of some of the necessaries of life was coming down." Thus prices behaved during the Civil War much as they did during later wars. It is difficult to say whether the farmer benefited to any great extent by the rise in prices, since higher prices of farm commodities were accompanied by higher costs of things purchased by farmers. Certainly many farmers incurred indebtedness in expanding their operations, particularly in wheat farming, and so mortgaged their futures. Later they were faced with the prospect of paying off their debts in a period of low prices and deflation. Further, the war resulted in burdening agriculture with higher taxes and a permanent tariff.[21]

In addition to wheat farming, some other branches of agriculture received an impetus because of the war. Sorghum and tobacco growing were tried, but with no great success. Quite a little pork was packed for the army, but swine production was held back because of the high price of grain and the small amount of corn produced in the state. The main interest in livestock in the later years of the war centered on sheep, because of the high price of wool brought about by army demands. The height of the sheep craze came in 1866, after which there was a decline of interest, since the hopes of many farmers were not realized.[22]

Taking it all in all, large numbers of Minnesota farmers lived through the years from 1861 to 1865 rather undisturbed by events of the war. According to Henry V. Arnold of Houston County, "During the continuance of the Civil War the prairie people were influenced thereby merely in the way that great events, transpiring far away, would be apt to affect any country community." Of all the farmers' diaries in the collections of the Minnesota Historical Society, only that of John R. Cummins, who lived near Eden Prairie, makes many comments about the war. In January, 1861, Cummins noted that there was deep feeling in his neighborhood against the separation of the states. Again, in April, he wrote: "There will be fighting times down South, they are in open rebellion, and it is the duty of the President to put it down. I would as soon go as stay." But he must have had a change of heart, for he did not enlist. When, in June, 1864, he learned that he had been drafted, it was a serious blow. "It is a good deal of injustice to compel one to go now," he complained. After going to Shakopee and St. Paul to see what he could do about the "cursed draft," and failing to find a substitute, he paid the three hundred dollars required of those drafted who did not want to serve.[23]

During the Civil War years two laws of importance to the agricultural interests of the state, in addition to the Homestead Act, were passed by Congress. One of these, enacted in 1862, established the federal Department of Agriculture, and Isaac Newton of Pennsylvania was chosen as the first commissioner of the department. Newton was not popular, and Minnesota newspapers printed numerous derisive articles about him. In 1862 also was passed the Land Grant College Act, allowing to each state federal lands to aid in establishing colleges of agriculture and mechanic arts.[24]

As early as 1858 a serious effort was made to establish a state agricultural college in Minnesota, when a bill to that effect passed the legislature. Concerning the plan, the St. Paul *Pioneer and Democrat* was enthusiastic: "It will be a glorious record for Minnesota, the youngest of her sisters in the confederacy, to send greeting that she has taken the initiative in the establishment of an Agricultural College." Evidently, however, it was mainly the overconfidence and optimism of a young state that prompted the attempt to create such a college, for, in October, 1858, Henry H. Sibley, addressing the Dakota County Agricultural Association at Nininger, said that the state's finances were too limited as yet to start the school, which it was hoped would be located at Glencoe. Nevertheless, in April, 1859, John S. Prince, chairman of the executive committee of the state agricultural society, advertised for bids for the erection of the proposed Glencoe college and, in June, the president and the executive committee of the society visited Glencoe to choose a location for it.[25]

The citizens of that community naturally wanted the school, and they subscribed liberally in land and money. The legislature placed the school in charge of the society, which elected a "Board of Education for the State Agricultural College," with John H. Stevens as president. The project made little headway in 1860, but in 1861 Stevens reported that ten thousand dollars had already been subscribed; that the state had purchased three hundred and twenty acres of land for thirty-five hundred dollars; and that all other expenses would have to be borne by the state. In April of the latter year it was reported that the contract for the erection of the building would have been completed had not Governor Alexander Ramsey been in Washington. The contractor, Edward White, was confident construction would start, and he had gone to Peoria, Illinois, for his family. Then the war and the Indian uprising of 1862, plus interest in the Morrill Land Grant College Act, delayed action at Glencoe. After the war, a correspondent in a St. Paul newspaper said that the agricultural college lay buried under a fog. It excited the interest of only a few people, although land had been donated for it and five thousand dollars had been appropriated by the legislature to start it. In 1866, Governor Stephen Miller, in his inaugural address, suggested that it might be best to unite the agricultural college with a normal school. As a result, the legislature of that year repealed the grant of five thousand dollars for the Glencoe college. The legislature of 1868 passed an act to unite the farm school with the state university and to remove the school to St. Anthony. At the same session a conditional grant was made to "Stevens' Seminary," to be located at Glencoe. Thus was ended all hope of locating the agricultural college at Glencoe, but the efforts made to erect such a college were early evidence of a desire to advance the study of scientific agriculture in the state.[26]

During the last half of the 1860's the population of the state increased by 189,607, or almost 38,000 per year, to a total in 1870 of 439,706. Of this total, 327,698 persons were classed as rural, representing a gain of 167.4 per cent in the country population between 1860 and 1870, somewhat greater than that for the total population. By 1870, however, there were eleven municipalities, each having a population of at least 2,500, and the late 1860's were not particularly prosperous years for the average farmer. The peak of prices was reached in 1866, after which deflation and overproduction led to a decline. In 1866, for example, the average price of wheat in New York was $2.19 a bushel, while in 1869 it was $.94. In Minnesota a similar decline occurred, wheat at Waseca on November 15, 1869, for instance, being listed at $.57 for number 1, and $.52 for number 2. High transportation charges, war in Europe, unfavorable weather conditions, and plant diseases further complicated the situation in Minnesota. The wheat crop of 1866 was light because of "the blight," and that of 1867 was hit by excessive moisture, rain "reigning supreme" until the middle of July. In 1868 the summer was hot and dry and prices were low, while in 1869 the harvest was reduced by blight, rust, rain, and high wind.[27]

The status of agriculture at the end of the 1860's is evident in the United States census report of 1870. Farming was still carried on mainly in the hardwood region, lack of transportation facilities and of fuel holding back the settlement of the prairie region. The principal farming communities in the north were found in Stearns and Douglas counties, in the hardwood belt on the route to the Red River Valley. In the coniferous forest areas agriculture was practically nonexistent. The aggregate value of farm products was reported by the census for the first time in 1870, and the figures reveal that agriculture in the 1860's developed chiefly south of Anoka and east of Brown County. The number of farms between 1860 and 1870 increased from 17,999 to 46,500, and their average size decreased from 150.7 to 139.4 acres. Unimproved land in farms increased 93.1 per cent, but improved land increased more than three times as fast. Thus, there was more improved land in farms for every one hundred of the country population in 1870 than there had been in 1860. In the words of Robinson: "It follows, therefore, that, in spite of the movement of the population westward, the principal agricultural development of the decade was a more complete use of the land, the average improved acreage per farm being 49.9 in 1870, against 30.9 in 1860." The value of farms, land, and buildings increased by 255.7 per cent during the 1860's to $97,847,442; the value of implements and machinery advanced to $6,721,120, representing a gain for the decade of 560.1 per cent; and the value of livestock grew to $20,118,841, or 452.3 per cent. Hence, all these factors developed more rapidly than did the country population. The census, however, suggested reducing the above currency values by 20 per cent in order to arrive at gold values. When this reduction is made, it is found that the percentage increase in farm values for the 1860's was only 184.6. Thus, farm values did not keep pace with farm improvements, and an indication was given of approaching depression in agriculture.[28]

A BIRD'S-EYE VIEW

During the decade of the 1870's, depression did strike agriculture, as it did other branches of economic life. In 1873 occurred a severe financial panic, the result of years of speculation, especially in railroad securities. A panic on the Vienna exchange in May, 1873, caused Europeans to liquidate large American holdings on New York, and this strain proved more than the shaky financial structure of the United States could stand. Finally, on September 18, the Philadelphia banking firm of Jay Cooke and Company, "the Gibraltar of American finance," collapsed, precipitating panic and a rush of liquidation. Bankruptcies followed with startling rapidity, and wholesale farm prices took a disastrous tumble.[29]

While the effects of the panic were felt more severely in the East, they were not negligible in Minnesota. John Edgar wrote from Rochester on October 20: "Our prospect through the immediate region has not been so good since I have been here, as it was before Jay Cooke and Co. tumbled over. But the panic struck us and stopped everything." In a similar vein John Rhodes in Hastings reported: "It is fearful hard times for many in this section of the country, and there will be no report of collections for May 1873 as there should be." However, by late 1873 both men reported that the panic was subsiding somewhat, although "everything has been thrown back."[30]

But the panic of 1873 was not the only foe which the Minnesota farmer had to combat in this period. From 1873 until 1877 large portions of the state were scourged by grasshoppers, and to a lesser extent by chinch bugs, blizzards, prairie fires, and plant diseases. There was, however, a brighter side to the picture. A growing urban population and the development of new milling processes during the decade furnished new and expanding markets to the farmer, and improved transportation facilities made it possible for him to get his products to these markets more rapidly than formerly.[31]

Between 1870 and 1880 the population of Minnesota increased from 439,706 to 780,773, a gain of 77.6 per cent. The increase was considerable in the first half of the decade, the population being 597,279 in 1875, but it was even greater in the second half, probably because of the effect of the new milling processes. By 1880 the bulk of the population was still found east and south of Stearns County, although settlement had extended west and northwest to the boundaries of the state, and settlement of the prairies was well under way. Nine counties in the southeastern section, from Mower and Fillmore to Dakota and Nicollet, had from 60 to 80 per cent of their total land area under tillage or otherwise improved for agriculture.

AN IMMIGRANT TRAIN IN A WESTERN TOWN
[From the *Independent Farmer*, 1:126 (June 1, 1879).]

On the west and northwest frontiers the percentage of such land was much less, while east of the Mississippi only Washington and Ramsey counties had as much as 20 per cent of their land improved.[32]

Even a superficial study of Minnesota agriculture in the 1870's leads to the conclusion that farming was relatively unprofitable during that period, and a study of the census statistics of 1880 bears out this conclusion. For one thing, the rush to the cities was beginning. The absolute increase of the country population was greater in the 1870's than that of the urban population, but the relative increase was 105.3 per cent for urban and 72 per cent for rural population. Indeed, farm population did not increase in the same ratio as total acreage in farms or acreage of improved lands. Total land in farms grew from 6,483,828 acres in 1870 to 13,403,019 in 1880, a percentage increase of 106.7; and improved land in farms increased by 212.1 per cent during the same period, from 2,322,102 to 7,246,693 acres. The main factors responsible for the discrepancy between growth of farm population and that of farm acreage were the increased use of farm machinery and the multiplication of large farms. These two factors also resulted in larger production of farm products; wheat production, for example, was 83 per cent greater in 1880 than in 1870. The average size of farms grew from 139.4 acres to 145.1 acres, and the total number of farms between 1870 and 1880 increased from 46,500 to 92,386, a gain of 98.7 per cent.[33]

But the value of farm products between 1870 and 1880 did not keep pace with the increased technical efficiency of production. For example, the value of farm products in 1880, as reported by the federal census, was $49,468,951, a percentage gain of only 47.9 for the preceding decade. Further, the value of farms, including fences and buildings, showed a gain of only 98 per cent, from $97,847,442 in 1870 to $193,724,260 in 1880. As indicated earlier, values in 1870 were inflated, but even when gold values are used, the percentage increases of the value of farms, of livestock, and of farm products during the decade were only 147.5, 98.2, and 87.1, respectively. Beside these percentages should be placed the percentage increases in the value of farm machinery and in the acreage of improved land during the same period, 143.4 and 212.1, respectively. Hence, it is apparent that there was a decline during the decade in the value of farm products per acre, and that farm values did not advance as rapidly as did the acreage of improved land. The major cause of this condition was the overproduction of farm products, especially wheat, and the resultant downward trend of prices. If the farmer could find some consolation during the 1870's, it was in the fact that farm values and acres in farms increased more rapidly than did the rural population, thus allowing him to accumulate something through a rise in land values. Also on the brighter side was the growing diversification of agriculture, a movement which resulted during the early 1880's in increased prosperity for those farmers who took part in it.[34]

Before concluding this general survey of the farmer's economic status in early Minnesota, it seems wise to mention three payments on the debit side of the farm ledger—interest payments, insurance premiums, and taxes. During the territorial period the legal rate of interest was five per cent a month, an extremely high rate. By the middle 1870's it was still one per cent a month; and, as one journal said in 1879: "Our farmers are being eaten up with high rates of interest. . . . In Southern Minnesota, and indeed throughout the State, our farmers are terribly mortgaged at 12 per cent, and this is creating ruin in every direction." At that time Illinois, Iowa, Michigan, and Wisconsin did not allow interest charges of more than ten per cent a year. Many people in Minnesota felt that the farmer should insist on eight per cent annually as the maximum.[35]

Before the 1880's much, if not most, of the fire insurance on Minnesota farms was carried by big stock companies, such as the St. Paul Fire and Marine Insurance Company and the Continental of Hartford, Connecticut. The insurance man, like the peddler and the lightning-rod salesman, was a familiar figure on the country roads. As early as the middle 1860's, however, there were a few harbingers of a new era in which the old-line companies would be supplanted by local mutual companies. The Minnesota Farmers' Mutual Fire Insurance Association, started in 1865 and incorporated in 1867, was one of these forerunners of the new day. W. A. Nimocks, editor of the *Farmers' Union,* was secretary of the association, whose membership in 1869 was over four thousand. The group claimed to insure at the rate of seventeen cents for a thousand dollars. In 1873 the Minnesota State Grange took steps toward absorbing the association and appointed a special committee to investigate the plan. In December of that year the committee reported that fifteen thousand farmers were insured, that one hundred thousand dollars had been paid out in losses, and that the association insured at one-third the usual cost. But the executive committee of the Grange reported that the association was financially unsound, as it had only $50,762.15 on hand to meet policies covering $9,622,084; and it condemned the management of the company.[36]

More soundly managed was the German Farmers' Mutual Fire Insurance Company, organized in Washington County in March, 1867, by German farmers who had picked up the idea of mutual aid in New York and in the fatherland. Dues were twenty-five cents a member and the rate of insurance was twenty-five cents per one hundred dollars. During the first year no policies were issued; the directors wrote insurance for the members and kept their records in a little book. No loss was incurred until 1873, when one of the members suffered a two-hundred-dollar fire damage. The next year the company took an interesting action, when it voted to pay no insurance if a fire was caused by a steam thresher. In 1879 the group incorporated under the state law, and in 1880 agents were hired to handle the expanding business. Until the late 1890's cash on hand was lent to members at a yearly interest of seven per cent, considerably less than the current rate among private lenders. So well did the officers and directors handle their trust that the company is still in a flourishing condition.[37]

The opportunity to pay taxes has seldom aroused enthusiasm on the part of any people, and the average Minnesota farmer was no exception to the rule. Grumbling over tax assessments is no modern phenomenon. Before 1860 appraisements of property were left almost entirely to owners and assessors, and the results presented the grossest inequalities. To remedy this situation the legislature of 1860 passed an act creating county and state boards of equalization. In the same year the appraised value of real estate returned was $27,947,290, an amount equalized by the state board to a total of $32,026,303. The average rates of taxes on a one-dollar valuation levied in the state in 1859, exclusive of city taxes, were as follows: state, 5 mills; school, 2.5 mills; county, 7.5 mills; and town and road, 2.5 mills. Delinquent taxes due the state from the counties for several years up to December 1, 1859, were $149,790.67.[38]

In 1862 the passage of the Homestead Act raised a taxation problem. Some people thought a homestead should be tax exempt until the patent for the land passed to the settler, while others felt that the settler should pay taxes during the first year he settled on his claim. In the face of this argument the state auditor on June 16, 1863, ordered that homestead land be placed on the assessment books. The action was sustained in several opinions by the attorney general of the state. As a result, homestead conventions held in many places passed resolutions opposing support for candidates for office who favored taxing homesteads. Finally, in 1869, the legislature passed an act providing for taxation of improvements on homesteads, but exempting from taxation "any *lands,* held or occupied by settlers under said act of Congress . . . so long as the fee of the same remains in the United States." The act proved a delusion as a relief measure, however, since the improvements on a homestead and "the interest of the claimant therein" could be taxed, and the last cow of the settler could be taken for taxes.[39]

During the middle part of the Civil War, the tax levied in Waseca County was about the same as that levied in 1859. It totaled seventeen mills on the dollar, of which twelve and one-half mills were for county and four and one-half for state purposes. By the end of the war taxes had gone up somewhat. In 1868, for example, the farmer near Rochester found his state tax rate six mills, but in 1869 it was reduced to five mills, the same as it had been ten years earlier.[40]

In 1874 the legislature reformed the tax law. Under the old law property was assessed only one-third of its value; hence all taxes were paid on one-third of the real valuation of property. The new law provided that the assessment of property should be at its fair cash value and that taxes for state purposes were not to be made until the annual assessed returns were in. Farmers generally favored the new law, as it would compel wealthy real estate owners and speculators to pay taxes on their numerous tracts of land. Heretofore these men had found it cheaper to contest tax titles than to pay taxes, but the new law inflicted penalties for tax evasion severe enough to influence people to pay taxes if possible.[41]

To us today, taxes paid by the pioneer farmer may seem small, but to him they were at times an unbearable burden. One settler near Glencoe said in 1874 that at least three-fourths of his neighbors were tax delinquent for from two to six years, but that most of them would have paid their taxes if they could. The penalty on delinquent taxes was twenty-four per cent, and few farmers wanted to pay that if they could avoid it. Another person, writing in a Winona paper about the same time, stated that the bulk of the taxes in the state were paid by farmers. One farmer, Andrew Peterson, who lived near Waconia, has left records of his tax payments. In June, 1860, his property was assessed at $87, and in January, 1861, he paid $2.90 in taxes. In July, 1862, his real property, including 30 acres of swamp land, 9 acres of broken land, and 121 acres of unbroken land, was valued at $330, which Peterson thought too high. His personal property was valued at $120, and included four bullocks, three cows with calves, one heifer, three calves, two ewes with lambs, five pigs, and household goods. The last were valued at $10, as was the log cabin. Peterson does not say what taxes he paid on this property, but the list throws much light on worldly possessions of the average farmer of the 1860's. In 1865 Peterson's taxes were nearly $57; and in 1866 and 1867 his real estate taxes alone were $30 and $23.50, respectively. In 1874 he paid his personal tax in January and his real estate tax in April, but he does not give the amounts. Finally, in June, 1875, he noted the fact that he paid his real estate tax, which amounted to $43.15. In the same year his wheat harvest was 475 bushels, his barley crop was 101 bushels, and his oat harvest was 83 bushels, and these were his main sources of income. Hence, his real estate tax alone represented a goodly percentage of his year's earnings.[42]

Here, then, are some of the major influences which helped to determine the degree of prosperity enjoyed by the average farmer of pioneer Minnesota. In addition to panics, wars, taxes, interest charges, insect visitations, and plant diseases, another powerful determinant of the farmer's welfare was, of course, his own initiative and intelligence, qualities possessed in abundance by some men and almost entirely lacking in others.

The intelligent farmer used fertilizer on land which needed it, whereas the ignorant or prejudiced settler considered the use of manure a sign of weakness. Further, the capable man kept farm accounts, diversified his agriculture, and budgeted his time. In January or February, our intelligent farmer took good care of his stock; he hauled wood to his woodpile; he split rails; he took good care of his machinery; and he hauled out some manure. In March, he might market grain left on hand; sow vegetable seeds in a hot bed; plow; and plant some potatoes, spring wheat, and vegetables. April and May were the months for sowing most of the small grains, potatoes, corn, sorghum, Hungarian grass, and some vegetables. In June some late vegetables might be planted, but the main work for June, as well as for July, was keeping the weeds down. Also in July there was haying to do, and sometimes rye and winter wheat to harvest. During August little was done on the farm except in the harvest field, where cutting and stacking wheat and oats was the order of the day, although some grain might be marketed at that time and tools might be put away. During the first part of September harvesting continued; in addition, potatoes were dug and grain was hauled to the mill. Later in September, plowing for next year's wheat crop, sowing winter wheat, cutting up corn, and attending fairs were the usual procedures. In October more potatoes remained to be dug, and other root crops and garden vegetables waited to be gathered. There was threshing to do, corn to husk, hogs to fatten, and beef to "make." Plowing and preparing for winter often continued into November, but that month and December were usually devoted to chores, husking corn, threshing, and marketing grain and other farm produce. At the end of this round of activities, many farmers no doubt could say with John Cummins: "Another year rolled round, and has not added much pecuniarily to my condition, though probably I have benefited some little by experience."[43]

A Powerful Determinant

On New Year's Day, 1862, a Minnesota farmer started a new volume of his diary with this sentence: "The commencement of my diary begins with something about the weather; indeed, it is the only thing that is sure to occur each day, and it must go a great way toward the filling of the book."[1] Weather and other factors of physical environment, such as soil and topography, were matters of vital concern to the pioneer farmers, even as they are to contemporary farmers. All too often did a settler see his hopes of a good crop blasted by a hailstorm, a dry spell, or an early frost. Was it any wonder that he filled his conversations with talk of the weather, and that the almanac was a second Bible to him? From prehistoric times the tiller of the soil has been aware of his simple and direct relationship to his environment. He has realized how forces beyond his control have determined the characteristics of agriculture in different parts of the world, and he has tried in many ways to please and appease these forces.

A word of caution must be interjected, however, for the geographical factor must not be overemphasized. It is but a limiting and conditioning element. Population movements and industrial developments also are important in determining types of agriculture. The most intensive developments of the industry are usually found near industrial centers where land values are high, and, as the distances from such centers increase, successive grades of land utilization are found, from floriculture lands and truck and fruit lands through various other types to stock-farming and ranching lands. Further, land utilization is affected by the invention of farm machinery and the discovery of new techniques. Indeed, it has been said, and quite correctly, that the agriculture of a country is as dependent upon the knowledge and power of its people as it is upon the qualities and characteristics of the land. Even politics, as we have been well aware in recent years, may affect types of agriculture. Especially was this true in the 1930's in Europe, where each country was struggling desperately to achieve what the Germans called "autarchy," or self-sufficiency. Then it was a question not so much of adjusting agriculture to its natural environment as of attempting to grow what the government said should be grown.[2]

Finally, forgetting politics, certain economic principles influence the types of crops grown in various regions. The crop or other product most limited in climatic or other physical requirements of production, if demand for it is sufficient, will have first choice of the land. For example, wheat could be grown in the cotton belt, but little is grown there. Also, the crop or product small in bulk or weight per unit of value can best bear the cost of transportation, and it will be grown in those regions offering the most favorable physical conditions; but some bulky crops must be grown there to meet local demands. Enough corn is grown in the cotton belt, therefore, to meet the demands of the locality. Furthermore, the varying seasonal requirements of agricultural products for labor tend to diversify the agriculture of a region. The farmer must do a particular task at a definite time in the year, and he can hardly afford to lie idle for long stretches.[3]

These social, economic, and political factors must always be kept in mind in a study of agriculture in any state or country; but an explanation of developments which ignores physical conditions is incomplete. The permanence of the influence of physical environment upon agriculture is attested by history. In fact, as Dr. Oliver E. Baker has pointed out, physical conditions actually become more important as population increases, as the knowledge and practice of agriculture advances, as transportation facilities improve, and as the supply of labor and capital increases and becomes better distributed. With each advance in technique and organization, agriculture is increasingly responsive to conditions of temperature, moisture, soil, and topography. The commercialization of agriculture and the resultant competition between regions make the production of a crop extremely sensitive to the geographical advantages or disadvantages of a district. Hence, even in modern scientific agriculture, physical environment is a powerful determinant.[4]

A POWERFUL DETERMINANT

Minnesota offered the pioneer farmer contrasts, challenges, advantages, extremes, and variations in physical environment, and most of the agricultural history of the state could be written around the theme of the farmers' attempts to adjust to this environment. The early settlers had little or no scientific knowledge to aid them in this process of adaptation, but, through trial and error and after many hard knocks, they developed patterns and techniques that have proved remarkably valid in the light of modern research.

Minnesota is in almost the geographical center of North America, and it contains the sources of three great drainage systems flowing in opposite directions, to the St. Lawrence, the Mississippi, and Hudson Bay. As in France and England, where the rivers have formed the basis of an excellent transportation system, short distances separate the navigable waters of the state; and these waterways have made a thoroughfare for white men—a matter of vital importance to the first farmers—as they did for the Indians earlier. The total area of Minnesota is 84,286 square miles, of which 80,858 is land and 3,428 water surface. The distance from the northern boundary line to the southern limit is about 400 miles, while the greatest width, 357 miles, is found in the area directly north of Lake Superior.[5]

In the early days many people in the older states thought that Minnesota's growing season was too short for the production of staples. To dispel such misconceptions in the minds of prospective immigrants, Minnesota editors and boosters wrote much about the "salubrious" and healthful climate of the territory. The following quotation from a railroad bulletin, while written a few years after the territorial period, is typical of the booster literature: "Minnesota is the most healthful, beautiful, fertile and attractive State in the World for Eastern and European immigration. Health, prosperity, and education are accessible to all. A delightful climate and exceeding richness of soil, combine with favorable natural and artificial means of transportation, to insure the success of all industrious and enterprising settlers in Minnesota."[6]

After a particularly long, cold, and snowy winter, the modern Minnesotan may feel that his progenitors were dealt a stacked hand by the pioneer booster who induced them with glowing prose to migrate to the state. But there have been many seasons when Minnesota has lived up to the most extravagant claims made for it. More information is available on Minnesota's climate in later years than on that in the earlier period; but, since the climate probably has not changed greatly since the 1850's, later statistics will throw light on the pioneer environment. Minnesota has a distinctly continental climate, marked by wide extremes of temperature. Hallock recorded a high of 109° Fahrenheit in July, 1936, and St. Vincent, in the same county, shivered at 45° below zero in February of that year! According to the United States weather bureau at Minneapolis, the longest growing season, one hundred and sixty days, is in the southeastern part of the state along the Mississippi River. In the north, near the Lake of the Woods, the season is just short of one hundred days. For most seasons one hundred days are too few for the successful growing of corn. The growing season is of such a character, however, that it produces a hard wheat rich in gluten, a fact of no little significance in the state's agricultural history.[7]

As is characteristic of continental climates, the average annual temperature for Minnesota as a whole has varied considerably, and it may well be that the effect of the extremes is more significant for vegetation than is the mean temperature. Between 1886 and 1912 the average annual temperature fell once, in 1888, below 39° Fahrenheit, and three times, in 1894, 1900, and 1908, it went above 43°. In the years between 1838 and 1879, the average did not fall below 39°, though it dipped to 40° in 1843 and again in 1875; while in 1839, 1846, 1851, 1870, and 1878, it went over 45°. Generally speaking, the mean annual temperature for the state falls between 41° and 44° Fahrenheit. The highest average is found in the Mississippi River Valley near the Iowa line and in the relatively low lands south of the elbow of the Minnesota River. Between October and March it varies from 27° in those two regions to 17° along the northern border. During the period from 1838 to 1879, the average winter temperatures ranged between 10° and 20°, the coldest winter being that of 1874-75 and the warmest, that of 1878.[8]

The cold winters and heavy snows added to the farmers' burdens, as winter grains were sometimes winterkilled, stock was hard to care for, and roads were often blocked. The blizzard of 1873 was the most severe manifestation of winter prior to the 1880's. Many people were frozen to death, livestock was lost, and transportation was impeded. But even during ordinary winters settlers suffered many hardships. George Biscoe in 1866 told of a neighbor's trip to bring back grist that had lain in the mill for about three weeks. The trip took all day and the neighbor reached home in the evening on horseback, "having been obliged to leave his load out on the pra[i]rie three miles from home. It has been a dreadful week to be out. This morning the thermometer stood -22° and the wind blowing a gale."[9]

In some ways the cold winters were an advantage. Frost promoted the disintegration of pebbles in the glacial drift and thus constantly produced new supplies of plant food; and, under certain conditions, it facilitated transportation in an age of poor, or no, roads, no airplanes, and no railroads.[10]

The heat of the growing season, however, is more important to Minnesota agriculture than are winter temperatures. From April through September the highest average temperature is 63° Fahrenheit in the southeast section and south of the Minnesota River elbow; the lowest is 55° near Lake of the Woods and near Lake Superior. The long summers and the lingering heat of the autumn are important factors for agriculture in a continental climate. During the years before 1880 the average temperature for June, July, and August hovered around 70°; the hottest summer was that of 1868, when the average was over 75°. The average date of the last killing frost varies from May 1 in the southeast to May 30 in the extreme north. Around Lake Superior frosts occur no later than at Winona because of the moderating effect of the lake. The average date of the first killing frost is September 10 on the iron ranges and October 10 in the southeastern lowlands. Earlier frosts hit the highlands and parts of the Minnesota River Valley. But, despite temperature variations, Minnesota's climate has been termed one of its most valuable geographic assets.[11]

In precipitation, as in temperature, the state has experienced great variations. These are connected with the passage eastward of areas of low atmospheric pressure followed by areas of high pressure. The surface winds constantly veer, though on the whole southwest winds predominate in summer, while northwest winds are most frequent in winter. A northwest wind in the summer is refreshing, but in the winter it is apt to bring a cold wave in its wake. The average annual rainfall in the southeast is thirty-four inches, and in the northwest it is twenty inches, while the average for the state from 1886 to 1912, inclusive, was twenty-six and a half inches. The rainfall is of the summer type, usually about seventy-five per cent of it falling during the growing season from April to September, and evaporation is less rapid than in regions farther south. Between 1838 and 1879 the wettest season was that of 1849, when the average for the state was nearly fifty inches. Other particularly wet years were 1865, 1869, and 1877. Particularly dry years were 1852, 1863, 1864, 1870, 1871, and 1872. In 1852, for example, the annual precipitation was only fifteen inches, and even more startling was the fact that during the summer of that year a meager five inches fell. During such a season farmers were especially weather conscious. One farmer reported in July of another dry year that no rain of any account had fallen since June 3, and that he did not see how anything could grow in such weather.[12]

If farmers generally were weather conscious, they were equally interested in the surface features, soils, and rock formations of their farms. Naturally they wanted land that was easily tillable and soil that responded bounteously to their efforts. If the Minnesota farmer found himself so favored, he almost invariably had an ancient glacier to thank for his good fortune, since nearly the entire area of the state was covered for ages by successive fields of ice. Only a small part of southeastern Minnesota, mainly in Houston County, escaped glaciation and became part of the "driftless area."[13]

Apparently in the later days of the ice age three main sheets invaded the state from the north. The first moved southeast from west of Hudson Bay across the Superior basin, covering most of the state and extending well into southern Iowa; the second moved southward from the region of present-day Quebec across eastern Minnesota to points a little beyond the site of St. Paul; and the third, like the first, moved southward from a center west of Hudson Bay through Manitoba and across western Minnesota. These glaciers covered the state with the finest soil-making material in depths varying from a few feet in places in southern Minnesota up to five hundred or six hundred feet in regions west of the Mississippi and north of the Minnesota River. The glaciers themselves frequently were many thousands of feet in depth. The great weight of the ice caused the earth's surface to sink, but gradually it rose again. The period of elevation was followed by warmer temperatures and the melting and retreat of the ice. The story of this retreat can be read in the numerous moraines to be seen in the state. One of the glaciers seems to have disappeared in its retreat by melting fitfully away up the Minnesota River Valley and down the valley of the Red River of the North; a second retreated from the vicinity of the present Lake Itasca in a northeasterly direction toward James Bay; and the third disappeared by way of Lake Superior.[14]

As a result of these ice invasions, the soils of the state are almost wholly glacial. "This means," according to one writer, "that the chemical composition is so varied, the rock contents being derived from every neighboring rock formation, that the soil is fertile for every kind of crop middle-temperate seasons will mature." Or, as another author has said, the drift area "provides the soil of the farms, and the foundation upon which cities, railroads and highways have been built. Except to those who dig ore it is the only part of the earth that really counts."[15]

In the glacial retreat, the ridges and cross ridges of glacial material impounded lakes, more than ten thousand in number, for which the state has become famous. Lake Superior itself, according to geologists, began as a marginal lake on the west side of a great ice lobe. At about where the boundaries of Minnesota and North and South Dakota meet, ancient Lake Agassiz spread northward. From Maple Lake its shoreline ran northeastward and embraced Red, Vermilion, and Rainy lakes. Finally Lake Agassiz disappeared, and Lake Winnipeg was left as a vestigial reminder of the once-great water formation. The formerly inundated lands were left as level as a floor and were covered with a thick layer of soil rich in all the chemicals essential to successful crop production. While all but about two per cent of the area is suitable for profitable farming, the flatness of the old lake bed necessitated much tiling and ditching to obtain the drainage to make it so. The beaches of the various levels of the lake are still visible, rising a few feet; affording dry and sightly spots and good drainage for cellars, they have served as locations for farm buildings. Moreover, their wells yield better water than do those drilled in adjacent clay areas.[16]

The land formations of Minnesota are the results both of glaciation and of conditions as they existed before the coming of the ice sheets. "Prior to the ice invasions," writes Robinson, "the valleys were generally deeper, the surface more rolling and more thoroughly drained, than is now the case outside of the driftless area." The highlands north of Lake Superior seem to have been in existence before the ice invasions. During or since the glacial age there has been a differential tilting of the surface. Minnesota as a whole is a level state, but there are some elevations important enough to be noted. The average altitude of the state is 1,200 feet above sea level, with the lowest elevation 602.2 feet at the surface of Lake Superior and the highest 2,230 feet in western Cook County. Two other regions exceed 1,500 feet. One is north of the Minnesota River and west of the Mississippi, culminating in Hubbard, Becker, and Clearwater counties and containing the divide between the Red and Mississippi river basins, which reaches a height of about 1,750 feet. The other is the ridge commonly known as the Coteau des Prairies, which crosses southwestern Minnesota and forms the divide between the Missouri and Mississippi river basins. This elevation can scarcely be appreciated by one crossing it, so gradual are the contours of its long, green slopes. It is covered deeply with glacial drift and it marks the southwestern limit, in Minnesota, of the last stage of glaciation. Finally, there are the Leaf Hills, another morainic region which stretches from northern Wisconsin through Chisago, Ramsey, Hennepin, Carver, Scott, Dakota, Rice, Le Sueur, Waseca, and Freeborn counties to central Iowa, reaching a height of 1,412 feet and being in places rather thinly covered with drift. In fact, glacial drift generally lies much thicker over the western than over the eastern part of the state.[17]

After the glacial period many forms of plant and animal life appeared in the region. "One would need moving pictures to present adequately the rapid stages of development which resulted in the typical Minnesota landscape which the first explorers saw and described—great woods and wide prairies, abounding with wild life," one writer has said of this postglacial period. In this development Minnesota became a woods country, two-thirds of the area, or 52,000 square miles, being timbered, with openings here and there. Two main exceptions were the ancient bed of Lake Agassiz and the area south and west of the Minnesota River, which were prairie regions. In the northern two-thirds of the state were great stands of coniferous trees, which extended from the eastern margin of the Red River Valley and the Canadian line to within a few miles of present-day Minneapolis. On its southwestern border the coniferous area was bounded by what was popularly called the "Big Woods," a region containing oak, elm, ash, maple, birch, poplar, box elder, and cottonwood trees. Adjoining the Big Woods on the west were prairies, which presented a problem of housing, fuel, and fencing to the early settlers; while to the east across the Mississippi were oak openings. The Big Woods ran along the Mississippi River south from the Crow Wing River for nearly a hundred miles, and their southwest corner extended to the valley of the Blue Earth River. In all, the Big Woods contained five thousand square miles, one-fifth of which was south of the Minnesota River. Many lakes were found in the region, as well as open prairies heavily covered with grass. According to Warren Upham, a geologist of Minnesota, 81 species of forest trees and about 125 species of shrubs are indigenous in the state, and about 125 species of native grass and numerous varieties of wild flowers are to be found. With flora such as this, plus many species of American wild life, Minnesota offered great advantages to the early pioneers who moved to the region.[18]

The forests as well as glaciation played a big part in determining the types of soil in Minnesota, since vegetation in timbered areas

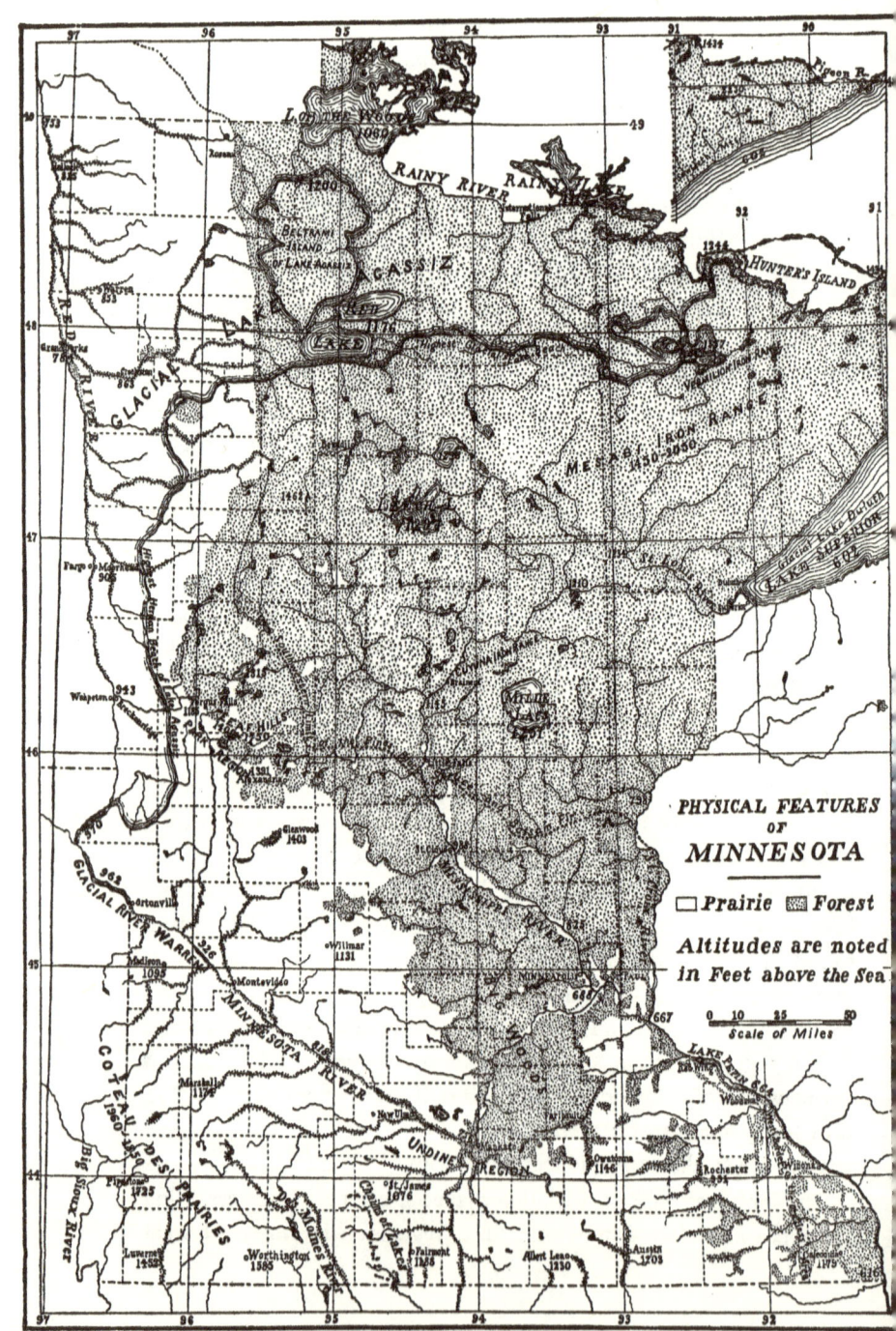

[From Folwell, *Minnesota*, 1:10.]

both grew and decayed more slowly than it did on the prairies. As a result the prairie soils possessed a darker color and contained a larger proportion of vegetable humus than did the forest soils. Early descriptions of the soil generally were not scientific, but they usually agreed that Minnesota's soil was excellent. Dr. Thomas Foster in 1850 described the soil as sandy, calcareous loam, derived mainly from the disintegration or decay of the magnesian limestones and the sandstones, "with erratic drift from the granitic and igneous rock regions farther north." Girart Hewitt some years later described it as a "dark, calcareous, sandy loam, containing a various intermixture of clay, abounding in mineral salts and in organic ingredients, derived from the accumulation of decomposed vegetable matter for long ages of growth and decay. The sand of which silica is the base, forms a large proportion of this, as of all good soils." And the chief engineer of the Southern Minnesota Railroad Company reported thus in the 1850's: "Throughout the whole of Southern Minnesota, a similarity of soil is observed, and a description of any one part, will be correct for the whole, it being rich vegetable mould, upon the high ground, and alluvial in the valleys of the streams."[19]

If these early descriptions of soil seem amateurish, it should be remembered that not only is "soil science . . . largely a product of the twentieth century," but also that "the whole subject of soil science" is still in a somewhat "formative state," and that it is "important to recall Robinson's (1915) admonition, that all soil classifications were provisional." It used to be thought that geology and chemistry were the all-important subjects needed by the student of soils of an area, since parent materials and chemical composition, it was believed, determined soil types. Gradually, however, people like E. W. Hilgard, a professor of agriculture in California in the late nineteenth century, came to realize that climate affected soil and might be considered a soil-forming factor, and the Russian school of soil scientists reached a similar conclusion. Also, more and more attention was devoted to the relationship between vegetation and soils and between animal life and soils. No longer could the soil be considered "a somewhat stationary reservoir of plant food," but it became an organic, living entity, "an object of nature in equilibrium with environment." Even today many aspects of soil microbiology are only dimly understood, and much soil research remains to be done. It is apparent, however, that soil science is a complex subject, and that "even in one small locality . . . a score or more of types of soils that were intricate mixtures of stone, gravel, sand of many qualities, loam, clay, muck, or other substance, each requiring a different treatment for successful farming," might be found. Is it any wonder that the pioneer farmer was discouraged or bewildered when he moved to a new frontier?"[20]

In the light of these generalizations concerning soils, it is not surprising to find several major types and many subtypes of soil in Minnesota. Part of the explanation for these varieties is to be found in the glacial movements over the state. The ice sheet entering the state from the northeast carried the red drift of the Lake Superior region southward, while the sheet entering from the northwest spread a gray drift over the western and southern parts of the state. Southeast from Red Lake, part of the latter glacier deposited gray drift on top of the red drift for more than two-thirds of the distance to Lake Superior. Also, a large arm of the sheet turned northeast through the Minnesota River Valley and covered the red drift to a little beyond the present course of the St. Croix River in Washington and Chisago counties. Both types of drift form good soils, but in general the gray drift, derived mainly from limestone and shale, is the more fertile. In both southeastern and southwestern Minnesota, drift older than that of the last glaciation is exposed. A part of this older drift is covered with loess, or wind deposits, and both of these soils are very fertile. In the northern and northeastern areas of the state the glaciers stripped off most of the soil and left these regions unfit for agriculture, but suitable for timber production.[21]

In 1938 the United States Department of Agriculture devoted its entire yearbook to a discussion of *Soils and Men*. Included in the volume is an excellent soil map of the United States, which shows clearly the soil groups of Minnesota and their relations to groups in neighboring states. According to this map, most of the state's soil can be classified into four great groups with well-developed characteristics, "reflecting the dominating influence of climate and vegetation." Most of the northern half of Minnesota east of the tier of counties bordering the Red River is blanketed with podzols—light-colored, leached soils typical of cool, humid, forested regions. Exceptions to this rule are found in the northernmost tier of counties, where there are bog soils and shallow soils, consisting largely of imperfectly weathered masses of rock fragments. Extending along the entire western boundary of the state are chernozem soils—dark brown to nearly black soils, typical of cool and temperate subhumid grasslands, and probably the richest of all soils. The third group of soils is found in a triangle-shaped region, whose base is practically coterminous with the Iowa-Minnesota line and whose apex falls roughly between Brainerd and Moorhead, in the central western part of the state. This group, "very dark brown soils of cool temperate, relatively humid grasslands," is classified as prairie soils, and it is even more productive than the chernozems because it receives greater rainfall. Finally, lying to the east of the prairie soils and south of the podzols, in a narrow strip of eastern Minnesota, are the gray-brown podzolic soils—leached soils characteristic of temperate, humid, forested regions.[22]

Using soils, topography, and flora as a basis, Robinson in 1915 divided Minnesota into five geographical provinces with special reference to agriculture, and these divisions have sufficient validity even today to warrant repeating. One is the "driftless area" in the southeast, which is well drained and has a rolling surface, but only moderately fertile soil. Another is the drift-covered prairie and deciduous forest zone outside of the bed of Lake Agassiz. The soil varies greatly in fertility, and drainage is imperfect in some places, but there is a large proportion of arable land of high fertility. A third province is the bed of glacial Lake Agassiz, which contains heavy clay soils that have made the Red River Valley world renowned for its wheat production. There are some patches of sand and gravel in the midst of the best soil, and there is a lack of natural drainage channels, as already noted; but these disadvantages are more than offset by the fertile soil and the level nature of the region, which is perfectly adapted to machine agriculture. A fourth province is the former bed of Lake Superior, which lies in the coniferous zone. There is considerable good soil and cheap water transportation to be found in this region. Lastly, there is the coniferous zone, outside of the Lake Agassiz and Lake Superior basins. In the western part of this province, sand and sandy loams predominate, while in the eastern part rock outcrops and drift boulders are numerous. In general, the region is better adapted to forests than to ordinary agriculture, and, of course, little farming was found in either the north central or northeastern parts of the state during the early period.[23]

Settlers and Speculators

In his *Social History of American Agriculture,* Joseph Schafer writes that "among the earliest and most persistent social problems was that of making land available for ever-growing numbers. So eager and determined, at most times, was the quest for new lands that one would almost be justified in maintaining the exact opposite of the usual thesis that in America the supply of that commodity has always exceeded the demand."[1] This statement applies to pioneer Minnesota as well as to the rest of the United States. The early settler wanted good land; he wanted it cheap; and he wanted a secure title after he had chosen his location. Indeed, so strong was the desire for land that many were unwilling to obey the country's land laws and became squatters.

The basis for the United States land system is to be found in the colonial systems, especially in the practice most general in early New England. More specifically, the land ordinance of 1785 was the foundation upon which the later land laws of the nation were superimposed. This ordinance, and subsequent legislation, provided for the rectangular survey of the land and the division of it into townships and sections, for survey before the sale and settlement, and for sale at public auction.[2]

In spite of its wise aspects, some features of the ordinance met with unfavorable reactions. Land was sold in parcels too large for the average settler. Moreover, many settlers refused to wait for the surveys, and they squatted on unsurveyed tracts, hoping to be able to maintain their tenure. This practice was always a problem to the government. Sometimes squatters were forcibly removed, and again acts were passed by Congress giving relief in special cases. Finally, after much argument pro and con, a general pre-emption law was passed by Congress in 1841. This law applied to many lands in Minnesota, and under its provisions thousands of settlers secured farms in the state. Another general land act which affected early Minnesota immigrants was the law of 1820 abolishing the credit system of paying for land, which had been in force from 1800 to 1820, and reducing the minimum price from two dollars to a dollar and a quarter an acre.[3]

Persons able to secure land warrants, however, did not have to pay the minimum price for land. Warrants, good for various amounts of land, were issued from time to time by the federal government to soldiers of the Revolution, the War of 1812, and the Mexican War. Also, Indian and half-breed scrip and agricultural college warrants, as will be seen, were used to locate land in the state. Often the original grantee of the paper did not locate the land, but allowed his scrip or warrants to fall into the hands of speculators, never very popular with the average settler.

Administration of the public domain in the early period was under the supervision of the commissioner of the General Land Office in Washington. This officer owed his existence to an act of Congress passed on April 25, 1812, which placed his bureau in and subordinate to the Treasury Department. Appeals from the actions of the commissioner were made to the secretary of the treasury. In 1849, Congress created the Home (now Interior) Department, and provided that the secretary of the new department "shall perform all the duties in relation to the General Land Office of supervision and appeal now discharged by the Secretary of the Treasury." Thus, during Minnesota's territorial period, as well as later, the General Land Office was in the Department of the Interior. The procedure for a disgruntled land seeker to follow was to appeal first to a local land office for redress of grievances, then to the General Land Office, and finally to the secretary of the interior.[4]

After the extension of surveys to new areas was authorized by Congress, the commissioner of the General Land Office directed the surveyor general of the particular district, whose office was created by law prior to extending the surveys, to begin them. The surveyors general, whose offices were conveniently located in their districts, entered into contracts with professional surveyors, whom they commissioned as their deputies. To protect the government from fraud, the deputy surveyors were placed under bond and their assistants were sworn to perform their duties with fidelity.[5]

Before any surveys could be made in the Minnesota region, it was necessary to quiet the Indian title to the land. This was accomplished by various treaties between the United States and certain of the Indian tribes. By the first treaties, negotiated in 1837 and ratified in 1838, the United States acquired title to the land between the St. Croix and the Mississippi rivers as far north as the mouth of the Crow Wing River. These cessions were relatively small and were located largely in the forested region. Furthermore, the surveys were delayed, so that title to land in Minnesota could not be obtained before 1848.[6]

Two principal meridians, the fourth and fifth, governed the establishment of ranges in Minnesota. The fourth meridian began in the middle of the channel of the mouth of the Illinois River, at latitude 38° 58′ 12″ north and longitude 90° 29′ 56″ west, and governed the surveys of Illinois west of the Illinois River and west of the third principal meridian lying north of the river. It extended also north through Wisconsin and northeastern Minnesota, and it governed all the surveys in the former state and those in Minnesota east of the Mississippi and the third guide meridian north of the river. The fifth principal meridian started from the mouth of the Arkansas River and, with a common base line running due west from the mouth of the St. Francis River in Arkansas, governed the surveys in Arkansas, Missouri, Iowa, Minnesota west of the Mississippi and the third guide meridian north of the river, and in Dakota Territory east of the Missouri River. It was coincident with 90° 58′ longitude west.[7]

When the deputy completed his survey, the work was inspected by the surveyor general or a competent agent and, if it was approved, the township plats of the land were made in triplicate—one for the office of the surveyor general, one for the General Land Office, and one for the local land office for the district in which the townships were located. When the local office received the plats, notice was posted announcing the date, not less than thirty days after posting, when applications would be received for entry of the lands. Notices were also posted in the offices of the clerks of court of the district and in the post offices, and were published in the newspapers.[8]

Mention has been made of the local land office. This agency was undoubtedly the most important part of the whole government land administration as far as the average settler was concerned. In fact, the pioneer's main contact with his government frequently was through the local land office. It was there that he "filed his claim," paid his fees, and secured a patent to his land. The local land officers were two, the register and the receiver. They were appointed by the president, by and with the advice and consent of the Senate, and held office for four-year terms, unless removed sooner. They had to give bond, and they were allowed salaries of five hundred dollars a year each, plus fees. Appointments to land offices were among the most lucrative and sought after under the patronage of the federal government. While his salary and fees were not to exceed three thousand dollars annually, the average officer received much more than that for his private services. He had considerable evidence to put in writing in nearly every pre-emption case, for which he was permitted to receive private compensation. Many of the officers were lawyers, a convenient circumstance, since there were frequent occasions to decide on litigated land claims.[9]

An event of great importance in any town was the establishment of a local land office. Such an office was a magnet, drawing people from far and wide and creating good business conditions. For example, the removal of the United States land office in May, 1879, from Detroit to Crookston was an event of the first importance in Polk County's history. Government land business in the district was at that time very large, and "in land contests and other matters before the office for two or three years, more was made by the lawyers than the district court practice has ever brought in a like period of time."[10]

Considering the importance of the land office in pioneer communities and the lucrativeness of the positions of register and receiver, it was but natural that many persons sought appointments to those offices. Paul C. Sletten, receiver of the office at Crookston, serves as a good example of the important role played by early land officers. Born in Norway, he worked in railroad construction camps for a time after coming to the United States. In the early 1870's he turned to farming in Becker County. In 1874 there was a contest between John T. Averill of St. Paul and William S. King of Minneapolis for the Republican nomination for Congress in the third district. Judge Reuben Reynolds, receiver of the land office, favored Averill, but Sletten secured delegates in his part of the district for King, who was nominated and elected. As a result, King obtained Sletten's appointment as receiver, a position he held until his death in 1884.[11]

The first local office for lands in the Minnesota area was established at St. Croix Falls, Wisconsin, in 1847. Samuel Leech was the first receiver of the office and Charles S. Whitney, the first register. In 1848 a presidential proclamation placed twenty-seven townships and fractional townships, embracing 436,737 acres, on the market. At the first sale, on August 14, 1848, 3,326 acres were sold at the minimum price of $1.25 an acre.[12]

The first public sale for land located west of the St. Croix River was held on September 15, 1848. At the St. Croix Falls office the townsites of Stillwater, St. Paul, and St. Anthony were entered by the claimants at $1.25 an acre. To guard against speculators on the St. Paul site, Henry H. Sibley, who bid the site in, was accompanied by a large, armed force of Canadian Frenchmen. It would have been a sad day for any speculator who might have bid against Sibley. As it was, none bid against him and his bodyguard was not needed. From the opening of the office until October 1, 1848, 131 certificates were granted for private entries and purchases at public sales.[13]

Not long after the first sale at St. Croix Falls the land office was removed, in the face of opposition from Wisconsinites, to Stillwater, some thirty miles to the south on the west bank of the St. Croix River. Notice of the removal was published in Minnesota's first newspaper.[14] The first public sale of the lands at Stillwater occurred on October 9, 1849, under the direction of N. Green Wilcox, receiver, and Abraham Van Voorhes, register. The land office continued at Stillwater until October, 1858, when it was removed to Cambridge in Isanti County. Unfortunately, in April, 1859, the office burned and some valuable papers were destroyed. In July of the same year the office was again removed, this time to Sunrise, where it remained until October, 1868, when it was removed to Taylor's Falls, to remain there during the rest of the period covered by this volume.[15]

On May 16, 1850, the *Minnesota Pioneer* reprinted an article from the *Pennsylvania Telegraph,* entitled "Original Sketch of the History and Geography of Minnesota Territory," by Dr. Thomas Foster. In it Foster indicated the public lands in the territory subject to private entry at that time, along with some interesting comment on them. The lands available included the rich delta between the St. Croix and Mississippi rivers, extending up the east side of the latter to Indian country, over a hundred miles above St. Paul. This area Foster described as a rolling country, well watered and sufficiently timbered. He mentioned the treaty of the previous fall for the cession of over 200,000 acres by the Sioux half-breeds on the west side of the Mississippi at Lake Pepin, and stated that the treaty would be ratified by the Senate at its current session. Plenty of good locations, he said, were to be had within from three to five miles of the main towns and rivers, and land warrants good for 160 acres could be purchased for from $130 to $150; and, he continued, "if a settler is not ready to purchase at once, he can make a location, put up a small improvement, and have a year's credit on his *pre-emption,* before he will be required to pay for it, in cash or with a warrant."[16]

To understand this last statement, it is necessary to know the provisions of the land laws then in effect in Minnesota. The main law, as has been mentioned, was the general pre-emption act of 1841, and interest in its provisions was keen among land seekers. Newspapers in the territory devoted much space to clarifying the law and answering questions about it, and many settlers' and land buyers' guides were published.

As has been indicated, a person could not avail himself of the privileges offered by the law of 1841 unless the Indian title to his land had been quieted and the land had been surveyed and offered for sale. All southeastern and southern Minnesota, including the prairie region, remained Indian country until the treaties of Traverse des Sioux and Mendota were negotiated in 1851; and the first government survey west of the Mississippi in Minnesota was not made until the summer of 1853. A line was then run northward for a distance of eight townships and thence eastward to the river. The first subdivision of townships was made in the early summer of 1854. William Ashley Jones of Dubuque had the contract for townshipping, and it was found later that much of his work was faulty. The first land office west of the river was opened in August, 1854, at Brownsville in Houston County. It served the Root River district, an area thirty miles wide, west from the Mississippi.[17]

When a settler had satisfied the land officers that he was entitled to pre-emption rights, he was expected to pay for his land as soon as practicable after the notice of the date of sale was posted, and before the day set for the sale. If he failed to do so, he forfeited his claim. Some settlers wanted lands offered for sale early, while others preferred to have the day of sale postponed as long as possible. A champion of the first position, who signed himself "A Settler," criticized severely people who did not want lands offered for sale. He contended that postponing sales allowed men to hold farms for years without paying taxes, while at the same time they enjoyed the protection of the government. Further, capital and improvements were kept out of regions long unoffered for sale.[18]

On the other hand, there were good and sufficient reasons why many settlers did not want the president to offer for sale lands upon which they had settled. The average settler was poor and, after coming to a new region, building a home, and making a few improvements, he had little money left for buying his land. The newspapers of the 1850's were filled with protests against proposed land sales. The editor of the *Minnesota Pioneer,* for example, commented that, while he had no information as to whether there would be a sale of part of the region west of the Mississippi, there was much feeling against such a sale. It was thought that it would hurt the settler and aid the speculator.[19]

On occasion relief was sought from the president in Washington.

Such a course was followed at one time in Freeborn County, where announcement was made on October 29, 1860, of a proposed land sale. The sale would have impoverished the people by depriving them of their claims, improvements, and homes. A meeting was held at Albert Lea, and G. W. Skinner was sent to Washington to determine what could be done. In addition, a petition was addressed to President Buchanan. Skinner returned to report that the land could not be withdrawn from sale, but that land not sold could be filed on the day after the public sale. A committee was appointed to appear at the sale and to make certain that no bids were made on land already occupied. No land was sold, and the occupants refiled the next day on their own claims.[20]

Sometimes, of course, settlers on surveyed lands had the money or scrip to pay for the land when it was offered for sale. Instructions aplenty were available in the newspapers and elsewhere for such individuals to follow. The settler must never before have had the benefit of pre-emption under the act of 1841, nor could he at the time of making the pre-emption own 320 acres of land in any state or territory of the United States. He was expected to settle upon and improve the land, which could be no more than 160 acres in extent, in good faith for his own exclusive use or benefit, without intention of selling it on speculation. He could not make, directly or indirectly, any contract or agreement by which the title he might acquire from the United States would inure, in whole or in part, to the benefit of any person except himself. The settler had to be twenty-one years old, if single, or the head of a family, or a widow. He must be a citizen of the United States, or must have filed his declaration of intention to become a citizen, as provided by naturalization laws. He was required to build on the land a house at least twelve feet square, with a door and a window. Further, this house must be his exclusive home and habitation at the time of his application for pre-emption. Before the middle fifties, a single man could board with his nearest neighbor and still qualify under the law, but by 1855 that practice was no longer permitted. Some improvement was required, such as breaking or fencing at least half an acre. No other person entitled to the right of pre-emption could reside upon the land at the same time. No person could remove from his own land to make a pre-emption in the same state or territory. The settler was required to bring to the land office a written or printed application stating that he had never pre-empted before, that he did not own 320 acres of land, and that he intended to use the land for himself exclusively. This application, supported by an affidavit, had to be signed by the register and the receiver. To make affidavit of the other requirements, a respectable witness had to accompany the pre-emptor. In addition, a foreigner had to bring his naturalization papers to the land office. Finally, every settler was required to file a written declaratory statement of intention to pre-empt before he could proceed at all. The register collected a fee of one dollar for filing a declaratory statement, and he and the receiver each received fifty cents for granting pre-emption.[21]

Until 1854 the only lands subject to pre-emption were public lands with the Indian title extinguished and surveys completed. By an act of July 22, 1854, pre-emption of unsurveyed lands was recognized as legal. Exceptions were reservations, lands within the limits of any incorporated town, lands which had been selected as the site for a city or town, lands actually occupied and settled for purposes of trade and not agriculture, and lands on which were situated any known salines or mines. Evidence for the need for such an act can be found in a statement by the receiver of the Sauk Rapids land office that the Sauk River Valley, at the time unsurveyed, was claimed and occupied for more than twenty miles west from the mouth of the river.[22]

The act of 1854 stated that "the provisions of the pre-emption act of fourth September, eighteen hundred forty-one, and the acts amendatory thereof, shall be extended to the lands in Minnesota Territory, whether surveyed or not; but in all cases where pre-emption is claimed on unsurveyed lands the settler shall file his declaratory statement within three months after the survey has been made and returned, and make proof and payment before the day appointed by the President's proclamation for the commencement of the sale of the lands including the tract claimed: *Provided, however,* That if, when said lands are surveyed, it is found that two or more persons have settled upon the same quarter section, each shall be permitted to enter his improvement, as near as may be, by legal subdivisions."

When the land had been surveyed before settlement, the pre-emptor, within a period varying from ten to thirty days as the different offices decided, was required to file with the register of his district a written statement describing the land settled upon and declaring his intention to claim it under the provisions of the pre-emption law. Then, within twelve months of the date of settlement, he had to make the requisite proof, affidavit, and payment. When a settler pre-empted unsurveyed lands, it was necessary, under the act of 1854, for him to file with the surveyor general, within three months after the survey had been made in the field, notice of the specific tracts claimed. If a person swore falsely before a land officer regarding a pre-emption, he was subject to the penalties of perjury, and he forfeited the money he had paid for his land, plus all right and title to it; and any grant or conveyance which he might have made, except in the hands of a bona fide purchaser for a valuable consideration, was null and void. When two or more persons settled on the same quarter section, the right of pre-emption was accorded the person who made the first settlement.[23]

Such were the main legal requirements for the pre-emption of land in early Minnesota. The provisions of any law as set forth in the statute books, however, seldom describe fully the actual operation of the law. Certainly many activities were associated with pre-emption that will not be discovered in the *Statutes at Large* of the United States. A writer in the *St. Croix Union* of August 11, 1855, speaking of pre-emption in the middle 1850's remarked that squatting or claim making was "among the romances of frontier and pioneer life." After improvements are made on the claim "to live off and on until 'matters come round right,'" he continued, "you go to the Land Office, 'prove up,' pocket your duplicate, and wait till the record of your case can pass the inspection of the Department in Washington, and then receive from the United States a patent. . . . all this is an experience of adventure, anxiety, exertion, and success."[24]

Sometimes claim-jumping occurred, though perhaps the extent of that practice has been exaggerated. As the author of one of the older county histories of the state wrote, "All through the country the trees were covered with notices posted up by claimants who made little or no pretense of living on their claims. But rather than waste time in law suits the settlers pushed farther on." It was customary for immigrants to stake claims in a new area in the summer or fall, and to return East for the winter. When they returned West the next spring they expected to find their claims unmolested. Sometimes men were hired or asked to watch over claims during the winter. Naturally the temptation presented by an unoccupied claim was more than some individuals could withstand, and so jumping was practiced. Then, again, the requirements of the pre-emption law were so complicated that many claimants, by some trifling neglect, made themselves liable to a forfeiture of their claims.[25]

Notices such as the following, from the *Glencoe Register* of April 16, 1859, were common in the newspapers of the 1850's:

> To Adam Blean: You are hereby notified to appear at the U. S. Land Office, at Forest City, Minnesota, on Wednesday, the eighteenth day of May next, at 10 o'clock A.M. for the purpose of contesting my right to the north east quarter of section 12 in township 119 of range 25, as I intend to offer proof in support of my claim to the said land on that day. ANSEL G. THAYER

Legally, of course, no right of pre-emption could be established when a claimant forcibly took possession of land already settled upon, improved, and enclosed by another, but it was not always easy to prove who was the prior claimant. Claimants often popped up and demanded fifty or a hundred dollars of farmers who had settled and improved land, and many farmers paid to avoid legal tangles. These grafters usually moved on to take up other claims and continue their extortion, and no law forbade the pre-emptor from selling his improvements to another and relinquishing his land to the government. It was a sad fact that the purchaser often thought he had bought land when he had purchased only the privilege of pre-empting the land—a privilege he could have had free of charge in many cases.[26]

But ignorance was not the only reason for irregularities surrounding pre-emption. Among many cases of outright fraud and corruption was one that occurred in pioneer Faribault County, where four quarter sections were pre-empted by four young men who stayed on them only a few days. For a house these "gentlemen" used four rails laid in a square. This square was moved from quarter to quarter so that the men might sleep on each quarter one night. A few grape vines stretched around a small tract constituted a fence. In another case, pre-emptors swore that they had built a house sixteen by twenty-four, with two doors and four windows; but it turned out that the house was sixteen by twenty-four inches, and twelve inches high. Another individual claimed that he had built a house with a stone foundation and a board floor. In reality he had constructed a shanty of poplar poles, each corner resting on a small stone, while the floor was earthen with a hole bored in it. Some pre-emptors, no doubt of sporting character, resided on their land by duck-hunting on Sundays."[27]

But in spite of irregularity and fraud, many honest and well-intentioned farmers came into possession of farms through the operation of the pre-emption act. These farmers paid for their land either with cash or with scrip of one sort or another. Paying with cash was often a great hardship, as has been indicated, and at times settlers had to sell half of their land to obtain money to pay for the rest. Sometimes farmers had to borrow money to buy their land. Often usurious rates of interest were charged by some Shylock who would ask "a bond and without mercy exact when due." The author of one county history reported that land was mortgaged and interest at the rate of from two to five per cent a month was exacted; and that a map of the county with the mortgaged farms marked on it would have looked like a checkerboard.[28]

If a settler did not care to pay cash for his land, he might use scrip or warrants, of which various kinds circulated in Minnesota in the 1850's. Around every government land office were the signs of land agents or bankers who had warrants to sell. The value of warrants fluctuated like stock values, and quotations on warrants were published in the newspapers. In fact, the main reason why

SETTLERS AND SPECULATORS

many people used scrip was that private dealers sold it at less than $1.25 an acre. One type of scrip used was the military bounty land warrant, issued by the commissioner of pensions for service in wars before 1855. Such paper called for 40, 60, 80, 120, or 160 acres and was assignable. To receive one of these warrants, a person must have performed at least fourteen days' service at the seat of war. If a veteran's widow married another veteran and survived him also, she was entitled to only one bounty, although surviving minor children of the husband whose bounty was not selected by the widow were entitled to land.[29]

Another type of paper which could be used to secure land was Chippewa half-breed scrip, issued in accordance with the treaty of 1854 with the Chippewa Indians of Lake Superior and the Mississippi. Each piece of scrip was good for eighty acres of land. Sioux half-breed scrip, issued under an act of July 17, 1854, and good for from 40 to 160 acres, also was available.[30]

Colorful events were associated at times with the use of scrip in Minnesota. An example was an occurrence in Goodhue County. In 1854 Congress provided for the survey of the Wabasha Reservation on Lake Pepin, which had been set aside for Sioux half-breeds in 1830, and authorized the president to issue to the half-breeds, in exchange for their claims to the tract, scrip which might be located on any unoccupied lands subject to pre-emption or private sale. Those entitled to the scrip were mainly children under age. When the tract was surveyed and the Red Wing land office was opened in 1855, the names of the mixbloods were sent to Washington and scrip was issued to each name. The scrip was brought to Minnesota, where most of it passed to the parents and guardians of the children and from them to speculators. At that time about two hundred white families, many of whom held quitclaim deeds from individual half-breeds, were living on the tract. The land officers, however, refused to recognize the quitclaims, and held that only scrip was valid. The speculators then "laid the scrip"—their term for registering it in the land office—for the land already settled and improved. The settlers naturally rallied in self-defense, and there was an exciting time in Red Wing. They raised funds among themselves and sent a representative to Washington. Settled lands were marked on the plats in the land office, and speculators were warned away. At a meeting on March 17, 1856, a vigilance committee of twenty-one was chosen to prevent the laying of any more scrip on occupied lands. Two members of the committee kept guard at the land office with loaded revolvers, and obstreperous speculators were threatened with drowning or a less pleasant death. At last a decision was obtained from the General Land Office, which allowed the settlers pre-emption rights on the half-breed tract and granted to the scrip holders the privilege of taking up other pieces of public land.[31]

While military bounty land warrants and half-breed scrip were the most common types of warrants in use in Minnesota in the 1850's, mention should be made also of the scrip issued in 1852 for the commutation of all warrants issued by the state of Virginia for services in the Revolution. This scrip could be located upon any of the public lands of the United States subject to sale at private entry.[32]

The greatest drawback to the warrant system, from the point of view of the average settler, was the fact that the documents tended to fall into the hands of speculators. Just how much land was secured by warrants for speculation rather than for settlement it is impossible to say. Bits of information here and there, however, indicate that the amount was large. For example, of three thousand claims made at the Henderson office, only three hundred were purchased with gold. The rest were secured with warrants, of which only three were given by their original recipients. Indeed, the speculator was generally considered to be the villain of the public-land drama.[33]

One of the characteristic organizations of early Minnesota was the "claim association," formed by settlers as a mutual-aid society for the protection of land claims. As early as 1850 the following item appeared in a St. Paul paper: "Persons making claims on public lands are invited to meet at the Central House in St. Paul, on Saturday next, at seven o'clock in the afternoon, to form an association." This association was to buy land at $1.25 an acre, and thus protect the poor from capitalists who would bid higher. The course of action to be followed was embodied in a resolution: "Resolved, That the Association will assemble whenever called upon by its officers or members and remove any intruder or intruders upon the claim of any bona fide settler or member of the Association, peaceably, if they can, forcibly if they must."[34]

One of the earliest of the associations was organized after Congress reduced the Fort Snelling reservation without making provision for the relief of settlers on the land. A member of the association wrote that in only one instance did it have to resort to severe measures, and in that case "a cat-o'-nine-tails well laid on the bare back of a trespasser on a claim down toward Minnehaha had the desired effect." Often claim contestants arrived at compromises.[35]

But compromises were not always the order of the day. Many people undoubtedly agreed with M. Wheeler Sargeant, who said in an address before the Winona Lyceum in 1858 that "a claim is a *fighting interest* in land, ostensibly based upon priority of possession and sustained by force." Also, it seems that claim jumping was not always a criminal offense in the opinion of the public. The wrong was generally forgiven and forgotten if the attempt was successful, especially if the claim proved to be valuable.[36]

A. G. W. Anderson relates an interesting account of an early claim club in Carver County, where a group of settlers located at Gotteborg in 1854. They laid out 160-acre farms with a compass as an aid, since no surveys had then been made, nor were they made for two or three years after the settlement began. Anderson's account follows:

"There was no law that would protect such squatters. We had to do something to protect ourselves, and so we organized for self defense, drafted our own law, and called it Clublaw, I mean to say that it was no joke to get at variance with the Club. There was no one who dared attempt to take the land from a worthy settler, and, if he did, the Club was after him.

"On one occasion we saw what the Club could do. There was a Norwegian by the name of Peder Thompson, who came late in the fall from Illinois, and bought the claim-right to a valuable piece of land along the Mississippi River. On account of early winter he could not return until spring. In the middle of winter two young men came from St. Paul to jump Thompson's claim. They tore down the house that Thompson had built, moved it a couple of feet, and built it up again. The law was that you had to live upon the land twenty-four hours before it could be preempted. The lads had moved into Thompson's house, with a stove and all the necessary household goods. The Club had observed what they were doing, and foregathered there in the evening, surrounded the shanty, and proceeded to tear the roof off. The young men came out, one with a loaded gun, and the other with an axe and threatened to shoot the first one that touched their house.

"One of the club-members edged up to the one with the gun and grabbed it and pointed it up, another struck him across the arms with his gun and he dropped the gun. Then the other one threw his axe away. Then the rascals begged for their lives. We were not such bad Vikings. On the promise to leave and never return, we let them go. The house was torn down, the stove smashed, and the gun thrown out in the snow. But they came back, cut a few rails, and disappeared. They had been to the Land Office which was then at Red Wing, proved up, and pre-empted the land. Thompson sued and won, and the young men lost their $200 in gold and their pre-emption right."[37]

Such disputes were often fought out in the regular courts, although the claim associations sometimes acted as courts in cases of land troubles. It was important in either case to have a counsel who had some knowledge of the claim laws. One man in Wabasha seems to have had a lucrative business in the 1850's, since he sometimes acted as counsel on both sides in the same suit and, in addition, as confidential adviser to the claim committee.[38]

An example of how land cases sometimes dragged out is to be found in an episode that occurred in Waseca County. In January, 1856, a group of townsite speculators of Owatonna hired men to jump the claims of four settlers. The claim jumpers built houses on the lands and set up counterclaims against the settlers, maintaining that the settlers claimed over 160 acres each, that the settlers were not citizens, and that they had not declared their intentions so to become. The last was true; there was no court nearer than Mankato, but the settlers intended to make their declarations when they got to the land office in Winona. At an impromptu meeting of the settlers it was decided to tell the claim jumpers that their action would not be tolerated. The jumpers, when confronted, did not fight, but stood aside while their buildings were torn down. The Owatonna speculators then signed warrants before a justice for the arrest of five men on the charge of maliciously tearing down a building. Many witnesses were subpoenaed and, after a farcical trial, three of the defendants were found guilty and two in due time were discharged without cost because of an error in the proceedings before the justice. Then followed about a year of expensive litigation at the Winona land office. Finally, two of the original settlers had to give up forty acres each and take up other forties elsewhere. During the whole affair there was actual danger of bloodshed, and some of the men involved went about armed.[39]

This episode shows clearly the aversion of the average settler to the land speculator. While practically every farmer was a speculator in the sense that he expected and hoped that his land would rise in value, he rarely thought of himself in such a role, and he read gleefully the numerous attacks on speculators in the columns of frontier newspapers. The following, from the *St. Paul Weekly Pioneer* of January 4, 1867, is a typical example of these attacks:

"Almost two whole counties have been entered with college scrip and land warrants by speculators. . . . These two counties had far better have been visited by the locusts of Egypt or the grasshoppers of the Red River than by these speculators. Look at the East side of the Mississippi, north of St. Paul, where the lands were sold to speculators, and compare it with the West side. The east is almost a wilderness. . . . The East side was cursed with speculators. The West side was blessed with actual settlers.

"Whole townships have been *doomed* as the homes of whippoorwills and owls—and 'No ADMITTANCE' written over them with 'agricultural college scrip,' to the hardy pioneers in search of homes.

"Let suitable petitions go up from every town and city in the State, to the Land Department at Washington to withhold our lands from sale except to actual settlers."[40]

Now and then a kindly editor would be more solicitous of the welfare of the large land owner. For example, one wrote: "We presume . . . that as small an amount of land has been entered in Minnesota by speculators as in any State or Territory." In another instance, speculators were advised to purchase in good townsites—in two or three, not only one, for protection. One speculator invested six thousand dollars at St. Paul about 1850, and within six years he sold over thirty thousand dollars' worth of the land and had as much more land left. "This," said the enthusiastic reporter, "is but an ordinary instance."[41]

Interesting, though undoubtedly not usual, was a group of swindling land brokers and counterfeiters who operated in southern Minnesota and northern Iowa. They were organized as a regular secret society, with passwords, signs, grips, and oaths, and they succeeded in disposing of nearly $100,000 worth of land before they were detected. They heaped warranty deeds of tax lands upon each other until a veritable labyrinth was formed, and forged recorders' names on certificates. Provided with forged abstracts of titles and forged certificates, the swindlers proceeded to Madison, Milwaukee, and Chicago and disposed of land to which they had no title. The disclosure of their activity came when their victims from Chicago or Milwaukee came to claim their lands.[42]

The years just preceding 1857 were a period of speculative fever, with great activity in town lots, sites, and farm lands. The country was undeveloped; agriculture was neglected; and real estate alone was high. Before the crash of 1857 some men came into possession of vast tracts of Minnesota land. William Holcombe, receiver of the land office at Stillwater, wrote on December 10, 1855, that Henry McKenty of St. Paul had entered 18,000 acres of farm land at the Stillwater office; Hersey and Staples of Stillwater had entered 15,000 acres of pine land; D. Morrison of Bangor, Maine, had entered 14,000 acres of pine land; and James Stinson of St. Paul had entered 8,000 acres of farm land. During the same year, men from Milwaukee, Philadelphia, and Virginia entered large tracts—one of them 4,300 acres—at the Minneapolis and Winona offices. While the boom period lasted money was made in land. Henry McKenty sold to a company of Pennsylvania farmers at five dollars an acre five thousand acres which he had entered at a dollar and a quarter an acre. Another man wrote that in 1855 he bought land "of Mr. Moss of St. Paul, agent of the owner, for $5.00 per acre. The land speculator had bought it two or three years before by land-warrant for about $1.00 per acre." It was said in 1850 that when a man earned a few dollars he could easily invest it in land and double his money in three months, or perhaps even in one month.[43]

This condition was not destined to last without interruption, and in 1857 the bottom fell out of the land market, as it did in other branches of economic life. Many settlers gave up when the panic came, loaded their belongings into dilapidated covered wagons, and trundled their ways across the hills, valleys, and prairies of Minnesota back to Wisconsin, Indiana, Illinois, Ohio, and other states. Persons of foresight and grit, as well as those too lackadaisical to move elsewhere, stayed on and many prospered, as a few years' time brought a change for the better.[44]

Some ten years after the panic, the *Glencoe Register* of August 19, 1869, printed a little item noting the fact that Colonel Henry McKenty had shot himself in St. Paul on the evening of August 10. This death was the occasion for a story in one of the agricultural periodicals of the state. In speaking of the suicide of McKenty, an "honest, kind-hearted, enterprising and brave man," the magazine commented:

"His story, with that of his contemporaries of our city in the wild 'flush times' of the last decade, and in the crash of imaginary fortunes which followed, with the sequel of their histories, could not fail to be instructive.

"Here is a text for one chapter: Early in the morning of August the 12th, many old settlers saw two plodding, prosperous and cheerful *cultivators* of 'broad acres,' who were notable magnates of our speculating fraternity in the 'flush times' of 1856, but on that bright morning, manfully engaged in the public market place."[45]

After the panic of 1857 land values were put on a firmer basis in Minnesota, although, of course, speculation was by no means entirely discontinued. But speculative fever during the pioneer period did not again reach the peak of the boom years of the 1850's.

The prices paid for farm land during the territorial period have already been indicated. Land pre-empted sold for $1.25 an acre, but that bought at auctions or from speculators brought varying amounts. The register and receiver of the Red Wing land office reported that the average price paid for land purchased between February, 1855, and February, 1856, was $1.42 an acre, and that the highest price paid was $16.25. At Stillwater, up to December, 1856, according to the receiver, only 80 acres ever sold for more than $1.25 an acre, and that small area brought only $1.50. At Minneapolis the highest priced land brought $22 an acre, while at Winona $14.50 an acre was the biggest price. Thus, it would seem that much land sold near the government minimum of $1.25 an acre, and that very little brought over $8 or $10 an acre.[46]

During the decade ending in 1858 the various land offices in Minnesota sold some 5,859,000 acres of land. Of this total, approximately 4,113,000 acres were entered with bounty land warrants, and the remainder sold for cash in the amount of $2,335,652.79. More pre-emptions, claimed one newspaper, were made in Minnesota in 1855, 1856, and 1857 than in all the other territories and states combined. Seven land offices handled this business, and by 1858 they were located at Cambridge, St. Cloud, Chatfield, Forest City, St. Peter, Henderson, and Buchanan.[47]

Free Land and Railroads

In 1858 Minnesota was admitted to the Union, and a new phase in her land history began. Before that date the United States government had jurisdiction over the land in Minnesota, except that belonging to the Indians, but after 1858 the state was in possession of land both for itself and for certain railroad companies. Hence, it became possible for a settler to buy state as well as federal land.

Minnesota, like other states, upon her admission was ceded certain lands by the federal government. Sections 16 and 36 of each township, 1,280 acres, were granted by the Minnesota enabling act to aid in sustaining public schools; while 500,000 acres more, under an act of 1841, were granted to the new state for internal improvements. Later, an act of March 12, 1860, granted to the state a type of land known as swamp land. By this law Minnesota was given all legal subdivisions in which more than one-half of the land was "wet and unfit for cultivation," with the exception of any lands which the United States "may have reserved, sold, or disposed of (in pursuance of any law heretofore enacted) prior to the confirmation of title to be made under the authority of said act." The selection of the lands was to be made by the surveyor general or his deputies, or from the field notes of the government surveyors. The selection of swamp land from lands already surveyed was to be made within two years after the adjournment of the legislature at its next session after the date of the act; and the selection from lands surveyed thereafter was to be made within two years after the adjournment of the legislature at its next session following notice by the secretary of the interior to the governor that surveys had been completed and confirmed.[1]

By June 30, 1880, Minnesota claimed 3,755,073 acres under the swamp land act. Further, under an act of February 26, 1857, the state received 46,080 acres of saline lands, which included twelve springs together with six sections of contiguous land for the use of each spring. This land had to be selected by the governor within a year after the state's admission, and it could be disposed of as the legislature saw fit. No salt springs in private hands, however, could be taken. Another grant, included in the enabling act of 1857, gave ten sections to aid in the construction of public buildings at the capital. Finally, under acts of February 26, 1857, March 2, 1861, and July 8, 1870, 92,548 acres were received as a university grant; and 94,439 acres were obtained under the Morrill Act of 1862 for the benefit of a school of agriculture and mechanic arts. This last grant should have been 120,000 acres, but less was received because some of it was double-minimum land.[2]

Procedure for disposing of state land suitable for agriculture was somewhat different from that for federal land. For one thing, by a legislative act of 1861, the care and supervision of all state lands was made the duty of a board consisting of the governor, the attorney general, and the superintendent of public instruction. Further, the lands were to be appraised, none for less than seven dollars an acre, before being offered for sale. After appraisal, six weeks' notice was required before auction sales could be held. Auctions were held at the county seats, and no bids were received for less than the appraised price. On the day of the sale twenty-five per cent of the purchase price had to be paid, and the remainder was allowed to run for twenty years at six per cent interest. In 1862 the law was amended in three respects: the state auditor was made ex-officio commissioner of the land office, the minimum price was reduced to five dollars an acre, and purchase terms were liberalized. Thenceforth only fifteen per cent of the purchase price was payable on the day of sale. The next year the rate of interest was reduced and time payments were extended to forty years. Certificates of purchase, which were assignable and could be recorded, were issued by the state. All land on which the interest was delinquent for more than a year was forfeited unless previously redeemed. To redeem such land it was necessary to pay double the interest overdue.[3]

Minnesota decided to use swamp land proceeds for schools and charitable institutions, one-half of the income from the principal to go to the common school fund and the rest to educational and charitable institutions. An amendment to the law provided that swamp lands could be sold for one-third less than the amount fixed as a minimum for the sale of school lands. Much of the swamp land grant, however, went to railroads or other bodies and the state realized little profit from it. The first list of swamp lands transferred in Becker County, for example, was a three-thousand-acre area granted to the Cannon River Improvement Association and sold to E. G. Holmes and A. H. Wilcox in 1882.[4]

School lands were offered for sale at various times, and many notices of such auctions are to be found in the early state newspapers. For example, in 1862 the state auditor toured southern Minnesota selling school lands in Goodhue, Rice, Winona, and Olmsted counties. Sales in each county averaged between $20,000 and $45,000, and the highest price received for any of the land was $150 per acre. In the same year the state began to sell school lands in Washington County, in areas of 40, 80, and 160 acres. Robert Watson wrote that that fall he bought forty acres there for seven dollars an acre, and a neighbor bought an adjoining forty-acre tract for eight dollars an acre. Some people complained that there was much stealing of timber from unsold school lands, and that the method of selling the land was bad.[5]

Within a year or two after Minnesota became a state the country was emerging from the depths of the panic of 1857, and land values became sounder than they had been in the boom period before 1857. In July, 1860, it was said that there "never had been a time within the last five years more favorable for those who wish to purchase improved farms, or wild lands near thriving cities and villages, than the present." There was little or no speculative movement in real estate, and land prices had sunk below the actual value of property. According to one of the newspapers: "The reason for this is obvious. . . . Much property has passed into the hands of mortgagees who have no use for it, who would gladly sell for the bare amount for which it was given as security, and that was not in most cases more than half its actual value. . . . Within a circle of ten miles from St. Paul, lands may be bought that have been entered for years, for a less sum than first cost, and interest compounded, which may be made into farms and gardens that will net much more than lands purchased at government price twenty, fifty and one hundred miles distant."[6]

President Lincoln, on May 20, 1862, signed the Homestead Act, one of the most important land measures ever enacted by the Congress. For years there had been agitation for such a law, and one was actually passed in 1860, but it was vetoed by President Buchanan. The South generally opposed such a measure as being a threat to the slave interests, and so it failed to become law until the South had seceded from the Union. In Minnesota the reaction to the act was quite different. State newspapers exulted over it and spoke of its stimulus to immigration. "Not since early times has there been so wonderful an accession to our people as at the present writing," was the enthusiastic comment of a Rochester paper. "Train after train of white covered wagons, accompanied by droves of horses, cattle and sheep, are passing through our streets, forming one continuous caravan from morn till dewy eve."[7]

Most of the newspapers published the full text of the act. Under its provisions, any citizen or person, who had applied for citizenship, who was head of a family or twenty-one years of age, and who had never borne arms against the United States or given aid and comfort to its enemies, was allowed, after January 1, 1863, to enter 160 acres or less of government land, open to pre-emption at $1.25 an acre, or 80 acres or less of land at $2.50 an acre, after the land had been surveyed. An affidavit attesting to the qualifications of the homesteader was required at the time of filing, and a residence of five years upon the homestead was necessary before a patent to the land would be issued. Land acquired under the act could not be seized for a debt incurred before the issuance of the patent.[8]

The mode of procedure under the act was something like this: A prospective settler looked over the quarter sections in a surveyed region until he found one he liked. Then he went to the government land office and had his name entered as a claimant, if it was found that there was no prior claimant. The expense involved so far was about fourteen dollars, for which he was given a receipt.

He was then at liberty to take possession of the land within a six months' period. If he failed to occupy the land within that time, his claim was liable to be "jumped"; that is, another person might appear at the land office to request that the validity of the original claim be tested. On the strength of such a request and the payment of five dollars by the applicant, a suit would be ordered and advertised, and the parties would be notified to appear at the land office on a certain day to give evidence in the case. The original claimant had to prove that he had not abandoned his claim, and that he had been deterred by unavoidable occurrences, such as death or illness, from occupying it, or the case would be decided against him. If, however, he won the case, or no case was brought against him, he was entitled to a deed from the government after five years' occupancy of the land. It was then his to sell or dispose of as he saw fit. Of course, if he desired title before the five-year period was up, he could secure it by paying the minimum price asked for the land.[9]

All this sounds fairly simple. In practice, however, homesteading frequently was a complicated business. As one Chippewa County settler wrote, "Locating one's homestead and getting it filed . . . was not as easy as to read about it. One had to be sure that one settled on government land opened to homestead entry and not on railroad grant land. For the railroad land tract given away by congress, to the railroad construction promoters . . . on July 4, 1866, and approved by the Minnesota legislature March 7, 1867, was exactly one half of all the land in Tunsberg, Big Bend and Kragero Townships. It was every odd numbered section, or every other section. . . . It often took a lot of walking, searching and painstaking sighting to locate the quarter section corner markers even after one or more section corners had been found. That is, probably, why one homesteader started digging a dugout on his neighbor's land. His neighbor . . . watched him work until the dugout was nearly completed. Then he stepped in and claimed it for his own."[10]

Despite the difficulties involved in homesteading, however, large tracts of Minnesota land went on to the tax lists of the state via the Homestead Act. According to one report, 1,851,627 acres in the state were filed upon under the law in a four-year period, while the

Winnebago City Homestead reported that 25,555 acres were taken up at the land office there under the act during the single month of May, 1864. Unfortunately, the persons who filed on homesteads, like those who pre-empted, "were not all bona-fide settlers. Some of them were the pawns of grasping lumbermen who took advantage of the generous impulses of the nation to despoil it of its resources." The majority of claimants, however, were farmers looking for a chance to improve their condition. Between May 20, 1862, and June 30, 1880, a total of 62,379 entries, involving 7,346,038.96 acres or nearly one-seventh of the state's area, were filed under the law.[11]

As time passed the Homestead Act of 1862 was amended, mainly by extending its privileges. On June 8, 1872, an amendment was passed providing that honorably discharged soldiers and sailors could take up homesteads and deduct from their five years' residence requirement their term of service during the Civil War. A minimum of one year's residence plus cultivation, however, was still necessary before a clear title could be secured. It was provided also that honorably discharged soldiers and sailors who had served at least ninety days were eligible to homestead 160 acres of $2.50 land. A soldiers' additional homestead provision of March 3, 1873, enabled soldiers who, under the act of 1862, had homesteaded less than 160 acres to take up additional land to total that amount. This could be done under the amendment of 1872 if the additional land was contiguous to the original homestead. Under the provision of 1873 the additional land did not have to be contiguous, but could be on any surveyed public land not otherwise appropriated. By an act of March 3, 1879, civilians were allowed to take up additional homesteads, although the additional had to be adjacent to the original homestead. As an alternative, the settler might relinquish his original homestead to the government and take up 160 acres elsewhere. Finally, the act of March 3, 1879, and others of July 1, 1879, and June 15, 1880, did away, within certain broad limits, with the distinction between $1.25 and $2.50 land as far as homesteading was concerned.[12]

The act of 1872 was the foundation of "soldiers' additionals," which were treated as transferable and became an important article of commerce. Many thousands of them were located by enterprising speculators in northwestern Minnesota on the pine lands and prairies. While the additionals were never made legally transferable, the law was circumvented by taking powers of attorney from the soldiers when they relinquished their certificates. These letters of attorney authorized persons, whose names were not filled in, to make entries of land at local offices in the name of the soldiers, and to sell and convey these lands. The blank for the name of the attorney was filled with the name of the last holder of the certificate before its surrender at the local land office. Here was just another way of prostituting the land laws to the purposes of the land grabber and the speculator.[13]

In fairness to the soldiers, it should be pointed out that all military men did not take advantage fraudulently of the Homestead Act. Furthermore, another person could file a lien on 160 acres for a soldier, who then had six months to make his entry at the land office and an additional half year to move on to the land. Other homesteaders had only six months in which to do both. On one occasion the *St. Cloud Democrat* stated that during the preceding six months more than four hundred homesteads had been located by one man at the St. Cloud land office for soldiers who planned to settle on them as soon as their terms of service expired. Most of the claims were in Stearns and Benton counties.[14]

In the same year that the Homestead Act became law, Congress passed an act granting public lands to the states for the purpose of establishing colleges of agriculture and mechanic arts. Some states, which did not have enough public lands within their borders to equal their bounty from Congress, were given agricultural college scrip good for enough land to make up the difference. The scrip could be used in locating on the surveyed and unappropriated public lands in other sections of the country, or it could be used in payment of pre-emption claims and the commutation of homestead entries. Homestead entries could be commuted to cash only after the homesteader had actually occupied the land, made improvements on it, and cultivated part of it for at least six months. A settler who commuted his homestead lost his right to make another homestead or pre-emption entry.[15]

Even after the passage of the Homestead Act many persons continued to buy land from the state, from the federal government, from railroad companies, or from individuals. Strange as this practice may seem, it was quite logical, since much land open to homesteading was far distant from markets or transportation facilities. And, of course, scrip and warrants were available for the purchase of land. For example, during November, 1868, the St. Cloud land office disposed of 514,154 acres of land, of which only 15,438 were taken up under the Homestead Act. The rest was located with agricultural college scrip and military warrants. One man from St. Cloud reported that nearly two whole counties had been entered by speculators with scrip and warrants; and letters were written to Congressmen to stay the "ruinous system."[16]

Thus, as during earlier periods, was the cry raised against the speculator, who now was armed with a new means of acquiring land—agricultural college scrip. So great was the blast against the speculator that Governor William R. Marshall, in his annual message of January 10, 1868, noted that evils connected with the public sales of United States land and the rapid absorption of it with college scrip by nonresidents continued. He recommended that the legislature send to Congress a memorial requesting that the lands be sold only to actual settlers.[17]

Like Marshall, another of Minnesota's outstanding figures, Ignatius Donnelly, was active and ardent in his opposition to the land speculator. Particularly at this time did Donnelly become aroused over the handling of the land in the Sioux reservation on the west side of the Minnesota River, a tract of 721,172 acres which President Johnson offered for sale on August 28, 1867, at the request of Senators Alexander Ramsey and Daniel Norton and the St. Peter land officers. Donnelly and others, notably William Windom, felt that the sale was unfair. Settlement of the tract had been provided for originally by the act of March 3, 1863, which decreed the removal of the Sioux, whose outbreak of the preceding year was all too fresh in the people's minds. On June 1, 1865, the reservation was opened for pre-emption settlement, but most of the settlers then residing in the area could not pre-empt, as they had exercised that privilege earlier. Indeed, from June 1, 1865, until October 1, 1866, only 198 declaratory statements, covering 28,000 acres, were made, and only 36 statements covering 5,000 acres were proved up and paid within a year, as required by law. During the same period, however, much lumber was stripped off the area.

On October 12, 1867, the settlers on the former reservation petitioned President Johnson as follows: "Our first crops raised in 1866 were at once destroyed by swarms of grasshoppers, so that a great famine was only averted from us by means of rations and supplies of voluntary contributions from other States. And this year our crops have suffered again severely from hail." Two weeks later Governor Marshall pointed out that a famine would have swept the region during the preceding spring and summer if the state had not helped the settlers. He said that the sale would sacrifice the poor settler to the grasping speculator, and he asked that it not be held. Finally, Donnelly and Windom succeeded in getting a law passed by Congress to protect the actual settlers, but only after the whole affair had worried the settlers and cost them the expense of sending an agent to Washington. Furthermore, the speculator also had his day. Between August, 1867, and May, 1868, a large portion of the former reservation was sold in extensive tracts, with some men buying as much as 4,700 acres. In the single month of May, 1868, the enormous amount of 27,262 acres was sold—20,787 acres to thirteen men, which, according to Donnelly, would have provided homes for 130 families. The speculator, Donnelly continued, "who improves his land is an extraordinary exception to the rule, and ... in all the older portions of the State there are large tracts bought for speculation which have been held unimproved for ten, fifteen, or twenty years."[18]

From 1862 until 1873 no major land law affecting Minnesota was passed by Congress. In the latter year, after the frontier line had penetrated subhumid, treeless areas, the Timber Culture Act was placed on the statute books. This law provided that any person who planted, protected, and kept in a healthy growing condition forty acres of timber for five years—the trees not to be over eight feet apart each way—on any 160 acres of public land, was entitled to a patent for the quarter section at the end of ten years. Proof of the tree culture must be attested by not fewer than two creditable witnesses, and only one quarter in any section could be thus granted. Persons entering timber-culture tracts were required to pay a ten-dollar fee upon entering and to make an affidavit to the effect that the entry was for the cultivation of timber. If the conditions of the law were not met, the land reverted to the government. A homesteader under the act of 1862 who, at the end of his third year's residence, had had under cultivation for two years one acre of timber trees, not more than eight feet apart, for every sixteen acres of his homestead, could, upon the word of two creditable witnesses, receive his patent. Timber-culture land, like homestead land, could not be seized for debts contracted by the applicant before he received his patent.[19]

At first very few settlers availed themselves of the advantages of the Timber Culture Act, for its conditions were onerous. In 1873, only 95 entries covering 14,710 acres were filed in the state, but in 1874 the number jumped to 804, covering 113,131 acres. On March 13 of the latter year the law was amended so that ten acres in timber and eight years' care sufficed to meet the basic requirements. At the end of eight years, or within five years thereafter, the settler or his heirs, supported by two witnesses, could prove up and receive a patent of title. Many farmers, after the terms of the law were liberalized, then took "tree claims." From 1873 to 1880, inclusive, 8,478 entries, embracing 1,166,059 acres, were made in the state under the Timber Culture Act and its amendments. The years 1878 and 1879 witnessed the largest number of entries made in this period, 2,693 and 1,847 respectively.[20]

There were frauds and abuses under the act, as under previous land laws, but some good was accomplished by it. One writer maintained that the law was of immense value to the Red River area as an incentive to planting trees. "Hundreds of settlers," he wrote, "who planted five or ten acres of trees, at first merely in order to secure title to the land, found later that they could not have made a better investment of either time or money, and the magnificent groves of timber resulting have, in fact, changed the face of the earth, influenced the climatic conditions, and added literally millions of dollars to the value of the lands." Writing in one of the farm journals, John Grimm stated that many pieces of land were taken up under the "Tree Act" in the western part of McLeod, Sibley, and adjoining counties. Everyone was naturally interested in the question of which trees were the best to plant. The *Farmers' Union* suggested the soft maple, but solicited more information on the subject. In answer to the query, a letter signed "Farmer" recommended willow, cottonwood, box elder, white maple, Norway, rock, and sycamore maple, white and blue ash, white elm, oak, hickory, laurel, and European larch trees.[21]

Not only the federal government and the farmers of Minnesota, but the state government also endeavored to cover sections of the prairie with trees. In 1873 an act of the Minnesota legislature provided for a bounty of two dollars annually for ten years for each acre of prairie land planted with any kind of forest trees, except black locust, and a like bounty for each half mile planted with forest trees along any public highway. The law stipulated that the trees must be planted within five years after the passage of the act and must be successfully grown and cultivated for a period of three years. Trees planted along public highways were to be not more than one rod apart, and if they were planted on both sides of a highway the planter was entitled to four dollars a half mile. Bounties ceased if the care of the trees was discontinued. Bounties could not be obtained until a plat of the land planted to trees had been filed with the county auditor; and the plat had to be filed annually. The act allowed $20,000 to be paid in bounties.[22]

In the first year of the law's operation about 8,000,000 saplings were set out. In 1880 the state commissioner of statistics reported that 25,331 Minnesota acres had been planted to trees. This total did not include 329,809 rods of tree rows along public roads and on boundary lines between farms. Many of the trees were short-lived cottonwoods and box elders, but many others were still standing more than fifty years later. And, if an author of one of the older county histories can be taken as an authority, the act deserves much praise. Said he: "Under the timber culture act, many of our farmers have beautified the drives around their respective farms, by planting forest trees along each thoroughfare, thereby improving their farms and the highways at the same time. The framers of the timber culture act should be canonized. They builded better than they knew."[23]

One other source of land open to the pioneer farmer of Minnesota was railroad land. Early in the nation's history land grants had been used to aid in the building of roads and canals, and in 1850 the state of Illinois received land from the federal government as a railroad subsidy. In Minnesota during the middle 1850's there was much discussion as to whether there should be free land for settlers or for railroads. Governor Willis A. Gorman, for example, favored the former, but there was much agitation for the latter, especially on the part of railroad interests and settlers who were distant from good water transportation facilities. Finally, on March 3, 1857, Congress answered the demands of the railroad advocates and voted land to Minnesota for railroad building. The grant gave alternate sections of land in a strip six sections wide on each side of the railroad right of way for 1,167 miles of track, or a total of 4,481,280 acres.[24]

No actual construction took place, however, until 1862, when the St. Paul and Pacific Railroad Company, incorporated as the Minnesota and Pacific, built ten miles of road from St. Paul to St. Anthony. In 1864 the company began to build toward Breckenridge, with a branch line north to Watab. The branch was completed in 1868, but Breckenridge was not reached until 1873. The Winona and St. Peter Railroad got under way in 1863, and by 1873 it had pushed westward through Rochester, Owatonna, Waseca, and St. Peter to New Ulm. The Minnesota Central Railroad, begun in 1864 at Mendota, extended south through Northfield, Faribault, Owatonna, and Austin, reaching the Iowa line in 1869. In 1865 the Southern Minnesota started west from La Crosse, and by 1870 it had reached Albert Lea and Winnebago City. Between 1868 and 1872 the Hastings and Dakota Railroad Company built tracks between Hastings and Chaska and Carver. The St. Paul and Chicago Railroad Company completed a line to La Crescent in 1872. The Minnesota Valley Railroad, later the St. Paul and Sioux City, was begun in 1865 and in 1870 it reached St. James. In the same year the Lake Superior and Mississippi Railroad was completed between St. Paul and Duluth. This road later became a part of the Northern Pacific Railroad, which was chartered in 1864 and was to receive 12,800 acres of land per mile of track built through the state. Work began in 1870, and by the end of the next year Moorhead was reached. Other lines built in this period were the Stillwater and St. Paul, finished in 1870; the Winona, Mankato, and New Ulm, with four miles in 1870; the Minneapolis and Duluth, with fifteen miles in 1871–72; the Minneapolis and St. Louis, with twenty-seven miles in 1871; and the Chicago, Clinton, Dubuque, and Minnesota, with twenty-five miles in 1872. The first decade of Minnesota railroad building saw a total of nineteen hundred miles of track laid in the state. Then came the panic of 1873, and building generally was halted for the next four years. Between 1873 and 1876 only eighty-seven miles of track were laid, mostly minor jobs, such as connecting Crookston and Grand Forks, and Worthington and Sioux Falls, South Dakota. Many of the roads already built had been aided by land grants, and their companies were busy trying to revive and continue grants which otherwise would lapse. By the winter of 1876 most of the grants had been renewed.[25]

Some of the companies received, in addition to federal lands, swamp lands from the state. These roads were the St. Paul and Duluth, the Southern Minnesota, the Duluth and Iron Range, and the River Division of the St. Paul and Chicago. Between 1861 and 1875 these roads were granted over 1,600,000 acres, of which over 1,450,000 were certified to the companies by the end of 1877.[26]

The largest building projects carried out during the last few years of the 1870's were those of the St. Paul and Pacific, the Minneapolis and St. Louis, the Southern Minnesota, the Hastings and Dakota, the Western, and the St. Paul and Sioux City railroads. Also, some six new lines entered the field. This burst of activity after the worst effects of the panic had worn off resulted in 1,112 miles of new track, giving the state nearly 3,100 miles of railroads in 1880.[27]

By consolidating the statistics of land grants to Minnesota railroads, it is found that Congressional gifts certified to the roads amounted to 7,621,131 acres by December 31, 1877, and state grants certified equaled 1,450,133 acres—a total of 9,071,264, over one-sixth of the area of the state. At the same time the state had nearly 2,200 miles of track, so that the land grants equaled 4,132 acres per mile. And, lest the reader marvel at the size of the public largess, it should be pointed out that by 1877 the railroads could have had 12,595,756 acres—an area equal to the combined areas of Connecticut, Massachusetts, and New Hampshire—if they had fulfilled all their bargains with the governments, state and federal.[28]

The granting of land to railroads raised a problem for some settlers—those who had pre-emptions on the land before the railroad received it. On August 21, 1860, the commissioner of the General Land Office ruled that settlers who did not pay for their claims prior to the date set for public sale forfeited them, and, if the claims were on odd-numbered sections, the land went to the railroad company. If, however, the pre-emptions were made before the date when the railroad plats were filed in the district land office, and they were paid for before public sale, the pre-emptions were valid. The railroad company in such cases was permitted to choose other land to make up the total allowed in a grant.[29]

When the railroads received their land they generally deeded it to some firm or group of men in trust. For example, the Southern Minnesota Railroad Company, which received 8,960 acres per mile of track built, deeded the land to Samuel B. Ruggles and Albon P. Man of New York. These men then used the proceeds of land sales to take up the bonds of the Southern Minnesota. In 1868 the First Division of the St. Paul and Pacific Railroad Company mortgaged its lands covered by the grant of 1857 to Edmund Rice, Horace Thompson, and Samuel J. Tilden to secure $3,000,000 in bonds. Again, in 1865, it mortgaged the lands in a grant of that year to the same men and George L. Becker to secure the payment of another issue of bonds. In 1879 both mortgages were foreclosed and the property was sold to the St. Paul, Minneapolis and Manitoba Railroad Company for $1,600,000. The latter then mortgaged the land to John S. Kennedy, John S. Barnes, and James A. Roosevelt to secure its bonds in an amount not to exceed $12,000 per mile of road built. The lands covered by mortgages were released as fast as they were sold by the several mortgage holders, and, for the most part, they went to settlers.[30]

This method of financing allowed the accumulation of large areas of Minnesota land by some individuals. During the dark days of the old St. Paul and Pacific Railroad Company, before the foreclosure of its two mortgages, the bonds of the company could be purchased for a few cents on the dollar. John H. Camp, a retired wholesale merchant of St. Paul, then obtained nearly 11,000 acres of the company's land, using the bonds as payment. In the five years succeeding the failure of Jay Cooke in 1873, the sale of Northern Pacific lands aggregated 1,723,500 acres to 2,988 different purchasers, realizing to the company $7,887,250. These sales represented an average of over 575 acres per buyer. One of the largest purchases was made by a corporation composed of families from Amenia and Sharon, about ninety miles north of New York City. The corporation was formed in July, 1875, with a capital of $100,000, which was exchanged for Northern Pacific bonds. In the same month E. W. Chaffee, as a representative of the corporation, visited the Red River Valley and selected odd-numbered sections in four townships in Cass County. Many such examples could be repeated. In fact, most of the great farms of northwestern Minnesota were created by purchasing alternate sections from railroad companies. Many of the intervening portions were obtained by purchase from the settlers who had received land from the government in good faith, "but in some instances claims were also obtained from the government by fraudulent agents, who professed their intention to comply with this legal requirement in taking land by pre-emption."[31]

The railroad companies naturally wanted the lands along their tracks settled as rapidly as possible, and they were active therefore in encouraging immigration to Minnesota. The Northern Pacific, for example, had local agents in England, Wales, Scotland, Germany, Switzerland, Norway, and Sweden to sell its land and to encourage immigration. Pamphlets, circulars, and folders praising Minnesota and telling how land could be secured were published in various languages and distributed widely. Another device used to attract settlers was the sale of land exploration tickets. These tickets were sold at full fare by the Northern Pacific, but if the purchaser bought forty acres or more from the company within sixty days, he could use the fare toward buying the land and his family and goods were given free transportation when he came to settle. Some of the companies maintained "reception houses," "receiving houses," or "immigrant houses," where settlers hunting a farm could get infor-

A COLONISTS' RECEPTION HOUSE
[From *Guide to the Northern Pacific Railroad Lands in Minnesota*, 48 (New York, 1872).]

mation, food, clothing, and shelter. And, if a settler purchased timberland, the railroad company sometimes agreed to buy wood from him. In these and other ways Minnesota railroad companies did much to encourage settlement in the state.[32]

Railroad land could be purchased by the average settler either for cash or on credit, or, as has been indicated, with company bonds. Cash prices generally were slightly less than credit quotations, although either one, in comparison with most modern land values, seems cheap indeed. The Southern Minnesota Railroad Company sold its land at from four to twelve dollars an acre, ten dollars being the average for good prairie land. Its credit terms for forty acres at ten dollars an acre were as follows:[33]

Cash down, $100 principal, advance interest $21 . . . . . . $121
Cash in one year, $100 principal, advance interest $14 . . . 114
Cash in two years, $100 principal, advance interest $7 . . . 107
Cash in three years, $100 principal 100

Total 442

In 1872 the main line of the St. Paul and Pacific sold land at from $5.00 to $15.00 an acre, with ten years' credit if desired. The cash price was $1.00 less per acre than the credit price. Northern Pacific lands in 1877 were bringing from $2.50 to $10.00 an acre, and a settler could secure them by making a ten-per-cent down payment and seven yearly installments at seven-per-cent interest. The St. Paul and Sioux City Company offered its lands at from $2.50 to $5.00 an acre cash, or double that price if purchased over a five-year period, with interest at seven per cent. Winona and St. Peter Railroad lands sold for from $2.00 to $9.00 an acre, with five years' credit offered or twelve and one-half per cent discount for cash, and the Lake Superior and Mississippi Company land brought a minimum of $5.00 an acre in 1879, ten per cent down and eight years to pay the rest. Sometimes rebates were given settlers for breaking and cropping land. The St. Paul and Pacific Company allowed a purchaser of its land as much as $3.00 an acre on three-quarters or less of the land bought, if certain conditions were fulfilled. If ten acres or more were broken on an eighty-acre tract, or a hundred acres or more on a section in a year, the settler was allowed $2.50 an acre, while he received $.50 an acre if he raised a crop on or before the third year on fifty or sixty acres out of eighty, or four hundred or four hundred and eighty out of a section.[34]

Not only did the railroads make land available for settlers, but they also provided the transportation facilities needed by farmers willing to venture out on to the prairies away from rivers. Before

1870 farmers clung to the hardwood regions of the state, but by 1880 they had ventured northwest and west to the Dakota and Canadian boundaries. Moving in the same directions were the various government land offices. In 1871 there were seven land offices in Minnesota, as there had been in 1858, but, while in 1858 the offices were located generally in the southeastern part of the state, in 1871 they had begun to push farther north and west, to Alexandria, Litchfield, New Ulm, and Duluth. The other three offices were at Taylor's Falls, Jackson, and St. Cloud. By the end of the 1870's there were nine offices, and their locations—at Taylor's Falls, St. Cloud, New Ulm, Duluth, Fergus Falls, Worthington, Benson, Redwood Falls, and Crookston—reflected even better than in 1871 the northwestern movement of settlement.[35]

By 1875, of the state's total area of 53,449,840 acres, about 37,595,000 had been surveyed. Of the latter, 16,500,000 acres, or 43.88 per cent, were in private hands; 8,400,000 acres were in farms; and only 2,816,413 acres were tilled. Thus, a very small part of Minnesota's total area was actually under cultivation, while 27.29 per cent of the state still remained to be surveyed. Three years later 39,282,418 acres were reported as surveyed. Of this amount the following distribution was given:[36]

Cash sales and warrants	8,920,285.70 acres
Homestead and Timber Culture acts	5,829,042.64 "
Agricultural college lands	1,033,908.75 "
Railroad grants (certified)	7,621,131.22 "
Swamp land selections (approved)	1,361,125.13 "
Internal improvement lands	500,000.00 "
School lands	2,969,990.00 "
University lands	92,548.35 "
Indian scrip	244,672.29 "
Float scrip	400.00 "
Saline lands	26,435.00 "
Public buildings land	6,400.00 "
Total	28,605,939.08 "

As would be expected, the price of privately owned land had

increased considerably by the late 1870's over the price it had brought twenty years earlier in the older sections of the state. In 1878 land in Fillmore County sold for $30.00 an acre, while in Olmsted County $40.00 to $50.00 an acre was said to be the general price, and farms sold near Rochester for $75.00 an acre. Such land, of course, had improvements on it and was located advantageously near markets and social facilities. In a later chapter an attempt will be made to show the relationship between this rise in land values in the southeastern part of Minnesota and the change in farming methods accompanying it.[37]

The Farmer's Home

As late as 1870 four-fifths of the population in Minnesota was concentrated in the southeastern part of the state, accessible to the Minnesota, St. Croix, and Mississippi rivers. This area, in general, was wooded, the kind of area congenial to the pioneers, for it furnished them with materials for fuel, fences, and houses. Only with reluctance did they venture out on the open prairie, where tradition maintained that the soil was less fertile, and where winds, blizzards, fires, insect pests, Indians, and lack of transportation facilities seemed to doom the settler to failure or death.[1]

The homes of the early farmers were invariably shanties or log cabins, hewn out of the surrounding woods. While these primitive structures for the most part adhered to a common pattern, there was enough variation among them to make a description of the "typical log cabin" as erroneous as would be that of the "typical Midwest home" of today. In the words of one writer, the "range in technical skill and financial resources of settlers led to wide variation of the method of cabin construction." Some settlers were fortunate enough to live near a sawmill, where they could purchase black walnut and butternut for the inside furnishing of their cabins, while others had to rely entirely upon their ingenuity and few tools for the fashioning of the entire building. Some had been able to bring considerable furniture with them from the East, while others had to make most of it on the spot. In any event, the early Minnesota farmer lived in a dwelling far from spacious.[2]

While the cabin was being built, the farmer and his family might live in their prairie wagon, sleep on the grass, build a temporary shanty, or crowd in with neighbors—none of these choices too pleasant. Mrs. Anna S. Apgar, who settled in Excelsior in 1854, reported that six families all lived in one little cabin until their homes were built and their furniture arrived; and John A. Jones, an early settler near Mankato, recalled years later: "We set our stove up in the yard by a tree and lived in the shanty until our new log house was completed. The shanty was covered with seven loads of hay to make it warm inside and a quilt was hung over the door. Here we lived for two months, suffering at times from rain penetrating."[3]

Most cabins were completed in far less than two months. Lewis Harrington in 1855 built one near Hutchinson in five days; and many another settler, in spite of lack of experience in cutting and dressing logs, put together a habitation in a matter of days. Where several families settled an area together, "cabin raisings," as they were called, became occasions for pleasant social get-togethers, truly welcome breaks in a rather drab and harsh existence. When all were assembled, several men were chosen to "carry up the corners," and each was provided with a sharp ax. It was their job to cut notches in the ends of the logs chosen for the walls, so that the logs of each side of the cabin would be interlocked with logs in adjoining walls. In this way a rather substantial structure could be erected, often without the use of any iron. The logs were carried to the building site or rolled there by men using "hand-spikes," or sticks of hard, tough wood, about six feet long, from which the bark had been removed and the ends slightly tapered. After being notched, the logs were rolled on skids or lifted with forked sticks and guide ropes to their places. Frequently the roof was made of clapboards, or "shakes," split from straight-grained timber with a frow and held together by poles running the length of the cabin and fastened to the end logs with wooden pins. Shingles were sold in St. Paul in the 1850's, but they were too expensive for many people, who relied on rough dirt or straw for roofing materials.

Spaces for doors and windows—or window, as was usually the case—were cut out after the walls were built. Doors generally opened inward, and they might be fastened to the frame with wooden pins and wooden hinges. A wooden latch fitted with a latchstring, often of deerskin, locked the door. When the latchstring was allowed to hang through a small hole in the door, the door could be opened from the outside. This custom naturally gave rise to the expression of hospitality: "The latchstring is always out." Some cabins had small panes of glass in the window. The floor might be of tramped earth, but better was a puncheon floor made of split logs, the rounded sides buried in the earth and the flat sides forming the surface. If a fireplace was desired it, too, was made of wood, but it was lined with stone or clay to protect it from the fire. Part of the fireplace extended outside the cabin, and the chimney paralleled one of the walls. After the framework of the building was completed, the spaces between the logs were chinked with split wood and a mixture of clay mortar and marsh hay. Mud plastering also was common in some localities.[4]

A few families brought from their old homes "a bureau, two or three chairs, and perhaps other cherished articles of furniture, but such families were an exception." Most of the furnishings of the cabins and shanties were homemade and usually quite primitive. In a corner of the room a one-legged bedstead was often built by placing a post upright about four feet from one wall and six feet from another. Logs from this post to the walls served as rails for the bed, and slats or cords from the wall to the longer log furnished the foundation. Trundle beds and cradles, which could be put under the larger bed during the day, took care of the children. If a cabin was large enough, two single-post or even two four-post beds could be accommodated. Clapboards laid across wooden pins in the walls formed shelves, and a large box or a packing case sometimes did duty as a table. Logs split in two, with the flat sides smoothed, could be converted into benches by inserting legs into the curved sides. A traveler's description of a cabin with such crude furnishings is quoted by Theodore C. Blegen in his *Grass Roots History:* "They lived in a rude log cabin, sixteen by eighteen, plastered with mud, and with a huge fireplace and mud chimney pushed out at one end. This one small room served as kitchen, parlor, bedroom, pantry, cellar, and all other purposes. The furniture was equally rude, there being but one chair with a back to it, and that quite rickety. For seats, there was a large trunk, two stools, and two empty boxes. ... There were two beds—the settler and wife occupied one, myself and chum the other, while the children made a bunk on the floor."

THE FARMER'S HOME

To add a touch of coziness and warmth to the cabins, some women placed on the floor buffalo robes and skins or carpets and rugs brought from the old home. Later, when time was found for handiwork, braided and crocheted rugs replaced the skins and robes.[5]

Beyond the wooded areas materials for log cabins and frame shanties were not easy to obtain, and, after the vanguard of settlement had pushed into the treeless areas, a different type of shelter was needed there until the railroads came and until the farmers could afford to import lumber. Once again the pioneer exercised his ingenuity and utilized the materials at hand. He found an answer to his need in the thick prairie sod everywhere available, which he cut into bricks suitable for building. In the 1860's, 1870's, 1880's, and even later, western Minnesota was dotted with sod houses of various types and sizes. When Ole Hedman arrived in Cottonwood County in 1870, he dug a hole four feet deep and roofed it over with bark, slough grass, and sod; and most of his neighbors did likewise. These dugouts were fairly waterproof, except in unusually hard rains, when straw was spread over the muddy floor. Families survived in these crude shelters even when winter snows completely covered them. In fact, on the prairies, sod houses were warmer in winter and cooler in summer than wooden shanties. Near Sleepy Eye a Danish family built a sod house large enough to accommodate not only themselves, but their cows and oxen as well. Within it copper utensils brought from Denmark seemed almost out of place. Some houses were built completely of sod while others had sod bricks laid on the outside of frame shacks. The walls of sod barns frequently were three or four feet thick; yet rain, sun, wind, mice, and rotting grass reduced them to piles of dirt in a few years. The surprising thing to us today is not the perishable quality of sod houses, but the fact that people could live in them at all, to say nothing of living in them for years.[6]

Keeping house in a log cabin or a sod house was no simple matter. Even the wives of veterans in trailer camps on our college campuses today would find the task quite a challenge. One early Minnesotan wrote: "My mother had to do all the cooking on a flat stone on the floor with another standing up behind it. She nearly lost her sight the first winter from the smoke." Often the flickering light from the hearth was the only break in the blackness of night, although most cabins had a supply of candles or their substitutes. If mutton tallow, a candle mold, and a candlewick were available, the housewife could make very acceptable candles. If they were lacking, she had to be satisfied with improvisations. Lard, goose grease, or venison fat could be melted and placed in a dish or a hollowed-out turnip or beet along with a rag wick to make a lamp which "emitted some smoke, much odor and a little light." In 1859 kerosene lamps were on the market and came gradually into use. "We had our first kerosene lamp in '61," related one woman. "We were terrible frightened of it. It did smell terrible but this did not keep us from being very proud of it." In Rice County inexperience with a kerosene lamp caused the tragic death of a settler's wife, "such a thing as a lamp being at that time a novelty and a curiosity." Lanterns were developed for use outside. At first candles were used in the lanterns, but later kerosene tanks and wicks were substituted for them.[7]

Cooking utensils, like everything else, were primitive and few. A large iron pot, a long-handled skillet with an iron lid, a cast-iron teakettle, and a coffee pot were the principal ones. Bread was baked in a skillet placed on a bed of coals, with coals also on the lid to produce an even temperature for the tops and bottoms of the loaves. The fireplace furnished the heat frequently, but by no means always. Not all cabins had fireplaces, since many settlers brought along with them cooking stoves with tin pipes. Where stoves were used, the cook's problems were lessened but not completely solved, for the task of gathering and chopping wood remained. Wood was the principal fuel for heating homes at first, but later, in the prairie sections, wood was not available. A common substitute was hay twisted into sticks. During extreme cold weather it was no simple task to twist hay fast enough to meet the demands of the roaring fire in the stove. In some dwellings a large stone hay-burning box or furnace, with walls a foot thick, was built into the main room. Hay was fed into the contraption through a fire door opening into a lean-to shed attached to the house. When the walls of the box were warm they heated the whole house.[8]

THE FARMER'S HOME

Securing water was another task for the housekeeper. In summer, water could be dipped from springs and streams, but in winter it was not always so readily available. Then ice or snow was usually melted on the back of the kitchen stove. Most settlers, of course, dug wells and installed pumps sooner or later. Pumps were offered for sale in St. Paul as early as 1851, but many farmers could not afford them, or lived where they were unavailable. M. G. Cobb, for example, tells of walking from High Forest to Austin, a distance of thirty-five miles, on a hot July day in 1857. Along the entire route he passed only three houses, each with a well but no pump. Water was drawn by the primitive means of a rope and bucket. Unfortunately, since none of the families was home and the ropes and buckets were locked inside the cabins, Cobb went thirsty. When settlement reached the Red River Valley in the 1870's, the water problem was even more acute than in the wooded sections. Buffalo wallows were relied upon at first, and the water from them had to be boiled. In dry seasons the wallows dried up and deep wells were resorted to. One early settler remembered the well water as being bluish, smelly, and extremely distasteful. Serious illness often resulted when people were not careful to boil such water before using it.[9]

In the face of such handicaps it may seem surprising that the pioneer mother was able to feed and clothe her family, but frequently she did the job exceptionally well. In most parts of the state, at least during the seasons other than winter, nature was her ally in providing food. As late as 1871 a visitor to Minnesota wrote: "In the timber and on the prairies you can shoot deer, bear, fox, wolf, badger, and muskrat, and if you go far west you may be lucky enough to meet with buffalo. The rivers and lakes teem with pike, perch, and trout." And he went on to say: "A settler . . . told me that during one forenoon alone he had shot forty-two blue-winged teal. . . . The families that live here find it much cheaper to have pheasant, prairie chicken, wild duck, or venison on the table than to buy meat at the butcher shop." Moreover, sweet potatoes, turnips, artichokes, beans, nuts, berries, plums, apples, grapes, wild tea, and wild rice were growing in many parts of the state when the white man arrived. And maple sap and honey could be gathered for use on the dinner table. All these foods helped to tide a family over until the first crop could be harvested.[10]

On the other hand, nature had also its darker side. Blackbirds were a constant menace, and farmers resorted to all sorts of devices to frighten them away from the crops. Prairie fires were a constant threat in some sections each fall, destroying crops, killing birds, and endangering humans and animals alike, and many a family remembered forever afterward all-night battles against an advancing wall of flame. In mixed prairie, lake, and wooded areas millions of fleas, flies, mosquitoes, and grasshoppers plagued all forms of animal life. Particularly bad were the mosquitoes, and it was necessary to build smudges in the evening to make life bearable. And, as if these were not enough, there were snakes, lizards, skunks, gophers, and chipmunks. Mrs. G. M. Way, who settled south of Blue Earth, related: "The rattlesnakes were very thick. We used to watch them drink from the trough. They would lap the water with their tongues just as a dog does." Another settler of the 1850's in Fillmore County remembered killing seventy-eight rattlesnakes in a single day. Even the lowly mouse had to be considered, and one pioneer mother claimed that "if women had mounted chairs to escape, they would have occupied permanent places on top of the furniture." In the winter, snow, cold, and blizzards made life miserable and even hazardous. The farmer who froze to death less than forty rods from his house in Clay County in the winter of 1871-72 unhappily was not unique. Then, in the spring, floods added another danger.[11]

The first winter in the new country was apt to be the worst. Supplies were often cut off and the farm families had to rely upon stored-up provisions and game. One Mower County family in 1857 for two months had no bread except buckwheat cakes made of flour ground in the coffee mill. John A. Jones' father, when supplies ran low, was able to make a trip from his farm near Mankato to St. Paul to buy flour, salt, sugar, and apples, but all pioneers were not so fortunate. Particularly needed was salt. In fact, Mrs. J. R. Beatty, who arrived in Mankato in 1853, declared that the "want of salt bothered the pioneers more than anything else." Salt was used not only to flavor otherwise tasteless foods, but also for livestock and for preserving meats.[12]

One kind of meat always associated with the frontier was pork, an all-too-common article of diet in the cabins and shanties. Before Martha Gilpatrick married her husband he had been "baching it" in a little shack. "In the winter his diet was pork! pork! pork!" she wrote. "Mrs. Birmingham, who helped him sometimes, said she bet if all the hogs he ate were stood end to end, they would reach to Fort Snelling." Corn was another frontier product, and it loomed large in the diet of early settlers, most of whom ground their own corn. One settler placed his corn in a trough and ground it by rolling over it a heavy cannon ball obtained at Fort Snelling. Others used burned-out stumps and blocks of hardwood as a mortar and pestle. Because wheat flour was expensive, corn bread, or johnnycake, was eaten far more generally than wheat bread or biscuits. Pastry was popular in many households, especially those of New Englanders who were used to pie at every meal. Potatoes, as well as tea and coffee or substitutes for them, were included in the menus of even the poorest families. And if the family had a garden, as most of them had, rutabagas were almost certain to be found in it.[13]

Preserving foods was not easy, and the housewife had to be ingenious as well as careful. Smoking and salting generally insured meat against spoiling, but milk and butter were not so easily kept fresh. One woman set her butter dish in water and covered the whole with an inverted flower pot, which she drenched and set in a cool place. Springhouses or cellars were almost necessities on the farm, and it was a good idea for the farmer to spend part of the winter putting up ice for the next summer.[14]

Difficult as it was to satisfy the appetites of hard-working members of her family, the frontier housewife could not devote her entire time to it. Even if she did not work in the fields, as she usually did, there were endless other tasks to occupy her time. Spinning yarn, weaving cloth, manufacturing soap, making clothes, and laundering were a few of her additional jobs. Hog grease and lye made by pouring water over wood ashes were the ingredients of homemade soap, and the early newspapers printed soap recipes for the benefit of their inexperienced readers. Brooms, many of them homemade also, were auxiliaries of soap in the constant struggle against dirt. The same was true of dyes. "And oh, the old blue dye tub! Such an odor was never on land or sea, save in the old dye pot. I am too modest to tell you what was used to dissolve the indigo! But the blue never faded," said one pioneer housewife. The odor made similar impressions on others. "I made all the clothes the men wore," reminisced Mrs. Mary Weeks, who arrived in Minnesota in 1853. "A tailor would cut out their suits and then I would make them by hand. I made all their shirts, too. . . . Then I knit the stocking[s] and mittens for the whole family and warm woolen scarfs for their necks." Warren Wakefield's mother served as a tailoress for settlers in her vicinity in her first year in Minnesota. She made shirts for her family from woolen sheets she had woven in the East. Wakefield had no coat until he was sixteen years old, and he wore no underclothing as a boy. He wore thick shirts in winter, and the colder it was the more shirts he put on. His pants were thickly lined in lieu of underclothing. At times his father bought leather, which an itinerant cobbler fashioned into shoes for the family.[15]

Undoubtedly there were pioneer wives and mothers who were no more deserving of praise than are some of their counterparts today. Some were lazy, shiftless, cowardly, nagging, ignorant, and faithless, even as were some of the men. Complained one settler: "I was despondent, owing to a little difference between my wife and me. She is discontented because we are poor." On one occasion this man borrowed for friends a horse and buggy from a neighbor. As a result his wife "was exceedingly angry because I got the horse and buggy for them, and declared she would go visiting also and compelled me to go more than 8 miles in search of some conveyance for her to go to her cousin . . . but I could not make a raise of a conveyance." But unco-operative wives were certainly in the minority, and it is difficult not to speak in superlatives of "wilderness Marthas." As Grace Lee Nute has said: "The housewife's lot has never been an heroic one. Who has written epics on making beds or sweeping floors? Even historians . . . have had little to say regarding the methods of operating that interesting economic unit, the family." The soldier, the missionary, the trapper, and the frontiersman have all had their due, but the women who made possible their exploits have all too often been hidden in a twilight zone of obscurity. One Minnesota historian as early as 1882 tried to redress this lack of balance when he wrote: "The value of the part taken by the noble women who first came to this uninhabited region cannot be overestimated. . . . they practiced the most rigid economy, and often at critical times preserved order, reclaiming the men from utter despair during gloomy periods; and their example of frugal industry and cheerfulness, constantly admonished him to renewed exertions, the instincts of womanhood, constantly encouraging integrity and manhood."[16]

It has been customary to stress the dramatic incidents of pioneer life and to highlight singular examples of courage. And certainly such incidents and examples are not hard to find. Particularly during the Indian uprising of 1862 did many Minnesota women prove their mettle. Guri Endreson, for instance, saw her husband killed by the Indians and her son Ole shot through the shoulder. Then she found another son who had been shot dead. "For two days and nights," she later wrote to relatives in Norway, "I hovered about here with my little daughter, between fear and hope and almost crazy, before I found my wounded son and a couple of other persons, unhurt, who helped us get away to a place of greater security." Yet she did not give up after this tragic experience; rather, as soon as possible, she returned to the farming which she had carried on with her husband before the uprising. But it may be that the phase of pioneering which merited emphasis was the deadening monotony of the day-by-day routine, the drabness, and the loneliness, not the "glaringly, glowingly, and awfully wonderful," to borrow the words of a student of frontier life. Year after year there were babies to bear and children to care for, usually without the aid of a doctor. Three weeks after Mrs. Martha Thorne moved into a log cabin at Lake Crystal in 1854 her baby was born. No doctor was available and the only aid she received was from her sister-in-law. Births under such circumstances were commonplace.[17]

The mother usually served as nurse and doctor for the family, and seldom, except in cases of childbirth, was anyone outside the home called in. She needed at least a rudimentary knowledge of home remedies for everyday ills. These remedies varied with families and localities, but some practices were fairly uniform. Skunk oil rubbed on the chest, bloodroot taken internally, and ginger or cayenne pepper in hot water or milk were standard remedies for colds. Black pepper in hot water supposedly "settled the stomach," and pennyroyal reduced a fever. Laxatives were rhubarb root, senna leaves, and castor oil. Sprains and bruises yielded to camphor, opodeldoc, and a liniment of vinegar and salt. Alum eased the misery of cold sores, sore lips, and the like. In the spring sulphur and molasses, dandelion-root tea, and mustard, dandelion, cowslip, or beet greens were a must as tonics to "thin the blood." A decoction of boneset leaves made a patient sweat; tansy was used as an emmenagogue; and wormwood served as a vermifuge. For "general debility," a tonic of tincture of iron, goldenseal, and wormwood was considered excellent. Blackberry juice or brandy stemmed diarrhea. Vaccination was practiced, but hardly in the manner of today. One member of a family was vaccinated by a doctor and after the vaccination had "worked" well, others in the family were vaccinated, usually by the father or mother, with matter from the scab. Cuts and open wounds were encouraged to bleed freely and were then "wrapped in the blood" with a clean cloth. If infection developed, strong salves were applied and at times saleratus was used. Soothing ointments and salves were used on burns, and carbuncles and boils were treated with poultices of dried bread mixed with sweet milk, to which the white of an egg, crushed boiled onion, corn meal, or wheat bran might be added. During the ordeal of teething most mothers used some sort of teething rings and bibs and let the baby drool. Camomile was used for coughs and colds, as was a syrup of onions and sugar or molasses. In severe cases of croup, sweetened urine was administered. Young people who were "run down" were frequently given a fat rind of salt pork to suck or chew. When measles attacked, treatment consisted of a week in bed and doses of cayenne pepper or tea of ginger.[18]

The remedy for one of the most painful afflictions, toothache, was usually to have the tooth "yanked out" by a doctor or by someone in the family using a shoemaker's or carpenter's pincers. We can sympathize with the farmer who recorded in his diary of 1858: "Suffered all night with the toothache and consequently got up quite late. I have suffered more or less for two or three days past with this horrid complaint." The next day he "went to Dr. Cummings to get a tooth pulled, the back tooth on the right side. He pulled four or five times at it—broke off the top—finally split and took out one prong, and left the other in which is in yet. My teeth are in very bad condition." A few months later he was bothered again. "I suffered with the toothache until noon, when I put in some prepared arsenic which I think killed the nerve, and my tooth has stopped aching," he related. The sufferer was not thirty years old at the time. Another method of relieving pain was to pack the cavity of a decayed tooth with a wad of cotton soaked in camphor or tobacco juice.[19]

Sanitation on the frontier was almost impossible, in spite of the best efforts of many housewives. Bathing was an ordeal not to be endured in winter, and it was far from universal in summer. Flies were a constant problem; wells or springs were polluted in some localities, often because of their proximity to the privy or the stables; and the knowledge of the causes and cures of diseases was meager. As a result, people who today would have been saved often died. Some of the common diseases of the time were typhoid fever, diphtheria, congestion of the lungs, lung fever, consumption, inflammation of the lungs, inflammation of the bowels, summer complaint, liver complaint, dyspepsia, and catarrh. When scarlet fever threatened, parents hurried to hang asafetida bags around the necks of their children next to the skin. The resulting smell in a crowded country school can only be imagined. Suffice it to say that someone composed an appropriate prayer: "Dear Lord, take away the bags, and let the fever come." Some of the frontier ailments are now known by other names—inflammation of the bowels as appendicitis, and catarrh as hay fever or sinus trouble—and relief can generally be given the sufferers. In the pioneer period the victim died, went on suffering, or eventually got well.[20]

Surely life under these conditions was not easy for pioneer women. And the menfolk, though perhaps better suited by temperament and physique for pioneering, worked hard and suffered much. Further, many of them endured their hardships without the solace and comfort of a good wife, since as late as 1900 men in the state outnumbered women by more than 110,000. Even children bore a heavy share of the burden. Indeed, one writer would give them much of the credit. "To be barefoot on a burnt-over prarie or woods is next to hell," he declares. "That is exactly what boys and even girls had to endure when at work in pioneer days. They had to be on the run constantly. . . . what I would like to see most of all is a monument erected to the noble ox and the barefoot boy. They were good companions in all sorts of hardships." Yet, while spells of melancholia must have gripped the hearts of most settlers at times, there was plenty of gaiety too. C. N. Brainerd, while traveling near Winnebago City in 1867, commented that in no section had he "ever seen more universal, unadulterated, happiness than that exhibited on these Western prairies." There was a spirit of independence, along with one of generous hospitality, combined with a faith in the future, a feeling on the part of thousands of people that they were helping to build a great, democratic state under God. Minnesotans were young and optimistic; more than eighty-five per cent of them were under forty-five years of age in 1880. Comforts and luxuries were absent—so what! The present condition was only temporary. A bright, new world was in the making.[21]

And with the passage of time "the initial ordeals of pioneering were met, and for many there came the better days that had beckoned." No longer must they live in the log or sod house built when the family first came to Minnesota. New frame and brick farmhouses, more roomy and livable than the former houses, appeared in the older areas of the state as population and wealth increased. John Thompson erected his cabin in Rice County in 1856, and he moved into his frame house in 1863. A resident of the same county, Hans O. Stenbakken, built his log house in 1856 also, but he did not construct a frame house until 1871. Still a third Rice County resident, Osmund Osmundson, went his fellows one better. He lived in his log cabin from 1857 to 1861, when he built a frame house, and in 1880 he replaced the latter with a brick dwelling. Henry Grote, Peter Odegard, and Friedrich Helberg, all log-cabin settlers of the middle 1850's in the same region, built their brick farmhouses in 1870, 1876, and 1877 respectively. Farther west, in the prairie section near Sleepy Eye, a Danish couple lived in their sod house from the middle 1860's until 1883, when they built "the first decent frame house in the settlement." Even then their neighbors, who generally still lived in one-room sod houses, thought the couple extravagant and suggested that it would have been wiser to use the money to purchase additional land. But in a few years the neighbors also yielded to the lure of more comfortable living.[22]

By the early 1870's people in the older settled areas of Minnesota were living under conditions that contrasted sharply with those of the 1850's. Kerosene lamps, cookstoves, heating ranges, and factory-made clothes were becoming more and more common; the same was true of comforts and conveniences in country homes. The new frame and brick houses that were sprouting up in the 1860's and 1870's contained furnishings that the most elaborate log cabins of the period before the Civil War could not attempt to rival. But here again, as in the case of log cabins, there is a danger of generalizing, for there was great diversity in rural homes. Some farmers merely added sections to their old cabins as the size of their families increased. On the other extreme, wealthy farmers built elaborate houses, frequently of hybrid design, in which "Greek columns, Roman domes, Moorish minarets, Gothic buttresses and windows, Romanesque massiveness, mansard roofs, dormer windows, cupolas, battlements, and always an abundance of scroll and iron-trellis work" were combined "in the same nightmarish heap." Most of the new houses, however, were between the two extremes—simple, two-story, boxlike structures, with shingled hip roofs and, if it could be afforded, a porch or, as it was called in those days, a veranda.[23]

Many of the houses of the 1870's are still in use today, with some of the modern conveniences added. When first built they had no running water, no toilet, no gas nor electric lights, and no steam, gas, nor hot-water heat. Still, the people of the time did not miss what they had not known. Unlike the first crude dwellings, the second generation of houses usually had cellars for the storage of fruits and vegetables. The cellar generally had a dirt floor, and was unheated and unlighted except for a narrow window or two. It could be reached in summer through an outside cellar door, and in the winter via an inside trap door and steep, treacherous stairs. Sometimes a cistern, to which rain water was piped from the eaves, was built under the kitchen. In the better houses, which were equipped with sinks, hand pumps drew water from the cistern. Drinking water was still carried from a well or spring. Bathtubs were a rarity, and the Saturday night bath was taken in a laundry tub in the kitchen. Daily lavations were performed in a washbasin on a bench outside the house in warm weather, and in the kitchen in the winter. Toilet facilities were housed in the familiar little structure down by the barn, or out back of the house. Trips there in the summer were pleasant enough, but in zero weather they called for real fortitude. The kitchen or, as was often the case, the combination kitchen and dining room, was heated by the iron cookstove. The sitting room and perhaps the main bedroom downstairs were provided with wood-burning heaters. Pipes from these stoves ran through drums in the rooms above and helped somewhat to temper the winter cold in otherwise unheated bedrooms. One pioneer recalls the experience of going to bed under such chilly conditions. The men left their footwear, "a motley and aromatic array of woolen socks, felt boots, German socks, shoepacks, and overshoes" around the stove, and then "stripped down to their pants and red flannel underwear they made a dash for the beds upstairs." Getting out of bed in the morning in frigid temperatures was a thrill not soon forgotten.[24]

Some houses had at least three rooms that were lacking in the old cabins. One was a parlor, a regular sanctum sanctorum, which was opened only on rare and special occasions, such as weddings, funerals, or visits from distinguished friends. Children usually remembered it as a dark, musty-smelling, mysterious place from which they were excluded. For everyday activities, the sitting room was the center of family life. A second addition in the newer houses was a "back" or summer kitchen, a sort of lean-to where cooking was done in the summer to avoid unnecessary heating of the house. Finally, there was the "buttery" or pantry, where eatables of all kinds and crockery, glass, silver, and cooking utensils were kept. Oscar Hallam viewed it as a great place "for clandestine resort between meals, for there were always cookies, pies, bread and butter, plum preserves, jelly and jams." Undoubtedly other farm boys shared his view.[25]

The interior walls of the new house were frequently plastered and papered or whitewashed, and the windows were adorned with decorative shades. Rugs and carpets covered the floors; fancy quilts and bedspreads enlivened the bedrooms; and a melodeon, a square piano, or an organ might grace the sitting room. Looms and spinning wheels were probably gathering dust in the attic, but a foot-powered sewing machine indicated that the mother had not completely given up responsibility for the family wardrobe. The beds might well be walnut, with cord springs and straw mattresses, although it was not uncommon for the girls in the family to have a feather bed. Straw in the straw ticks was changed every fall after threshing. A whatnot was a necessity in the well-appointed home, as was a bookshelf and a corner bracket to hold a vase. Various types and pieces of furniture helped give the home individuality. William A. Marin always remembered the "old cherry center table on which reposed a pressed leather family album" and the "rocking chairs, cane-seated dining room chairs, and a sofa covered with large figured Brussels." Haircloth sofas and chairs were also typical of the period, many of them of local manufacture, since furniture factories were well established in Minnesota by the 1860's. On the walls hung chromos, tintypes, crayon pictures, paintings, and daguerreotypes. One settler was impressed by a chromo of Valley Forge which bedecked his sitting room wall, but he took great pride in the fact that the usual enlarged crayon portraits were conspicuous by their absence.[26]

The bookcases and tables of the homes displayed various reading materials, according to the education, wealth, and interests of the family. Books, magazines, and newspapers held a great allure for those members who could read. They gave news of the world outside the rural community and provided an escape from the narrow confines of the farm. Mrs. Alice George illustrated the intense appeal of reading matter when she recalled the habits of one of her pioneer neighbors who subscribed to the *New York Ledger,* a weekly story paper. "When the paper came," she wrote, "whoever got it first dropped her work, no matter what she was doing, locked herself in a room, and read it through. Then there was a scramble to see who should have it next." A similar scramble occurred in countless other rural homes.[27]

According to a New Englander in Stillwater in the 1850's, the publications of Harper, Putnam, Graham, and Godey were commonly found in the homes of that day, and Horace Greeley's *New York Tribune* was popular. Joseph Haskell of Afton subscribed to the *Boston Journal of Chemistry,* Judd's *American Agriculturist, Scribner's Magazine,* and the *Atlantic Monthly.* Levi Countryman, who was particularly well educated, being able to read Greek and Latin, kept a record of his reading in his diary. In September, 1858, he recorded: "I bought 4 books. . . . Alexanders *Evidences of Christianity, Pilgrim's Progress, Practical Piety, Natural-goodness,* were the books I bought." A few months later he read in Hall's *Journal of Health,* Sallust's *Jugurtha,* and a biography of the Reverend H. Mowes, a German pastor. In March, 1859, a life of J. B. Finley and Schaffer on baptism provided his reading material. At this stage in his life he was seriously considering the ministry as a life work, and his choice of books clearly reflects that interest. In December he sent for some back numbers of the *New York Tribune.* His next two books were a life of Fremont and a history of the United Brethren in Christ. In the fall of 1860 he mentions receiving books from Harper's and Stanley, but he neglects to mention their titles. His later reading included the poems of Scott and Byron and a life of the latter, a life of Peter Cartwright, and the *Swiss Family Robinson,* which he read aloud for the benefit of his family. On November 8, 1862, his diary ends, as he left home for service with the army, but before that date he had read at least three more books, *Life and Historic Incidents in India*, Finley's *Memorials of Prison Life*, and Hickok's *Science of the Mind*. Andrew Peterson said little about reading in his diary, but on one occasion he noted that he "took out a draft on $19.10 to send . . . to pay for the books," and the next month he sent a volume of Spurgeon's sermons "to Carl." Le Roy G. Davis, whose family moved to the Sleepy Eye area in 1867, remembered that his father had a leather-bound copy of Prescott's *History of the World* and received the *Weekly New York Sun* and Brown's *Shakespearian Almanac*. Dime novels were popular and circulated from home to home. Most towns had a weekly newspaper which was read in the surrounding countryside, and numerous farm journals were common. Finally, but by no means least in importance, was the family Bible. In it were kept the vital statistics of the family, and it served as a source of inspiration daily in large numbers of farmhouses.[28]

As the houses assumed a more imposing and dignified appearance, so did the other buildings and appurtenances of the farm. In the early days about the only structures on a claim or homestead were the cabin, a crude shelter for livestock, and a bit of rail fence. Cheapness was the thing, and each settler built according to his individual ideas and present needs. Rude and simple straw stables were common. They were made of crotches and poles, with three or four feet of straw for a roof. The straw was held down with anything heavy that could be put on it, and sometimes a thatch of long prairie grass was used in an effort to make the roof waterproof. The walls were made of straw several feet thick, packed solid, and held in place by poles. Windows and ventilation were nonexistent, and if rain came in the floor soon took on the aspect of a quagmire. Instead of swinging doors, a sort of platform was put over the opening and held in place overnight by braces. Usually there was a feeding manger also made with poles. As late as 1865 George Biscoe wrote from Cottage Grove that for twenty or twenty-five dollars he could "have as good a stable as half the farmers about here. A shed 14 feet square 12 feet high on one side and 8 on the other will do. . . . Lumber is $16.00 per thousand at the mill and shingles

THE EARTH BROUGHT FORTH

from 3 to 5 dollars per thousand according to quality." Some farmers constructed rough pens to hold stocks of wheat, oats, and other grains, and a few built granaries. But the early settler who had a fine array of buildings was almost unique.[29]

The passing years brought many changes. Old fences were torn down and replaced by new board ones, which could be painted to

EDWARD B. DREW'S FARM IN WINONA COUNTY
[From Andreas, *Historical Atlas of Minnesota*, 108.]

give a neat and tidy look to the farmyard. As soon as possible a new barn, an item of basic economic significance, was built, probably before the new house. Charles E. McColley recalls that his father built the first large frame barn in his neighborhood in 1865 with money earned in the army. It was thirty feet wide and forty feet long and had two stories. On the first floor were stalls, grain bins, a haymow, and a threshing floor, and at each end were double doors through which a wagon and a hay rack could be driven. On the second floor was an oat bin built over the horse stalls, a grain bin, and a scaffold. The barn was put together with mortises and pins, as were most of the barns of the period, and it was still standing

THE FARMER'S HOME

secure seventy-five years later. Corncribs, granaries, smokehouses, and sheds of various kinds were fitted into the pattern around the house and the barn, and, in prairie sections, groves of trees were planted as windbreaks for the house. Often a real effort was made to beautify the farm by spacing stately elms or evergreens along the drive leading to the yard and by arranging flower beds and shrubbery in attractive designs around the house. Pictures of the 1870's testify to the success of many farmers in providing their farmsteads with warmth and charm. Surely these individuals felt sincere satisfaction and more than a touch of pride when they surveyed their homes in 1880 and contrasted them with what they had been in the 1850's. The early struggles had been worth while; much of the pioneer dream had come true.[30]

Rural Social Life

"It seemed at first in those early days impossible to have social relations with anyone," recalled Judge Lorin Cray, who settled near Shelbyville in the fall of 1859. "Neighbors as we had known them, we had none. The nearest settlers were a mile distant from us, and there were but four or five families nearer than two or three miles distant. But we soon learned that we had neighbors even though the distance was considerable. First one neighbor and then another would extend to every family in the vicinity an invitation to spend an afternoon or an evening. Someone would hitch his oxen to his wagon or sled, and going from house to house, gather up a full load well rounded up and then at the usual gait for such conveyances, we rode and visited and sang until we reached the appointed place, where perhaps eight, ten or a dozen persons spent the afternoon or evening, in the one little room, where the meal was being prepared and the table spread. There were no sets or clans, no grades of society.... Friendships were formed which were never broken, and when recalled always revive tender memories." [1]

How often could this picture be repeated in the early days of Minnesota! Settlement was sparse, facilities were meager, and simple pleasures were about all that could be devised. Just getting together with a few neighbors was an event anticipated eagerly by people living a lonely, isolated, harsh existence. Nearly sixty years after coming to Minnesota, one housewife related somewhat nostalgically: "For amusement we used to go visiting and always spent the day. We would put the whole family into a sleigh or wagon and away we would go for an outing. We had such kind neighbors—no one any better than the other—all equal." It is easy to visualize the scene of a "visit." The men, wearing blue denims and heavy boots, are in one group, discussing such topics as crops, the new neighbor, the schoolteacher, the road just laid out, on which they are to work, or politics. The women, in their best attire, are comparing notes on housekeeping, the latest remedy for croup, or clothes. The youngsters are playing games. At nine o'clock the ladies slip out to the kitchen—if the house is large enough to have a separate kitchen—and the menfolk and children await eagerly the call to hot biscuits, butter, and perhaps honey.[2]

While the early settler had to be content with simple pastimes, he would not have wanted sympathy. If hours were long and work was arduous, ways were usually found to mix business with pleasure. Since labor was scarce, families had to pool their resources for such tasks as clearing land, building cabins and barns, harvesting grain, and husking corn. Like "house raisings," logrollings were real events. At these gatherings the men piled and burned excess logs and trash, while the women prepared dinner, each woman having brought some particular dish. By the time the men sat down to eat, the table groaned under its burden of food, but sometime later it usually looked as if a cyclone had struck it. The completion of a cabin was an occasion for a housewarming. Mrs. Duncan Kennedy, who settled near Nicollet village in 1856, remembered that the "first party we went to was a housewarming. We went about seven miles with the ox team. I thought I would die laughing when I saw the girls go to their dressing room. They went up a ladder on the outside. There were two fiddlers and we danced all the old dances. Supper was served on a work bench from victuals out of a wash tub." As late as 1883, when a new frame house was completed near Sleepy Eye, a Fourth of July celebration, attended by some three hundred people, was held in it.[3]

Husking bees were common after the first year in a settlement, and they were gala affairs. The main interest centered on the search for a "red ear," for that gave the lucky finder permission to kiss any girl present, "a privilege never denied." In speaking of these happy events, a Minnesota newspaper of 1858 remarked that they "have been in vogue, of late, and were the means of enlivening the spirits of old and young. On several occasions within a fortnight, and especially at the mansion of our neighbor Clayborne Chandler, one evening last week, the men had no occasion to sigh and wish they were boys again, for they were apparently young, in feeling at least. . . . The ladies, too, were all young equally with those of 'sweet sixteen.' Better corn; ladies with healthier bloom upon their cheeks; gentlemen more worthy to be—ahem!—sweeter kisses; better people—cannot be found elsewhere." Unquestionably machinery has lightened the farmer's burden, but when he thinks back on the old-time husking bee he may regard mechanization as something of a mixed blessing.[4]

Starved as they were for social relaxation, the settlers put forth great efforts to attend a party or a dance. One woman near Blue Earth, when her baby was only three weeks old, "drove fourteen miles to a dance and took in every dance all night and wasn't sick afterward either." Who watched her baby she does not say, but she took him to the dance with her. Another settler told of entertaining winter visitors in his Red River Valley home in the early 1880's. A dancing party was held, with the usual square dances accompanied by a fiddle. Some of the most popular songs played were "Little Brown Jug," "Goodbye, My Lover, Goodbye," "Beautiful Isle of the Sea," "My Brave Laddie Sleeps in His Faded Coat of Blue," "Where Is My Wandering Boy Tonight?" "Dem Golden Slippers," "Silver Threads among the Gold," and "Ten O'Clock the Rain Begins to Fall and Nellie Is Far from Home." But all families could not enjoy dancing. There was a strong puritan element on the frontier, and certain churches, such as the Methodist and some branches of the Lutheran, frowned upon dancing as a lure of the Devil. Mrs. C. A. Smith, who settled in Watertown in 1858, said: "We lived just as we had in Sweden, as we were in a Swedish settlement. We were Lutheran, so there were no parties. Going to church was our only amusement."[5]

But going to church should not be minimized as a social activity. In an age when automobiles, radios, television, movies, bowling alleys, and country clubs did not vie for popularity, the church, whether held in a schoolhouse, hotel, log cabin, or structure of its own, was the leading social center of many communities. And even before settlement was dense enough to warrant the founding of a church, visiting ministers and circuit riders, carrying Bibles, hymn-

RURAL SOCIAL LIFE

books, a few tracts, and perhaps another book or two in their carpetbags, penetrated isolated areas and brought vivid pictures of Heaven and Hell to eager listeners. In the middle 1840's, for example, a Methodist preacher, Joseph Hurlburt, visited cabins all the way from Fort Snelling and Red Rock to Osceola and St. Croix Falls, thirty miles up the St. Croix River from Stillwater, as his regularly assigned duty. Another minister on one occasion traveled forty miles in below-zero weather to hold a meeting at which the collection netted him fifty cents. The Reverend William McKinley in 1856 journeyed all day, on horseback and by foot, over snow-covered, trackless areas in Rice County, to attend a watch meeting. He arrived at his destination about ten o'clock in the evening, after two other men had already preached sermons. Nevertheless, McKinley preached also and his listeners apparently were eager to get as much of the gospel as possible.[6]

Denominationalism was strong and rivalry among various sects was keen. Immigrant groups, such as the Swedes and Norwegians, brought their old world churches with them; but if members of such groups became disaffected, they were free to become communicants in other faiths. Religious freedom was one of the great attractions of America, and Minnesota offered a full program of choices to the settler seeking a church where he could feel at home. By 1870 the Catholic church was the largest in the state, followed by the Methodist and the Lutheran; but the Baptist, Presbyterian, Episcopal, and Congregational churches also had substantial memberships. Not only did all these denominations, and others, minister to the spiritual needs of the early farm families, but they also provided outlets in varying degrees for their social drives as well. Hospitality on the frontier was proverbial, and no more honored nor welcome guest than the preacher ever paid a visit. Many of the pioneer ministers were hardy, vigorous specimens, who not only brought news of the outside world, but also might "help the farmer get in the last load of hay, dig the potatoes, milk the cow and after supper lead in singing the old camp meeting songs that were well known and great favorites." A Norwegian pastor's wife has left a charming diary, in which she tells of the warm treatment accorded her and her husband by parishioners in Iowa and Wisconsin, but the locale might just as well have been Minnesota. At one home she was given homemade wild-grape wine and *fattigmand,* and then was seated at a table "loaded down with fried pork, spareribs, sausages, bread and butter, cake, and excellent coffee." [7]

When a parsonage was available, it developed into a social center alongside the church. At times it was the setting for a donation party, a means by which the congregation supplemented the pastor's modest salary and had an enjoyable social gathering. In 1857 at such an affair in Winona, money and provisions worth three hundred dollars were left for the preacher. A more elaborate, if less productive, party was given for the Reverend B. A. Kemp of Sauk Centre in 1866. For this occasion the hall was decorated with evergreens, and people attended from as far away as Alexandria. Two cakes containing rings, a guess cake, and a fish pond were the attractions, in addition to tables loaded with good things to eat. The cakes were auctioned off, bringing from $.25 to $4.50 each. Net receipts were $150, and the pastor was presented with a study gown. Another way of raising money for the minister or for the church was a supper. In 1875 the ladies of the Worthington Methodist Church held a supper and spelling school, with a prize for the best speller. On another occasion, in St. Cloud, an oyster supper, supplemented by vocal and instrumental music, yielded a profit of $180 for the benefit of the minister. In the winter months sociables, sleigh rides, and festivals were popular, and in summer icecream socials, picnics, excursions, and May parties were the order of the day. In 1863 the Methodist Sunday School of Rochester joined with the other Sunday schools in town for a picnic. The children formed in line at ten A.M. and marched to the grove on College Hill. There the exercises consisted of singing, prayer, addresses by the different pastors and others, and refreshments. Before 1870 steamboat excursions were held, but with the advent of railroads train excursions became popular. One example is typical. In 1875 nearly a hundred and fifty people went by train from Hastings to Lakeville Lake, where they were joined by two hundred more from Castle Rock and its vicinity. Baskets of cake, pie, sandwiches, pickles, and other foods, and singing, short addresses, boating, croquet, and swinging made the affair a truly notable and thoroughly enjoyable event.[8]

It is impossible and useless to attempt to list and describe all the social diversions offered by the pioneer churches. There were sewing circles, coffee parties, quilting bees, ladies' aid societies, mite societies, temperance groups, church tableaux, men's groups, revivals, and camp meetings. The last two particularly were associated with some of the American churches, such as the Baptist and the Methodist, and with the frontier. At times they were given over to emotional excesses, and the people who "hit the sawdust trail" frequently backslid and had to be "saved" year after year; nevertheless they were an important and colorful part of the life of early Minnesota. A revival in St. Paul seems to have made quite an impression on Colonel A. P. Conolly, who came to that city in 1857. A large crowd, he wrote, was in attendance, some people having to stand outside the church. When the revival was at white heat, a well-known individual, whose custom of lending money at five per cent a month was common knowledge, was overcome with religious fervor and, falling to his knees, cried out: "Oh, Lord, give us more interest in Heaven." Hearing this plea, a wag in the crowd outside the door exclaimed: "For God's sake, isn't five per cent enough?" But in spite of the ridicule heaped on the revival services, they induced scores of people to lead better lives.[9]

Even more elaborate and dramatic than the revival, and a revival service itself, was the camp meeting. The pioneer newspapers of Minnesota during the warm months were filled with notices of camp meetings, and their attraction was considerable. Tents were erected to house those who attended them, a platform was built for the leaders, plank seats were set up, and facilities for serving food were provided. For several days people gave themselves over to the enjoyment and inspiration of a religious experience. There was something about the beauties of the noonday in the forest and the glare of torches and camp fires at night that had a profound effect on emotions. Apparently the excitement and excesses attending earlier camp meetings in Tennessee and Kentucky, the jerkings and faintings, were uncommon in Minnesota, but deep religious feeling was certainly not missing. Year after year hundreds of city and country people looked forward eagerly to the annual camp meeting as an outstanding experience in their lives. One of the first, if not the first camp meeting in the state, was held in 1855 in an oak grove near Red Wing. More than thirty ministers and a large number of laymen were in attendance, some having come more than a hundred miles on horseback, in wagons, or by steamboat. The captains of the steamboats set a precedent, followed for many years, by giving the camp meeting passengers a reduced rate. One interesting feature of the meeting was the location of the tents. Those occupied by English-speaking settlers were on the right of the speakers' platform, and those occupied by German settlers were on the left. Preaching was sometimes in English and sometimes in German.[10]

After this first meeting it is doubtful whether a summer passed without a camp meeting in Minnesota. Most of the services were similar, consisting of preaching, praying, singing, and general social intercourse, the last being not the least of their attractions. Camp meeting sites were found all over the state where settlement was dense enough to support reasonable attendance. The most important meeting of all, however, was the one started by the Methodists in 1869 at Red Rock on the Mississippi River and continued to the present day. On a Sunday in June, 1869, about two thousand people attended the services. From this auspicious beginning the institution grew year by year, until by the early 1880's the camp meeting site had grown to sixty-one acres, with numerous cottages, a large wooden dining hall, a "preachers' home," gasoline lamps, and a three-story hotel. Steamboats and railroad trains ran special excursions to the grounds at reduced rates each summer. On Sunday during the 1879 meeting, for example, the St. Paul and St. Croix Company ran three of their boats from St. Paul to Red Rock every forty minutes. With such facilities, it is not surprising to read that as many as ten thousand people visited the camp meeting during the Sunday services of 1883. More than two hundred tents were on the site the same day. Unfortunately, in the opinion of those whose interest was mainly religious, too many came merely from curiosity, or for the pleasure of the excursion. The grounds took on the aspect of a grand picnic, where people of all creeds, nationalities, and colors congregated to have a good time. But whether camp meetings were considered as excuses for gay outings or as opportunities for worship, the fact remains that they furnished a social outlet for thousands of rural families in the early days of the state.[11]

A COUNTRY STORE AT FOUNTAIN, 1874
[From Andreas, *Historical Atlas of Minnesota*, 144.]

In addition to the home and the church, at least three other institutions helped to enrich the social life of the farm folk—the country store, the country school, and the fair. Today people gather in clubs and taverns to settle the affairs of the world; in a frontier community the combined general store and post office was the center for such discussions. A trip to town to buy the few items not produced on the farm and some licorice for the children and to trade eggs for calico was a major event, a break in the routine, and a chance to exchange views with friends in the store. "On entering the store through the front double door one would likely see a counter on each side of a long room, a big cast-iron, wood-burning box heater near the middle, and a long table behind the stove," relates a farm boy of the period. "There was room for passing, however, on all sides of the stove. Around it the men of the community discussed politics, religion, history, crops, livestock, neighborhood gossip, and the events, causes, and results of the then recent Civil War. Nothing was avoided and no subject escaped scathing condemnation or warm commendation except the personal or family affairs of someone present." And to minister to the comforts of the debaters, a cracker barrel, a free tobacco box, and a cuspidor were usually handy.[12]

Most farmers had very little formal education, but, since many of them wanted all possible advantages for their children, schools were started wherever settlements sprang up. At first the log cabins were used as schoolhouses. Mrs. Gideon Pond, who came to Bloomington in the middle 1850's, often shared with other mothers the task of teaching the neighborhood children who gathered for lessons every morning around the kitchen table in her house. In another locality, an observer saw twenty-four Norwegian children "studiously at work" in the attic of a log cabin. As population increased, schoolhouses were built. Mrs. Margaret R. Funk attended such a school in Mankato in the winter of 1853–54. "The school house was built by popular subscription," she wrote. "It was a log structure of one room, and in the middle of this room was a large, square, iron stove. The pupils sat around the room facing the four walls, the desks being wide boards, projecting out from the walls. . . . I came from my home across the prairie, through the snow in the bitter cold of the winter. . . . The education the children received in those days had to be paid for either by their parents or by someone else who picked out a child and paid for his or her tuition."[13]

Well-trained schoolteachers were rare on the frontier. About all that was necessary to qualify for teaching was to pass an examination given by the most literate person in the community. Levi Countryman mentions frequently in his diary that he had examined this or that person "on qualifications for school teaching." Often a farmer in slack seasons, or a young fellow who hoped to enter law or the ministry, "took" a school for a term as a means of earning a few dollars. Countryman himself taught for a time. In November, 1858, he entered in his diary: "Commenced teaching this district school. The trustees have pledged themselves to give me $100 for a term of 4 months, and I feel that I could not employ a winter more advantageously since we at this time need so much external aid. . . . I had eleven pupils, some of whom come with a desire to learn, I am confident." Countryman, like all teachers of the period, earned his money. Not only was he expected to teach pupils of various ages and degrees of proficiency "reading, spelling, writing, mental and written arithmetic, Grammar, Geography & Algebra," but he was required to do janitorial work as well. "I must have fires prepared at 8 o'clock to warm well the room, and I must teach $6\frac{1}{4}$ hours, per day," he wrote. Most teachers had to "board around" with the families of their students, not always a joyous experience. Not the least of the teachers' tasks was to discipline young bloods whose interest in school was to discover how much insubordination the master would stand. The hickory stick was in frequent use. On one occasion Countryman noted: "The school was very noisy today and vexed me a good deal." Again, he confided to his diary: "Quite an unruly school today. I have promised the scholars to have a new set of rules, by which they will not be allowed to whisper etc." Finally he was driven to striking a boy. After this occurrence, the boy's father accused him of harming the boy, and he threatened to bring the matter before the church. Countryman then felt considerable contrition. "I acknowledge that I did wrong in the manner I whipped his child," he confessed, "but he did deserve a whipping. I have a very passionate disposition. God help me." [14]

Methods, as well as the quality, of teaching varied. Judge Loren W. Collins, who taught school near Cannon Falls in the fall of 1858, followed the New England custom of having each pupil read a verse from the New Testament at the opening of school every morning. There was much memorizing of rules and definitions, all too often without understanding. School terms were short and were sandwiched between busy seasons on the farm. Yet the pupils gained much, and enjoyed good times as well. Countryman recorded the pleasant events along with the trying ones. "Played with the scholars at recess, had a fine speaking time after recess and a spelling down," he wrote on one occasion. A few days later he "played ball with the students at noon." It was always fun to be sent after water, or to be allowed to pass the bucket and dipper around the room. On Friday afternoons there were recitations, and on the last day of school there was always an examination and an exhibition attended by the parents. Years later many people undoubtedly agreed with Thomas Kenny, who wrote: "Henry them were the sunniest days, I think, that will ever brighten the dark and dreary path of my after life." [15]

In addition to serving its main function, the schoolhouse, as one settler observed, "soon came to be used for dances, political and religious meetings, and social gatherings. Spelling and debating schools, also called lyceums, seemed to come as a natural result of the public school spirit." These events were held in the fall and winter months, and young and old alike thought nothing of driving fifteen miles in a sleigh to a dance or a spelling bee at the schoolhouse. Debates also were popular, as were the readings, recitations, and songs frequently contributed to the programs by the women. It is interesting and intriguing to contemplate the place of the country school and the meetings held in it in the evolution of our society. Undoubtedly Le Roy G. Davis, who grew up in the heyday of the country school, did not exaggerate when he claimed that the spelling bees and lyceums "exerted a profound influence upon the methods of thinking, the language, and the social instincts of the pioneer. Perhaps no other institution could have supplied similar benefits for the heterogeneous population of the new state." [16]

An institution that did little to enrich the social life of Minnesota, but one that cannot be ignored, was the saloon. In spite of the puritan element and the influence of certain churches, the sale of liquor could not be stamped out, and many farmers sought release from their routine drudgery by visiting a saloon, "having a few with the boys," and perhaps getting drunk. An incident like the following was not unique: "Just before supper," related a pioneer farmer, "I saw a man going along in a buggy, leaning back, and after a few moments, I saw the horse turned around towards the fence. I went down to him and found a man . . . dead drunk in the buggy. I took him and the horse to the house where I cared for both, getting him to bed." At every Fourth of July celebration it was all too common for men to visit the saloon instead of the afternoon festivities at the park. Even after the railroad penetrated a region, certain little hamlets persisted as sort of halfway stations for farmers who lived long distances from the railroad towns. Each of these little places had one or more saloons, frequently unlicensed, where the farmers enjoyed conviviality on a Saturday afternoon. Iberia, Golden Gate, and Leavenworth, near Sleepy Eye, were such places.[17]

Even the village blacksmith shop and the local gristmill had their social aspects. While waiting to have their horses shod, farmers found time to spin a yarn or two and exchange a bit of gossip. At gristmills, while their grain was ground, men passed the time in wrestling, pitching horseshoes, or running foot races. The women, unfortunately, had no such social centers in town. The only time they entered the saloon, for example, was when it was necessary to help their husbands out to the wagons.[18]

There were far fewer spectator amusements in rural Minnesota in the late nineteenth century than there are today. Perhaps twentieth century people are the losers, for they are merely passive spectators, watching movies, hearing broadcasts, or viewing athletic contests. Their grandparents, on the other hand, participated in the group diversions of their time. Although baseball was played to some extent in the 1860's and 1870's, competitive athletic sports did not occupy a large part in the life of rural Minnesota until after 1900. Circuses occasionally came to town, as did theatrical attractions, but some settlers regarded those pleasures, along with dancing, drinking, gambling, and card playing, as devices of the Devil. German farmers had no aversion to drinking beer and dancing, nor to enjoying themselves on the Sabbath; but their New England puritan and many of their Scandinavian Lutheran neighbors felt differently about such matters. Hence, skating parties, sleigh rides, picnics, and games of various kinds, along, of course, with that ever-attractive activity of courting—in those days by horse and wagon or buggy—loomed large in the life of the young people. Today the young man with a convertible and a girl thinks he is sitting on top of the world; his counterpart of the 1870's felt the same way when he had a cutter, a buffalo robe, a fast horse, and a girl.[19]

While smoking, dancing, and the theater—unless the performance was *Uncle Tom's Cabin* or *Ten Nights in a Barroom*—were taboo with some people, it is curious that kissing games were entirely acceptable. Some of the popular party games in which the object was either to get the desired partner or to kiss a girl, or both, were "Roll the Platter," "Drop the Handkerchief," "Happy Is the Miller," "King William," "Marching Down to Old Quebec," "The Needle's Eye," and "Post Office." In most of the games a rhyme was sung during the action leading to the selection of a partner. In "Happy Is the Miller," for example, the couples danced around in two circles, with the girls on the outside and one lone boy in the middle. Then all would sing:

> Happy is the miller, that lives by himself.
> As the wheel turns round he is gaining in his wealth.
> One hand in the hopper and the other in the bag.
> As the wheel rolls round he cries out—Grab!

At the shout of "Grab!" the boy in the center tried to get a girl. If the party was not properly constituted for kissing games, there were always singing games to enjoy, such as "Here Come Two Dukes A'Roving," "London Bridge Is Falling Down," and "I Come to See Miss Jennie-a-Jones." And charades, of course, were good old stand-bys. Popcorn, apples, and molasses candy were standard refreshments.[20]

Out of doors there were plenty of diversions for the youngsters, especially the boys. Woods filled with plums, hazelnuts, black walnuts, and butternuts promised pleasant outings, and streams, lakes, and rivers provided swimming holes beyond compare. There were hunting, fishing, trapping, and camping the like of which most modern boys will never see. After chores and supper were out of the way, time might be found for a few games of "pull-away" or "one old cat." The latter frequently was played with a homemade yarn ball and a piece of board in lieu of a regular ball and bat; but it was just as much fun. If the teen-agers found the games a bit childish for their tastes, they could always pair off and go horseback riding up and down the road in the neighborhood. In the winter skating and sliding beckoned. Certainly there is no need to feel sorry for the pioneer youngsters, especially after settlement increased. Families generally were large, providing plenty of playmates; and opportunities for recreation and pleasure, simple and homemade though they usually were, were far from lacking.[21]

Special days, such as the Fourth of July, Thanksgiving, Christmas, and New Year's, and occasions like weddings and funerals, provided excuses for social gatherings, services, and festivities. The Fourth of July was the big day of the year, and every village and city worthy of the name arranged a "rousing programme," which attracted country people for miles around. Even the immigrant groups adopted the celebration and made it a part of their community life. The main features of the day's activities became almost stereotyped. There must, if possible, be a parade in the morning. Mrs. Joseph Ullman recalled vividly some forty years later the celebration in St. Paul in 1860. Companies of state militia, resplendent in new uniforms and armed, together with members of the local lodges and musical organizations, aided by flags and banners, formed an impressive parade. Band music, singing, firecrackers, and a stirring oration were other essentials of a good celebration. And, of course, each family and group must have a real picnic dinner, at which fried chicken was the accepted main dish. After these activities were out of the way, various forms of amusement, such as ball games and foot, sack, potato, and horse races, were provided. In the evening a "grand display" of fireworks and dancing climaxed a day long to be remembered.[22]

Farmers' reactions to the Fourth of July festivities are found frequently in their diaries. Countryman, who had a strong puritanical strain, took a dim view of the celebration he attended in 1860. " 'Tis independence day!" he wrote. "Went down to Hastings to enjoy the day, expecting to see great things. And what did I see. I saw several men selling 'Lager Beer.' I saw men playing ball and cricket.

I saw men gormandizing with good things; boys shooting with crackers. To a small crowd a man read the declaration of Independence, and another spake on oration. A few drank freely and fought. Finally there was a foot race for a belt. The whole thing was a foolish affair." On July 4, 1862, Countryman and his family went on a picnic to Fort Snelling and Minnehaha Falls. Andrew Peterson cradled rye on the Fourth in 1870, but some of his family went to the celebration in Scandia. Likewise, in 1878, Henry Smith had to stay home and tend his bees, while the girls went to the ceremonies. The next year, however, the Smith family and six friends celebrated at home. They set their dinner table "in the shadows of the trees out of doors, had strawberries (last picking) basswood honey (2 years old) ice cream, lemonade, boned chicken, etc., etc." In Stearns County about the same time Edwin H. Atwood wrote in his diary: "We all went over to J. Martins, Fair Haven to a picnic had a good time. Harry cut his foot in the lake Clarence staid to the dance at F H." [23]

Thanksgiving, far more than the Fourth of July, had religious significance, but it also was the occasion for feasting and get-togethers. In 1850 the day was observed on December 26. On that day a family in Minneapolis "had a dinner of stewed oysters, boiled vegetables, baked pork and beans, cranberries, mince and cranberry pies, cheese, and nuts." Michael Teeter, who lived on the Iowa line in the late 1850's, missed fruit as part of his usual diet, so his family celebrated Thanksgiving by eating dried wild crab apples boiled in soda water and sweetened with molasses. At a later date turkey came to occupy the place of honor, even as it does today. Countryman felt much the same about Thanksgiving festivities as he did about those of the Fourth of July. Said he: "Thanksgiving day. A day which I think ought to be kept, as a fast day, but instead mirth and hilarity are most conspicuous, and feasting is a regular feature." But even he, three years later, went over to his sister Lany's for dinner. [24]

Christmas, of course, unlike the Fourth of July and Thanksgiving, was not an American-born institution, and the traditions and customs surrounding its observance sprang from many sources.

Catholic French-Canadians, their heirs the Indians, conventional New Englanders, Germans, Scandinavians, and others brought their methods of commemorating the birth of Christ to Minnesota. Here these methods tended to be modified and amalgamated, resulting in the evolution of what might be termed an American Christmas, less lengthy, for example, than the Swedish or Norwegian celebration. Each nationality group and religious sect perpetuated certain characteristic traits, yet each in turn was shaped by contact with the others. Religious services, the exchange of gifts, decoration of a tree, the Santa Claus myth, visiting, and feasting—these were the basic elements of Christmas as the pioneer Minnesota farmer knew it. In the primitive shanty or log cabin of an early settler Christmas was simple and meager. Mrs. W. L. Niemann, a resident of Sauk Rapids in the 1850's, wrote: "Christmas in those hard times did not mean to us little pioneer children what it does now. There was no spare money with which to buy presents. We always hung up our stockings, but got nothing in them but a little cheap candy, and perhaps a few raisins." Yet no effort was spared to make the Yuletide as gay as possible. A Swedish woman near Watertown described Christmas preparations in her home as follows: "Nothing could be cozier than our cabin Christmas eve. We had brought solid silver knives, forks and spoons. These hung from racks. Quantities of copper and brass utensils burnished until they were like mirrors hung in rows. In Sweden mother had woven curtains and bed coverings of red, white and blue linen and these were always used on holidays. . . . We covered a hoop with gay colored paper and set little wooden candle holders that my father had made all around it. This was suspended from the ceiling all aglow with dips. Then, as a last touch to the decorations, we filled our brass candle sticks with real candles and set them in the windows as a greeting to those living across the lake. A sheaf for the birds and all was done." In 1871 a community Christmas was celebrated in a schoolhouse in Martin County. A tree lighted with candles and loaded with stockings made of mosquito netting and piles of popcorn balls were the chief attractions. Scandinavian families ate their big meal and opened their presents on Christmas Eve; among other groups it was customary to do these things on Christmas Day. In either case it was a joyous time, made even more pleasant if some of the traditional fare, such as *lutefisk,* rice pudding, plum pudding, and turkey, were available. Sleigh rides, balls, and amateur theatricals enlivened the holiday season in many communities; and special church services gave it solemnity and meaning everywhere.[25]

New Year's Eve was ushered in with gaiety by some and by attendance at church services by others. On New Year's Day calls were customary, and they must have been very popular if the following item from a Winona paper in 1855 is any criterion: "New Year's Calls.—Several beautiful young ladies—God bless 'em—of our town, have requested us to say that the good old Eastern fashion, of receiving calls of gentlemen on New Year's day, will be observed by them, and we appreciate their resolution, satisfied that the gentlemen 'will be too happy,' etc."[26]

Marriage, quite naturally, was viewed in varying lights by Minnesota's heterogeneous population. On a new frontier it was not unusual to find a settler living in a common-law relationship with an Indian woman; conversely, there were large numbers who considered marriage a highly sacred matter, a state that must have the blessing of the church. At times some of the latter lived in actual marriage before the coming of a clergyman to their area, but they always secured church sanction as soon as it was available. German Catholic settlers at Winsted journeyed to Chaska to have the wedding mass sung in the church there until they were able to build their own church in 1869. Many immigrant groups were staunchly opposed to marriage outside their own fold, but as the years passed such marriages became more and more numerous. Some weddings were rather solemn and sedate affairs, but far more common was the type attended by feasting, a charivari, dancing, and not infrequently plenty of whiskey.[27]

Certainly no cause for merrymaking, yet a reason that brought people together all too often, was a funeral. Death struck suddenly in the pioneer period, and it was a rare family who could keep the unwelcome visitor away from the home for any appreciable number of years. In primitive areas little or no ceremony accompanied the interment of a deceased member of the family. A few words and a prayer mumbled over the grave by a lay preacher or a friend had to suffice. Countryman, referring to the death of a neighbor in 1859, wrote: "Attended funeral services at 10½ with my family. There was no sermon, but we repaired immediately to the grave and interred the mortals [sic] remains of a much esteemed man. . . . Quite a large concourse attended his burial." Even the coffin was homemade. On another occasion Countryman went into Hastings to get material for a shroud and to have a coffin made for a boy who had just died. The preacher did not arrive for the boy's funeral, and so Countryman "read a chapter, Sang a hymn and prayed, after which we repaired to the grave." A few weeks later a minister visited the neighborhood and "preached a funeral discourse to the memory" of the boy. As churches and houses were built, funerals became more elaborate and customs surrounding them were more fully observed. Undoubtedly it was comforting to the bereaved to be remembered in their sorrow, but it must also have been a great strain to endure the wakes, the meals, and the conversations that attended the preparation for a funeral. When death struck in Countryman's own family, he noted in his diary: "This has been a day of mourning and sorrow. We have had some company, but were without company a part of the time. This morning early, I went down to town and bought the graves clothes for Royal, and ordered the coffin made." [28]

During the late 1860's and the 1870's, a new social agency for rural people, the Patrons of Husbandry, or the Grange, as it was known, made its appearance. Oliver H. Kelley, the Minnesota farmer who won lasting fame as the founder of the organization, felt that "farmers were handicapped mainly by their lack of gregarious habits." Because of this belief, he and a few associates in 1867 established the Grange as a device for improving the social, intellectual, moral, and economic conditions of farm people. The organization was provided with a secret ritual, patterned after that of the Masonic order, and both men and women were admitted to membership. Farmers were slow to join at first, but with the advent of hard times in the early 1870's membership grew by leaps and bounds. By September, 1874, there were 538 local lodges in Minnesota. About that time membership began to decline, although there were still nearly three hundred local Granges in the state in 1876. The local groups met monthly, semimonthly, or sometimes weekly in schoolhouses, homes, or Grange halls to perform the work of the ritual, listen to programs, play games, and partake of refreshments. On other occasions groups of local lodges banded together to hold picnics or festivals or to celebrate the Fourth of July. The social influence of such activities was naturally considerable, and much credit should go to the Grange for its work in breaking down rural social isolation. Indeed, one writer maintains that the "old provincialism of the agricultural population had received such a shaking up that it never again sank quite to the old level." [29]

From at least the 1850's on, the strictly masculine fraternal orders, like the Masons and the Odd Fellows, made their appearances in the state. Catholics and Lutherans, of course, were prevented by their religion from joining these orders, but thousands of other farmers went through the various degrees. These groups did particularly good work in bringing country and urban dwellers together and in helping to dispel some of the bitterness that existed between them. Another lodge frequently encountered during the period was that of the Good Templars. Farmers interested in stamping out the liquor traffic found congenial company in this order, which was organized on a state-wide basis into a grand lodge. One evening Countryman "took dinner with Alte at the Festival of the Good Templars at Elfelts Hall [in St. Paul]. After dinner heard a number of toasts and responses, to one of which 'The Ladies' I was called upon to respond." [30]

In these ways the pioneer farmer tried to make his life full and abundant. The picture is necessarily general; much has been omitted; and the social patterns of the various immigrant groups, together with the effect of the American environment upon their thinking and way of life, have barely been touched. The obvious and the usual have not been noted, yet the day-by-day activities when there was no opportunity or occasion for a social get-together accounted for far more of the farmer's time than did the dance, the visit, or the church festival. Countryman felt this monotony and complained: "I go through about the same routine of duty daily, milking, feeding hogs, husking corn, etc." But the picture is a changing one. No two large sections of the state were in the same stage of social development at one time. While the northern part was a wild, unsettled frontier, the southeastern region was well populated and socially mature, with schools, churches, roads, opera houses, railroads, and comfortable homes. By the early 1880's social life in parts of the northern region was still in the stage of cabin raisings, visits, and occasional dances, while in the southern section it had progressed to a stage of numerous well-organized and regularly scheduled activities. Exceptions there were in all areas. In 1879, Owen H. Roche of Chicago created a truly baronial estate in western Jackson County and held "rare goings-on" in his twenty-six room "farmhouse," quite in contrast to the social life of his "God-fearing Swedish" neighbors; but he, like the log-cabin dweller in a neighborhood of frame houses, was the exception and not the rule. The trend was clear. Well-organized rural community life and agricultural diversification went hand in hand across the state. Both sprang from many sources and both suffered through many ordeals, but together they presented a way of life and a manner of making a living which not a few persons regard as the best that America has produced.[31]

Toward Mechanization

One of America's main contributions in agriculture has been the invention and development of laborsaving devices which have enabled farmers of the United States to cultivate more land per man than has been possible in any other country. The story of this development is a fascinating one. The easing of the farmer's toil, better farming, the displacement of horses and mules, the freeing of acres formerly devoted to forage crops, the relation of farmer and machine agent, improved machines—these are only a few of the topics related to the history of farm machinery. That history has been marked by almost constant improvement and development, and one of its most amazing features has been the fact that most of the action has taken place during little more than a hundred years. It was only in July of 1831 that Cyrus McCormick tested his reaper before a little group of interested, if skeptical, spectators on a Virginia farm. Before that date agricultural mechanization had made little advance, but it has since progressed to such an extent that practically every farm job can be done by a machine. Playing a role by no means passive in this drama were many pioneer Minnesotans.

Little is known about the agricultural implements used by Minnesota pioneers of the 1840's, but one student of local agricultural history believes that "most of their implements were made of wood." It is quite possible, however, that metal tips and other small pieces of metal were used to reinforce the wooden parts. William R. Brown of Red Rock recorded in his diary on May 20, 1846: "Davis plowing. Struck a Bolder & broke 2 inches off the point of the Boston plow ground it & went to work." Again, on May 30, Brown wrote: "yesterday Harrison commenced plowing for potatoes & Rutabagas plows 10 to 12 inches deep. . . . We hoed the Beets parsnips & Carrots." And on June 1 he recorded: "Sold my Large

Prairie Plow to B. L. Rockwood he agrees to Break next year between the 20 of May & 20 of June 8 acres for me for the Plow." [1] Thus it is evident that some crude machines were used in Minnesota in the 1840's, notably a breaking plow, perhaps a smaller plow, and a hoe. In addition to these implements, Brown and the other farmers of his day probably had sickles or cradles, spades, wagons, flails, and a few other primitive agricultural devices to aid them in their efforts to wring returns from the land. But the inadequacy of these tools was undoubtedly a real handicap.

Few of the earliest settlers in any part of the state had many farm implements when they arrived. Lurett Whiting, who emigrated from Fremont County, Iowa, to Clitherall, Minnesota, in 1865, gives an interesting account of farm machinery in the middle sixties, and the essentials of his story will fit the case of many Minnesota farmers of earlier decades. Whiting and his party took with them only a few plowshares, one breaking plowshare, a small set of blacksmith's tools, and some carpenter's tools. For plow beams and handles they were dependent upon their own skill, fashioning them of wood cut in the forest. Their breaking plow "had a large beam of about six feet long made of wood, with a piece framed into the back end of the beam to fasten the plow-share to. There were four-and-a-half-inch rods bolted above the share to take the place of a moldboard, and a wooden axletree about four feet long. To this was fastened the plow with two wagon-wheels attached to the axletree and a gauge made out of wood, so arranged that one could set it at any depth desired. Two yoke of oxen were hitched to this plow. It would run without being held up by hand and worked fine, all our land being broken in this way." [2]

The drags used by Whiting's group were made of wood, teeth and all, as iron teeth were not available. One was called the "A drag," and it was hinged in the middle so that it could be cleaned by raising only half of it at a time. One member of the group fashioned a drag from a forked tree and drove teeth about twenty inches long into holes bored through the two prongs of the fork. "This was surely a comical looking affair," Whiting recalled, "and on account of its being so narrow and high it would often upset on the side-hills. This drag was drawn by oxen, and they had to work very steadily all day to smooth up an acre." Sometimes, when Whiting used it, he "let it run lying on its back . . . for it did just about as good work that way." Another invention used at Clitherall was a corn cultivator, which "never gave satisfaction. It went twice in a row and was never known to scour. After using it a while" the colonists "decided to call it a 'corn aggravator' for it lived up to that name to perfection." For cutting their grain, the Clitherall settlers used cradles with which "a man who was good at it" might cut five or six acres a day. After the grain was cut it was raked with a hand rake and bound by hand into bundles with straw. One other device mentioned by Whiting was a pair of wool cards, used in the process of preparing wool for spinning into yarn.[3]

Such inventions as Whiting used and such difficulties as he encountered probably were typical of the experiences of thousands of other early farmers. He mentions threshing with a horsepower machine, but even earlier, in the 1840's and 1850's, horses or oxen were commonly used to tramp out the grain. Edward B. Drew, who farmed near Winona in the early 1850's, tells of the latter method in his reminiscenses. "We stacked our wheat of course," he writes. "We wanted our winter wheat threshed for seed. We knew the primitive way was to tread it out with oxen. We had never seen anything of the sort done, except shelling out corn in Indiana by horses treading it out on the barn floor. . . . We fixed a place by the side of the stack, smoothing off a circular piece about twenty feet in diameter, and making the ground as smooth and hard as we could by using a maul made for that purpose. We made a temporary fence around it to keep the cattle off from it. . . . We were not long in threshing out the stack and it was very satisfactory too. But when it came to cleaning the grain without a mill it was very poor business. . . . We watched for a windy day. We heard of a fanning mill in Winona. A man had sold his farm . . . and brought his mill to Minnesota. I found the man and borrowed or hired the mill. It was a streak of good luck."[4]

Another common method of threshing was to beat the grain with a flail. This instrument was composed of two rods of hardwood of varying lengths, one about four and the other about two and a half feet long, fastened together at one end with a cord or a piece of rawhide. The operator held the loose end of the longer piece in his hand, whirled the shorter piece over his head, and brought the flail down upon the grain. To perform this task a man needed a certain amount of skill to avoid hitting himself over the head. A Mower County pioneer recalled that as a boy in 1858 he did not know how to use a flail, and so he and his brothers and sisters "took the grain by the handful and whipped it out on the sides of a wagon box, letting the grain fall into the box." [5]

But the hand labor of the frontier agriculturist was not confined to threshing time. Most of his work was performed by hand. He often cut his hay and grain with a scythe, sickle, or cradle; he raked his hay and grain by hand; he bound his bundles in the same way, and shocked them without benefit of machine; his corn was planted, picked, husked, and often shelled by hand; and his fences, house, and barn were the products of his ingenuity and skill. Such tasks could and did become deadening, but they might also provide occasions for co-operative effort and social get-togethers, as we have seen. [6]

The village blacksmith was a mighty figure. He was very necessary to the farmer, not only as a maker of implements, but as a repairman as well. As late as 1925 one Minnesota pioneer liked his old shovel plow, made in 1856 by David Smith, a Belle Plaine blacksmith. This plow was similar in shape to a cultivator shovel, but was much larger and more convex. A strip of iron sharpened on one side was attached to the beam perpendicularly ahead of the plow to cut the sod. It was recalled that in his shop Smith turned out hundreds of farming implements for the early settlers of the Big Woods area. [7]

Neither the inventiveness and ingenuity of the farmer himself nor the hammer and anvil of the blacksmith, however, were sufficient to meet the needs of Minnesota's growing rural population in the late 1840's. The earliest territorial newspapers frequently mention the importation of agricultural implements into the region. One rather typical item notes the fact that a certain Irishman who traveled up the Mississippi by boat had on board three plows brought from Ireland. With them he expected to break the prairie, and they were made of iron—beam, handles, and all. "Such plows will be of no manner of service breaking prairies," was the newspaper comment. And some early settlers recall in their reminiscences that the river boats transported many implements to Minnesota, Iowa, and Wisconsin in the early 1850's. One pioneer recalled "seeing grain cradles carried off the boat" in 1852.[8]

An essential implement was the breaking plow, which made the tough prairie sod ready for agriculture. Sometimes, also, city lots were broken. Drew recalls that he "started the breaking-plow" at Minnesota City early in May, 1852. "We made it quite a business breaking city lots for members [of the Western Farm and Village Association], or half a lot for some," he writes. "We got $3 per acre for breaking, and called a lot two acres." It was no easy job to cut the prairie sod, and sometimes as many as ten yoke of oxen were used to pull one giant breaking plow. Another difficulty was the failure of many of the plows to scour in the rich prairie soil. Joseph Haskell and James Norris at Cottage Grove used wooden and cast-iron plows that would not scour; so the plowmen had to carry paddles to clean the plowshares frequently.[9]

Another implement prized by the farmer fortunate enough to possess one was a reaper. There seems to be some doubt as to the exact date when the first reaper appeared in Minnesota, but it probably was not later than 1854. In February of that year George W. Farrington of St. Paul wrote to Cyrus H. McCormick that the prospects were favorable in the vicinity of St. Paul for an increased demand for the McCormick reaper. In conversations with farmers during the winter of 1853–54, Farrington was led to believe that several of them planned to order reapers in the spring. Later in the spring J. C. Burbank and Company of St. Paul wrote to Norton and Hempstead of Chicago about obtaining reapers. The Minnesota concern had orders for two reapers manufactured in 1853 without mowers attached and for two complete machines. And in August, 1854, Farrington complained to McCormick that he had received a bill of lading for a McCormick machine which had been shipped from St. Louis but had arrived too late to be sold that year. This was regrettable, as Farrington had had many earlier opportunities for disposing of it. "Shall I pay charges on it and hold it until next season?" he asked. The freight charge, incidentally, was $55.95. The first reapers were crude machines designed for cutting both grain and hay, the hay mower being optional on a reaper. The reaper proper in 1854 was still rather crude, though it was equipped with seats for both the driver and the man who raked the cut grain from a platform to the ground. The grain was bound by hand.[10]

It is thus apparent that McCormick early invaded the Minnesota market. Farrington acted as his agent at St. Paul as early as 1854, and other agents were appointed at various places in the 1850's and later. These agents wrote numerous letters in longhand to the McCormick Harvesting Company of Chicago, giving not only details of sales, but also information on market conditions, rival machines, weather, and a host of other matters. In return came replies from McCormick urging the agents to expand their business, telling how to keep books, directing the disposition of machines neglected by incapable agents, and giving other information and advice.[11]

But McCormick did not have the Minnesota reaper business all to himself in the 1850's. James J. Hill later recalled that a Manny reaper was used in the territory at an early date. Mention is made of this reaper in Illinois in 1851, but no record has been found to tell when the first Manny machine appeared in Minnesota. It seems to have been crude, however, until 1854, when a greatly improved machine was placed on the market. Another reaper and mower that competed with McCormick's machine was the Esterley. George Esterley originally patented a header in 1844, but in the early 1850's he abandoned that device and began to manufacture a combined reaper and mower. A good deal of rivalry existed among the agents representing the various implement manufacturers. In 1858 one of McCormick's agents complained that other agents had the advantage over him. It was claimed that the McCormick machines were older and that they ran harder than the Manny and Esterley reapers, and the writer noted that the latter especially had taken well during the season just past.[12]

In addition to the reaper, other implements found their way to

Minnesota in the 1850's. A Fillmore County pioneer enumerates the various farm machines owned by the farmers of his neighborhood in that decade. He lists "lumber wagons, bob sleighs of home manufacture, sleds with long runners of home manufacture, 'A'-shaped harrows, wood-beam crossing and breaking plows, cradles to cut the grain, scythes to cut the grass, hand rakes to rake the hay and the grain from the swath, single and double shovel corn plows, spades, shovels, axes, hoes, iron wedges, bettles or mauls used to split rails for fencing, frows to rive out the shakes or clapboards to cover the log cabin, and a limited number of carpenter tools." Often "five or more settlers would own a fanning mill to clean their grain, and in the first few years of settlement an eight-horse sweep power separator threshed all the grain grown in two or more townships." Corn was dropped by hand, covered with a hoe, and plowed with a one-horse shovel plow; the weeds in the cornfield were kept down with a hand hoe; and when the corn was picked the stalks were cut by hand and then shocked.[13]

Although many of the plows were homemade or were fashioned by the local blacksmith, some were factory made. By 1860 cast-iron plows were being made in numerous foundries and factories in the Middle West; and steel plows, which would scour, though they were often brittle and inclined to warp, were being manufactured in various places, notably by John Deere at Moline, Illinois. Breaking plows manufactured in Galena, Illinois, were extensively used in Minnesota in the early 1850's. Gradually, plow factories began to appear in Minnesota itself. The date of the first one is unknown, but in 1856 a St. Paul newspaper mentioned the fact that a plow factory was in operation at Cannon City in Rice County. This plant was owned by Honeyman and Andyke, and its breaking plows were said to be better than those made in Galena. The factory, however, unfortunately could not supply half the demand for plows in its vicinity. New developments in plows were being made constantly, some practical and some not, and many people had visions of great and rapid future progress. Governor Sibley, in an address before the Dakota County Agricultural Association at Nininger on October 8, 1858, predicted that the steam plow would supersede all others. Although his prediction was incorrect, there was an element of truth in it. On farms today steam is not the motivating power for plows, but another force, gasoline, furnishes fuel for the tractors that pull many Minnesota plows.[14]

Another machine that reached Minnesota in the 1850's was the mechanical thresher. Although the West lagged behind the East in the use of the threshing machine, the Case thresher was manufactured at Racine, Wisconsin, as early as 1844, and the better-known Pitts machine, at Alton, Illinois, in 1847. In 1852 the Pitts company produced machines at its new plant in Chicago. Thus, the thresher became easily available in the West at about the time that Minnesota was beginning to fill in with settlers.[15]

According to James J. Hill, the first threshing machine in Minnesota was operated by John Cormack, a river pilot, at Eden Prairie back of Fort Snelling. The Pitts company was early in the Minnesota field, and Hill's company made a contract with it "to try to sell three threshing machines." Hill was asked if he thought he could set up a thresher, and after watching Cormack's machine run at Eden Prairie, he was convinced that he could. Soon he had a customer near Shakopee.[16]

Louis H. Powell, however, maintains that his great uncle, Nathaniel Newell Powell, in 1850 purchased, at a cost of three hundred dollars, the first threshing machine used north of Prairie du Chien. No record of the make of this machine has survived, but there is reason to believe it was bought in Galena and shipped to Minnesota by river steamer. It operated in southern Washington County and in the vicinity of St. Anthony in Ramsey County. A three-man crew, which included Powell himself, traveled with the machine during the 1850 season. Powell's two helpers received thirty-two and twenty-five dollars a month, respectively. Much of the threshing was done on shares and, although the 1850 venture paid the costs involved, Powell reduced wages in 1851 and increased the price for threshing grain. The charge for threshing wheat in the latter year seems to have been ten cents a bushel.[17]

Most of these early threshers were little horsepower treadmill machines, which separated the grain and the straw, but threw them out together. Then all the straw had to be pitched on to a stack by hand, and the grain had to be cleaned with a fanning mill. Still, this was better than using a flail. The Pitts thresher, however, from the first combined the three operations of threshing the grain, separating it from the straw, and winnowing it. Gradually other machines added to the cylinders shakers which separated the wheat from the straw; and then fanning mills, which cleaned the grain of chaff, became integral parts of the threshers. Nearly all machines seem to have had winnowers attached by the early 1860's.[18]

THRESHING WITH HORSEPOWER
[From Minnesota Board of Immigration, *The Agricultural, Manufacturing, and Commercial Resources of Minnesota*, 37 (St. Paul, 1881).]

Many a farmer, however, did not have access to an improved thresher. Small machines provided with separators were much more common than the larger type. Before grain was fed into the cylinder, the bands on the bundles were cut by hand. Then the bundles were thrown into the machine by a feeder, who wore goggles to protect his eyes from stray kernels of grain flying from the cylinder. The feeder's task was considered the most laborious of all the operations connected with threshing. To operate the early threshing machines, from one to eight or ten horses were used. In the late 1860's, threshers "with from one to four-horse powers" were generally used in the East, but at the same time and even earlier, in Minnesota, eight- and ten-horsepower machines were frequently employed.[19]

Operating a horsepower machine was not always easy, as Lurett Whiting later recalled. "I well remember that the first threshing done in Otter Tail County was with a second-hand horsepower machine which Uncle Lewis Whiting bought near Sauk Center," he writes. "As we had only a few horses we hitched in two yokes of oxen and started up, but the merry-go-round, so to speak, was too much for the oxen and they would get dizzy after two or three rounds and lie down, so we took them off and managed to thresh out what little we had with the horses by feeding the machine light. After a year or two farmers began to settle all around us, and we were then able to get all the horses we needed."[20]

The introduction of a thresher into a pioneer community was heralded with delight. Typical was the notice of the purchase of a machine at Glencoe: "This is an institution that was required, it being the second one introduced into the county. The proprietors will find plenty of work for their machine. We hope to hear it 'rattle' before another month rolls around. There will be some fun in threshing grain this year. It will not be all chaff."[21]

Another device much needed by farmers who were distant from an adequate water supply was a well-drilling machine. In Fillmore County in the 1850's, for example, some farmers hauled water five miles or more before well drillers became available. Finally, in 1858 or 1859, a drilling machine was put in operation on a local farm. "It consisted of a kind of spring pole arrangement and was operated by the foot. The hole drilled was about four inches in diameter, and about twelve inches [*feet?*] . . . constituted a day's work drilling." When water was reached, only about four pails a day could be drawn.[22]

As the decade of the 1850's came to a close, the United States government, for the third time through its census bureau, inquired into the status and progress of agriculture in each of the states. By studying the census findings it is possible to gain at least a rough picture of the place occupied by farm machinery in Minnesota's agricultural pattern in the decade. The rural population increased 3,119.4 per cent; the number of farms, 11,364.4 per cent; the value of farms, land, and buildings, 16,884.4 per cent; and the production of field crops, 12,248.4 per cent. Thus the number of farms, the value of farm property, and the total value of field crops each increased four or five times faster than the total population. Although the average value of agricultural implements per farm decreased from $102 in 1849 to $56 in 1859, farm machine values for the state as a whole increased by 6,271.2 per cent in the same decade. Nearly all the farm machinery used in the state was imported at heavy expense from the East, for only such simple utensils as plows and fanning mills were manufactured in Minnesota in 1860. All grain cradles, horse rakes, forks, spades, shovels, straw cutters, and hoes were imported, and only about thirty of the thousand reapers sold in Minnesota in 1861 were manufactured there. This represented expenditures amounting to about $150,000, a "pretty large sum to go out of our State in one year for a single implement used by the farmer," according to the state's leading farm journal, which asked, "When will these machines be made at home?" [23]

Fifteen years later the state had many farm implement plants, and manufacturers from other localities had developed elaborate distribution agencies in Minnesota. The loud complaints from Grange orators, debt-ridden farmers, and crusading editors were voiced against the machine manufacturers and agents. Some urged that the farmers scrap their machinery and return to the cradle and the hoe. But whatever the evils associated with the production, sale, and distribution of farm machinery, one thing is certain—man's, and later woman's, lot was eased and the constant fear of famine was removed by the invention, production, and use of mechanical devices on the farm. Even today we may be only on the threshold of agricultural mechanization, and a century hence observers probably will consider our farming methods just as primitive as we do those of 1850.

Mechanization Gains Momentum

The decade of the 1860's saw many improvements in farm machinery, as well as the more general use of implements by the farmers. The fact that the Civil War resulted in a scarcity of labor stimulated the adoption of machinery. In 1860, according to a St. Paul newspaper, more reapers and threshing machines were brought into Minnesota than in all previous years put together. No accurate statistics have been found to measure this importation, but nearly a hundred threshing machines and more than two hundred reapers had been landed and purchased at the St. Paul levee alone by the latter part of July. In Winona, three hundred reaping machines had been sold by late July, and a dealer at Marion, near Rochester, disposed of ninety McCormick reapers during the spring and summer. Much of the crop of 1859 was not forwarded to market until the spring and summer of 1860 because of insufficient machinery to thresh it in the earlier year.[1]

It was hoped that a similar difficulty would be obviated in 1860. Certainly the machine trade of that year was extensive. Reports like the following were typical: "The levee was well covered yesterday with almost every variety of agricultural implements, including no less than a dozen ponderous and elegant threshing machines—some in complete running order, others with the parts separated for transportation to the Red River, and other points in the interior of the State."[2]

One improvement that came into general use was the self-raking reaper. Although the self-rake was first placed on the market in 1854, its output during the 1850's apparently did not approximate that of the leading makes of hand-rake reapers. The purpose of the self-rake was to dispense with the labor of the man who raked the grain off the machines, but the early self-rakes were extremely crude. In August, 1860, it was reported in the press that B. M. Smith, who lived two miles from St. Paul on the St. Anthony road, had some of his wheat, of which he had a hundred acres, cut by one of Esterley's self-raking reapers. This machine cut an average of two acres an hour in grain that yielded twenty-five bushels an acre, for it eliminated the delays caused by the fact that a person raking by hand could not work for more than five minutes at a time without resting. When gathered the grain was in as good condition as if it had been harvested by the most experienced cradler. According to one newspaper, in 1860 Temple and Beaupre of St. Paul sold "quite a number" of self-rakes, "which have given general satisfaction." The self-rake was indeed a boon to the wheat growers of Minnesota, where a labor shortage was apparent in the late summer of 1860. At the Minnesota State Fair of 1860 Dorsey's self-raking reaper was exhibited. This machine was equipped with a reel rake; that is, the reel served as a rake. It was one of the first of this type to be successful.[3]

McCormick began to manufacture self-rakes in 1861, and so successful were they, and so great was the shortage of labor, that by 1864 fully two-thirds of the reapers he produced were self-rakes. The old hand-raking reaper continued to be widely used, however, especially in the East, because many farmers desired a combined reaper and mower. McCormick did not produce a self-rake which combined the two operations until 1869. Even the McCormick self-rake of the 1860's was somewhat crude, as one farm wife recalled. "There was a big red wooden arm that went around and around," she wrote, "and to balance it there had to be a large iron ball on a long iron rod, as a sort of counter weight. When the big red wooden arm came up over the reaper it looked as though it would come down on the horses' backs as it revolved. The horses were frightened and it was a hard task to get them used to it so they wouldn't shy at it and run away."[4]

To a greater extent than during the 1850's was there rivalry in the reaper business in the succeeding decade. In 1867, for example, one agent wrote that "there has been and is still, a most fierce competition. Last year was so good for machine men, that all rushed in with a vast amount of machinery, and the county has been overrun with the most active class of agents." Naturally each company claimed that its machine was the best, which was very confusing to the farmer. As a result, trials of rival reapers were suggested and held at various times. In 1861, for example, the *Farmer and Gardener* suggested that, since so many reapers were offered to the public, a trial be held to determine the merits of their performances and not of their paint jobs. One such trial was held on the fair grounds of the Minnesota State Agricultural Society in 1867. The first premium for reapers went to the Manny machine, that for combined

A McCORMICK SELF-RAKING REAPER
[From Rogin, *Farm Machinery*, 101.]

self-raking reapers and mowers was awarded to the Kirby machine, and the sweepstakes were given to the Wood combined reaper and mower.[5]

At another trial held in the same year on the Gournsey farm near Cottage Grove, it was found that the McCormick machines were heavier to draw than the others, although the parts were more accessible for oiling and tightening. The Massillon Excelsior won this trial, and the Johnston self-rake was designated the best for cutting on uneven surfaces. Some reapers were manufactured in Minnesota at this time. A notable exhibit at the state fair of 1869 was devoted to home-manufactured implements. Among them was the Valley Chief self-raking reaper and mower made by the W. W. Eastman Company of Minneapolis, and a self-rake invented by L. H. Johnston of Rochester for attachment to the Weston and Curtis reaper. The latter attracted much attention.[6]

In addition to the hand- and self-raking reapers, some "headers" and "droppers" were used by Minnesota farmers. The dropper delivered the grain to the rear of the machine instead of to the side, as did the self-rake. Since it dispensed with the revolving rake, it was a light machine, but the grain had to be bound fast in order to get it out of the way before the machine made its next round. The header dispensed with binding by cutting off the tops of the grain, but it never became very popular because climatic conditions were not favorable for its use. Most grain needed drying before stacking in order to prevent spoilage. Very few headers were used in Minnesota in comparison with other machines.[7]

The biggest advance in the reaper field in the 1860's was the introduction of the Marsh harvester, which made "its commercial debut in 1864" with about twenty-five machines. By 1867, when a Marsh machine was exhibited at the state fair, 825 of the harvesters were on the market. This machine was a great improvement over those previously used. Two men standing on a platform bound the cut grain into bundles with straw. The backbreaking task of following a reaper and binding the grain off the ground thus was eliminated. Most of the cutting and bundle binding had to be done when dew was on the straw in the early morning or the evening, however, for the straw of midday usually broke when used in binding.[8]

The advantages of the Marsh harvester were enthusiastically advertised in the newspapers. It was claimed that the machine saved the board and wages of three men, walking and stooping in the hot sun, half the expense of binding, the labor of one man in raking off, and, finally, at least one bushel of grain per acre wasted with other machines. These claims were not exaggerated, if farmers of the period are to be believed. Such a statement as the following was common: "I have bound my half of 12 to 15 acres a day, easier than 5 of us did before on the ground."[9]

MECHANIZATION GAINS MOMENTUM

The prices of reapers varied, but an average figure in the middle 1860's was about two hundred dollars for the combined reaper and mower, and somewhat less for the reaper. About 1866 P. P. Quist purchased a Champion self-rake reaper and mower for $225, payable in three annual installments, with interest at ten per cent. The installment method of paying for agricultural implements was general then, as later. Credit played a big part in the farm machinery business, and most agents complained that making collections was difficult and often unpleasant. As a result an attractive discount was offered for cash, but cash was difficult to secure. McCormick usually demanded cash on delivery equal to a third of the purchase price, with the balance plus six per cent interest due on the following December 1. If the notes were not paid on time, they were generally renewed at ten per cent and were secured by a mortgage on the farm or the personal property of the buyer. An annual rate of sixty per cent was not uncommon in Minnesota.[10]

Naturally many farmers cried out against exorbitant interest rates and the efforts of agents to make collections. "The state of public opinion here about the wealth of the McCormicks and their grace and mercy," wrote a McCormick agent in 1868, "are badly against collections at any time—and are worse now. It will take years to cultivate a good healthy state of feeling about paying promptly the McCormick notes. Some men even take it in high du[d]geon because I send them a simple notice that their notes are coming due, as I do to *every man*. I actually have to explain and almost apologize."[11]

The late 1860's, following the Civil War, were difficult years for collections. The deflation after the war pushed farm prices downward at a time when the average Minnesota farmer was in debt for almost everything. Thus the implement agent had to be a sharp snatcher to get the farmers' money before someone else did. A Rochester agent described conditions well when he said: "The low price of wheat and the downward tendency for the last three years has altogether ruined many men and creditors are pushing so hard as almost to make a panic. *Money is coming very hard and slow.* . . . We shall have to secure [our paper notes] in any way we can

Harvesting on a Dakota County Farm

and in many cases be glad to get security on long time." About three weeks later the same agent informed McCormick that Minnesota "is badly in debt, hopelessly in debt. . . . Through the high prices of grain during the war, men were lured on into buying and running into debt, many of them extravagantly, some of them recklessly, and perhaps nearly all of them foolishly." Many farmers put one mortgage on top of another from 1866 to 1869, going deeper and deeper into debt. As a result, the lawyers, sheriffs, and constables were swamped.[12]

When notes given for machinery fell due, the price of grain generally was low, so the farmer borrowed money at from twenty-four to thirty per cent. "Are not two-thirds of our farmers machine poor?" asked one newspaper, which even suggested that farmers would be better off if they went back to the flail and cradle. The *Glencoe Register* advised caution, expressing the belief that many farmers in the vicinity were making a big mistake by buying so much machinery on credit. Some were purchasing machines that had never been tried in the region, and the practicability of such implements was not known. "From the best calculation we are able to make, the surplus of the present crop will hardly pay for the machinery that will be purchased in this county this season," said the editor of the *Register*. And in a similar vein were the remarks of a farmer who wrote in the *Lake City Leader:* "I think a great many of our Minnesota farmers buy things they might get along without, and would if they had to pay cash for them. This credit system is ruining us. . . . I have known farmers to buy three reapers in seven years, at an expense of over six hundred dollars; that is only one article. A reaper will last ten years if properly taken care of at a very little expense. . . . Anyway stop this credit system. Let farmers try the cash system for one year."[13]

Undoubtedly it was true that many farmers failed to take proper care of their machinery and that they bought more than was necessary. Particularly did this fact impress an observer near Crookston, who recorded: "The prairie farmer should have been proud of the magnificence of his machine shed, for the roof was the high dome of the blue sky and the floor the size of his farm. The sun lighted it by day and the moon and stars by night. The machinery was washed by rains and dried by the sun; it was protected by the snow banks in winter; and it was always easy of access when needed. Usually the plow, binder, harrow, and seeder were left just where last used in the field. Most farmers were thoughtful enough to remove and put in the granary the canvases from the binder. Around the yard was a miscellaneous assortment of farm machinery,—rusted, faded, and dilapidated,—broken parts, hayracks, old wagons, piles of manure, half-used haystacks, logs hauled from the river for firewood, all landscaped in a shrubbery of ragweed, thistles, and sunflowers." [14]

Despite newspaper complaints, agents' dissatisfaction, and farmers' protests, however, the farm machinery business grew in Minnesota. In addition to improvements on reapers, new developments were made during the 1860's on many other types of implements, notably the plow. At the state fair in September, 1860, Boston steel clipper plows, clipper cross plows, clipper breaking plows, and iron beam plows were displayed. [15]

A much larger proportion of plows was manufactured in Minnesota during the 1860's than earlier. Cannon City had a plow factory in 1856, as has been noted, and Alonzo Leaming, who has been credited with being the earliest plow maker in the state, opened his factory in 1851 and carried on the business in St. Anthony for several years. Plow manufacturing in Minnesota, however, had only faint beginnings before 1860. One of the first plow factories in the state was the firm of Woodley and Berry of St. Anthony. As early as 1861 it received orders for plows from as far away as Wisconsin. Between the fall of 1860 and the summer of 1861, the plant made four hundred plows of different sizes, a large number of which were sold in St. Paul. An early farm journal congratulated this "pioneer plow factory of Minnesota" on its success, and expressed the hope that "the day will come when the Saint Anthony plows will be sold in Moline and Rock Island." [16]

In 1860 the firm of Wells and Smith established a plow factory at Belle Plaine. This plant advertised that it made the only plow that "cleaned satisfactorily in the sticky timber soil of Scott and Sibley Counties, being the same that gave universal satisfaction to our customers last year," and that it had the "largest and best equipped Foundry and Machine Shop" in Minnesota. Originally the Belle Plaine plant manufactured and repaired steam engines and mill gearing, but when these activities proved unprofitable, its owners turned to plows. Specimens of various plows in use in Minnesota — the Moline, Galena, Grand Detour, and St. Anthony — were collected, and farmers were asked about their qualities. Then an experienced plow maker was secured from the East and a plow dif-

MOHAWK VALLEY STEEL CLIPPER PLOW
[From an advertisement in the *American Agriculturist* 27:164 (April, 1868).]

ferent from any other in use was designed. The new plow proved to be popular in the vicinity, but it could not be made cheaply enough to compete in the wholesale trade with those manufactured in Illinois. As a result, the Belle Plaine manufacturers went to Moline and elsewhere and examined the machinery with a view to adopting the best. In the winter of 1860-61 they added eight new machines to their former equipment and made plans to introduce their plows in the Minnesota Valley.[17]

Another factory established in 1860 was the Monitor Plow Manufacturing Company of Minneapolis. St. Paul lagged behind some other towns in establishing implement factories, but during the winter of 1861-62 the firm of Davison and Connelly started a plow factory there. Leaming, whose St. Paul Clipper plow took second premium at the state fair in 1861, was placed at the head of the plant; and he expected to have four hundred plows ready for the spring trade in 1862. They were of all sizes, from a breaker that would take off six-inch roots down to a little corn plow.[18]

As agriculture expanded in the state, more and more machine factories were established. For example, the Noble plow was manufactured by Harrison and Company of St. Anthony, the Gopher State by C. L. Snyder of Faribault, the Monitor by Ferguson and Clark of Minneapolis, the North Star of Winona by B. W. Sutherlin at Winona, and Nelson and Gunderson's was made in Rochester. Of 438 plows sold in 1867 in Mankato, 78 were manufactured in that city; while of 510 sold there in the following year, 245 were produced locally, by either Mohr and Danber or Hatch and Roberts.

The largest plow factory west of the Great Lakes was owned by Laraway, Perrine, and Company of Minneapolis and was housed in a building which measured 157 by 44 feet. In 1869 this plant turned out five thousand plows, with a daily production of twenty-five. Its plows were an improvement on the C. K. Perrine brand, a model which had been extremely popular west of the Big Woods. A new process of hardening the metal made possible plows that would scour, and the moldboard was shaped in such a way that the furrow could be turned over with greater ease than previously.[19]

The year 1864 marked the introduction on a small commercial scale of buggy plows, as they were called, and two years later they were displayed at the state fair. The exhibit caused Oliver H. Kelley, the Grange founder, to say: "Won't it be fun to be a farmer, when we can ride while doing all our farm work? Now we can ride while plowing, drilling in the seed, reaping and mowing, ride while raking our hay, and if fortune favors us, we can ride to prosperity." Few Minnesota farmers, however, had riding plows before 1870. Gang plows for four horses and two plows were tried out at the same fair, but they did no better than a single plow with two horses. A plow made for general use by William B. Young and Company of Chicago was the only one on the grounds that did not clog.[20]

The introduction of the riding plow and the invention by James Oliver of a method of hardening cast iron that improved its wearing and scouring qualities constituted the two major improvements in plow manufacturing of the 1860's.

In general, it would appear, the average pioneer Minnesota farmer did a poor job of plowing, and his work was constantly criticized in the farm papers. "Here in the west, especially," said the *Farmer and Gardener,* "there is almost a universal practice of turning over about four or five inches of the surface, and continuing this same process from year to year." The paper suggested a motto, "Plow deep while sluggards sleep." It advised plowing fewer acres a day, and "running the plow deeper." Farmers were told that it would pay to get a subsoil plow and put on three horses for deep plowing, which "is, in short, a system of trenching on a small scale," and would put the ground in good condition to "withstand a drouth."[21] Nevertheless, plowing methods remained poor, for their improvement was retarded by lack of machinery, ignorance, and fertile soil that required little working.

New developments in threshing appeared during the 1860's, although many farmers continued to use the primitive flail or to tramp out the grain with horses or oxen. Horsepower was generally used for threshing machines, though steam was introduced before 1870. The horses and the thresher generally required a dozen men and boys to handle the various operations. Three or four men usually accompanied the outfit and the rest were gathered from the neighborhood. But the threshing itself was not the biggest task. Serious difficulties in moving their outfits were encountered by "Old Man" Boomhower, who operated an eight-horsepower thresher, and J. J. Mihin, who had a twelve-horsepower machine, near Lake Wilson in 1866. There was constant danger of breakdowns, and when they occurred it was often necessary to drive to the nearest blacksmith shop for repairs. The possibility of injury to one of the operators was a source of worry. Although a state law required owners of threshers to box the tumbling rod on the machine, it probably was not enforced on two occasions out of ten. Hence, men were frequently injured, sometimes fatally. A writer for the *Farmer and Gardener* felt that "of all the work that has to be done on the farm, there is hardly anything that is so unpleasant as threshing with machines that are tended by a large number of horses."[22]

The amount of grain which a horsepower machine could thresh in a day varied, of course, with its size. Boomhower's eight-horsepower machine turned out about three hundred bushels of wheat in a day, while the Mihin twelve-horsepower unit threshed five hundred. A report in 1861 stated that a man near Faribault threshed 217 bushels of oats in an hour and fifteen minutes. "It was probably a large machine," said a farm paper, "and exceedingly well handled. If any . . . beat this, we should be glad to hear from them and receive their figures." In 1868, L. Martindale of Redstone, using a Tornado thresher with a thirty-inch cylinder, threshed 247 bushels of wheat in two hours and seven minutes. The grain was usually taken out of the separators in half-bushel measures, a method that required much extra stooping and hard work and resulted in a great deal of waste. Horsepower units generally charged about five cents a bushel for threshing wheat and ten cents for flax.[23]

The Pitts thresher, which was popular in Minnesota in the 1850's, continued to be used there extensively in the next decade, but other makes were well liked also. The Massillon machines, manufactured by C. M. Russell and Company of Massillon, Ohio, were popular with many southern Minnesota farmers as early as 1861, although few if any of them were then in use near St. Paul. Ruble Brothers of McGregor's Landing sold the Massillon, as did S. P. and P. F. Hodges of St. Paul. Particularly popular was the Sweepstakes threshing machine of C. Aultman and Company of Canton, Ohio, which was exhibited at the state fairs of 1860 and subsequent years. According to Bigflow, Murdock, and Company of St. Paul, who sold the machine, it was "the accredited head of the Threshing Machine family," for "it threshes clean from the heads, separates perfectly from the straw, cleans fit for market without waste, saves all the grain, does its work with the utmost speed, safety and economy. . . . Our 'Patent Cleaning Apparatus' enables the operator to control the direction of the blast, and position of the sieves, and clean either heavy or light grain, without waste, as fast as it can be threshed,—the chaff and dirt being separated from the grain *before it strikes the sieve at all.*" Some of these claims doubtless were true, as the Sweepstakes won a prize at the state fair of 1866. Among the threshers exhibited at the fair of 1868 were the Invincible Vi-

TWO HORSE POWER AND THRESHER AND CLEANER.—Weight 2,900 Pounds. For Sale by Gilman & Seager, Saint Paul, Min.

[From the *Farmer and Gardener*, 1:206 (July, 1861).]

brator, made by Roberts and Throp at Three Rivers, Michigan, the Tornado, and the Case thresher. The latter, with a Woodbury power unit, sold for $639. Also shown was Taylor's Alarm Register, which would "keep a correct tally of grain measured" when attached to a thresher and so dispense with hand measures.[24]

The steam thresher made its appearance in Minnesota not later than 1867. In that year Sylvanus Jenkins raised wheat on more than four hundred of the 1,036 acres of his Dakota County farm. This was then the largest farm in one tract in the state, and naturally many machines were to be found on it. Outstanding among them was a steam-powered threshing machine. An appeal to farmers to make general use of steam threshing machines was published by a rural journal in 1869. There were then in the state a number of portable steam engines that were being used to run ordinary threshing machines. Most of these engines were from the works of N. Wood and Company of Madison County, New York, and they sold in St. Paul for about twelve hundred dollars. They were eight-horsepower engines which required about half a cord of wood a day to operate. Farmers were urged to get together before the next harvest and purchase steam threshers, for they would thresh from nine hundred to one thousand bushels a day while the horses were free to do the plowing.[25]

Many Minnesota farmers who used improved plows, cut their grain with a Marsh harvester, and had it threshed with a mechanical thresher nevertheless continued to sow their seed by the primitive broadcast method. As late as 1867 one of the state's leading newspapers reported that broadcast sowing prevailed, and that the broadcasting machine was not much better than broadcasting by hand. A farmer who signed his communication "De Novo" recommended the drill and described his own experience as follows: "I well knew that this subject of drilling grain is pretty generally tabooed among farmers, but I also know that many who argue the loudest against the drill know the least about it. I have used the drill for four seasons. If the season proves dry the advantage in the yield is most decided . . . yet I expect to see the broadcast system prevail for years to come." Although there were advantages in planting corn with drills, farmers continued to plant it with hoes. Drilling corn was faster than the old way, and a field needed to be marked only one way. One enthusiastic writer expressed the hope that "our readers will this season try this new way of raising corn. If corn will yield as well in drills as in hills, and we are inclined to think it will, this system will certainly bring about a revolution in corn culture." [26]

Not until the late 1860's and the early 1870's, however, was there a rapid transition from broadcasting to drilling in the Mississippi

A DRILL IN OPERATION
[From an advertisement in the *American Agriculturist*, 26:305 (August, 1867).]

Valley winter wheat region. For spring wheat, the main crop of Minnesota, drilling was used even less than for winter wheat. Small patches of land, stumpy ground, and land with cornstalks on it were better suited to hand planting than to drilling. In addition, many impecunious pioneers were slow to buy drills. [27]

Various types of drills nevertheless were offered for sale in Minnesota. At the state fair of 1860 Pennock's wheat drill, patented in 1841, was exhibited by D. C. Jones of St. Paul, who, a little more than a year later, was advertising strongly the Buckeye grain drill and advising every farmer with fifty acres of wheat to buy one. By 1866 the McSherry grain and seed drill was well known, and in that year it won the prize for drills at the state fair. Lowth and Howe's seeder, manufactured in Owatonna, won first place among the broadcast machines at the same fair. Another device used by some Minnesota farmers was Cahoon's hand rotation seed sower. This implement was simply a box which held seed and was carried by a planter who broadcast the seed by turning an attached crank instead of by throwing it out by hand. Such a machine was exhibited in the state as early as 1860. In 1868 it was reported that a hundred and fifteen seeders sold at Mankato for ninety-two hundred dollars—an average price of eighty dollars. Many of them, however, were undoubtedly hand seeders and broadcasters, which must have sold for smaller sums.[28]

Other implements in use as early as 1860 were harrows, straw cutters, horse hay rakes, wheat-field gleaners, potato diggers, iron corn shellers, corn brushers, horse hoes, and fanning mills. By the middle 1860's Hunter's patent well was attracting considerable attention, because of its simplicity and low cost. At the state fair of 1866 a man sank a Hunter tube ten feet and pumped water, all within fifteen minutes. The tube cost a dollar and a half a foot and the pump attached to its top was priced at five dollars. On display at the same fair was a horse-drawn hay fork which would unload a ton of hay from a wagon to a stack or mow in ten minutes. Revolving horse hay rakes were exhibited as well, but they were out of date as compared with sulky rakes. Exhibited also were many handsome buggies, wagons, and cutters from the Winona Carriage Works, the largest establishment of its kind in the state.[29] In spite of mechanization, the lowly pitchfork continued to hold the respect of the pioneer. In the summer of 1869, O. E. Slotte walked to New Ulm and "bought himself a pitchfork and walked right back home to his dugout again, and this fork he displayed with a great deal of pride pretty nearly as long as he lived."[30]

Some idea of the extent of agricultural mechanization in the 1860's can be obtained by comparing the census figures of 1870 with those of 1860, incomplete as they undoubtedly are. Since the federal government did not collect statistics for 1865, it is impossible to measure the effects of the Civil War, which without doubt stimulated the use of machinery. In line with other agricultural gains the value of implements and machinery advanced from $1,018,183 in 1860 to $6,721,120 in 1870, an increase of 560.1 per cent, which was greater than that for any other property classification on the farm. The average value of agricultural implements per farm at the end of the 1860's was slightly over $144.50, as compared with $56 in 1859. The census, however, suggested reducing currency values of 1870 by twenty per cent in order to arrive at gold values. Even when this suggestion is followed, the average value of machinery per farm in 1870 was twice that of a decade earlier, a fact which

Patent Steel Tooth Self Delivering Horse Hay Rake.
[From an advertisement in the *American Agriculturist*, 19:222 (July, 1860).]

emphasizes the growing mechanization of the 1860's. Accompanying this mechanization was a marked change in the type of animal power used on the farm. In 1860 there were ten thousand more oxen than horses in Minnesota, but by 1870 horses outnumbered oxen by fifty thousand.[31] The newer machinery operated more efficiently with horses than with oxen.

No decade since has witnessed so great a relative growth in the value of machinery as did the 1860's. Today it is not uncommon to see machinery valued at from three to four thousand dollars on a Minnesota farm; nevertheless, it is doubtful that the impact of mechanization on agricultural and agrarian life was greater in the 1940's than in the 1860's.

Mechanization Takes on Modern Aspects

During the decade of the 1870's the outstanding advance in the field of farm machinery was the development of self-binding devices for reapers. Today, where reapers are used, grain is generally bound with twine, but such was not always the case. Various materials were tried until twine proved to be the best. For a time wire served, and in 1866 Oliver H. Kelley described a binder that could be attached to a reaper and worked by hand. One man passed the gavel of grain to the machine while another, with two movements of levers, instantly bound the bundle with fine wire. A farmer who had tried the device for two years did not like it, as the cost of wire amounted to a dollar an acre; but Kelley's enthusiasm was not dampened. "I should favor the machine," he announced, "if it cost twice that as more economical than sore fingers."[1]

About 1868 John H. Whitney of Rochester evolved the idea of a wire binder that would gather and tie bundles automatically on a harvester and throw the bundles on the ground, tied up ready for the stack. He had worked on the invention for over a year, and in the season of 1868 he put it in the field. It was simple in construction, apparently a merchantable machine, and a number were made and sold; but for some reason they never came into general use, and the enterprise failed, despite the fact that a gold medal was awarded the machine by the Minnesota State Agricultural Society. Edward Chapman, a skilled machinist, soon afterward invented a self-binder that seemed excellent. C. H. Chadbourn and Alan K. and J. M. Williams formed a company, established a factory, and turned out a number of machines, but here again the manufacture was abandoned.[2]

Undoubtedly there were other experiments with wire binders in the state, but not until 1874 was a very successful machine patented. The owner of the patent was Charles B. Withington of Wisconsin, and his device, manufactured by McCormick, "was widely used for about a decade." In the same year, 1874, the Walter A. Wood Company sold twenty-five wire binders. Another well-known machine was the Osborne wire binder, and one early settler recalled in 1930 that the first wire binder in his family was an Osborne. It cost three hundred dollars, plus twenty-five dollars for freight from Auburn, New York. The machine, which required three horses to pull it, worked very well.[3]

The introduction of the wire binder saved the work of binding the grain by hand, but it also inaugurated a controversy over the machine's merits. Some people complained of the expense of the wire, and others said that bits of wire got into the grain and made it unfit for feed. On the other hand, a member of the Farmers' Club at a meeting at the Capitol in 1879 mentioned a farmer who had used wire for six years and had never lost a cow from eating wire. One of the strongest protests against the wire binder came from the millers. A committee of the Minneapolis Millers' Association in 1878 found that the millstones at the Washburn A Mill were marked and glazed by wire, and that the bolting cloth frequently was cut. Several quarts of wire, from a quarter of an inch to two inches long, were taken from the stones. It was the unanimous opinion of the millers that the wire in the wheat was greatly damaging the mills, and they resolved to pay ten cents a bushel less, whenever practicable, for wheat containing wire. William H. Dunwoody, John Crosby, and George Hineline, members of the millers' committee, issued this statement: "We earnestly recommend that the farmers discontinue the use of the wire binders."[4]

The credit for inventing a twine binder generally goes to John Appleby. His device was invented in 1859, but it was not put on the market until after 1875. In the meantime others in Minnesota and elsewhere tinkered with the idea. In 1869 a Rochester newspaper reported that N. F. Gilman had invented a new self-binder which used twine; and in 1873 it was stated that A. S. Hoyt of Minneapolis had invented a twine-binding reaper which he expected to put on the market that season. Competition in the field of automatic binding increased rapidly, and trials were held, as in the earlier days with the older reapers. Thus, in one of the McCormick letters we read: "The Fassett twine binder agent here has challenged all binders to come into a trial tomorrow, and I intend to go in with full expectation of winning."[5]

Each of the numerous automatic binding machines had its peculiar advantages. Yet each had certain drawbacks. Particularly vex-

AN ELWARD SELF-BINDING HARVESTER
[From the *Independent Farmer*, 1:60 (March 1, 1879).]

atious was the difficulty of binding badly lodged and tangled grain. Self-binders could cut and elevate such grain, but when the grain, interlaced and twisted, came on the binding table, it was found impossible to separate the bundles or prevent the tangled grain from dragging after the machine and pulling the binding cord out of place, so that the machine would not bind. In 1882 the Reverend Charles A. Ruddock of Benson patented an attachment for harvesters to handle lodged grain. During the harvest of 1881 Ruddock cut fifty acres of tangled oats at Granite Falls in two and a half days, a "result which had hitherto seemed impossible." At an exhibition near Benson a year later, agents and experts of the Osborne binders were loud in their praise of the attachment. Not until the coming of the small combine, however, did the average farmer have a good answer to tangled grain. Yet by 1882, according to one early commentator, the twine self-binder was almost universally used. It was drawn by three or four horses, and cut ten acres of grain a day. The driver of the binder rode, and he was followed by two men who shocked the bundles.[6]

The economic depression and the grasshopper scourge which hit the state in 1873 intensified the old rivalry between machine agents In that year a McCormick agent expressed the hope that McCormick prices would not be raised, as farmers were in a mood to meet any raise with a stiff protest, especially since the prices of some of the other machines were coming down. Ten months later, in January, 1874, a Wood reaper sold for $165 cash or $175 on time; the Little Champion of Janesville, Wisconsin, was listed at $160 cash or $180 on time; the Excelsior listings were $165 and $175; the Manny reaper could be obtained for $160 cash or $175 on time; the Ohio Champion cost $185 or $190 cash or $200 on time; the renowned Marsh harvester came a little higher, at $195 or $210; and the Elward harvester of St. Paul could be purchased for $190 cash or $200 on time. Shortly after these figures were quoted, a McCormick agent wrote: "Marsh Harvester seems to about have possession of the field." Yet other makes managed to find buyers, and Massillon, Edwards, Advance, Werner, Madison, Hubbard, Osborne, and Esterley machines, in addition to those listed above, were in use on the farms of Minnesota. No wonder a McCormick agent exclaimed: "We are having a desperate fight here, the worst we have ever had. We have no less than eight firms here selling Reapers and Mowers that represent ten different machines and they are all bound to ruin the McCormick."[7]

In their efforts to collect machine bills, McCormick's agents resorted to various devices, among them the following amusing form letter, dated Austin, March 8, 1876, and signed by M. T. Grattan:[8]

"Dear Sir:—Are you aware of the fact that you have not yet paid C. H. and L. J. McCormick what you owe them? It must be that you have forgotten the obligation, and the task again devolves upon me of reminding you of it. Allow me to ask if you have any regard for a promise to pay or any comprehension of the need of people for money who hold your note: if you have why don't you pay! One thing is certain: if you are in the least responsible, the money will speedily be made by legal process, while if you are execution proof, and do not desire to pay, I will endeavor to amuse you with

A Marsh Harvester
[From Rogin, *Farm Machinery*, 107.]

duns of this character often enough to inform those at least who handle the mail, that it is a dangerous thing to give you credit. I have been tempted at times to publish in the newspapers a 'black list,' comprising the names of those who will not pay their debts. Make haste to place yourself in a position where your name cannot *be* used, or mayhap it may have prominent position and lead all the rest."

If letters such as this did not bring results, recourse might be had to the courts. McCormick, however, preferred not to go into court and incur risks and losses of time and money unless it was absolutely necessary. Farmers avoided firms that sued too much, whereas they frequently renewed notes at from ten to twelve per cent interest with a firm that did not sue. Then, of course, there were exemptions which protected farmers from suits. The law allowed a man eighty acres and all the improvements he could put on them, with some stock, farming utensils, and other articles. Homesteads of a hundred and sixty acres were exempt from all debts and claims made prior to the date on which the patent for the land was issued. Finally, a judgment ran at seven per cent, even if the note or mortgage was drawing twelve per cent. Nevertheless, suits were brought once in a while. Writing of one, an agent said: "In the case of the man who said 'bad Advance' we did not even swear a witness, or make a plea, but let the case go to the jury on the testimony of the man himself. His own lawyer gave him up, while we sat back and laughed, the judge and jury shaking their sides with us." [9]

In addition to selling machines, collecting notes, and keeping the home office informed of local conditions, the machine agent spent much time repairing machinery. Thomas Jordan of Belle Plaine, agent for Osborne and Plano machines, for example, was so busy at times with repair work that he had to work at night with the aid of a lantern. And many of the McCormick letters were written as orders for spare parts, such as cams, shafts, links, cranks, castings, crank boxes, and sickles. "We have some flax sickles," said one letter, "but order more expecting a demand for them and don't want to miss the sale of a machine by being out of sickles. There is about 10,000 acres of flax in this vicinity and we expect to sell some machines where others fail to cut it." [10]

The hard times of the 1870's led Minnesota farmers to flock into the Patrons of Husbandry, which attacked, among other things, the high price of farm machinery. Interesting indeed was the reaction of McCormick's agents to the Patrons, or Grangers. "They talk big, and say some severe things about Reaper Agents making money at expense of farmers, just as though we were responsible for the high price of machinery," said E. W. Brooks. He told his men to "get about as smoothly as possible" with the Grange members, and to talk quietly of the merits of the McCormick machine, in the hope that the Patrons "will probably fail in their grand scheme of getting *cheap* Reapers." Grange speakers told the farmers that the McCormick reaper cost about forty-five dollars to manufacture and that the farmer had made McCormick rich. "One of their speakers," wrote Brooks, "told an audience last week of a bank somewhere in Minnesota who hold for collection $200,000.00 of farmers' notes belonging to the firm of C. H. McCormick and Bro., and when they wind up a harangue on monopolies, they finish off with: '*and especially the McCormick*.' " [11]

Some unflattering descriptions of Grange leaders found their way into the letters. Ignatius Donnelly, once in Congress, it was said, tried every party by turns in an effort to get re-elected, but without success. William Paist of St. Paul, secretary of the state Grange, was called a "broken down politician" and "busted up real estate man." The grand lecturer for the United States, T. A. Thompson, it was reported, was a Minnesotan who tried farming and gave it up. He bought a McCormick machine in 1866 and finished paying the principal and interest, amounting to $342, in 1873. The editors of the *Grange Advance,* the state organ, were described as two lawyers who "have *both together* just about brains enough for one decent lawyer, but not near enough for *one good Reaper man!* They could not make a respectable living in the law business, so now they are giving advice to farmers." The purchasing agent of the Goodhue County Grange council was reported to have owed a mower note for five years, and the president of the council to have owed a reaper note for the same length of time. Of course, it was admitted, there were good, reliable men in the Grange, too. [12]

In the long run, the Patrons were not able to compete with private manufacturers, although they may have had some effect on machine prices. The *Farmers' Union* gave a good deal of publicity to the Grange's state agency and distributing headquarters, but after 1875, when the Grange's Iowa plants failed, the movement declined rapidly. Prophetic was a comment by a McCormick agent:

MECHANIZATION TAKES ON MODERN ASPECTS

"I find that the opinion is growing stronger with our best Reaper men that if manufacturers just go on as usual, the *Grange Agency business* will 'dry up.' " [13]

While perhaps the greatest advances during the 1870's were made on reapers, other farm machines also were improved. In threshing, as we have indicated, horsepower machines were most common in the 1860's, but by 1880 steam threshers were commonly used. These machines used straw or coal for fuel and threshed from six hundred to nine hundred bushels of grain a day. Their cost was around seventeen hundred dollars, and the charge for threshing was four or five cents a bushel for wheat and two cents for oats. It was the duty of the farmer to furnish the fuel and all the labor except the fireman, engineer, and feeders. The whole work cost the farmer about nine cents a bushel. [14]

During the early 1870's McCormick was thinking about entering the thresher field, and he consulted his agents on the idea. One wrote him that if he should go into that line he must do two things: get a machine that in some leading feature was better than those then sold, and make it a little cheaper, since a thresher cost as much as a good farm. In 1873 the Case threshers had about driven out all other makes, and Case agents did not need even to canvass farmers for business. [15]

Just at the close of the decade a new machine made its appearance in the state—a steam traction engine. The first one shown was exhibited by J. I. Case of Racine, Wisconsin, at the state fair of 1879. The arrival of such a steam monster in any community was a sight to attract people from miles around. In 1882 the unloading of an Aultman and Taylor ten-horsepower wooden-wheel traction engine at New Prague was attended by considerable activity. "The boiler was filled with water, a fire lighted in the box and steam raised," runs an account of the event. "When sufficient steam was raised the journey to Heidelber[g], six miles distant, was started. . . . in late afternoon the people of the little village were eagerly awaiting the arrival of the machine that traveled without horses or oxen. Upon hearing the engine's whistle, a delegation from the village rushed to the outskirts to greet the first traction engine in Le Sueur County.

The engine and the crew were met north of the village and the townsfolk watched it labor up a steep hill successfully." That fall the engine put in a long season threshing.[16]

It appears that the combine was first patented in 1828, that it was used in Michigan in the late 1840's, and that it was operated in California in 1854; but it was not until 1869 that the *Minnesota Monthly* noted that a "machine has been invented and put in operation in California, which, it is said, has cut, thrashed, cleaned, and sacked the wheat from 20 acres in ten hours, with only three men to work it." No mention has been found of the use of the combine in Minnesota before 1880.[17]

Plowing machines too numerous to mention were found on Minnesota farms in the 1870's, though more important innovations in plows came in the 1860's than in the succeeding decade. Much space in the newspapers was devoted to steam plows, but the average farmer could not afford them. The Evans and the R. C. Parvin steam plows bid for support in 1873 and 1874, but apparently they found few buyers in the state. Sulky plows were becoming increasingly common and more efficient. The Ferguson sulky plow, for example, could be raised well above the furrow for cleaning, and the plow could be turned over on the platform of the frame to protect it from rain and dew. The Browne sulky plow, manufactured by the famous Rock Island Plow Works, was managed by one lever, and in a moment it could be set to plow various depths. Gang plows, iron-beam plows that cut from ten to sixteen inches, wooden-beam plows, Nebraska prairie breakers, and Wisconsin brush breakers were manufactured by the same concern.[18]

Sulky hay rakes, like sulky plows, were easing the labor of the farmer in the 1870's. Widely advertised was the Monitor self-dump rake, manufactured in Minneapolis. It had no cogs, gearing, nor springs, and it could be changed easily in the field from drop tooth to rigid, or vice versa.[19]

Interesting indeed was an advertisement for a machine that was far in advance of its day—a "Self-Acting Cow Milker" manufactured by Stent and Company of New York and sold for two dollars. A veterinary surgeon for the Society for the Prevention of

MECHANIZATION TAKES ON MODERN ASPECTS

Cruelty to Animals endorsed it, but it was condemned by the Elmira Farmers' Club, which also castigated smooth-tongued salesmen. The farmers claimed the milker caused cows' milk to become lumpy, bloody, and dried up.[20]

About the middle of the 1870's farmers began to get open buggies and, in some cases, light two-seated wagons. These were better to get around in than was the ordinary farm wagon. Of the latter, the "Old Reliable Peter Schuttler" was the favorite in Minnesota. All wood used in the Schuttler wagons was aged for from three to five years and was thoroughly air seasoned. Windmills were first erected during the early 1860's for grinding and elevating grain, and gradually they were adapted to the chore of pumping water for livestock. As early as 1867 the state's leading farm journal predicted that "in prairie portions of the State they will be invaluable," and a few years later the same paper was carrying regular advertisements for mills. Apparently the advertising was effective, for the Faribault Wind Mill Company in 1878 claimed that it was flooded with orders. Between June, 1878, and May, 1879, the company sold 115 mills, two of them to purchasers as far away as California and Nevada. And when one considers the work involved in watering stock before the day of the pump and the windmill, the popularity of the latter is easily understood.[21]

But it is useless to attempt to list all devices found on the Minnesota farm of the 1870's. Some idea of the proportions of the implement trade can be obtained from the reports of the state commissioner of statistics for those years. In 1876 it was reported that the sale of farm machinery was a business of immense proportions, laborsaving machinery being in demand and finding a ready sale. It was estimated that during that season alone the farmers of the state purchased more than 5,000 grain harvesters and reapers at a cost of $900,000; and the trade was increasing yearly at a very rapid rate. Annually about 600 threshers were sold in Minnesota at an average cost per machine of $700 or more. The number of plows purchased each year was estimated at 25,000, worth about $450,000.[22]

As earlier, this great trade was detrimental to the many farmers whose optimism was greater than their judgment. Governor John

S. Pillsbury, who made frequent visits to various parts of the state in the middle 1870's, found in some townships "the farm of nearly every resident incumbered," and scarcely a horse, cow, or farm implement that was not mortgaged. Among the oppressors of the farmer he found "agents of certain agricultural machines from other states, who, under fair promises of great leniency towards buyers, if unfortunate, induced farmers to purchase more than they need, taking from them notes with peremptory conditions, and then, immediately upon nonpayment, enforce their inexorable forfeitures." In his message of 1877 Pillsbury expressed his surprise at the extent to which farmers had mortgaged their all for "the latest assumed improvement in farm machinery," which they then left with the old machine "to perish unprotected from the weather, while the needless debt thus incurred is accumulating its burden against the improvident debtor." [23]

As may be inferred from Pillsbury's remarks, much of the criticism of the farm implement business was due to the fact that it drained money out of the state. Had all the machinery been manufactured in Minnesota, less criticism would have been heard. It must not be overlooked, however, that local manufacture was reaching significant proportions. Several of the firms dating from the 1870's deserve special notice.

One of these was the St. Paul Harvester Works. This company was incorporated in 1872 by a group of nine St. Paul business men, who invested $150,000 in it. Grounds were purchased near Lake Phalen, and the right to produce a harvester was secured. The machine selected was the Elward, invented and patented by John H. Elward of Illinois. During the first season three hundred harvesters were made, and by 1876 the number had increased to three thousand. The value of the latter was over fifty per cent of the entire amount paid by Minnesota farmers for harvesting machinery in that year. The company employed 250 men in 1876 and sold its machines from Canada to the Gulf, and from eastern Ohio to the Pacific; and a few of its harvesters were used even in Europe. Its capital by 1876 had increased to $500,000, all paid up, and there was a surplus. Where its site had been a waste area, four years later

St. Paul Harvester Works
[From Andreas, *Historical Atlas of Minnesota*, 35.]

there was a village with a public school, a chapel, a store, and a post office. By 1878 the factory could turn out twenty-five harvesters, ten binders, and ten mowers a day. During the summer months a harvester was produced every twenty minutes.[24]

Another firm still in a prosperous condition was the Monitor Plow Works established in Minneapolis, as has been noted, in 1860. The business of the firm to March 1, 1872, was over four hundred per cent above that of the previous year, and the business to March 1, 1873, was over five hundred per cent above that of 1872–73. By December, 1873, the company had already received over three hundred orders for plows and breakers for the spring trade.[25]

In St. Paul, in the spring of 1876, was established the St. Paul Plow Works, a small company employing only thirty men. In the fall of 1877 the company erected extensive works on Seventh Street at "Post Side Track," about two miles northeast of the heart of the city, at a cost of $40,000. William B. Dean was president and Louis Berthiaume was superintendent, and the moving mechanical spirit, of the concern. Berthiaume was experienced in plow manufacture, having started a factory in Osseo in 1861–62. The equipment of the factory included a fifty-horsepower engine, a foundry, a blacksmith shop, a fitting room, a stock room, nine forges, six furnaces, two trip hammers, drilling machines, welding machines, machines that cut off plates of cast steel one-half inch thick, an emery room, wood and paint shops, and a warehouse with a capacity of from four thousand to five thousand plows. In this warehouse could be seen aristocratic sulky plows, great twenty-four-inch grub breakers, trim little nine-inch stirring plows, long graceful prairie breakers, timber plows, gang plows, and fin coulter plows. These plows found a market in Dakota, Minnesota, Wisconsin, Manitoba, and Nebraska. Between fifty and sixty men were employed in 1879, and over a thousand plows were turned out in April alone.[26]

Minneapolis was the site of at least two harvester firms. The Minneapolis Harvester Works produced the Dewey harvester and the Werner harvester for the Granges for a time. The Dewey machine seems to have had a good sale, and it drew much praise from farmers, particularly for its lightness. One man said two mules could draw it easier than four strong horses could a McCormick Advance. The Hubbard Harvester Company was organized in Minneapolis in 1873 with a capital stock of $200,000. Its machine was invented by one Hubbard of Rochester, New York, who removed to Minneapolis to direct manufacture of the harvesters, which, it was claimed, combined strength and durability with lightness of draft and efficiency.[27]

Minneapolis by 1878 had seventeen firms manufacturing agricultural implements, wagons, and carriages valued at $702,500. By 1880, or shortly thereafter, Minneapolis claimed to be the recognized headquarters in the Northwest for agricultural machinery, its business being surpassed only by Kansas City. About that time representatives of the Walter A. Wood Manufacturing Company made known their intention to make Minneapolis their chief distributing point in the Northwest. This announcement caused the *Minneapolis Tribune* to wax eloquent over the machine trade of Minneapolis. About 1875 W. H. Jones, an agent of Deering and Company, which made Marsh harvesters, set up an agency there. Then came D. M. Osborne and Company's warehouse, which annually did business in the hundreds of thousands of dollars. The one little ewe lamb left to St. Paul, said the *Tribune,* was the general agency of the Champion Reaper and Mower Company. In addition to the firms mentioned, there were in Minneapolis in 1881 agents for the Buckeye mower; the Sweepstakes thresher; Russell and Company of Massillon, Ohio; the La Belle Wagon Works of Fond du Lac; Avery and Sons Plow Works of Louisville; Furst and Bradley; Studebaker Wagon; Pitts Agricultural Works; N. C. Thompson of Rockford; Madison Manufacturing Company; Adams and French of Illinois; Kalamazoo spring tooth harrow; Deere and Company; Moline Plow Works; Grand Detour Plow Works; McDonald Manufacturing Company of Fond du Lac; Peerless Reaper Company of Canton, Ohio; and the Wayne Agricultural Company of Richmond, Indiana. The business done by these general agents at Minneapolis amounted to $4,330,000 a year.[28]

In 1878 the wholesale trade of St. Paul in agricultural implements, carried on through 7 houses by 90 workers, amounted to $1,500,000. In addition, 2 firms manufacturing implements employed 190 workers and did a $375,000 business; 18 firms making carriages and wagons and employing 160 workers did a $200,000 business; and 6 pork packers with 58 workers accounted for a $350,000 business. The manufacture of farm implements ranked third behind boot and shoe ($700,000) and flour manufacture ($600,000) in St. Paul.[29]

Outside of the Twin Cities there were other farm machinery

FARM MACHINERY DEPOT AND FEED STORE AT ROCHESTER
[From Andreas, *Historical Atlas of Minnesota*, 114.]

plants. Lowth and Howe of Owatonna, already mentioned, manufactured 610 of their seeders and cultivators combined during the winter of 1872–73. This amount was nearly double the number produced during the previous season, yet all the machines were disposed of without difficulty. The plant was burned in 1870 with a loss of $150,000, but it was soon rebuilt; and in 1873 it covered nearly three acres and employed twenty-five men.[30]

The largest concern in the state by 1880 was Seymour, Sabin, and Company of Stillwater, established in 1875 with a capital of $325,000 to manufacture the Minnesota Chief, a thresher of Minnesota invention. In 1876 this machine was awarded the first premium at the state fair, and in the same year the company sold 100 threshers, not supplying half the demand, at $650 each. During the next two years 300 and 500 machines respectively were manufactured. In August, 1878, more than 400 men were on the payroll and 220 convicts from the state penitentiary were under contract. Some of the Minnesota Chiefs were shipped as far away as Australia, and many of them were sold in Ohio, Indiana, Illinois, Kansas, the Red River Valley, and on the Pacific coast. General agents were placed in strategic locations and under them were local agents and field men. During 1879 a total of 1,250 separators were made and sold, and there were orders for 700 more which could not be filled. Sales that year aggregated over $1,000,000. Materials for constructing the machines, which included the Pitts Horse Power, Woodbury Horse Power, and Elward's Equalizing Power, were secured from many sources —iron from Pennsylvania and Michigan and lumber from half a dozen states. To bring in these materials and to ship out the machines required more than 3,000 cars yearly. Dwight M. Sabin was president of the company; C. M. Seymour, vice-president; W. S. Goodhue, secretary; and John H. Elward, of Elward harvester fame, was the chief inventor of the thresher.[31]

Seymour, Sabin, and Company, however, was not destined to enjoy a long and prosperous life. It failed in 1884, after less than ten years of existence. Sabin gave as the reason for the failure the fact that he took a large amount of paper from farmers who could not pay their obligations because of poor crops, low prices, and high freights.[32]

Although the use of farm machinery, especially drills and reapers, was constantly increasing during the 1870's, the statistical summaries for that decade were by no means as impressive as they had been for the preceding decade. It will be remembered that the value of implements and machinery in the state in 1870 was $6,721,120. Ten years later, the total was $13,089,783, a percentage gain of 94.8. Undoubtedly a fairer picture would be secured by translating the 1870 figure into gold values. Yet even when this is done the percentage gain for the 1870's was only 143.4, far less than it had been for the 1860's. Still, it placed Minnesota eleventh among the states and territories in the matter of farm machinery values, and it was sufficient to allow the country population, whose relative growth for the 1870's was half that of farm machinery, to boost the number of acres of improved land in farms during the same period by a significant 212.1 per cent. And it was nearly five times greater than the corresponding increase for the 1880's. Also, the average value of implements per farm in 1880 was $141.69, a fairly substantial figure when placed alongside the average for 1859 of $56, or that of 1870, of $115.63, when expressed in gold values. Mechanization had come a long way from the primitive beginnings of the 1840's.[33]

Wheat: King or Tyrant?

Minnesota has not always had the diversified type of agriculture that it has today. At one time nearly every farmer in the state concentrated on wheat production. Wheat was the great cash crop. It opened the way to fortune, and so attractive was it to the average farmer that he neglected other phases of farming almost entirely. The story of the rise of this one-crop system of farming in Minnesota and the beginnings of its decline is one of the most interesting as well as one of the most revealing in the state's entire agricultural history.

According to one early commentator, Alexis Bailly of Wabasha, it was in 1820 that the first wheat was raised in Minnesota. It was spring wheat produced on an island at the junction of the Minnesota and Mississippi rivers by Jean Baptiste Faribault, who obtained the seed at Prairie du Chien. In 1831 Joseph R. Brown grew spring wheat on ground now within the limits of Hastings, and in 1835 he raised both spring and winter wheat at Lake Traverse. Generally speaking, however, wheat was not commercially important in the state until 1858. In earlier years low prices, the panic of 1857, and sparse farming population held back the production of that staple commodity.[1]

With the removal of these handicaps, Minnesota wheat production skyrocketed in a manner that would have pleased even that enthusiastic booster of an earlier period, James M. Goodhue, whose pleas for the growing of wheat filled columns of the *Minnesota Pioneer* between 1849 and 1852. In much the same manner were the papers of 1859 and 1860 filled with comments about wheat. From the middle of September, 1859, until the beginning of December, 103,000 bushels of the cereal were shipped from Winona, and 5,000 more were awaiting shipment. A visitor to Hastings in 1859 observed that there "was wheat everywhere; wheat on the levee; wagon loads of wheat pouring down to the levee; wheat in the streets; wheat in the side-walks; warehouses of wheat; men talking of wheat; and, verily, wheat was the one idea of Hastings the afternoon we arrived there." In the same year Chicago received its first lot of wheat from St. Paul, a fact which prompted the *Chicago Journal* to report: "It is a good article of spring wheat, better than the average received here. It sold for 78 cents on track. We welcome this first tribute to our industrious Minnesota grain-raisers, to the great grain market of the Northwest. We hope they will send along much 'more of the same sort.'" At Shakopee, early in April, 1860, there were from 25,000 to 30,000 bushels of wheat awaiting the opening of Lake Pepin, and later in the same month it was estimated that four Northern Line steamers had taken 120,000 bushels of grain to St. Louis from Minnesota. And as early as 1860 orders for Minnesota spring wheat were received from as great a distance as Lockport, New York. The total state production in 1860 was 2,186,973 bushels, while exports amounted to 1,576,666 bushels. These figures seem truly impressive when placed alongside the figure for Minnesota's 1850 wheat production of 1,401 bushels. [2]

As in all frontier areas, so in Minnesota did the lack of adequate transportation and marketing facilities prove a handicap to the development of commercialized wheat farming. Even the river towns felt this lack because of congestion on the streams and winter ice. As George B. Merrick, a prominent steamboatman, put it: "There was no question about getting it [*wheat*]. Every boat got all the wheat it could carry, and the shippers begged, almost on bended knees, for a chance to ship five hundred sacks, or a hundred, or fifty—any amount would be considered a great favor. Wheat was shipped at that time in two-bushel sacks." [3]

Shipments to St. Louis in 1859 were smaller than they would have been had freight rates been lower, and farmers around Shakopee would have made a greater profit could they have saved the cost of handling and transshipment at St. Paul of their St. Louis bound grain. Low water and high freight rates went hand in hand. In April, 1860, the freight charge on a bushel of wheat from St. Paul to St. Louis was about fifteen cents; from St. Paul to Milwaukee it varied between nine and fifteen cents in September of the same year.[4]

As wheat production increased, middlemen appeared to handle the product. They carried on their trade along the navigable rivers and shipped their purchases down the Mississippi to larger markets. Thus the river towns became the first centers of the local wheat trade. Fortunate was the farmer who lived near such a market, but the farmer on the frontier often had to go great distances to sell his wheat for cash. In frontier communities the storekeeper was usually the middleman, and he often lacked competition. There was no grading of wheat, and cash payments were rare. Gradually, however, cash wheat markets developed in the interior, the earliest probably being Chatfield, where a federal land office was located. Milo White, a general merchant, began to buy wheat there for cash in 1859. He stored it in a warehouse, which he himself built, and shipped it later by team to La Crosse. Another type of cash wheat buyer in the interior was the miller, but mills were sometimes slow to appear in smaller communities. Even the best interior markets paid comparatively low prices. Not until the coming of the railroads did specialized wheat buyers operate in most of the interior towns.[5]

Many dramatic stories could be told of trips made by farmers with loads of wheat hauled by oxen to distant cash markets. Such hauls often were difficult, as roads were rough and the temperature might be very low. Some farmers were frozen to death; others at times encountered robbers and hostile Indians. Gilbert I. Larsen, in an account of early Lincoln County, said that much of the wheat raised there sold for from thirty to forty-five cents a bushel and that it took two or three days to haul it to Marshall, the nearest market. A committee of the state legislature in 1861 reported that the mean distance to a navigable river for the average farmer was eighty miles. Those who lived within three days of a stream by ox team were considered lucky, despite the fact that a load of wheat seldom consisted of more than thirty bushels.[6]

Naturally, the pioneer farmer wanted to have in his locality mills where he could sell his wheat or have it ground into flour. In 1850 there was only one mill in the state with an output valued at five hundred dollars a year. Ten years later eighty-one gristmills were reported, one of which, in Rice County, cost over thirty thousand dollars, yet interior towns long after 1860 were inconvenienced by the lack of mills. A resident of Glencoe in 1869 complained that the "demand for a Grist mill in our town, is becoming an actual necessity, owing to the great quantity of wheat that is produced

A FLOUR MILL AT FILLMORE, 1874
[From Andreas, *Historical Atlas of Minnesota*, 144.]

in this vicinity, which, if conveyed fifteen or twenty miles to mill —counting the farmers time and expense at fair wages—will soon pay for a mill." [7]

Wheat sold outside of Minnesota during the period of river transportation usually was shipped in the spring, when prices were highest. Unfortunately the average farmer could not hold his wheat until spring in order to take advantage of the better price. He ordinarily sold his grain upon taking it to market in the fall, because he was often in debt, interest rates were high, and he saw no guarantee in warehouse receipts, since warehousemen were not under public supervision. The farmer could not watch prices for the most opportune time to sell, and he could not, in many cases, go to town later to dispose of his grain. Grain storage rates in the middle sixties were about four cents a bushel for six months. Sometimes warehousemen loaned money to grain storers, but the terms apparently were not liberal.[8]

All in all, the raising and marketing of wheat was pretty much of a gamble. The situation in 1866 was well described by an early pastor at Cottage Grove: "People have no money till they sell their wheat, and they cannot draw it off till they finish putting in this springs crop. . . . Wheat is very high now. Nothing interests the people of this community more than the price of wheat. The selling of wheat is the blindest business any one can engage in. No one can tell a fortnight in advance whether wheat will be $.75 or $1.50 per bushel. . . . On Monday wheat was $1.50 per bushel on Wed. it was $1.40. . . . Where a man had a thousand bushels as many of our farmers had and sold it a few months ago for .95 they mo[u]rn over their ill luck that they did not keep it till the present time."[9]

When the railroads were built they furnished a new market for the wheat farmer, and railroad grain elevators or warehouses began to dot the landscape. The locations of these elevators were fixed by railroad officials, many of whom, with their friends, made comfortable little fortunes by dealing in town lots. The order in which the store, the blacksmith shop, the saloon, the school, the church, and the post office arose around the depot and the elevator became almost stereotyped. Yet "but for the elevator it would have been impossible to handle the Minnesota wheat crops."[10]

The rush of farmers to the elevators usually began in the second half of September and lasted until about the middle of November. The wheat dealers hired buyers who stood on the streets from morning until night bidding for the grain as fast as the wagons came in. Each buyer had tickets on which appeared the date, the current price of wheat, his name, and blank spaces in which to write the farmer's name and the number of bushels of grain he had for sale. The day's business normally began with a price agreement, and the traders adhered to the figure decided upon until competition forced it higher or bad news from the East pushed it lower. The buyer would jump on to a wagon, open a sack, and offer the farmer a price.[11]

In 1858 the Chicago Board of Trade began grading wheat, and thereafter three grades of wheat based on weight were recognized. A difference in price of about ten cents separated numbers 1 and 2, while the difference between 2 and 3 ranged from ten to twenty cents. Farmers complained bitterly about grading and weighing, but they had little or no choice in the early days. There were no public scales, and public inspection of weights and measures was unknown. The earliest attempts to combat dishonesty came from the towns themselves. These attempts were bred by a desire to secure trade by establishing a good reputation. Boards of trade were organized to make rules, and public weighing was tried. In 1862 Winona provided for a public market, where all grain was to be sold, and for the appointment of a public weighmaster, but the plan was in force only a short time. Then in 1867 a bill "to prevent fraud in inspection, weighing and transportation of grain" was introduced into the state legislature, but it came to naught.[12]

St. Louis and Milwaukee were the principal primary wheat markets for Minnesota before the Civil War. After the war Milwaukee forged ahead of St. Louis because Minnesota trade with the latter city had been cut off for a time during hostilities, and St. Louis never regained its former position. Chicago began to rival Milwaukee in the early 1860's, but Milwaukee prices remained slightly higher than those in Chicago during the whole era of river trade. The rivalry between the two markets was felt somewhat in the Minnesota river towns, which, in spite of telegraphic connections, found it difficult to get reliable data from the primary markets. There was always a disparity between the prices received by Minnesota farmers, even in the river towns, and prices quoted in Milwaukee and Chicago. Freights, handling charges, and manipulation accounted for this difference, which at times was as much as fifty-nine cents at Winona.[13]

Wheat prices were particularly low in Minnesota in 1869 and 1870, and farmers were looking for a scapegoat for their unhappy

WHEAT: KING OR TYRANT?

plight. One foe appeared to be the railroad. Said Governor Horace Austin in his inaugural address of 1870. "It is alleged that grain and other products are still hauled by teams, right beside the tracks of these roads and in competition with them, to and from markets many miles distant, and that the farmer, through whose land the railway runs, can better afford this than submit to the tariff exacted for carrying his products. It is also asserted that the freight for some classes of goods upon the railroads, though carried from fifty to eighty miles, is higher than was formerly paid over the wagon roads between the same points when transported by horses." While not entirely justified, the farmers' complaints against the railroads did have some basis in fact. Freight rates did not drop in proportion to the price decline in wheat after the Civil War. In 1868, for example, the rate on wheat from St. Paul to Milwaukee or Chicago was about thirty cents a bushel, and not until February, 1870, did the St. Paul and Milwaukee Railroad reduce the rate to Milwaukee to twenty-one cents.[14]

Another thing that irritated the wheat farmer was the manner in which wheat was graded. At times the farmer was at fault, since he was careless about cleaning the grain, but frequently incompetency or dishonesty on the part of inspectors resulted in number 1 wheat being graded as number 2. And wheat invariably seemed to have more screenings and light-weight or discolored kernels at the local elevator than at the terminal market. Finally, in addition to high freight rates, false grading, and dockage, the farmer at times had to contend with wheat buyers' pools.[15]

An act of the Minnesota legislature of 1871 stating that railroads were invested with a public interest prescribed maximum freight and passenger charges. Freight rates were to vary according to distance and classification, and the roads were to accept and expedite shipments in the order received. A punitive clause was included, and the office of railroad commissioner was set up, though the commissioner was without adequate power. Governor Austin, in his message of 1873, said that the railroads defied the law, and it was not long before its constitutionality was tested in the courts. John D. Blake and Company of Rochester sued the Winona and St. Peter

Railroad Company to replevin goods. The Blake company offered to pay fifty-seven cents for freight and the railroad demanded a dollar. In the district court the railroad was upheld; but the state's highest court, which was supported by the United States Supreme Court in 1876, reversed the decision of the district court. All in all, the farmers' protest against high freight rates, expressed mainly through the Grange movement, did have some effect in reducing the charges. In the 1870's, both in the state and nationally, there was much talk of a revival of water trade, and towboats pulling long strings of light draft barges began to appear on the rivers in increasing numbers. But the river revival was only temporary, and the railroads remained the dominant commercial carriers of the North and West.[16]

"Indications were consequently not lacking early in the seventies," writes one authority, "that the craze for wheat had almost run its course, and that conditions were ripe for a return to mixed farming." Various factors prevented the change at that time—among them lack of capital by many farmers, the opening of new lands by the railroads, and the introduction of new milling methods. The influence of the millers in obtaining further regulation of the marketing of Minnesota wheat has been investigated by Charles B. Kuhlmann, who made an extensive study of wheat marketing. "The immediate effect of their [*the millers'*] activities was to create a cash market for wheat and so to encourage one-crop farming," he writes. "And yet the early millers generally stood for progressive farming. Before 1880 they were alarmed at the declining yields and quality of Minnesota wheat crops. They advised the bringing in of selected Red Fife wheat from Canada for seed and opposed the introduction of the softer varieties. In the next decade they attempted to increase the sale of mill feeds by advocating live stock growing.... Available evidence seems to show that, on the whole, they have stood for a progressive type of agriculture." On the other hand, farmers did not by any means always feel that the millers gave them a square deal. For example, John R. Cummins wrote in his diary in 1874: "Went to town with a load of wheat. I have some reason to think the millers in town do not give fair weight."[17]

WHEAT: KING OR TYRANT?

In 1878 the St. Paul Chamber of Commerce charged that the Minneapolis Millers' Association was an oppressive monopoly, but the *Minnesota Farmer* branded the charges as ridiculous. A few months later, however, the editor of another farm journal stated that he had examined a wheat tester known as the "brass kettle," which had been adopted and used by the millers. The editor found that it had been used to defraud farmers, with the result that there was feeling against it over the state. On January 8, 1879, Representative Edward Larssen, a farmer of Swift County, gave notice in the Minnesota house of representatives of a bill to regulate the grading and inspection of wheat in the state, and other representatives gave notices of bills to regulate weights and measures and to make the half bushel the only unit for grading wheat. The fight on the "swindling brass kettle" had begun.[18]

Anti-brass-kettle meetings were held by farmers in various parts of the state. At one in Litchfield on February 4, 1879, a farmer whose sentiments were probably characteristic of his group said of the "'wheat ring' that 'the devil would kick them out of the nethermost recesses of hell on the ground of total depravity.'" Finally, in the spring of 1879 the governor signed a bill which allowed the Farmers' Board of Trade to select the measure to be used for wheat grading. The half bushel was to be the legal standard, although a two-quart tester could be used if both parties agreed. The board chose the Stacey filler—a small tin vessel shaped somewhat like an hourglass, into which wheat was poured. Below it was a tin kettle. The advantage of the measure was that the running of the wheat from the hourglass vessel seemed to give the grain a "uniform packing."[19]

But the farmers' battle against the wheat alliance, the railroads, the elevators, and the millers was not yet won. Farmers wanted the right to load on cars and ship direct to a terminal market without having to pass their wheat through elevators, which graded it and charged for handling it. This rural agitation led to the organization of the Farmers' Alliance, and it bore fruit in the Minnesota legislative session of 1885. An act approved on March 5, 1885, regulated railroad companies and provided for the Board of Railroad and

Warehouse Commissioners. Under the law, railroad companies were required to make annual reports to the commissioners showing the amount of stock subscribed, their assets and liabilities, the amount of their debts, the estimated value of their roadbed, rolling stock, stations, and buildings, the mileage of tracks and branches, the number of tons of through and local freight hauled, the monthly earnings for carrying freight and passengers, expenses incurred, the rates charged for fares, the tariff of freights, and various other figures. The commissioners were empowered to examine the books of railroads, make investigations, and require new information in the annual reports. Every railroad company was forced to permit any person or company to build and operate elevators at any of its way stations, and to furnish cars on application for transporting grain stored in any and all elevators or warehouses without discrimination. Rates were not to be extortionate and penalties were provided for violations of the law.[20]

At the same session of the legislature an act was passed to regulate elevators and warehouses and to provide for the inspection and weighing of grain. It declared public all elevators and warehouses at Duluth, Minneapolis, and St. Paul, and required the proprietors to take out licenses. Elevators and warehouses were to receive grain for storage without discrimination, to give receipts therefor, and to deliver grain or return the receipt. The owner or lessee was required to make and post weekly in a conspicuous place a statement of the kind and grade of grain received, to send a daily report to the state registrar, and to publish rates for storage. Mixing grain of different grades was prohibited. A state weighmaster and assistants were to be appointed to weigh grain at points where it was inspected. A chief inspector and deputies likewise were to be appointed to inspect and grade grain as prescribed by the commissioners. For inspection a fee was to be charged to cover the cost of service. Finally, the commissioners were to establish and publish Minnesota wheat grades. Thus, by 1885 the Minnesota wheat farmer was fairly well protected against the transportation companies, the elevators, and the millers. A comparison of freight rates on wheat from selected points in Minnesota to Duluth or Minneapolis will show that the 1873 rates were nearly double those of 1891.[21]

WHEAT: KING OR TYRANT?

During all the period in which the farmer was struggling against recurrent low prices and wheat rings, total wheat production was increasing, areas of production were shifting, and methods of production were changing. During the Civil War and until 1867 high prices were the order of the day, a condition which naturally stimulated wheat production. By 1868 sixty-two per cent of the cultivated land in Minnesota was devoted to wheat, as compared with fifty-three per cent in 1860, and wheat was a matter of paramount concern to almost everybody. The Reverend George Biscoe caught the spirit of the times when he wrote: "Minnesota or that part of it known as Cottage Grove has gone to wheat. Men work in wheat all day when it does not rain, lounge round talking about wheat when it is wet, Dream about wheat at night and I fear go to meeting Sabbath Day to think about wheat." [22]

For a few years after 1868 the tendency toward exclusive wheat growing was somewhat checked. Lower prices, lower yields per acre, and marketing difficulties caused many farmers to diversify their agriculture to a certain extent. Governor Austin even "proposed perhaps for the first time in an official state paper" a more diversified agriculture, and the newspapers admonished farmers to shift to other crops. Said a contributor to one paper: "To *live* . . . we must change our system of farming; there is no article of farm produce in this State but commands a better price to-day than wheat; yet, there is nothing that will impoverish our land and ruin the farmer so quick as wheat. After one or two crops it is very difficult to raise No. 1 wheat." [23]

But the decline in wheat farming did not last long after 1870. The total state production was then 18,866,073 bushels, and Minnesota ranked twelfth among the wheat-producing states. It has been noted that production in 1860 amounted to only 2,186,973 bushels. The leading wheat counties in 1870 were about the same as in 1860, and six of them—Olmsted, Goodhue, Fillmore, Wabasha, Dakota, and Winona—were producing over a million bushels each. [24]

During the decade of the 1870's many factors influenced the development of wheat production—among them the railroads, which brought new lands within reach of markets and connected Minnesota more effectively with the East. It was in September, 1870, that the Lake Superior route to the East was opened by the connection of St. Paul and Duluth by railroad; in October of the next year the St. Paul and Pacific reached Breckenridge on the upper Red River; while the Northern Pacific, also in 1871, connected Duluth with Moorhead, the usual head of Red River navigation.[25]

With the building of the railroad the great wheat growing area of the Red River Valley began to pour its grain into the markets of the world. Early settlers in that region, however, lacked faith in the ability of the valley to produce a crop. After the Sioux Outbreak of 1862, Henry H. Sibley expressed his belief that the area was "fit only for the Indians and the devil." His error became more and more obvious as settlers began to appreciate the region and to stream into it after 1870. Vere Ether of Neche, Nels Larson of Moorhead, and three farmers who lived south of Moorhead—Ole Thompson, Hogan Anderson, and Jens Anderson—were among residents of the valley who raised wheat in the first half of the 1870's. But perhaps the most important was Henry A. Bruns of Moorhead. In the winter of 1871-72 he bought five hundred bushels of seed wheat in central and southern Minnesota, transported it to the valley on sleds, and distributed it to farmers in Clay and Norman counties. Although grasshoppers were destructive in 1872, an important start was made, and in 1873 Bruns shipped the first carload of wheat from the Red River to Duluth. Later he was instrumental in erecting the first flour mill in Moorhead and the first steam elevator in the valley.[26]

Closely related to the railroad in promoting settlement in the Red River Valley was the bonanza farm, which demonstrated on a large scale the practicability of producing wheat in the region at a profit. Among the earliest farms of the type was that of Oliver Dalrymple, who had had earlier experience in large-scale agriculture in eastern Minnesota. In 1875 he broke 1,280 acres of Red River Valley land, and in 1876 he harvested 32,000 bushels of excellent wheat, averaging a little over twenty-three bushels to the acre. The fame of the valley was established. The land had been purchased at from forty to sixty cents an acre, but, according to Dalrymple himself, speak-

A BONANZA FARM
[From the *Independent Farmer*, 1:174 (November 1, 1879).]

ing about 1909, it "immediately took on a value of $5.00 per acre in 1875—and has increased a dollar per acre per annum since, and has a present value of from $30.00 to $40.00 per acre."[27]

Much of the activity in the valley occurred so shortly before 1880 that the census returns of that year did not reflect to any great degree the development of the region. Practically the same counties led in wheat production in 1880 as in 1870. While still leading, however, few of those counties increased their total production during the decade, and Olmsted and Winona actually registered decreases. Total state production nearly doubled between 1870 and 1880, reaching a figure of 34,601,030 bushels, which placed Minnesota fifth among the wheat-producing states, following Illinois, Indiana, Ohio, and Michigan. In 1874 wheat occupied 66.3 per cent of all tilled land, but thereafter a reaction set in for a few years. It was caused by the panic of 1873, the almost complete cessation of railroad building, lower prices, lower yields, grasshoppers, and agrarian discontent. The year 1877 marked the low point of this decline, but even then a larger percentage of land was in wheat than in 1867, the high point of the preceding decade. Wheat prices were high in 1877, largely as a result of the crop failure of 1876, and farmers consequently rushed into wheat production in the spring of 1878, devoting 68.98 per cent of all tilled land to the crop, a record equaled in no other year. Most of the increase in production of the 1870's, as has been implied, was due to the opening up of new fields along the Minnesota River and in the central and northwestern parts of the state.[28]

Developments of great significance to the farmer, as well as to the state as a whole, occurred in the field of flour milling during the 1870's. Mere mention of them here will be sufficient to show their effect on Minnesota wheat farming. One was the introduction of the middlings purifier, which by 1876 was in general use. That invention revolutionized spring-wheat milling. As a result spring wheat became "king" in the Northwest, and Minnesota flours commanded the highest prices in Eastern and, eventually, in foreign markets. There was an advance of from a dollar to three dollars a barrel in the selling price of spring-wheat flour, and a premium of a dollar a barrel over winter-wheat flour. One writer declares that

"Minnesota farmers now had a market for a grain suited to the climate and soil of the state, which, but for this revolution in milling, if produced at all, must have been marketed at inferior prices." [29]

Another improvement in general use by 1880 was the metallic roller process of milling. Like the middlings purifier, it caused a rise in spring-wheat prices. Since the process was perfected in Minneapolis, the wheat trade of the Northwest tended more and more to be directed toward that city, where the Minneapolis Millers' Association controlled mills, elevators, and warehouses. The millers' monopoly resulted in certain abuses and much criticism. Hence, in 1881 the Minneapolis Chamber of Commerce was formed to remedy evils in the wheat market. It helped matters somewhat, but practices still persisted which necessitated the legislative acts of 1885. The grain trade grew, however, and by 1885 Minneapolis had elevators with a total capacity of 9,515,000 bushels. One of them, the Great Northern, built in 1879 with a capacity of 780,000 bushels, was the largest elevator west of Chicago. In 1876 Minneapolis wheat receipts passed 5,000,000 bushels; in 1880 they reached 10,000,000; and by 1898 the figure was 77,159,980. In 1881 Minneapolis ranked third among the primary wheat markets; by 1885 the city was first. [30]

Duluth also was a good wheat market by the late 1870's, favored as it was by its position on the Northern Pacific Railroad and on the Great Lakes. At Duluth there were fewer complaints about grading, and prices tended to be higher than at Minneapolis. Furthermore, freight rates on the Northern Pacific seem to have been lower than on some other roads. In Europe, Liverpool was the big market, and to that place Minnesota wheat in large quantities began to find its way, especially after 1873, much to the dismay of the English farmer. Some of the wheat went by way of St. Louis and New Orleans, while some was shipped to Liverpool via New York. Notices about Minnesota wheat destined for Europe often appeared in the press. A report of 1879, for instance, records that 72,000 bushels were received in Barcelona—the "first cargo of wheat that was ever imported to that place from America." The bill for freight amounted to $18,000. [31]

Struggling as he was to improve his lot, it was natural for the pioneer farmer to experiment with various types of wheat in order to find those best suited to Minnesota. Right from the beginning both winter and spring wheats were tried, though many doubted the success of growing winter wheat so far north. Booster newspapers tried to prove the doubters wrong by frequent accounts of successful winter-wheat production. "Those who think winter wheat cannot be produced in this Territory, are invited to call at our office, and examine for themselves," reported one St. Paul paper in 1856, asserting that in "several of the Territorial papers received during the past week, we have glowing accounts of the great success that has attended the efforts of our farmers to produce winter wheat." Yet in 1859 the same paper had to admit that the amount of winter wheat grown was "foolishly small," and about the same time almost two-thirds of the wheat marketed at Chicago was of the spring variety.[32]

Winter wheat yields were heavier than those of spring wheat if the crop was a success, often running to forty bushels or more per acre, but the uncertainty of the crop caused farmers to neglect it. Just how much winter wheat was grown in the early period is impossible to determine, since the census did not enumerate the two types separately by bushels until 1870.[33] Many varieties of wheat appeared in the state before the middle eighties. During the late 1850's and early 1860's Scotch Fife, Canada Club, and Rio Grande were the most common, especially Canada Club, despite its susceptibility to rust. Red River wheat from Pembina did well in Stearns County, and it was used for the first crop of spring wheat in Benton County. White China was mentioned early near Winona, and Black Sea and Tea wheats had their followers in the 1850's.[34]

By 1867 decreasing wheat yields were to a large extent blamed on the seed in use. Undoubtedly many farmers were not careful enough in selecting their seed; they did not clean it sufficiently and did not buy new wheat often enough. Some farmers, however, did band together in many parts of the state to send to Canada for the native pure Canada Club. "This movement on the part of the farmers," commented one journal, "is the best news we have received for a long time." In Faribault County, when Fife wheat "ran out," farmers turned to a new Russian wheat, Red Osaka, which saved the local crop from failure in 1872. But Red Osaka in turn did not last long, as it proved especially subject to rust. Some large fields of it in the southern part of the state were not even cut in 1874, so destructive was the rust. According to one writer, the best varieties in that year were Halstead, White Michigan, Rio Grande, White Hamburg or Amber, China Tea, Fife, and Golden Drop. Two other varieties that received much attention were Hiller, or White Fife, and Blandin Fife. The latter barely missed the first premium at the state fair of 1878 in a field of twenty-six other varieties. It was accidentally discovered by an old farmer who noticed two ripe heads in a field where other berries were only about half grown. He saved the heads and cultivated the variety for six years before another farmer secured the wheat from him for exhibit at the fair. From time to time, farmers and newspapers became excited about this or that variety of wheat for which someone made fantastic claims, but the crazes did not last long.[35]

No matter what variety of wheat was grown, however, it would "run out," rust, or get smutty if conditions were not favorable. Hence, farmers were continually seeking new methods for making their seed sturdier and more resistant to disease. A characteristic recipe was given by one Charles H. Ford in 1861. To prevent "the worm" (what he meant is not apparent), he advised combining six bushels of seed grain with three pounds of a creamy mixture of sugar and chimney soot, and allowing it to stand for from twenty to forty hours. To prevent smut, it was suggested that farmers add one ounce of blue vitriol dissolved in one pint of water to each bushel of seed. Indeed, modern researches have established the fact that blue vitriol or copper sulphate will effectively control covered smut of wheat.[36]

Another foe of the early Minnesota wheat crops was the Rocky Mountain locust, or grasshopper, which invaded the Red River settlements as early as 1818 and 1819. From 1820 to 1855 there were no unusual invasions of the pest in the state, though slight inroads may have occurred. The years 1856, 1857, 1864, and 1865 saw extensive destruction, but the worst damage was done in the period from

1873 to 1877. The story of the plague of the 1870's is too well known to need retelling here. About forty counties felt the hopper visitation in 1876, some five hundred thousand acres of crops were damaged, and the average yield of wheat through the state was under ten bushels to the acre. Fortunately, weather conditions in 1877, as well as parasites, were unfavorable to the locusts, and by the middle of August, Minnesota was virtually free of them.[37]

Insect pests, unfavorable weather, low prices, transportation difficulties, and the like were not the wheat farmer's only problems. Often he was confronted by a labor shortage, accompanied by high wages. Even with the coming of self-binders and improved threshers in the 1870's the labor problem was not altogether solved, since there was a limit to what one man or one family alone could do. Although farmers relied much on the help of neighbors at rush seasons, they still had to depend to some extent upon hired laborers, especially at harvest time.

Wheat began to ripen in early and middle August—a signal for the whole countryside to spring to life. Incoming trains at St. Charles, Winona, and other stations brought with them sets of rough-looking fellows, each carrying a bundle or valise. These men, looking like a detachment of Goths, were harvest hands, who began the season in the vicinity of St. Louis and worked northward through Iowa as the grain ripened. After leaving the train, they went to a local hostelry, where they plied the landlord with questions regarding labor conditions and wages in the vicinity. Farmers drove into town and argued with the workers over wages, sometimes for several days, while the wheat was getting riper and riper. On some occasions the first comers would grow impatient and take a train to another town—Rochester, Kasson, or Owatonna—there to try their luck. Always there were fresh arrivals, however, from the East and South. At last the farmers would grow anxious, promise three dollars a day in wages, and drive off to their fields with a gang of laborers. Generally they were good workers, but they demanded meals fit for a "New York alderman." The preparation of such meals was a real task for the farm women, for often a dozen men had to be fed three times a day for as many weeks. Harvest hands, however, were not so particular about sleeping quarters, nor was their piety always strong, their swearing often drowning out the grace at mealtime. "The habit of swearing is very common in the Northwest," wrote one observer, "an oath at every ten words is perhaps a fair average. We omit them in our report." In 1867, even when all help was absorbed at three dollars a day, "hundreds of farms all over the State, still lay untouched by the scythe," and hands at Eyota and Rochester were paid as much as four and a half dollars a day. People became alarmed, and everyone who was physically fit felt an almost patriotic call to enter the fields.[38]

Just what profits the average Minnesota wheat farmer made between the 1850's and the 1880's it is impossible to say with accuracy. There were exceptional periods, such as those marked by the panics of 1857 and 1873, and the hard times of the late 1860's, during which both rural and urban populations felt the effects of economic depression. Hence, such years cannot be cited in a study of what might be called normal wheat profits. In order to calculate such profits it is necessary to know the cost of raising wheat, the total acreage devoted to the crop, and the prices received. A few examples may throw light on the question.

A writer of 1882 gives the following detailed list of equipment needed to operate a hundred-and-sixty-acre wheat farm, with a hundred acres under cultivation:

Three horses, at $150 each	$ 450
One pair of oxen	100
One sulky three-horse plow	50
Attachment to same for breaking	15
Two-horse cultivator	30
Three-horse reaper (self-binder)	275
Two-horse harrow	15
Fanning mill with cockle attachment	20
One wagon	75
One sled	35
One drill	85
Three sets of harness	45
Spades, shovels, hoes, forks, hayrack, &c	60
Total	$1,255

Of course every farmer did not have such extensive equipment, but all had to have a certain amount of capital before they could begin to grow wheat. Added to this expense was that of raising the crop. Various estimates are to be found of the latter cost, generally ranging from ten to fifteen dollars an acre. A typical estimate follows:

Plowing, per acre	$ 2.00
Seed (1½ bushels per acre)	1.50
Seeding and dragging, per acre	1.00
Cutting with reaper, per acre	1.00
Binding, per acre	1.20
Shocking, per acre	.35
Threshing 18 bushels, at $.15 per bushel	2.70
Teaming 8 miles to market	1.44
Interest on land at $10 per acre at 10%	1.00
Total	$12.19

In this instance the cost per bushel was sixty-seven and two-thirds cents. Other estimates might include greater costs for marketing, higher land valuations, taxes and insurance, depreciation, and other factors which would increase the cost of raising wheat. On large farms the cost per acre might be smaller, while on small farms using cradles it would be larger.[39]

Undoubtedly many men made money in wheat farming, and they made it in a short time. Robert Hews of Wasioja, for instance, in 1866 purchased 48 acres of broken but unfenced land for $1,183. He sowed 36 acres of wheat in the spring of that year, and secured over 19 bushels per acre at harvest, or 739½ bushels in all. He sold 95 bushels at $1.25 a bushel, and in the spring he sold the rest for seed at from $2.00 to $2.25 a bushel. His total wheat sales brought in $1,524.30, plus $93.50 for the straw. Since his expenses were about $200, he cleared about $234.80 on his first year's operations.[40]

For every Robert Hews, however, there were many farmers struggling along, year after year, raising wheat and still remaining in debt. When wheat brought a dollar or better a bushel, raising it was not an unhappy business, but when the price was down to forty-five or fifty cents a bushel, matters were different. Leonard B. Hodges, in a letter of December 14, 1878, told of a friend who invested all he had in growing wheat in Olmsted County until 1872, and who left that place with "worse than nothing." All his earnings went to pay store and machine bills. "Paying 'after harvest,'" warned the editor of the *Farmers' Union*, "has ruined a good many men. It may you." Particularly during the late 1860's was there ample evidence of the lack of profit in specialized wheat farming. John R. Cummins, a typical or above-average farmer who concentrated on wheat, wrote in 1880: "Moved from the old log, into the new house, where we had lived since 1857, excepting 2 years." Had he grown rich by raising wheat he probably would not have lived in his old log cabin all those years. One writer has said that in the first few years after the cessation of spring-wheat raising there came a transition period which gradually opened up more prosperous conditions than the older times ever produced.[41]

Considering the gamble involved in wheat raising, it is difficult to understand why the pioneer farmer placed so much stress on that branch of agriculture. J. R. Drake in 1868 undertook to explain the problem. He claimed that most farmers were poor and that wheat was the only crop which would ensure a return, the only one for which there was always a market. There was much truth in his opinion, but it did not tell the whole story. Poor farmers could not afford to buy stock, erect buildings, and experiment with little-known crops and methods. Lack of skill, knowledge, and experience was another factor. Wheat farming also was comparatively easy compared with mixed husbandry, and there was always the hope that wheat yields and prices would be high in another year. Thus many farmers raised wheat every year, often on the same land, although they knew better.[42]

Finally, however, natural forces, economic conditions, better understanding of farming methods, and general agricultural trends caused many a Minnesota wheat farmer to change his course of production. Diversification did not come all at once, nor did it affect all parts of the state equally. Some farmers carried on mixed agriculture in the midst of specialized wheat areas, and some clung to wheat almost solely in areas of diversification. General trends, nevertheless, show that as wheat farming moved north and west, the older southern and eastern sections of the state turned more to other types of agriculture, especially from 1878 onward. As early as 1873 evidence of the trend could be found in the older parts of Minnesota. Statistics collected by the state Grange in 1873 showed that the percentage of land in wheat and grain crops was lowest in the counties that had been settled the longest. Crops such as flax, cultivated hay, sorghum, hops, tobacco, peas, and beans were receiving increasing attention at the expense of wheat.[43]

Then in 1878 occurred a catastrophe that hastened the demise of wheat growing in southern and southeastern Minnesota—the poor crop of that year. Indications in June forecast a banner crop, but weather conditions in July, characterized by excessive rainfall and heat, blasted early hopes. Stem rust was the villain of the piece, and the poorest yields occurred in the two southernmost tiers of counties, Mower County having a low of six and seven-tenths bushels per acre. The only number 1 wheat produced in Minnesota in that year came from the western or northwestern sections of the state.[44]

A picture of the great change in the location of wheat areas that occurred in Minnesota after 1870 can be had by comparing county production statistics for that year with those for 1890. It is almost startling. Leading wheat counties of 1870 showed in all cases small production in 1890, while newer counties exhibited gigantic totals in the latter year. Olmsted and Dakota counties, for example, produced 2,117,074 and 1,435,874 bushels, respectively, in 1870; in 1890 their figures were 198,992 and 64,806. On the other hand, Polk County, which was not even listed in 1870, and Otter Tail County, which produced 8,406 bushels in 1870, produced 3,013,361 and 2,623,538 bushels, respectively, in 1890. In exhibiting this shift in wheat areas, Minnesota was not unique; rather, the state's history typified the course of wheat production in the United States. Until recent times wheat has always been attracted rapidly to new lands. It has been a frontier crop, and its center of production has moved swiftly across the continent.[45]

In contemplating this movement, one naturally wonders why the shift in wheat farming took place. Why did farmers abandon wheat raising and take up diversified agriculture? Some attributed the change to declining soil fertility and reduced yields, but that explanation does not suffice. True, wheat yields did decrease on particular pieces of ground where the grain was grown year after year, but it is doubtful that soil in Olmsted County in 1890, for example, was any less fertile generally than it was in 1866. The contour of the land in much of southern Minnesota, also, was as well suited to wheat as that of Stearns or Renville counties; while the cost of machinery, the price of wheat, the cost of farm labor, and the rate of interest charged on farm loans were such as to give a relative advantage to the southeastern over the northwestern counties. Wherein, then, lies the explanation? It has been noted that wheat production was considered best adapted to the conditions of frontier agriculture. Rising land values in southeastern Minnesota forced the farmers there to shift from wheat farming to dairying. Where a man farmed land that was free, his aim was to extend the use of a given amount of labor and capital over as large an area as possible, no additional expense thereby being added as rent. As soon, however, as the land acquired a value, thus involving a definite expense per acre, the farmer found it necessary to direct his farming so as to get a larger return per acre. Hence, in the long run, the wheat farmer had to leave southeastern Minnesota when land values increased, or shift to another type of farming. If he did neither of these things, he probably found himself getting more and more into debt, since the return per acre was generally greater in dairying than it was in wheat farming. Stem rust, chinch bugs, and hot, wet weather undoubtedly seemed like the addition of insult to injury to the wheat farmer of southeastern Minnesota in 1878, but in reality he benefited from them if they forced him to diversify his agriculture to meet changing conditions. The rise in land values in that section, of course, was not only a cause of more intensive farming, but was partly a result as well. The most important factor, however, in increasing land values was the growth of population and settlement, with attendant social and other advantages.[46]

The shift in wheat production in Minnesota did not mean that the state's importance as a wheat grower suffered any setback after 1880. On the contrary, Minnesota ranked first among the states in 1889 and again in 1899, and total state production in the latter year was nearly three times what it had been in 1879. It did mean, however, that the state was passing out of the frontier stage and that never again would the single-crop craze take hold of so great a portion of the farm area as it did in the 1860's and 1870's.[47]

Livestock

Although the pioneer Minnesota farmer placed much faith in spring wheat as a cash staple, he by no means neglected the livestock industry. In fact, domestic animals were introduced into the region before wheat was grown there. In the vicinity of missions, trading posts, and military forts the white man early carried on farming which included stock raising. Lieutenant Zebulon M. Pike in 1806 wrote that at the post of the North West Company on Sandy Lake he saw horses procured from the Red River country and from the Indians. In the next year George Henry Monk reported of Fond du Lac: "Here are two Horses, a Cow, a Bull, and a few pigs." By 1830 Joseph Renville at Lac qui Parle was reported to have owned "sheep by the hundreds and cattle by the score." Two years later the Reverend William T. Boutwell visited the Sandy Lake post and saw there stables for thirty head of cattle, three or four horses, and fifteen swine.[1]

As time went on, the number of head of livestock gradually increased, although until nearly 1860 much of the livestock in the Northwest was imported from other sections for slaughter, dairy, and draught purposes.[2] Little effort was made before the middle 1850's to improve breeds, and most farmers paid slight attention to their farm animals. On December 16, 1845, for example, William R. Brown noted in his diary: "E. Brissette & I went out on the hills to look for his hogs which have been lost for several weeks. I found them on the hills Back of Harrison's Claim. Brissette & I followed them all day but could not get to them." On the following day Brown recorded that Brissette and he "went out & built a pen over his hogs bed (we found where they slept) hoping at night we could slip up & shut the door at night & thus fasten them in so we made a pen & at night went down but only 3 of them were in we fastened those in intending to shoot the others & haul them home, next day his old Black sow had pigs this evening." Not

LIVESTOCK

until December 23 did Brown and a companion go "to haul Brissettes hogs home he had shut them all up but one little pig it ran away we tied them & put them in the sled." [3]

From these extracts it is apparent that some farmers of the 1840's made little effort to house their hogs, and other livestock fared little better. Most farm animals were used for home consumption, though some meat might be sold at a fort or a village if one happened to be near enough to make such a sale profitable.

At the beginning of the decade of the 1840's, according to the sixth census, there were in St. Croix County, Wisconsin, which included Minnesota east of the Mississippi, 58 horses and mules, 434 cattle, 6 sheep, and 187 swine. These statistics probably are inaccurate and they give no clue, of course, to the number of animals in Minnesota proper. Ten years later the census included statistics for Minnesota Territory by counties. The livestock population had grown appreciably, though the validity of the figures is again open to doubt. Most of the increase was due to importation, as items in the first newspaper of the territory testify. On one occasion it noted that the "boiler deck of the Senator . . . was crowded with cattle and horses migrating to Minnesota"; on another it spoke of cattle and horses that were destined "to be let down, as it were, in a sheet by the four corners, before St. Peters." [4]

Many head of cattle were driven overland along with the covered wagons of the settlers. One writer, F. D. Currier, however, stated that the majority of settlers in the 1850's reached their destination without a hoofed or horned animal upon which to draw for sustenance. Most early settlers had to be content with buying a calf and waiting for it to grow. No attention was paid to breeds, and the buyer had to be satisfied with "anything that walked on four legs, could grow horns and would resemble a cow when grown up." In 1850 Minnesota's "live stock comprised chiefly horses and work oxen, though some milch cows were reported, especially in Washington and Pembina counties." [5]

The lack of home-produced beef and pork was reflected in price quotations, which were extremely changeable. In February, 1851, for example, beef and pork had advanced to ten cents a pound in St. Paul, partly because hogs from Dubuque, Prairie du Chien, and other places had not yet arrived. At the same time good butter was scarce, all kinds bringing twenty-five cents a pound. Less than a year later, in January, 1852, when there was a good supply of beef on hand in St. Paul, it sold for from five to seven cents a pound by the quarter, or from six to eight cents by the piece. There was no fresh pork to speak of, only one wagonload having reached St. Paul during the previous few days. As a result, pork brought from eight to ten cents a pound and hams, twelve and a half cents.[6]

In the early 1850's good cows could be purchased in Iowa, Illinois, or Wisconsin for about twenty-five dollars each, and the cost of taking one from Galena to St. Paul by steamboat was between three and four dollars. This, however, was too expensive for the average farmer, who generally was short of cash. Hence, importation of livestock and improved breeding methods were carried on for the most part by the wealthier men of the territory. They performed a valuable service for Minnesota—a service, by the way, which did not go unnoticed. In 1854, for example, this item appeared in the weekly *Pioneer*: "As yet but little has been done towards the improvement of stock in the Territory, and we are highly gratified to see that at this time, many are making exertions to bring in improved breeds. Col. Stevens of Minneapolis, last year got up a fine Durham Bull and a heifer of the same breed, from which the farmers in Hennepin County are now breeding very extensively, which will of course make a general improvement in that region, and Mr. William Fowler of Red Rock prairie has just brought up a beautiful Devonshire Bull, which he purchased in Geauga County, Ohio." The writer mentions two other Minnesotans who "are now below for the purpose of procuring an improved stock of horses," and he concludes with the remark that "they will, probably, bring on some good stock, and our present race of ponies will soon disappear from the land."[7] Perhaps such importations of stock brought the desired results. At least Christopher C. Andrews, commenting on a trip to Minnesota in 1856, when he noted the absence of mules, declared: "Minnesotians are supplied with uncommonly good horses. I do not remember to have seen a mean horse in the territory."[8]

In the spring of 1855 the press once more reported on the activities of stock importers. It was expected that beginning in May extensive droves would arrive. Even in April, fifty or sixty milch cows, work oxen, and beef cattle were on their way from northern Illinois, and another herd was coming from Iowa. By June 1 a large lot was expected from Missouri. Some uncertainty regarding sheep importation was expressed, but of live pork there was plenty, and it was believed that Ramsey County could almost supply its own demand for that article.[9]

In addition to the importers already mentioned, recognition should be given Joseph Haskell, who in 1851 brought the first Devons into the region and bred them successfully for some years thereafter. John P. Miller also deserves notice, since he and John H. Stevens in 1853 imported the first full-blooded Devon cow and bull into Hennepin County at a cost of two thousand dollars. Devons, however, did not prove popular and were rarely profitable in Minnesota. At the same time, in the early 1850's, Herefords, Anguses, and Galloways were practically unknown in the region.[10]

The breed of horses in greatest favor was the Morgan. At the Minnesota Territorial Agricultural Society's fair of 1855 the first premiums for stallions went to "Flying Morgan, 2d," a full-blooded Morgan owned by Daniel Hopkins, and first on colts went to another Morgan owned by William Holcombe. There was not then a Percheron, a Belgian, nor a Clydesdale in Minnesota. At the same fair the first premium for bulls went to a three-year-old Durham, and for sheep to a Leicester. The hogs exhibited evidently belonged to no particular breed.[11]

In 1859, about the time when wheat was becoming commercially important in the state, the first shipment of cattle was made from Minnesota to the East. On November 10 Salathiel Olin of Rochester sent three carloads, comprising forty-five cattle in all, over the Milwaukee and La Crosse road directly to Boston. The cattle were purchased in the neighborhood of Rochester, and they averaged seventeen hundred pounds in weight.[12] The shipment was a welcome harbinger of the future to Minnesotans accustomed only to importing stock.

Shortly after Olin's venture, G. W. Piper of St. Peter took east a drove of Minnesota fattened cattle. He reported that they met with a ready sale in Buffalo and that "the speculation netted a handsome profit to those who embarked their means in it." The local market, however, did not always prove so attractive, for it was discovered by one owner of some fat cattle driven from Rice County to St. Paul that he could not find a purchaser among the city butchers, though he asked only four cents a pound on the hoof. He therefore resolved to drive the cattle to Superior.[13]

According to the census of 1850, there were only 80 sheep in all Minnesota Territory, of which 45 were in Ramsey County and 26 in Wabasha County. By 1860, however, there were 13,044 sheep in the state. Then came the Civil War with the accompanying demand for wool, and as a result the sheep population jumped to 97,241 in 1864 and to 193,045 in 1866. Then the movement subsided, and in 1869 there were only 135,450 sheep in the state. The end of the war and the general price decline caused this falling off in sheep production.[14]

Much ink was used by the papers of the territory and state in an attempt to interest farmers in sheep production. In 1853 one editor predicted that "within the time necessary for a farmer to get an extensive sheep farm in complete operation, we will be in a condition to avail ourselves of any and all the markets, both in Europe and America." Several years later the *St. Peter Statesman* published an account of P. S. Carson's experience as a sheep raiser. "All honor," said the writer, "is due Mr. Carson for his efforts in establishing the success of wool growing in this section of Minnesota, as it promises to be one of the most profitable branches of agricultural industry in the State." A farmers' club organized by members of the state legislature became interested in the question of sheep raising and devoted many discussions to it. One member pointed out that a good sheep yielded four and a half pounds of wool a year. Wool could be sent to New York and Boston for two and a half cents a pound, including commissions. Since the average price of wool in 1860 was forty cents a pound, as least a dollar and a half a year could be realized on each sheep. The speaker claimed that he had raised five hundred sheep himself, and he therefore knew from experience what he was talking about.[15]

Ample evidence of a craze for wool production can be found in the newspapers from 1860 to 1866. A flock of sheep from Vermont and another from New York were driven through Mantorville in one week in 1860. Richard Healy of New York and Russell Smith of Wisconsin let out sheep in flocks of five hundred to three farmers in Olmsted County in the fall of 1860. Half of the wool and half of the increase went to the owners, who claimed from thirty to fifty per cent dividends in the first year. J. G. Getty, who lived south of Sauk Centre, spent the winter of 1860–61 in Illinois, where he planned to buy two thousand sheep to take back to his farm the following spring. By 1863 there were many different breeds of sheep in the state, and each had defenders who vigorously proclaimed its merits. Some of the breeds most frequently mentioned were Leicester, Southdown, Sussex, Silesian, Saxon, and Merino. As late as September, 1866, forty thousand pounds of wool were at the railroad depot in St. Anthony ready to be shipped east—the largest amount exported from the state up to that time. A local newspaper commented on the year's shipment as follows: "Only half a dozen seasons since the entire wool clip of the State could not have filled a dozen burlaps. This year our exports of wool will exceed half a million pounds, and is almost doubling every season. It has become one of our most profitable branches of husbandry, or of any business, and numbers are embarking capital in it." [16]

But, however impressive the state's expansion of sheep raising was, Minnesota lagged far behind other states in the Middle West, as the following table shows:

POUNDS OF WOOL

	1862	1865
Illinois	5,800,000	12,000,000
Wisconsin	2,200,000	5,000,000
Iowa	2,000,000	7,000,000
Minnesota	150,000	450,000

The proportion of sheep to other livestock in the state can be seen by looking at a table based upon assessors' returns:

	1860	1863	1866	Per cent of increase
Horses	10,196	34,749	63,600	500
Cattle	40,928	194,736	210,921	400
Sheep	8,042	63,624	194,522	2,300
Hogs	21,317	87,857	95,472	350

The actual value of livestock in 1866 was about $21,286,697, more than double that of wheat. Fillmore, Olmsted, Goodhue, Dakota, Hennepin, Blue Earth, and Carver were banner livestock counties in the middle 1860's.[17]

The price of medium-grade wool fluctuated greatly during the war, but it seldom, if ever, sank below a figure remunerative to the farmer. The price range for 1862 was from $.40 to $.65 a pound; for 1863, from $.63 to $.75; for 1864, from $.70 to $1.10; for 1865, from $.45 to $.90.[18]

Despite high war prices, the sheepman's life was not always a bed of roses. Disease, wolves, and dogs were three of his worst enemies. The Minnesota State Agricultural Society and individuals bemoaned the dog menace and repeatedly petitioned the legislature to pass a stringent dog law. Typical was a plea from a well-known sheep raiser, R. H. Bennett of Cottage Grove: "I am confident the time is not far distant when Minnesota will rank among the *wool producing States* . . . *Provided, our intelligent Legislature* will pass a *law taxing all Dogs,* and creating a revenue, *sufficient to pay for the depredations of the canine race,* the only efficient protection that we can have." An act levying a dog tax was approved on March 6, 1862, but it was not stringent enough to please the sheepmen. An act of March 6, 1873, made the owner of a dog who killed or wounded a sheep liable for the value of such sheep. Diseases among sheep, especially foot rot, were prevalent between 1864 and 1867. Later the flocks appear to have been generally healthy.[19]

With the decline in the production of sheep after 1866, there was a noticeable decrease in public interest. In 1870 there were 132,343 sheep in Minnesota, fewer than the number given in the state returns of 1869; and in 1880 there were 267,598, exclusive of spring lambs. Ohio and California at the same time had more than 4,000,000 sheep each, and Texas and New Mexico had more than 2,000,000 apiece. The increase of sheep during the 1870's was relatively smaller than that of any other class of livestock except work oxen. It would seem that the postwar years dealt the industry a blow from which it did not easily recover. No organization to stimulate sheep and wool production appeared until 1879, when the Minnesota State Wool Growers' Association was formed.[20]

LIVESTOCK

According to the census of 1850, there were 734 swine in the territory, 580 of which were found in Wabasha and Washington counties. By 1860 the total number had increased to 101,371, yet Minnesota ranked twenty-fifth in the list of thirty-four states in the number of swine. Indiana, with more than 3,000,000 swine, was first, followed by Illinois, Missouri, Tennessee, Kentucky, Ohio, and Georgia, in that order, with well over 2,000,000 each. During the 1860's the percentage increase for swine was only 46.5, a smaller relative gain than was found in any other class of livestock on the farms in the state, even including work oxen. The total by 1870 was 148,473, and Minnesota ranked twenty-sixth on the swine-producing list. Illinois was then first, with over 2,700,000 swine, and next came Missouri, with over 2,000,000, and Indiana, Kentucky, Tennessee, Ohio, Iowa, Texas, and North Carolina, each with over 1,000,000. There were 82.7 swine per 100 of the rural population in 1860 and 45.3 in 1870. During the 1870's there was an increase in the hog population of 156.9 per cent to a total of 381,415 in 1880, or 70.2 swine for each 100 of the country population. Relatively, Minnesota was still twenty-fifth on the list. Iowa was first, with more than 6,000,000 swine; Illinois was second, with over 5,000,000; Missouri, with over 4,000,000, was third; Indiana and Ohio, in the 3,000,000 class, came next; and Kentucky and Tennessee could boast of over 2,000,000.[21]

Important factors in retarding swine production during the 1860's were the state's limited corn crop and the high price of grain. Thomas Lamb, whose dealings in pork were the most extensive in St. Paul, said that $300,000 worth of pork reached the city from Iowa during the winter of 1867–68. Slaughtered hogs valued at $500,000 probably were imported by the state during the same period. The *Minnesota Monthly* deplored this condition, and pointed out that, since Canadian farmers fattened hogs with peas, Minnesota farmers could do likewise. George Biscoe gave evidence of the scarcity of pigs when he wrote: "Mr. Van Slyke offered to give me a young pig if I would come and get it. Young pigs are very scarce and bring a high price for Minn. so it is worth going for."[22]

Prior to 1860 there seems to have been little commercial pork raising in the state. According to the St. Paul *Weekly Pioneer and*

Democrat of March 29, 1861, "very little was done in this city in pork packing until the winter of 1859-60—the time when we were relieved from the necessity of dependence on importations from below. In that winter a packing house was established by Messrs. Strong & Miller, which was quite successful. Last winter other firms commenced the business, and the results go to show that hereafter this will become a prominent source of occupation and profit."

Berkshire Boar "GEN. HANCOCK," Property of DeGraff & Hopkins, Janesville, Minnesota.
[From the *Minnesota Farmer*, vol. 1, no. 6, p. 9 (February, 1878).]

E. and H. Y. Bell, St. Paul dealers, sent pork to Chicago during the winter of 1860-61 and made a fair profit on it. The price for hauling the pork to La Crosse was a dollar a hundredweight. Thence it was sent on to Chicago by rail. Not only St. Paul, but Northfield, St. Peter, Winona, and Stillwater as well, figured in this early trade.[23]

Hogs were seldom sold alive. When freezing weather arrived the farmers had a hog-killing bee, with neighbors assisting one another, as they did at threshing time. As soon as the pork was frozen, it was taken to town, where on many a cold day the street would be lined with loads of dressed hogs. Buyers took the meat to the depot, where it was weighed and marked. When business was especially good, the railroads sometimes ran short of cars. Then if a thaw set in, the meat stored in the depot freight room was likely to turn green, and it would have to be sent to a soap factory. About 1870, men were paid from twenty-five to thirty-five cents an hour to load cars with frozen pork. Farmers generally rendered the entrails only for lard, as the leaf lard had to go with the hogs when they were sold.[24]

Prior to 1860 little if any attention was paid to any particular breed of swine. At the state fair of that year, however, a Chester White barrow attracted wide notice, and the breed took prizes at many other state fairs in 1860. It originated in Chester County, Pennsylvania, as the result of a very careful breeding of the common white hog for many years. It became larger than the popular little Suffolk, which it resembled, often weighing from five hundred to eight hundred pounds in the early 1860's. By 1861 Chester Whites were appearing on Minnesota farms, and many of the good hogs that went to market during the winter of 1860–61, eliciting "much praise," were of that breed.[25]

As time went on more interest was taken in improved breeds of swine. The lead there, as in other branches of the industry, was taken by wealthy, not average, farmers. Charles M. Reeve and William S. King of Minneapolis, Brockway Brothers of Eyota, and Charles de Graff of Janesville were among the leading swine raisers. As a result of the work of Brockway Brothers and others, the Olmsted County auditor was able to report that he believed the grade of swine in the county was improved fifty per cent between 1869 and 1871. These men were particularly interested in Essex and Berkshire swine. Reeve, in a letter dated February 2, 1877, said that he raised Berkshires, some of which he obtained from England. Although he raised 140 pigs in 1874, for two years he had been unable to fill all the orders that reached him. He received twenty-five dollars a pair for hogs four months old, fifteen for single pigs, and as high as fifty dollars each for choice sows in pig. Some of his swine were sent to Wisconsin and Iowa, and one of his pigs at

Charles A. de Graff's Farm in Waseca County
[From Andreas, *Historical Atlas of Minnesota*, 1874.]

two years weighed 502 pounds when dressed. He complained, however, that prices were very low in the state when compared with other parts of the country. De Graff, like the rest, raised some Berkshires, but he also had Chester Whites and Poland Chinas.[26]

Complaints of low prices were fairly general until the late 1870's. In 1873 the *Winona Weekly Republican* explained that the pork trade had been poor during the previous winter because of low prices, ranging from $4.00 to $4.10 a hundredweight most of the season. Such prices, however, caused farmers to devote more care to methods of fattening and more attention to improved breeds. During the season of 1872 the practice of summer packing was introduced in several of the large markets of the West, and the influence of this development was soon felt in Minnesota. Hogs could be fattened more cheaply in summer than in winter, so there was now a greater inducement to farmers to engage in the business.[27]

Another innovation of interest came with the establishment, in the spring of 1878, of a meat-packing business by Holbrook and Company of Minneapolis. This firm had a retail department where Minneapolitans could obtain for the first time the frankfurt sausage. By 1880 a large part of the Minnesota product was going to Chicago and Milwaukee, centers which maintained buyers in Minnesota and could be easily reached by rail. The cry then went up in many circles that Minnesota farmers should raise more pork and that capitalists should invest in meat packing, in order to put pork on a par with wheat in the state.[28]

The census of 1850 recorded 874 horses in the territory, a figure which included a small number of asses and mules. Pembina, Washington, and Wabasha counties accounted for the majority of the animals. In 1860 there were 17,065 horses in the state, and Minnesota ranked thirty-first in this matter among the thirty-four states. Ohio, with over 600,000 horses, was first, followed by Illinois, Indiana, New York, and Pennsylvania. In 1870 the number in Minnesota was 93,011, a percentage increase for the 1860's of 445, and the state had moved up to seventeenth place in the nation. Illinois, with over 800,000 horses, was then first, followed by Ohio, New York, Indiana, Missouri, Pennsylvania, Iowa, and Texas. By 1880 Minnesota's horse population had mounted to 257,282, for a percentage increase of 176.6 during the decade of the 1870's, and the state's position in the nation was fifteenth. Illinois, with over 1,000,000 horses, was still first; Texas had replaced Ohio in second place; Iowa was third; and Ohio, Missouri, and New York came next. There were only 13.9 horses in Minnesota per 100 of the rural population in 1860 as compared with 47.3 in 1880. An interesting contrast appears when the figures on horses are compared with those on work oxen. In 1860 there were 27,568 of these animals; in 1870, 43,176; and in 1880, only 36,344. The introduction of farm machinery, which operated more efficiently with horses, plus an improved standard of living, are closely related to the disappearance of oxen.[29]

As was the case with other farm animals, the average horse owned by pioneer Minnesotans was of a nondescript breed. For good blooded horses the state was indebted to men "not bred of farming"—Captain D. Haney of Rochester, John Farrington of St. Paul, a certain Wollgate of Fort Snelling, and Thomas Crosby of Ramsey County. Ruble Brothers of Freeborn County also raised fine horses, George S. Ruble's stallion "Red Eye" being known as the best in the state in 1861. Most experienced farmers welcomed these men as friends and benefactors.[30]

Although Morgans were in greatest favor during the 1850's, in time other breeds became popular in the region. As late as 1863, however, all the horses shown at the Minnesota State Fair were Morgans or Morgan crosses. At the 1870 fair, which was held in Winona, fine Clydesdales and Percherons were shown, but not until 1875 were the latter in considerable numbers exhibited at the state fair. Leonard Johnson of Castle Rock, Dr. O. O. Evans of Minneapolis, and S. B. Spearin of Empire exhibited Percherons, and the breed drew considerable comment in the press. The horses, however, were described as "huge creatures," and the general opinion was that they were "too large and clumsy and would cost too much to maintain to be of much use to Minnesota farmers." Spearin's gray draught stallion "Sensation" weighed two thousand pounds and stood eighteen hands high.[31]

Two enemies that particularly jeopardized farm horses in the

Percheron Norman Stallion Imported from France in 1876 [From the *Minnesota Farmer*, vol. 2, no. 1, p. 35 (September, 1878).]

pioneer period were thieves and disease. The disease that was most widely publicized was "epizoot," or "epizooty," which struck in southern Minnesota in November and December, 1872, and rapidly became epidemic. Veterinaries said it was acute catarrh and influenza, and that it originated in eastern Canada, where thousands of horses died. Next it appeared in the eastern states, and then it spread westward. Cities were especially hard hit. In the latter part of December, 1872, nearly all business in some counties was at a standstill because of the "epizooty." It was said that the best treatment was to give afflicted horses perfect rest and keep them warm and dry. They were to be fed no hay, oats, corn, nor barley, but only warm bran mash mixed with a little oat or rye straw. A small dose of bromide of potassium two or three times a day in the mash for the first two or three days was recommended, as was tar on the trough, manger, and horse's nose. Fewer horses actually died of the disease in Minnesota than in some other areas.[32]

Various associations were formed from time to time to combat horse thieves. In southern Minnesota thieves were extremely active in the 1860's and 1870's, and they were not unknown elsewhere. One such organization, the Waseca County Horse Thief Detectives, founded in 1864, continues to hold meetings and collect membership dues after more than eighty years. In March, 1872, the Anti-Horse Thief Association of Fergus Falls was organized, although, according to one writer, "there was not a horse in town valuable enough to tempt the most ornery horse thief." The tenth bylaw of the organization read as follows: "It shall be the sworn duty of any and all members of this society capturing a horse thief having in his possession the property of any member of the association, to promptly execute the said horse thief, by hanging, or in the absence of facilities for hanging, by shooting, or in any other manner, but in any and all events to take such effective measures as shall preclude the possibility of the return of said horse thief to commit any further depredations in the county."[33]

The interest in beef cattle during the 1850's and 1860's has been noted. In 1850 there were 1,395 cattle other than milch cows in Minnesota Territory, mainly in Washington, Pembina, Wabasha, and Ramsey counties. Ten years later the figure had increased to 51,345, and Minnesota ranked thirty-first in beef cattle production among the thirty-four states of the Union. Texas was far and away in the lead, with over 2,700,000 head of cattle. Illinois, with over 970,000 head was second, followed by California, Ohio, New York, and Pennsylvania. The increase in the number of cattle in Minnesota for the 1860's was 183.8 per cent, a smaller relative gain than for any other class of stock, except swine and work oxen. In absolute numbers, however, cattle ranked second to hogs. The total for 1870 was only 145,736, and Minnesota was twenty-fourth among the states in beef cattle production. Texas was still in the lead, but its total had gone up to only a little over 2,900,000 head. Illinois, with over 1,050,000 head, was still second, and Ohio, Missouri, New York, Indiana, Iowa, and Pennsylvania trailed in that order. During the 1870's Minnesota's beef cattle population grew to 347,161, a gain of 138.2 per cent, yet the state was still twenty-fourth on the list of beef cattle producing states. Texas then produced more than 3,300,000 head; Iowa had jumped into second place, with over 1,750,000 head; Illinois, with over 1,500,000 head, was third; Missouri was close behind, with more than 1,400,000 head; and Ohio and Kansas trailed, with slightly over 1,000,000 head each. In 1860 there were 41.9 cattle for every 100 country people in Minnesota, and in 1880 there were 63.9, though cattle still ranked second to hogs in numbers.[34]

The most popular breed of cattle in the early years was the Shorthorn or Durham. Well-known Shorthorn raisers were De Graff and Hopkins of the Lake Elysian Stock Farm at Janesville, N. P. Clark of St. Cloud, H. F. Brown of Minneapolis, Brockway Brothers of Eyota, George H. Smith of Carlton County, Dr. Charles W. Ballard of Albert Lea, and William S. King of Minneapolis. The latter gained international recognition. In 1868 he purchased some blooded stock in New York for his farm, located three miles from Minneapolis. Included were the "Sixth Duke of Geneva," a pure Duchess bull costing three thousand dollars, and "Blush," a Shorthorn cow. About the same time King also bought some Ayrshires and some Jerseys. By 1869 his was said to be one of the three most valuable herds in the United States. "Mr. King's enterprise will become historic as the pioneer adventure, on a comprehensive scale, in this highly classic department of Minnesota husbandry," read one press comment.[35]

In 1874, when King disposed of his herd of Shorthorns in Chicago, the sale received wide publicity, and it attracted buyers from as far away as England. The cows and heifers sold at an average

THE SHORT-HORN COW "BLUSH," THE PROPERTY OF COL. WM. S. KING.—COST $1,000
[From the *Farmers' Union*, September, 1869.]

price of $1,730, and the bulls at $1,210. For one bull, the "2 Duke of Hillhurse," King was offered $14,000, which was said to be the highest figure ever quoted on a bull, but the deal fell through and the animal was taken back to Minnesota. Fifty-eight cows and twenty-one bulls were sold for a total of $126,990. After the sale King still retained a fine herd of cattle in Meeker County.[36]

Dr. Charles W. Ballard wrote from Albert Lea, on January 14, 1877, that drovers traveling through Minnesota to buy stock to fatten in Illinois and Iowa could not obtain as good cattle as were available ten years before, even though the number of cattle was increasing. Steers two and one-half years old averaged from 700 to 800 pounds and heifers from 650 to 700 pounds. The reasons for the condition were lack of good care and the use of poor bulls throughout the state. Bulls were prohibited by law from running at large, but since many people figured that all animals under two years of age were calves, yearling bulls were found ranging with nearly every herd. The amount of pasture was being reduced each year, and prices were low during the 1870's. Of purebred cattle, Dr. Ballard claimed, Minnesota had produced fewer than 500, among which Shorthorns predominated. The American herd book of 1876 showed that breeders of the state had recorded only 49 bulls of their own raising, and of those probably a third had been sold out of the state. About 150 bulls were imported. Dr. Ballard makes it clear that, so far as breeding methods were concerned, the average farmer had not progressed far beyond his predecessor of the 1850's. In 1876 at public sales 774 Shorthorn bulls were sold in Minnesota at an average price of $242, and 3,230 cows brought an average price of $365.[37]

In addition to Shorthorns, Ayrshires, and Jerseys, other breeds, such as Guernsey, Galloway, Holstein, and Angus cattle, appeared as dairying began to develop. At the state fair of 1873 Shorthorns, Ayrshires, Alderneys, and Jerseys were represented, while Shorthorns and Alderneys were the leading breeds at the fair of the next year. In 1883 James J. Hill drew upon his herd, which had a national reputation, for the only showing of Polled Angus, and J. C. Easton entered the only exhibit of Scotch Galloways. A. V. Ellis of the Evergreen Stock Farm at Austin received credit for first introducing and breeding Holsteins in Minnesota.[38]

Fencing was a problem that sooner or later confronted most stockmen. At first stock were fenced out, not in. As one man put it: "In those days we used a great deal of board fencing as all our cultivated land had to be fenced in, all stock being allowed to run at large." Another, writing in the spring of 1867, complained that the "Legislature did not see fit to compel us to restrain our cattle, therefore we must fence our crops." At times local communities took action. At Waseca, for example, the subject aroused much debate among the people and the city fathers in 1868; and, as a result, on July 22 an ordinance was passed providing that cattle, horses, mules, or sheep found running at large within the village between one hour after sunset and the following sunrise should be impounded by the poundmaster, marshal, street commissioner, or constable. This was better than no law, but it was poor protection for gardens and lawns.[39]

In his message to the legislature in 1873, Governor Austin recommended "that the several counties or towns be authorized to determine for themselves the vexed question of 'fencing in or fencing out' livestock." Finally, in 1874, a herd law applying to certain parts of the state was enacted. Under its terms a farmer had no redress for damage done to his crops by stock in the daytime unless he could prove that he had a three-rail fence four feet high on the side from which the cattle entered. A law of 1878 gave the farmer damages whether or not he had a fence. Thus it became necessary to keep stock in fenced enclosures or to send them to ranges away from the farming district. Something of a business of summer herding was built up. The usual charge for herding stock from May 15 to October 15 was from a dollar to a dollar and a quarter a head. Some herders even went out of the state into Dakota.[40]

Another problem that the raiser of beef cattle had to face was how to market his animals. During the middle 1860's, for example, large herds of cattle were driven annually to Chicago from Blue Earth County. When the railroad was completed to the county it proved of great assistance in getting livestock to market. By 1880 the Twin Cities were the chief market and slaughtering center, and St. Paul soon took precedence over Minneapolis. In St. Paul there were three well-equipped stockyards, through which more than 28,000 head of cattle passed in 1878. By 1882 the livestock and dressed meat business of the city was valued at $3,515,700.[41] By that time the dairy industry had made great strides in the state.

The Beginnings of Dairying

When the subject of dairying is mentioned today it is natural to think of Minnesota, for its farms and creameries have placed it among the leaders in that branch of husbandry. Were the subject being discussed in the 1860's, however, few would have thought of Minnesota in this connection. It was not until the 1880's that dairying really began to make strides in the state, and even then wheat attracted more attention. A glance at Minnesota dairying as it existed before the middle eighties should prove interesting, and it should also serve to highlight the development which has since taken place.

In 1850 there were recorded in Minnesota Territory, which included part of what is now the Dakotas, 607 milk cows, a figure that probably is not accurate. By 1860 the state had 40,444 cows, and in 1870 the figure was 121,467, an increase for the decade of slightly more than two hundred per cent. During the 1870's progress was not so rapid, for in 1880 reports showed 275,545 cows in the state. Minnesota then ranked fifteenth among the states in this respect. New York was first, with more than 1,400,000 cows, followed by Illinois, Iowa, and Pennsylvania. In general, as would be expected, there was a high correlation between the number of cows at any particular time and the production of butter, milk, and cheese. An exception to this, however, was the increase in the production of factory-made cheese in the state during the 1870's, which was far more rapid than the increase in the number of cows.[1]

Dairying, as carried on by the average farmer of the pioneer period, was primitive indeed. During the cold winter months all dairy products were at a premium; but "when the winter broke and the spring grasses started, in May, the old cow was expected to 'come across,' deliver a calf and start her flow of milk, which she did, and another season of corn meal mush and milk opened up." A dugout or cellar served as a milk room. The milk was set in shallow pans or earthen crocks, which were placed on racks or some cheap structure. After the milk had set the cream was skimmed off, and the milk was fed to the family, the pigs, or the calves. The cream was placed in a dash churn and made into butter, a strenuous job.[2]

The quality of the butter produced varied greatly. Each farm wife seemed to have her own method of making the product, and the newspapers of the early period were filled with recipes for buttermaking. Generally, however, the homemade product was of a low grade, and many women refused to learn better methods. F. A. Richardson of Austin told members of the Minnesota Butter, Cheese, and Dairy Stock Association in 1883: "I have not forgotten instructions given me more than twenty years ago by my employer while behind the counter. Said he, 'you may strike a woman's child, abuse her husband before her face, but *never* find fault with her butter,' and I have seen it illustrated. A young man attempted to test a crock of butter by smelling of it, when the woman gave him a slap on the back of his head of sufficient force to leave an impression of his smelling organ in the butter."[3]

When a supply of good butter was obtained by a merchant, it often occasioned comment in the press. For example, in 1861 Watson and Eastman of St. Paul received a lot of excellent butter from Steele County, an incident which prompted one farm journal to remark: "We have seen so much poor butter in our market that we have sometimes half believed a superior article could not be made in our State. Not unfrequently have we purchased what the merchants would call a first rate article, which our women folks, who were brought up on Vermont butter, would not have on the table. No doubt most of what has been sent to our market has been made by women who knew but little, if anything, about the nice art of butter making."[4]

When butter was taken out of the churn, it was placed on a wooden tray and washed, worked, and patted with a hand ladle. Then it was salted and placed in a jar, to be kept for home use or taken to a store and traded at from six to ten cents a pound for family necessities. Some women skimmed their sweet cream for butter, and some waited until the milk had turned to clabber. Many cellars and root houses in which milk was kept lacked ventilation, and the milk was often allowed to stand near decaying vegetables, all of which did not help the quality of the butter. Store owners as a rule paid a better price for good than for poor butter, but they tried to keep quiet about this practice. Customers soon became aware of differences in quality, and they asked for Mrs. So-and-So's butter. Often, however, all butter obtained would be mixed in a common container, the good with the bad, and the customer had to take what he could get. The frontier stores of the 1850's and 1860's had no iceboxes and their cellars were not always the best. Sometimes a man would buy all the butter in a given store and throw it together.

[From the *American Agriculturist*, 41:40 (January, 1882).]

Then he would churn it in sweet milk, add other ingredients, and sell the resultant product to cheap boardinghouses. No wonder some people detested the taste of butter.[5]

The experiences of one or two early farmers in the dairying business may prove enlightening. H. J. Brainard of Little Canada related some of his experiences in a letter written in 1869. From 1853 to 1868 he kept from forty to a hundred and fifty milk cows. For several years he experimented with feed. At first he used hay, which by 1869 he considered little better than oat straw. One fall he fed his cows white turnips, which later he believed were injurious to the animals. Finally he found corn fodder to be a fine winter feed, fourteen acres of drilled corn sufficing to feed forty head of cattle. By feeding his cows corn rather than hay he saved from five to eight hundred dollars in a single winter, and his cows gave a larger quantity of milk. Brainard also fed his cattle barley grains from breweries, brans, and a mixture of a pint of corn to five pints of oats. He concluded that "dairy and stock farming, properly conducted, is a profitable business in Minnesota, notwithstanding the length and severity of our winters." [6]

H. P. Van Cleve, in a letter of March 8, 1861, from Long Prairie, wrote that the cows he reserved for family use the preceding summer furnished 650 pounds of butter, besides cheese, milk, and cream for from sixteen to eighteen persons. His butter alone paid for cutting and hauling hay for all his cattle and horses. "A careful estimate of the value of the increase of my stock, after deducting losses, has convinced me that I have realized from my cows fifty per cent. per annum, for four years," he wrote. He added that the "losses referred to were four calves destroyed by wolves, about three years since; and during this winter one young cow drowned, and one gored to death by another; not one by sickness or poverty." [7]

At a meeting of the Glencoe Farmers' Club on June 5, 1869, dairying was discussed. One farmer said he could put into his cheese vat milk from fifty cows at a cost of four cents a gallon. He estimated the cost of keeping a cow at $12.50 a year, and stated that she would give at least three hundred gallons of milk during that time. That amount of milk would produce three hundred pounds of cheese, which would bring twelve and a half cents a pound, or $37.50. Whey and butter would be worth at least $10 more, leaving a profit of $35 a cow. [8]

But dairying was not easy. One pioneer recalled that he had to care for thirty-three head of cattle one winter and that it took nearly

THE BEGINNINGS OF DAIRYING

all day to do the chores. He had to carry hay from stacks to the cattle in the stables, and for water he had to drive them to a spring on a neighbor's farm.[9]

Just when the first butter was exported from the state is difficult to determine. From scattered notices in the press it is apparent that the amount sold elsewhere increased constantly after 1860. A St. Peter newspaper of 1861 reported that twenty thousand pounds of butter would be shipped from that community during the current season, adding that "Minnesota, by and by, will be able to butter the bread for five millions of people." In 1869, after the opening of the Union Pacific Railroad, parties from California were in the state buying butter for the California market. This was good news to Minnesotans, since in the East, California competed with Minnesota in the wheat market.[10] Generally speaking, however, the lack of a dairy market held back the industry until after 1870, or even later, and the local store remained the main market for any surplus a farmer might have.

The first record that the present writer has found of cheese marketed in St. Paul was in 1852, but this was evidently a small amount. Yet it was sufficient to inspire a paper to prophesy: "We confidently expect soon to see large dairies in Minnesota. Climate, grass, water, everything is favorable to dairies. We have sometimes thought . . . that sometime Minnesota would be *the Dairy* land of the West." In 1859 the *Glencoe Democrat* reported that a few citizens at that place had turned their attention toward the manufacture of cheese. John H. Stevens remarked at the time that it had been eighteen years since he had lived where cheese was made. Cows had been too scarce on the frontier for cheese making.[11]

About 1868, some sixteen years after the first cheese factory was erected in New York, the first cheese factories in Minnesota were established. One at Owatonna attracted considerable attention. The plant was owned by Horton and Case, and the superintendent was C. W. Richardson, late of Erie County, New York. The building measured thirty by forty feet, with a wing eighteen by forty that was used as an engine room. The boiler of a twelve-horsepower steam engine was used to heat two cheese vats, each of which held

A Cheese Factory at Eyota, 1874
[From Andreas, *Historical Atlas of Minnesota*, 118.]

six hundred gallons. There was space for a third of the same size. The milk of six hundred cows, obtained within a radius of four miles, was used each day. The factory was conducted on a co-operative basis, each farmer receiving dividends according to the amount of milk he furnished. The proprietors received two cents a pound for making and selling the cheese, plus "all the butter which is obtained from the whey, by a new process." According to the *Minnesota Monthly,* there was a big demand for cheese both in the United States and in Europe. "Dairy farming, properly conducted," advised the *Monthly,* "is everywhere prosperous, and is soon to become, we think, an important branch of Minnesota husbandry. We hope so." From 1870 on, cheese factories multiplied rapidly, and within a period of less than ten years Minnesota cheese ranked with the best.[12]

The reputation of Minnesota butter, however, developed slowly, and butter factories were established later and less rapidly than cheese factories, not only in the state, but in the country as a whole. The first one was built in Orange County, New York, in 1861. As late as 1877 butter factories in Minnesota were considered something new. They were conducted on an associated plan. Milk was taken to the factories twice a day in cans, which were emptied and then refilled with sour milk for use on the farms. Among the state's earliest butter manufacturing concerns was the Langdon Butter and Cheese Factory Company, which was organized in January, 1876, as a joint stock company at Cottage Grove. The building and apparatus cost $4,500. Milk from two hundred cows was used during the first season, and fifty-two thousand pounds of cheese and three hundred pounds of butter were made and sold in St. Paul. It took nine and a half pounds of milk to make a pound of cheese and twenty-two and a quarter pounds for one of butter.[13]

Just as cheese and butter factories were being established in Minnesota, the dairy interests received a setback. In 1878 there was a big drop in dairy prices. Cheese fell to six and seven cents, and butter also dropped. Some blamed the decline on overproduction, especially of the common grades of cheese and butter, while others said it was due to the introduction of oleomargarine. Both factors, plus the depression of the 1870's, contributed to the situation. The decline in prices hit the cheese business harder than it did butter making. The production of cheese in 1880 was the smallest in ten years. In that year the state had forty-nine cheese factories, mainly in two regions. One group was in Dodge, Olmsted, and adjacent counties, the heart of the early wheat belt, where diversified farming was being introduced. The other was in the region east of the Mississippi, where wheat raising never had been very successful. Few cheese factories were located on main waterways or near cities, for in such areas it was more profitable to market butter or milk. On the other hand, cheese could be produced in remote districts, since it was less perishable than butter or milk.[14]

As late as 1879 there were many complaints about the quality of butter. The *Minnesota Farmer* bemoaned the fact that it did "not know of a single dairyman in the state, who makes what is generally considered a first rate article." The highest price paid for local butter went to George Morrison of Fairvale Farm, Minneapolis, and yet his product brought only thirty-five cents a pound among "select consumers." Wells creamery butter retailed at thirty cents, and Langdon's butter at about twenty cents a pound. In some other states, according to the *Minnesota Farmer,* butter was made that retailed at from fifty cents to a dollar a pound. Despite the low price paid for its product, the Langdon Butter and Cheese Factory was awarded the first premium for butter by the Minnesota Dairymen's Association at its 1879 meeting. With its entry, the factory submitted the following description of the method used in making its butter: "Skimmed the milk at thirty-six hours' setting; mixed the morning and evening cream together; let it stand twelve hours, stirring it often; and then churned; temperature of churning-room, thirty-eight degrees; time of churning, forty-five minutes; draw off the buttermilk; work the butter until the water is quite clear, then place the butter upon the worker and press gently with the lever until the butter is level; then add seventeen ounces of salt to twenty pounds of butter; then work until it grains right; pack in tubs directly from the worker, the result of each churning."[15]

W. A. Van Styke of St. Paul, who was said to handle more butter than anyone else in the state, estimated that Minnesotans produced five hundred pounds of poor butter to one of really good butter. It was difficult to induce the average farmer to improve the quality of his butter; yet the same farmer often thought that the butter buyer was trying to cheat him. One man, whose butter was extremely poor, said to a buyer at Owatonna: "You get lots of poor butter here; you go around to the stores and buy it and send it to Minneapolis and St. Paul and get forty cents a pound for it, and make thirty cents a pound; you are rich and I am poor and hardly make enough to buy my clothes and poor clothes at that!" In justice to the farmers, it should be pointed out that many buyers obtained unsalted butter at low prices and mixed it with Wells-Richardson's butter coloring, the staple article used "from ocean to ocean" for making white butter an even yellow color.[16]

Despite low prices, malpractices, and poor products, the dairy interests of the state were on the march by the late 1870's. One evidence of their development was the organization of associations to stimulate the industry. In 1878 the State Dairymen's Association was organized, fifteen years after the American Dairymen's Association united producers in the region east of Indiana; and in 1882 the Minnesota Butter and Cheese Association had its inception. The growth of dairying was due not only to natural evolution from the 1850's, but also to the fact that wheat farming was becoming increasingly unprofitable in some of the older sections of the state. Exhortations to farmers to diversify their agriculture appeared in the press almost as soon as the territory was organized, and the number of appeals increased rapidly after 1870. Farmers, however, were slow to adjust to new conditions until a change became absolutely imperative. Dr. E. C. Cross of Rochester, in an address of welcome to members of the Butter and Cheese Association in 1882, said: "Our lands are not seeded with grasses for hay or grazing, barns and comfortable stables unbuilt, and secure yards unprovided. We have not cows enough to make dairying profitable, and are generally ignorant of the best breeds and grades for milking uses. Much time and capital are necessary to convert the grain into a live stock farm. The change must be made slowly; yet we feel that the time is at hand when many of the grain elevators on the line of our railroads must give place to stock yards, and cattle cars become more common on the great lines of transportation from the Northwest." And Charles E. Marvin concurred: "In Minnesota at the present time, there seems to exist the same necessity for a change in the methods of farming, as has existed in some of the older and now more prosperous states." [17]

Slowly but surely economic forces, plus the efforts of enlightened and prosperous farmers, wrought the transition from wheat raising to dairying. Azro P. McKinstry of Winnebago City was sometimes described as the "first creamery man, perhaps in the State." In December, 1880, he proposed that if the farmers would bring in their cream he would do the churning. That was continued until spring, when he sent out teams of his own to gather cream. At first the farmers did not respond well, but as time went on their interest heightened, and by 1883 McKinstry's cream route extended as far as eighteen miles from Winnebago City. He kept from sixty to seventy-five head of Holsteins and Jerseys, and raised only enough grain for his own use. [18]

By the summer of 1883 there were more than seventy creameries in successful operation in Minnesota, and their products were known in the markets of New York and Boston. In 1884, when Mower County had four creameries in full operation, the benefits derived from them were the subject of comment. Eastern and foreign epicures were said to "readily pay forty and fifty cents per pound" for creamery butter, which they preferred "to the time-honored 'country butter' we used to brag about at an inferior price. Time was when 'farm butter' was king, but since the advent of creameries the product of the home dairy has lost caste, and cannot compete with the more modern article in quality nor price. A few years since the good farmers' wives of Mower County were glad to realize six to eight cents per pound for their butter, after performing all the labor of milking, caring for the cream, churning, packing and delivering at the store counter." [19]

No longer did the farmer have to take his milk and cream to the skimming station or cheese and butter factory. All he had to do was set the milk aside in cans furnished by the creamery. By 1880 the best can was that known as the "shotgun can." It was from eighteen to twenty inches high and eight inches in diameter, with a glass gauge on one side to show the number of inches of cream in the container. The can was so built that one inch of cream when churned would produce one pound of butter. The farmer of the early 1880's usually received from fifteen to eighteen cents for each inch of cream. As in other fields, however, the farmer was slow to use new equipment, and pans and crocks were not uncommon in 1880 and later.[20]

The age of mechanization in the dairy business was still in the future. At the meeting of the Butter and Cheese Association in 1882 the following products and articles were on exhibit: Ashton's Imported Dairy Salt, Higgin's Eureka Imported Dairy Salt, a dairy tank, Peerless Butter Color, Perry's Concentrated Butter Color, June Golden Butter Color, Calkin's Milk Cooler and Creamer, Haney's Creamer, P. S. Mont's Ventilated Cooler, a tin and wood butter package, a cream gauge, a transportation cream can, Bennett Brothers' Butter Worker, a combined milk and cream strainer, cooler, and setter, C. C. Buell's Graduating, Self-Ventilating Milk Can and Cooler, a barrel churn, the Belle City Feed Cutler, Hewe's Air Pressure Creamer, a square box churn, the Davis Swing Churn, and a new process linseed meal. None of the articles listed represented anything more than an improvement over primitive hand methods. The De Laval cream separator, invented in Europe in the late 1870's, and the Babcock cream tester, perfected about 1890, did not appear in Minnesota until late in the century.[21]

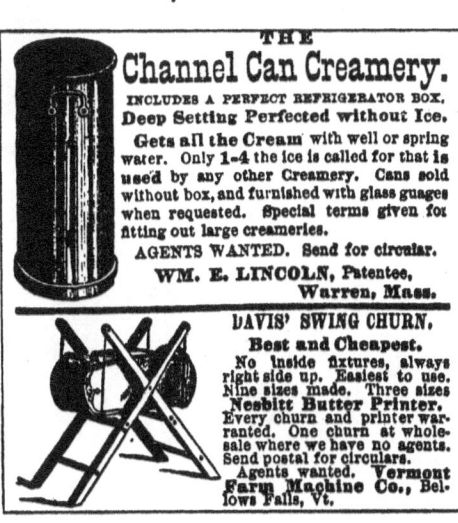

[From the *American Agriculturist*, 41:136 (March, 1882).]

Since there was no scientific method for testing the butterfat content of cream, disputes between farmers and creamerymen were frequent. Some farmers thought that creamerymen were getting rich by cheating the farmer; others devised methods for cheating the creameryman. Cream would be filled with air by stirring it, or it would be kept until it was sour, which would make the butterfat content appear greater than it actually was. In their defense creamerymen said that sometimes they had men collecting cream at a

[From the *Minnesota Farmer*, vol. 1, no. 9, p. 20 (May, 1878).]

wage of two dollars a day on a route of from thirty-two to thirty-four miles, who might come in with only sixteen or eighteen inches of cream; and one man said that in 1882 it cost him six cents a pound to gather cream. In the early 1880's some Minnesota creamerymen adopted the Schoch and Bolender system of testing cream. It consisted of "taking a half inch (56½ cubic inches) of each patron's cream, churning and weighing the butter by itself, thus determining the amount of butter he should be paid for." [22] After adopting this system, both farmers and creamerymen seemed better satisfied. In this connection it should be remembered that the early creameries were private or joint stock concerns. Co-operative creameries, for which Minnesota is now so well known, had not yet appeared.

By 1882 the breeds of cattle most commonly found in the state were Shorthorn Durham, Jersey, and Ayrshire. There were some Herefords, a few Polled Angus, and some Devons, but only a very few Holsteins. Much strife, some of which was personal, arose between owners of various breeds, especially of Shorthorns and Herefords. Leading dairymen contended that to be profitable a cow must give at least five thousand pounds of milk a year, an amount sufficient to make about two hundred pounds of butter. Too many "blizzard cows" were to be found—cows that could stand ill treatment and adverse weather conditions, but could not produce enough butterfat to be profitable. Furthermore, there were too few cows, only two and a half per farm in 1883. In that year N. C. McLean of Frontenac advised farmers to raise Jerseys for butter, Holsteins for butter and cheese, and Shorthorns for beef.[23]

Certain nationality groups were closely identified with dairy enterprises. Swiss settlers developed the cheese industry, and the Danes tended to go into butter making. The latter, particularly, established themselves in a leading position in the Minnesota dairy industry by their pioneer work in the Clarks Grove vicinity. During the early 1880's agriculture in that area was carried on in much the same manner as it was in other communities. Then in 1884 Hans Peter Jensen, a Danish immigrant of 1865, made a visit to Denmark, an event which was to be of great significance to the future of dairying in Minnesota. In his homeland he found that the dairy industry had made remarkable strides since he left for America, and that it was far in advance of the industry in Minnesota. In 1882 a co-operative dairy was established at Hjedding, Jutland, and from there the co-operative movement spread over Denmark. This development greatly impressed Jensen, who "made it the subject of many conversations with his friends" when he returned to his adopted home. In 1890 his work and that of his friends bore fruit when the famed Clarks Grove creamery, one of the first co-operative creameries in the state, was organized.[24]

Some of the men interested in developing dairying deserve special mention. In addition to McLean, McKinstry, and Jensen, there were Charles E. Marvin of Rochester, J. M. Thurston of Redwood Falls, H. M. Burchard of Marshall, G. W. Van Dusen of Rochester, Oren C. Gregg of Lyon County, W. C. Rice of Goodhue, Moses Hutchinson of Owatonna, Samuel Deering of St. Paul, and C. H. Chadbourn of Rochester. This list is not exhaustive, but it includes some of the most articulate and active proponents of dairying. Deering, for example, operated a seventy-five acre dairy farm about a mile and a quarter west of St. Paul, which was worth about $45,000. On his place were three barns, one of which was for his purebred Shorthorns, and he employed four men.[25]

The bugbear of the dairyman was oleomargarine. In 1884–85 leading commission men estimated that four million pounds of it were sold in Minnesota. The legislature of 1881 passed a law providing that all packages of counterfeit butter should be marked with the word "oleomargarine," but it neglected to appropriate money to carry the law into effect. Hence it was a dead letter. The addition of water to milk was another problem for the dairyman, and as a result a law was enacted on March 5, 1885, "to prohibit and prevent the sale or manufacture of unhealthy or adulterated dairy products." Less than a month later the law providing for a state dairy commissioner went into effect. Then, on November 11, 1886, the Minnesota supreme court, in the case of Butler *v.* Chambers, upheld the law prohibiting the sale of adulterated milk and butter substitutes. Minnesota was the first state to prohibit such sales.[26]

But evidence of the success of the state's dairy interests was to be found in places other than legislative halls and court chambers. In the winter of 1884–85, at the World's Industrial and Cotton Centennial Exposition at New Orleans, Minnesota won the highest award for a display of dairy products, including the "grand sweepstakes" for the best butter and the "grand diploma of honor" for an educational exhibit. What satisfaction this award must have given such men as Charles E. Marvin and O. C. Gregg![27]

The New Orleans award was symptomatic of the future of the industry—that it lay with the butter rather than with the cheese producers, although factory cheese led factory butter production until 1885. One writer has given eight reasons for the victory of butter over cheese: There were few Swiss in the state; Minnesota farmers, interested in enlarging their herds, were raising young stock, and for feeding it they needed skim milk, a byproduct of butter; the early leaders of the University of Minnesota school of agriculture encouraged butter rather than cheese factories; the school also favored butter production because of the feeding value of skim milk; New York and Wisconsin had become leaders in cheese production; cheese was bulkier in relation to its value and more expensive to transport than butter; the mechanical separator favored the development of butter; and the fact that cheese had to be cured caused returns to be slow in reaching the farmer.[28]

By 1885 dairying had become an extensive Minnesota industry. There were sixty-three creameries and forty-six cheese factories in the state, and the dairy farmer had become something of a political power. Ten years later a leading St. Paul journal proclaimed that the "most remarkable feature in the recent development of the State of Minnesota is beyond doubt the progress made in the dairying industry." That progress would not have taken place had not the pioneer farmer and his wife laid solid foundations upon which the later dairyman, equipped with the De Laval separator and the Babcock tester, could build. The frontier farmer, striving at first to provide dairy products for his family and later producing a surplus for an expanding market, had placed Minnesota on the threshold of a development which was to make it one of the most productive and progressive dairy states in the Union.[29]

Bizarre Experiments and Sound Agriculture

Prior to 1860, the approximate date when the state embarked upon specialized wheat farming, various expedients were tried by Minnesota farmers in their search for the best means of making a livelihood. Among the stories of this search none is more interesting than that of the ginseng episode in the Big Woods region in the lean years of 1858 and 1859. Ginseng, found an inch or so below the surface of the ground and between the roots of trees, was used by the Chinese for medicinal purposes. From the middle 1840's on, the trade in "sang," as it was called, was controlled by a firm in Philadelphia, which secured the product mainly in western Virginia and Pennsylvania, at the rate of sixty cents a pound in the raw state in Philadelphia. The early settler in Minnesota was an exception, however, if he had ever heard of ginseng; yet this product was destined to be of value to some of his fellow pioneers.

The years 1857 and 1858 were disastrous to most Minnesotans in the Big Woods region, as they were to settlers in other sections where the panic and grasshoppers raised havoc. Many were about to leave the region when a certain Robert Blaine of Virginia appeared, told the people about ginseng, showed them how to dig it, and offered to buy all they dug at six cents a pound. The farmers naturally were skeptical at first, and some dug "sang" secretly on Sundays to avoid "joshings" by neighbors. But Blaine paid cash for baskets, dirt and all, and so more and more persons began to dig, and agencies were put in operation in Buffalo, Kingston, Rockford, Monticello, Minnetonka, and Watertown. Some men and boys made from two to five dollars a day in this pursuit, and farmers found it more profitable to go "sanging" than to harvest crops. Many settlers even paid for their land by selling ginseng. Finally, one summer Blaine failed to come back, and local merchants wrote to

Chinese agents concerning the price of ginseng. When the answer was received that the price of the product had always been sixty cents a pound, the natives realized that "sucker," once their name for Blaine, had been applied to the wrong person. "The medical profession denies that ginseng has any medical value whatever," said one writer. "It is wrong; ginseng once cured an acute attack of Wright County gossip." In Anoka County ginseng digging continued to be important until 1863. St. Peter was the leading depot of the Minnesota Valley for the collection and preparation of the plant, and it was shipped out of the state chiefly from St. Paul and Hastings.[1]

There were other bizarre experiments during the 1850's, like those tried by early English colonists on the Atlantic seaboard, but these proved far less successful even than ginseng. According to the census of 1860, in the previous year 412 gallons of wine, 3,286 pounds of rice, and 52 pounds of silk cocoons were produced in the state. No doubt some enthusiasts viewed Minnesota as a future producer of exotics, but, of course, such visions were not destined to be fulfilled. The *Weekly Pioneer and Democrat,* nevertheless, tried to awaken Minnesotans to the possibilities of utilizing the state's resources of osier willows, sarsaparilla, and spikenard, the latter being used for spring beer and for anointing beards.[2]

A much sounder basis for later agriculture was found in the production of old staples, such as corn, oats, potatoes, barley, and rye. Indeed, the earliest farmers of the state, in the 1840's and 1850's, carried on a much more diversified agriculture than did most of their successors in the period between 1860 and 1880. In 1849 the main crops of Minnesota were oats, 30,582 bushels produced on thirty-seven per cent of the total area under cultivation; potatoes, 21,145 bushels grown on twenty-six per cent of the area; corn, 16,725 bushels contributed by twenty per cent of the area; and peas and beans, 10,002 bushels produced on twelve per cent of the area. The remaining five per cent of the arable land yielded some 3,400 bushels of various crops. Wheat had not yet come into vogue, and the crops grown were those mainly suited to local use. Agriculture was in large part in the subsistence stage, except near towns and lumber camps.[3]

As has been indicated, the farmers of Minnesota were incapable of feeding the territory's population during most of the 1850's.[4] Hence, prices of farm products were high during the early days of the territory. In 1849, corn and oats retailed at from fifty to seventy-five cents a bushel most of the time, and potatoes brought from seventy-five cents to a dollar a bushel. And, as was the case with winter wheat, many people doubted the success of corn raising in Minnesota, although one man declared: "Corn grows as well as in Southern Ohio. *Oats will average fifty bushels to the acre. . . . Remember I speak what I know, and not from the say so of others.*"[5]

James M. Goodhue never missed an opportunity to call to his readers' attention examples of successful corn growing in the territory. "Speaking of corn," he wrote, "Mr. Wm. Middleton, a farmer living a few miles southeast of us . . . has raised this year [*1850*] upon his farm, 90 bushels of Indian corn per acre." This corn was the large twelve-rowed, Pennsylvania flint variety. Governor Gorman, in an address before the Benton County Agricultural Society in January, 1854, reported that during 1853 twenty-five thousand bushels of corn were grown in Minnesota, at an average of fifty bushels to the acre. The safest and best varieties to grow, he suggested, were Golden Sioux or Northern Yellow Flint, Eight-Rowed Yellow, Canada Early White, Tuscarora, White Flour, and Rhode Island White Flint.[6]

Some farmers planted dent corn, also, in the 1850's. C. A. Sherwin of Belle Plaine, in a letter dated January 17, 1858, said that farmers around his vicinity grew white and yellow dent corn principally, as in Ohio, Illinois, and Indiana, where most of the seed was obtained. The dent corn ripened, he reported, if it was planted about May 20. The yellow flint, on the other hand, did not have to be planted before June 15, and it appeared to be better adapted to Minnesota than dent. For example, a "Mr. J." of Kaposia in 1857 raised seven acres of dent and secured only 250 bushels of corn at harvest. The next year he decided to plant flint.[7]

Some men tried corn breeding experiments in the 1850's in an attempt to develop a corn best suited to the soil and climate of Minnesota. An example was William B. Dodd who lived near St. Peter. About 1855 he began mixing King Philip Dent with two or more

BIZARRE EXPERIMENTS AND SOUND AGRICULTURE

other kinds in an effort to secure an early maturing and heavy yielding corn, and by 1860 he had achieved some success. The rural members of the state legislature got together and discussed corn varieties. Several said dent corn would ripen, but that it might freeze in the crib over winter, while flint corn was liable to rot. It was the consensus that King Philip corn ripened well, but that it was well liked by the blackbirds because of its open husks. The most favored kinds seem to have been the "Canada" varieties, which some of the legislators believed were best suited to Minnesota.[8]

By 1859, according to the census of 1860, the state produced 2,941,952 bushels of corn, or 2,401 bushels for every hundred persons in the country population, a ratio exceeded by none of the other bushel crops or small grains; and the crop would have been larger if it had not been partially destroyed by an early frost. Corn was grown as far north as Stearns County, but relatively little of it was exported from the state—40,376 bushels in 1859, to be exact. Most of this amount was shipped from Minneapolis and St. Anthony. Because it did not stand the cost of transportation well, corn was grown chiefly for local consumption. Hence, it was found at greater distances from the rivers than were wheat and oats. It had the preference on the frontier because it was easily planted and harvested on land imperfectly cleared or broken.[9]

More important to the farmer of the 1850's than corn as a commercial crop was the potato. Very early much attention was paid to this crop. Henry W. Hamilton in August, 1850, wrote about a professional friend who, in May of that year, went out a few miles from St. Paul and hired twelve acres of prairie land broken up and planted to potatoes. By August he had contracted for his crop, and he made a clear profit of two thousand dollars on the venture. Hamilton does not tell the price these potatoes brought, but in late April, 1850, potatoes were quoted at a dollar and a quarter a bushel at St. Anthony, and there was a great demand for them, as most of the potatoes consumed in Minnesota were imported.[10]

By 1855, however, potatoes began to be shipped out of the territory, evidence of the growth in production of the crop. As early as 1852 the *Pioneer* said it could see no reason why Minnesota should not have a monopoly of the potato trade for the whole valley of the Mississippi. "Men & brethren, why stand ye here idle, all the day, in the market place?" asked that newspaper. And in 1856 C. C. Andrews wrote: "The great staple article of Minnesota soil appears to be potatoes, for they were never known to be better anywhere else —Eastport not excepted—and at our table d'hote they were a grand collateral to the beef and pork." In the spring of 1859, 123,400 bushels of potatoes were shipped out of the state, mostly from the Twin Cities.[11]

Both Irish and sweet potatoes were grown, though the latter were unimportant. Of Irish potatoes, several varieties were tried. In the vicinity of Chaska in 1855 the Rachel potato was raised in large quantities. It grew to be very large, one specimen weighing two pounds and five ounces, and thirty-three of them making a bushel. "Huzza for the Minnesota Rachel Potatoe!!" exclaimed a newspaper. In 1856 Martin McLeod took the first premium on potatoes at the territorial fair with White Meshannocks. This variety yielded two hundred bushels from half an acre planted on the sod. John R. Cummins of Eden Prairie raised Mercer, Pink Eye, and Irish Grey potatoes in 1858, but his Mercers were hurt somewhat by rot and yielded only about a hundred bushels to the acre. An average potato crop in Hennepin County, according to Cummins, was from two hundred to three hundred bushels per acre.[12]

The prices received for potatoes varied greatly during the 1850's, according to supply and demand. In the spring of 1857 in frontier McLeod County, for instance, the price was $2.50 a bushel and only a few people could afford to eat potatoes. On the other hand, in April, 1858, Cummins reported the price at $.30; in June, at from $.25 to $.30; and in September, at $.25 a bushel. In the fall of 1860 the steamboat "Time and Tide" was loaded with seven thousand bushels of potatoes for New Orleans. This cargo was purchased near St. Paul, and $.20 a bushel was paid for the greater part of it. "This one shipment made the potato market quite active for some two weeks," reported the press, "and our farmers were pretty well satisfied with the price received, which was cash down, and at wholesale."[13]

BIZARRE EXPERIMENTS AND SOUND AGRICULTURE

In 1859 the total state production of potatoes was 2,517,277 bushels, of which 792 bushels were sweet potatoes. Like corn, potatoes were grown pretty generally over the state, with the greatest concentration in those areas from which part of the crop was shipped out of the state.[14]

Of the small grains, oats held the lead over wheat until nearly the end of the 1850's. In 1853 the oat crop, according to Governor Gorman, was 120,000 bushels as against between 35,000 and 40,000 bushels of wheat. By 1859 total oat production was 2,176,002 bushels, only about 11,000 bushels less than the state's wheat production the same year. The oat crop was produced mainly in the wheat belt, that is, in the two tiers of counties west of the Mississippi and south of the Minnesota River. Oats, however, were quite strongly represented east of the Mississippi. Like corn, oats were grown chiefly for local use, and less than half as many bushels of oats were exported from the state in 1859 as of wheat. The oats that were sent out were shipped mainly from Hastings, Winona, and St. Paul.[15]

Other small grains were of minor importance during the early period. In 1849, for example, only 125 bushels of rye, 1,216 bushels of barley, and 515 bushels of buckwheat were reported for the territory. Ten years later rye production was 121,411 bushels, barley 119,568, and buckwheat 28,052.[16]

After 1860 Minnesota farmers generally began to devote themselves to specialized wheat farming. Hence, other crops became relatively less important, the only one which nearly maintained its position being oats. A clear picture of this relative decline can be obtained by comparing statistics of 1860 with those of 1868. In 1860 oats occupied 15.85 per cent of the total tilled acres in the state, while in 1868 they occupied 15.28 per cent. The statistics for some of the other crops for the respective years were as follows: corn, 20.34 and 9.36 per cent; potatoes, 3.85 and 1.76 per cent; barley, 2.09 and 1.3 per cent; rye, 3.06 and .19 per cent; and buckwheat, 1.83 and .11 per cent. Even these figures, however, do not tell adequately of the decline in crops other than wheat, because there was a reaction away from wheat in 1868.[17]

In 1869, according to the United States census of 1870, Minnesota produced 4,743,117 bushels of corn, an increase of 61.2 per cent in production for the decade of the 1860's. Irish potato production was 1,943,063 bushels, a decrease of 22.8 per cent for the decade. Oat production was 10,678,261 bushels, an increase for the previous ten years of 390 per cent. Barley production for the decade increased relatively more than wheat, to 1,032,024 bushels, a percentage increase of 763.1. But barley, of course, was a minor crop. Rye production was 73,088 bushels, a decrease of 35.7 per cent. As Cummins said: "Rye at 20¢ a bushel is a losing business." Buckwheat production was 52,438 bushels, an increase of 86.9 per cent. Oats were grown mainly in the southeastern part of the state and continued to be used mainly for local consumption. Barley, like wheat, was a market crop and so was grown mainly along the Mississippi River in the southeast. Corn and potatoes followed pretty closely the distribution of the rural population, while rye was grown especially north of the Minnesota River.[18]

The prices of corn, potatoes, and small grain remained fairly low during the first years of the 1860's. For example, in November, 1861, Cummins received $.25 a bushel for some of his oats; in May, 1862, he received from $.30 to $.40; and in November, 1863, he secured $.65. Corn and potatoes remained around $.40 or $.50 a bushel during the same period. The last year or so of the Civil War saw corn rising to over $1.00 a bushel, and potatoes going up to from $.80 to $1.00. Prices in the late 1860's were generally better than in the first years of the decade, but markets were often dull. Thus, in 1870 Cummins told of taking some potatoes to town for a neighbor, but that times were so dull he could not sell them.[19]

During the late 1850's and early 1860's much notice was paid to various "prolific" corns. Some of this corn produced stalks that grew to great heights. In 1858, near St. Peter, one Carpenter grew, from seed obtained in Savannah, Georgia, some of Peabody's Prolific, whose stalks attained a height of twelve and a half feet; while a farmer near St. Paul in 1869 raised some of the same kind, planted in June, whose stalks were seventeen feet high. Other prolific corns were procured from southern Illinois, and some farmers swore by them. As earlier, however, dent and flint corns were the most common. John H. Stevens, in an address before the Crow River Agricultural Society in 1861, said that Ohio dent was most commonly cultivated south of the Minnesota River, but that common flint was the surest year after year. He recommended curing the cornstalks for use as corn fodder. A farmers' club of St. Peter in 1864 agreed that corn was a profitable crop even at twenty-five cents a bushel. The cost of raising it per acre was given as follows: rent of land, $2.00; plowing, $1.25; harrowing, $.25; marking, $.25; planting, $.75; cultivating, $1.00; harvesting, $3.00; total cost, $8.50. The most common method of planting corn in the 1860's seems to have been by hand, with from two to four grains placed in a hill.[20]

Some comments on rye, oat, and barley production were also made by Stevens in the speech just alluded to. Winter rye, he claimed, had become quite a staple among the German population, who used it in bread making. It was a safe crop and usually brought a good price, but it was not so profitable as were many other crops. Since 1859 the oat crop had been much neglected, because so many people had turned to wheat production. Wheat was so low by the fall of 1861, however, that Stevens advised farmers to turn again to oats. In the more thickly settled part of the state, where lager beer was generally used, barley was extensively and successfully raised.[21]

Various factors, such as lack of markets, increased emphasis on wheat, and insects, caused a decline in potato growing between 1860 and 1870. In 1865 the Colorado beetle or potato bug began to infest the potato fields of Minnesota, and each successive year saw the bug spread over a greater area. The newspapers of the period devoted much space to accounts of the pest, the damage done by it, and methods for its destruction. On July 18, 1867, the *Winona Republican* said: "Potatoes continue to be scourged by the . . . potato bug, and on old fields the crop will be light." The next year the *Mankato Record* reported that "those striped bugs which, for the past three years have so seriously damaged the crop west of us, have already made their appearance in large numbers"; and a Waseca paper said that they should be "attacked at first sight and exterminated if possible." That was not so easy to accomplish. Some people shook the bugs off the plants into an open space between the rows and buried them with a shovel plow, while others gathered them into pails of hot water. The most effective weapon proved to be Paris green, but many farmers were afraid to use it for fear it would poison the potatoes. Gradually, however, better ways of applying the insecticide were developed and greater control over the bugs was achieved, but not until after much damage had been done. The potato crop of Anoka County in 1869, for example, was less than one-half of the crop of 1859, and the same was true of many other counties in the state.[22]

During these same years the farmer was preyed upon by charlatans with potatoes which they claimed would give marvelous yields. In 1867 the Harrison potato occupied a big place in the advertisements, while in 1869 it was the Early Rose. One farmer, awed by these advertisements, paid ninety dollars for ten barrels of Harrisons. The yield proved to be fair, but the quality was inferior. The seed dealers also made great claims for various kinds of oats, which they sold for from fifteen to eighteen dollars a bushel for seed. The greatest swindle in oats appears to have been the so-called Norway oats. In 1868 these oats sold at the rate of fifty dollars an acre for seed, and when they were harvested it was hard to tell them from ordinary kinds. But the channels of communication were not the best, and farmers continued to be "taken' in" many times. In 1870, as a case in point, D. W. Ramsdell and Company appointed a certain Bollar to contract with farmers near New Ulm for the purchase of Norway oats for seed at five dollars a bushel. Many farmers bought the oats and gave notes payable after harvest. Bollar agreed to buy some of the oats at fifty cents a bushel and to furnish sacks for them. When the crop was harvested in the fall the farmers asked him about the sacks and the number of bushels the Ramsdell Company would purchase. To their amazement, Bollar said he no longer represented the company. Meanwhile the farmers' notes had been sent to the Brown County Bank for collection, and a court decision had been handed down to the effect that they must be paid. And, to make matters worse, the oats were not as excellent as they had been represented. "You know the old adage of the fool and his money," commented one editor.[23]

During the 1870's the biggest percentage increase in production of small grains and bushel crops was in corn, a 212.7 per cent increase, from 4,743,117 in 1869 to 14,831,741 bushels in 1879. The second largest relative increase was in barley, from a little over 1,000,000 to 2,972,965 bushels, an increase of 188.1 per cent. Rye production in 1879 was 215,245 bushels, a gain of 175.6 per cent for the decade. Irish potato production made nearly as large a relative gain, to a total of 5,184,676 bushels. Oat production was larger than any of the above —23,382,158 bushels—but its gain for the decade was only 119 per cent. Buckwheat production actually declined by 20.4 per cent during the 1870's, to a crop of 41,756 bushels. Oats in 1879 were less concentrated in southeastern Minnesota than wheat, and they advanced westward about as fast as the population. Ten years earlier barley had been confined almost entirely to the southeast, but by 1879 it had spread westward and northwestward. The bulk of the crop, however, was still produced in five or six southeastern counties, where diversification in agriculture was making headway. Rye was still a minor crop, but it had nearly tripled between 1870 and 1880, especially in districts formerly wooded. Being planted usually in autumn, it got a good growth before the season of hot and dry weather. Corn acreage was found mainly in the southern quarter of the state south of Hennepin County, though it had advanced west and northwest, being important in Otter Tail County. The corn yield per acre was about four bushels larger in 1879 than it had been ten years earlier. Potato cultivation had moved westward and northwestward with the population, and the yield per acre had increased; but the zone of greatest density in potato growing was found near the largest cities of the state.[24]

Prices received by farmers for corn, rye, oats, potatoes, and barley during the 1870's were not as high as those received during the middle 1860's. In February, 1871, John R. Cummins was paid from $.60 to $.70 a bushel for his corn in Minneapolis, but the next October 31 he gave the price as $.45. On October 16, 1872, corn was $.50, and it was the same a year later; in 1874, it ranged between $.60 and $.80; in the spring of 1875, from $.75 to $.80 was quoted; and on September 13, 1878, it sold at $.40 a bushel. Prices in New York during the same years generally averaged about $.20 a bushel more than in Minnesota. On September 1, 1871, Cummins reported oats at $.35 a bushel; on October 31, at $.40; and, on April 24, 1875, they brought $.65. On July 18, 1871, potatoes were worth $1.00 a bushel, but by September they were down to $.50, and there was not much of a market for them. The next spring the price was up to $.65 and they were quite scarce, but in April, 1873, the price was down again to between $.35 and $.40 a bushel. During the summer the price went over $1.00 again, and then it coasted down to $.60 in the fall. The springs of 1874 and 1875 saw potatoes up to $1.00 a bushel again, but by July of the latter year the price was $.40 and there was no sale. On October 8, 1875, potatoes were reported as "quite plenty" at $.30 a bushel. This low remained through the following winter and spring of 1876, on May 2 potatoes being worth $.25 a bushel if a buyer could be found. On June 12 potatoes at Minneapolis found no sale at from $.15 to $.20 a bushel. In 1877, however, the price went up to $1.00 by June, and potatoes were retailing at from $1.50 to $1.80 a bushel.[25]

At $.15 to $.20 a bushel potatoes were not very profitable, if at all, but at $.40 a farmer could usually make some money.[26] E. N. Larpenteur gave the cost and profit on five acres of potatoes in 1860 as follows:[26]

To plowing and planting, 3 men and team, 2 days	$ 14.00
50 bushels of seed	25.00
First harrowing, half day	2.00
Second harrowing, one day	4.00
First one-horse plowing, 2 days	4.00
Cultivating and plowing, one horse each, 2 days each	8.00
Harrowing down the vines, half day	2.00
Plowing out potatoes and gathering, man and team $4.00 a day, 6 days	24.00
Three men to gather potatoes, 6 days	27.00
Last harrowing at harvest, half day	2.00
Total	$112.00

The average crop for nineteen years was 250 bushels per acre. From five acres would come 1,250 bushels at $.40 a bushel, which would equal $500, or a profit of $388.

Some people urged that starch factories be started as a market for potatoes, but little action resulted.[27] No doubt a few small plants were erected, but not until 1886 was the firm of C. F. Leland and R. L. Hall established in Anoka at a cost of $25,000. It was claimed that this was the largest potato starch factory in the United States, but not until its third year were enough potatoes raised in the vicinity to give the plant a decent run. Then farmers awoke, land rose in value, and Hall built other factories at Harris, North Branch, and Monticello. The potato crop of Anoka County jumped from 68,000 bushels in 1879 to 717,000 bushels in 1899.[28]

Many varieties of potatoes were available for the farmer who desired to try his hand at the business. For example, the regents of the University of Minnesota, in their report for 1877, gave the results of potato growing on the state experimental farm and listed twenty-three varieties. Among the varieties yielding the most per acre were Peerless, Dunmore's Seedling, Calcutta Seedling, Burbank's Seedling, Victor, Extra Early Vermont, Eureka, Late Rose, Little Giant, Fluke, and Snowflake. In 1869 T. T. Mann of Cottage Grove reported that he favored Peachblow potatoes, while Cummins in 1871 raised the Peerless and Prolific varieties. In 1878 the Early Vermont brought five cents more a bushel at the Minneapolis City Market than any other kind, including the Early Rose and the Snowflake.[29]

Numerous varieties of oats were also procurable, according to the regents' report. Some of the best yields were secured with Canadian, Black Norway, Probsteir, White Schonen, White Dutch, Excelsior, Waterloo, Brunswick, and Silver White Queen. Of barley varieties, the Chevalier showed the plumpest and heaviest grain at the university's experimental farm, but it had not gained wide acceptance over the state.[30]

During the middle 1870's crops other than wheat also were damaged by the grasshoppers. The estimated losses of oats in 1875 were 1,127,780 bushels; of corn, 790,982; of barley, 41,059; of rye, 11,031; of buckwheat, 16,450; and of potatoes, 130,886. Two years later, in 1877, the losses were given as follows: oats, 1,757,570 bushels; corn, 1,665,993; barley, 146,985; rye, 34,252; buckwheat, 15,652; and potatoes, 350,831.[31] But, despite losses such as these, the diversification in farming of the late 1870's produced an increased amount of land in crops other than wheat. In 1878, for instance, oats, corn, and barley occupied 24.8 per cent of the total cultivated area in the state, while by 1882 these three crops accounted for 37.89 per cent of it.[32]

In addition to raising wheat, oats, corn, potatoes, and perhaps some barley, rye, or buckwheat, many early Minnesota farmers kept poultry on their farms. Unfortunately the United States census gave no poultry statistics in 1850, 1860, or 1870, and so the number of poultry cannot be given during those years. The census of 1840 reported 130 fowl in St. Croix County, Wisconsin, which included Minnesota east of the Mississippi, but this number is so small as to be of no significance. By 1880 the census listed 2,258,385 poultry for the state, which meant slightly over 400 for every 100 persons in the country population. Of course it is inaccurate to generalize, but, from what sources exist, it would seem that the average settler paid little attention to poultry, either as to breeding or as to care. George Gilbertson recalls that the poor things had to get along as best they could. When evening came they were forced to find their own shelter, usually on a fence or up in a tree. Where such conditions existed, a chicken with two legs was seldom seen; more common was one hopping along on two short stumps.[33]

The local storekeeper usually furnished a market for the farmer with eggs to sell, and the price before the middle 1880's varied from seven to twenty-five cents a dozen. On June 6, 1863, John Cummins reported that eggs were selling in St. Paul for ten cents a dozen, but in February, 1864, they were up to twenty-five cents. Nothing was known about candling them, so farmers were paid for floaters, blood-streaked and rotten eggs, and eggs with chicks in them. Since farmers did not have good hen houses, the hens laid all over the premises, and some nests went undiscovered for days on end. Nevertheless, eggs from such nests were often taken to market. At the store they were packed in oats or bran and kept in the cellar, because most stores had no iceboxes.[34]

Agricultural periodicals tried to influence farmers to give their poultry more attention and care. The *Minnesota Monthly* in 1869 stated that "in the markets of Saint Paul and other cities of the State, the supply of poultry is rarely equal to the demand"; and in

1870 the *Farmers' Union* pointed out that poultry had always brought a good price, from eighteen to twenty cents a pound in the fall, with eggs from twelve to twenty-five cents a dozen. "We are glad to know that a good deal of interest is being taken by our people in the new varieties of chickens," said the editor. "The poultry question will be an important one yet." And Peter Gideon wrote from Excelsior on December 31, 1867, that, with proper care, no stock would pay as well as the common hen, which in addition would devour insects of all kinds. But evidently farmers did not heed such advice, for it was reported that as late as 1879 Olmsted County, a big grain raising area, and probably Mower County, imported eggs.[35]

As in the case of livestock, however, so in the poultry field did some men strive to improve breeds in the state. This activity began to get under way in the late 1860's, and it was said in 1868 that the old-fashioned barnyard fowl was giving way to the Brahmas and Black Spanish. At that time genuine pure-blooded Brahmas sold for three dollars a pair if taken before they were fully matured. Outstanding poultry raisers in the state were Dr. Bryant of St. Paul; William S. King, whose recent importations from England were the "finest specimens of their respective kinds we ever saw"; Ed Bogert, who imported Light Brahmas from Massachusetts; P. Scherffius, who brought Dark Brahmas from the same state; George P. Wilson, who got Silver Speckled Hamburgs from Connecticut; and a certain Grant, who had Partridge Cochins from Massachusetts. E. W. Pierce of Winona in 1876 had the only large flock of Plymouth Rocks in the state. The work of these men naturally brought practical results in the flocks of farmers all over Minnesota.[36]

With the improvement of poultry breeds over the state, poultry associations were formed to advance the interests of farmers engaged in raising chickens and other fowl. One of these was the Winona County Poultry Association, which opened its first exhibition at the county courthouse on January 1, 1873. Fifty coops were entered by noon of the first day and more came in later. Chickens, ducks, geese, turkeys, and fighting cocks vied for attention. Among the poultry exhibited were Light and Dark Brahmas, Buff and Black Cochins, Dorkings, White and Spanish Leghorns, Silver Spangled Hamburgs, Black and White Polands, Houdans, and Bantams. The most unusual display consisted of two coops of Drahmas. Three of these birds sold for fifty dollars, and their eggs were worth five dollars a dozen. Elder Edward Ely delivered a lecture at the exhibition, and his remarks, although interrupted by the cackling of hens, apparently were interesting and "very satisfactory to all present." Also satisfying to the association was the importation of three hundred dollars' worth of blooded poultry into Winona County between January and March of 1873. Evidently the organization achieved some practical results.[37]

In 1874 the poultry men organized the Minnesota State Poultry Association, which held its first annual exhibition that year. In 1873–74 two journals, *The Northwestern* and *The National,* were started in Minneapolis to represent the poultry business. Thus, by 1880 much attention was being paid by Minnesota farmers to poultry as a regular part of agricultural operations, just another symptom of the general trend away from specialized wheat farming. During the season of 1882, as much as nine hundred dollars a day were paid for eggs in Rochester to farmers in the vicinity, whereas four years earlier eggs, when they were obtained at all, were imported.[38] The same situation prevailed in other cities in the state.

At the meeting of the Minnesota Butter, Cheese, and Dairy Stock Association in 1883, O. C. Gregg of Marshall inquired as to the number of men who had asked, "Can you raise *timothy* and *clover* in Minnesota?" His guess was that, as a general rule, farmers did not know whether or not these grasses would thrive in the state. And at the annual meeting of the same organization two years later, H. C. Howard stated that everyone before 1870 doubted that clover could be grown in the region. Along the same line, a correspondent who signed himself "De Novo" in 1867 reported that all his neighbors were weary of wheat, but that "year after year passes and no preparation for grass fields. It is a thing too far in the future for most men." From statements such as these it would seem that the average Minnesota farmer of the 1860's and 1870's paid little, if any, attention to the production of tame grasses. Generally speaking that was the case, but here again there were many exceptions to the rule.[39]

Most early settlers relied on the abundant wild grasses for their hay requirements. "Beta," writing in 1857, said that a field of tame grass was very rare in Minnesota, but that the hay generally was good. It ran from half a ton to two tons per acre, and as a rule it was cut with scythes. Some meadows bore a short round grass, while others had a thick burden of blue joint grass, especially on the banks of the Minnesota River. Hay was either stacked or drawn to market, where it sold at from ten to twelve dollars a ton in the late 1850's. And the fact that there was often a good market for hay was a fortunate thing for many settlers. In 1848 Simeon S. P. Folsom, who lived on the banks of the Rum River in Anoka County, made a profit of six thousand dollars by selling hay to the teamsters who hauled supplies to the Winnebago Indians in the vicinity of Long Prairie. Another hay market was provided by the military posts in the state. In the winter of 1858–59, for example, the government paid twelve dollars a ton for hay at Fort Ridgely, and that source of income was a great boon to the settlers who were hit by the panic and poor crops of that period. Again, in 1865, Daniel Rohrer of St. Paul received the contract for 2,400 tons of hay for Fort Snelling at $7.73 a ton.[40]

But all farmers did not rely entirely upon wild hay. According to John H. Stevens, "Major Joseph R. Brown opened a farm at Lake Traverse, near the head of Red River, and raised a fine crop of wheat in 1836. He was also the pioneer in raising tame grasses, having introduced timothy on his farm in 1831." And, in 1854, a St. Paul newspaper reported that many farmers had begun to cultivate red clover and timothy. One of the earliest of these men was probably Charles N. Larpenteur of Rose Township in Ramsey County. In 1861 he recalled that he had raised timothy for ten years and that there was no danger of its being winterkilled. He sowed his timothy in two ways. Sometimes he planted it in spring wheat or rye, sowing four quarts to the acre; or he broke new ground in July and sowed his timothy alone on that land. Usually he obtained two or three tons of hay per acre, and he felt that such hay not only was far superior to wild hay for horses, but also that it was more profitable than wheat where the land was suitable and a market was near. Another farmer, who signed himself "Subsoil," expressed similar sentiments in 1856. He argued that timothy sown with grain made excellent pasturage in the fall and that it would yield a good crop of hay during the next season. He recommended also raising clover to enrich the soil. "It may be set down as a fact," he wrote, "that though our soil is now fertile, it will not always, nor long continue so, *without manure.*" Mark Furber Libby, who began farming in Dakota County in 1863, followed the practice of these two men. "And in with the wheat," wrote Libby's son, "he sowed red-top, timothy and red clover, and the grass would take hold and come a runnin after the wheat was cut and the cows would be turned in about six weeks after with little Freddie to herd em." Libby sold his hay at the St. Paul Market, then on Minnesota Street between Fourth and Sixth. In 1858 John R. Cummins raised millet, sowing six quarts to the acre, and the next year he recorded that a good deal of his clover was killed, but that his timothy stood the winter well.[41]

A few farmers grew clover for seed, a profitable practice, according to J. Dickson of Chatfield. In 1869 Dickson threshed sixty-four bushels of seed from sixteen acres. The lowest price quoted in Chicago at the time was nine dollars a bushel, which would amount to $576 for sixty-four bushels. The same area of land in wheat, at eighteen bushels per acre, would have returned only about $360. To thresh his clover, Dickson purchased for $475 a machine which threshed forty bushels of seed in a day.[42]

Growth in hay production can be followed by referring to the United States census. In the year that Minnesota became a territory 2,019 tons of hay were reported. Ten years later, in 1859, the production was 269,483 tons; in 1869 it was 695,053, and in 1879, 1,637,109, produced on about a third of the area then devoted to wheat. The percentage increase in production for the 1860's was 157.9, and for the next decade it was somewhat less. In 1860 there were 219.9 tons of hay for each 100 people in the country population; and in 1880 the comparable figure was 301.4 tons. How much of this amount was wild and how much tame hay it is impossible to say. In 1862 it was reported that farmers in the older parts of the state were starting to raise timothy. Later, in 1871, the *Rochester Post* indicated that the native products of marsh and prairie were about used up in the vicinity; yet in Olmsted County at the same time there were 12,811 acres of native or wild meadow as against 5,889 acres of tame meadow. Still another bit of evidence comes from a commentator in 1885, who stated that, from 1879 on, clover was widely grown in southern Minnesota.[43]

The varieties of clover most frequently mentioned were Northern Red, obtained from New Hampshire; Large Red or Mammoth, from Chicago; Alsike, from New York; and Medium Red. James T. Price of Eyota, who had a hundred and fifty acres in clover in 1872, recommended the Medium Red, but other farmers, of course, swore by other favorite kinds.[44]

One variety of clover not widely grown during the pioneer period, but so important later as to merit mention of its early history, was Grimm alfalfa, named for Wendelin Grimm, who migrated to Carver County from Baden, Germany, in 1857. In the spring of 1858 Grimm planted some alfalfa seed which he had brought with him from his old home, but he did not achieve much success with the crop at first. The winters were severe and some of the plants winterkilled. Yet he saved the seed from those that survived and year after year he replanted the field. "After years of persistence," writes a leading authority on agricultural history, "the alfalfa became acclimatized and no longer winterkilled. The scientific importance of his work, Grimm probably never realized." Further, he made no effort to put his seed on a commercial basis. His alfalfa was grown only within a radius of ten miles of his farm, by his neighbors to whom he distributed seed. The sufficiency of open pasture and the practice, common in the early period, of grazing livestock on vacant lands undoubtedly combined to retard the spread of alfalfa in the state. As late as 1889 Carver County produced nearly fifty per cent of the alfalfa grown in Minnesota. It was only gradually that the superiority of Grimm alfalfa over other forage plants for the Northwest became recognized, and it was not until the decade from 1910 to 1920 that alfalfa was becoming a standard hay crop in the state; yet, during the years from 1858 on, Wendelin Grimm was performing a work of enduring importance to agriculture.[45]

Another plant that gained some fame for a time, especially in the 1860's, was flax. Not mentioned in the census of 1840 or 1850, flax appeared for the first time in the schedules of 1860, which reported 118 bushels of flaxseed and 1,983 pounds of flax fiber for Minnesota. During the succeeding ten years the relative increase in flax production was greater than that of wheat. Flaxseed production in 1869 was 18,635 bushels, a 15,692.4 per cent increase for the 1860's, and fiber production was 122,571 pounds, a 6,081.1 per cent increase. Charles Hoag, in a letter of December 14, 1868, from his Hennepin County farm, recommended that farmers turn to flax. In 1868 he raised four acres of the plant, which yielded him twenty-five dollars an acre and cost no more to raise than wheat. He purchased the seed for two dollars a bushel, and sold the straw for ten dollars a ton to Schiedlen, Bell, and Siedle, who operated an oil and cordage factory in Minneapolis. At that time, Hoag reported, the firm imported thousands of bushels of flaxseed from outside the state. Another market for flax was furnished by the Minnesota Linseed Oil Company of Minneapolis, which issued a little *Farmers' Handbook* telling how and why to raise flax. Also, here and there, local tow mills were erected, where flax straw could be made into tow. One of these was built in 1873 at Cottage Grove by S. W. Furber, who purchased unthreshed flax and threshed it with a machine made expressly for that purpose. In spite of such activities, however, flax raising in Minnesota remained a minor pursuit. In 1860 only .1 of a bushel of flaxseed was produced for every 100 persons in the country population, and only 1.6 pounds of fiber. By 1879 the production of flaxseed was up to 98,689 bushels, or 18.2 bushels per 100 of the country population, but fiber production was down to only 497 pounds. Most flaxseed was produced in the prairie counties of the southwest.[46]

Another product which became popular in the 1860's, when supplies of Southern sugar were cut off, was sorghum. Some 14,000 gallons of sorghum syrup were produced in 1860; ten years later the amount was 38,735 gallons; and in 1880 it reached 543,369 gallons. About 1869 a new sorghum hybrid, Minnesota Early Amber, was introduced; a syrup factory was built at Morristown; a sugar factory was established at Dundas; and great hopes for Minnesota as a sugar state were aroused. Generally speaking, however, Minnesota is neither warm nor dry enough for sorghum.[47]

Closely related to this branch of agriculture was the making of maple syrup and maple sugar, and many pioneer farmers engaged in these activities during the winters. For example, in 1856 Andrew Peterson wrote in his diary that he had made six troughs for maple sap; and in 1865 he jotted down the comment that he had finished cooking maple syrup. Similarly, John R. Cummins remarked in March, 1861, that the maple sugar season was nearly over. Cummins also at an early date raised sugar cane and made molasses from it. As Minnesota emerged from frontier conditions, maple sugar production, quite naturally, decreased in importance. Thus, in 1860 the state produced 370,669 pounds of maple sugar and 23,038 gallons of maple syrup; but in 1880 only 76,972 pounds of sugar and 11,407 gallons of maple syrup were reported.[48]

A few other crops which played but minor roles on the agricultural stage in early Minnesota were also reported in the census. Hop culture spread into the state from Wisconsin and reached its peak about 1869, after which it suffered an abrupt decline, as production figures for 1860, 1870, and 1880 clearly indicate. These figures were 140 pounds, 222,065 pounds, and 10,928 pounds respectively. Some farmers tried tobacco growing, but the results were not impressive. In 1860 a production of 38,938 pounds of tobacco was reported; but by 1870 the amount was down to 8,247 and in 1880 it was only 69,922. Of far greater importance was market gardening, which got an early start in Washington County. In fact, the only report on the value of market garden produce in the census of 1850 was that for Washington County, a total of $150. The report for peas and beans in the same census was obviously an error and hence of no value. In 1859 Minnesota produced 18,988 bushels of peas and beans, and the value of its market garden produce was $94,704. Some of the garden stuff of the 1850's was of magnificent proportions, if numerous newspaper accounts can be relied upon. For example, in 1853 an onion raised at Fort Ridgely measured five and a half inches in diameter, and a rutabaga raised on the sod west of Henderson weighed nineteen and a half pounds. Quite naturally, the greatest development in market gardening during the 1850's occurred in Hennepin, Ramsey, and Wright counties, since the St. Paul and Minneapolis markets were developing rapidly. By 1869 the state produced 46,601 bushels of peas and beans, an increase of 145.4 per cent for the decade, and the value of market garden products was $115,234, an increase of only 21.7 per cent. During the 1870's the production of peas and beans declined by 46.3 per cent, to 25,039 bushels in 1879; and the value of market garden produce increased by a mere 44.1 per cent, to $166,030. During the same decade the country population increased by 65.8 per cent. It is possible, however, that there was a change in classification in market gardening in the census report, which would account for the seeming decline in gardening; for there was money to be made in that branch of agriculture. Thomas Squires of Becker County, for example, in 1878 received a cash return of $832.75 from six acres devoted to garden truck, as follows:

2 acres of potatoes, 500 bushels, sold at $.35 a bushel	$175.00
2 acres of corn, 190 bushels, sold at $1.00 a bushel	190.00
⅕ acre of onions, 77 bushels, sold at $.75 a bushel	57.75
1 acre of squash, 9 tons, sold at $.015 a pound	270.00
½ acre of turnips, 100 bushels, sold at $.30 a bushel	30.00
⅓ acre of white beans, 10 bushels, at $2.00 a bushel	20.00
Sweet potatoes, 8 bushels, at $2.50 a bushel	20.00
Tomatoes, 10 bushels, at $2.00 a bushel	20.00
Other miscellaneous garden truck	50.00
Total	$832.75

Had Squires put the same land into wheat, his return would have been less than half as much. Of course, his labor might have been considerably less, also.[49]

BIZARRE EXPERIMENTS AND SOUND AGRICULTURE

To cater to market gardeners and others, a number of seed farms were established in the state. As early as 1858 it was reported that nurseries in Mower County were young but thrifty. This report, however, probably reflected more a wish than a fact, for it was not until later that much was heard of seed farms. Toward the end of the 1870's one of the most widely publicized was that of Hollister, Castle, and Company, known as the Silver Lake Farm. It was located on Silver Lake, six miles northeast of St. Paul, on a tract of nearly a thousand acres. Particularly interesting were the long rows of thrifty peas to be seen at the farm. Among the fancy varieties represented were the Little Gem, Tom Thumb, Carter's First Crop, Kentish Invicta, Blue Imperial Dwarf, and Blue Peter.[50]

Closely allied to market gardening was fruit raising, and, despite the severity of Minnesota winters, a good many farmers started orchards and vineyards. As early as 1854 Peter Gideon had 350 apple trees and 50 pear, cherry, and quince trees in his orchard. In the spring of 1862 Countryman recorded the fact that he set out apple and cherry trees, which he had obtained in Wisconsin the previous fall, as well as grapevines and raspberry bushes. Andrew Peterson was particularly interested in fruit, and he kept in touch regularly with orchardmen in the Lake Minnetonka district, where Gideon was developing the hardy Wealthy apple. In the fall of 1871 Peterson carefully noted in his diary that he received a three-dollar prize for large apples at the county fair. On another occasion he wrote: "This winter I have grafted 404 apple-trees, 13 pear trees, 30 plum trees and 12 cherry trees." To stimulate similar activity by more farmers, the *Farmer and Gardener* and the *Farmers' Union* included in each issue a section entitled "Horticultural," which gave advice on the production of flowers, fruits, and vegetables. Newspapers followed suit, as did the *Minnesota Monthly* under Daniel A. Robertson. In the columns of the latter much space was allotted to reports of the activities of the Minnesota Horticultural Society and to descriptions of nurseries and orchards. The work of professional gardeners in Ramsey County, such as Truman Smith, Dr. Jarvis, Judge Baker, and William E. Brimhall, of orchardmen at Lake Minnetonka, and of nurserymen in Rice and Dakota counties was pointed to with pride. All this activity was not without effect. In 1869 the orchards of the state yielded a crop of about ten thousand bushels, the first time such a record was achieved in Minnesota. Still, Ohio and Michigan did not view with any real alarm the emergence of Minnesota as a fruit-producing state. The winters of 1872–73 and 1874–75 were especially damaging to apple orchards, but total fruit production increased quite appreciably during the 1870's. At the start of the decade the value of orchard products was $12,654, but by the end of the decade it was $121,648. Placed alongside the value of livestock or of farm products, this figure seems almost infinitesimal. Yet it looms large when it is compared with the figure for 1860, a mere $649.[51]

Early Agricultural Societies and Fairs

One of the institutions deeply ingrained in the pattern of American life is the agricultural fair. Anyone who saw the motion picture "State Fair," starring the late Will Rogers, will appreciate better than through descriptive words how many families anticipate and enjoy the fair. Some people feel that such exhibitions are outmoded, that they are carry-overs from an earlier age; yet the tenacity with which they have hung on to the present day attests their importance even in modern society. Two eminent scholars have asserted that "no institution, perhaps, has exerted greater influence upon American rural life than the agricultural fair." [1]

In Minnesota, fairs are older than the state itself, for they first appeared in the early 1850's, just at the zenith of the golden age of such institutions in the United States. [2] Compared with later exhibitions, the early fairs were primitive indeed, yet they more than justified their existence. They gave the isolated pioneer farmer a chance to meet his fellows, to have a good time; and, by showing him late developments in machinery, fine livestock, and new techniques in farming, they gave him an incentive to improve his own farming. As one writer has remarked, until about 1870 "the whole burden of agricultural experimentation, instruction, extension and recreation fell upon the agricultural societies whose work was carried on mainly through State and local fairs." [3]

In the period before 1870 fairs were primarily educational, and amusement features were secondary or were subordinated to the instructional motive. Stock and crop exhibits and judging were the main features of most fairs, and the exchange of experiences by dirt farmers and lectures by experts played important parts. Also necessary was the annual address, delivered by the most renowned figure available. These addresses were usually flowery, elevating agriculture to a lofty pinnacle and praising it as the noblest of pursuits. Such discourses might not have helped a farmer to earn more money nor to raise better crops, but they probably made his chest swell with pride when he thought about his calling.[4]

But early fairs were not all work and no play. Concerning the medieval counterparts of later fairs, it has been written: "If the booths of the foreign merchants were of interest, even more so were the minstrels and jongleurs, the acrobats and trained animals, the magicians and human freaks, all for the amazement and amusement of the public." And it may logically be surmised that Minnesota farmers of the 1850's and 1860's attended fairs to have a good time as well as to learn. Plowing matches, reaper trials, and ladies' riding exhibitions were popular, and, although frowned upon by many, the horse race was a regular feature of many fairs. At the Washington County Fair of 1875 persons interested in amusement features could witness a pigeon shoot, a walking contest, a foot race, a baseball game, and a boat race.[5] But whether primarily educational or recreational, most fairs seem to have had a common feature—financial stringency. In fact, state aid for local agricultural societies, the sponsors of the fairs, was not made available until 1868.

There is some difference of opinion as to when the first agricultural society was organized in Minnesota. Some authorities and at least one early newspaper agree that the first move toward the organization of such a society was made in the winter of 1852 in Benton County, mainly near Watab.[6] An agricultural society existed as early as 1849, however, for in that year the St. Anthony Agricultural Association offered prizes in cash or implements for the best crops raised during the ensuing season. For the best crop of Indian corn in a quantity of not less than ten acres a prize of twenty-five dollars was offered. Contenders for the prizes were to make proof before a justice of the peace, a judge, or a notary before January 1, 1851.[7] The nature of this association and the success of the crop contest, however, are unknown.

But the date of the formation of the first agricultural society in Minnesota is of little interest except to the antiquarian. Of greater significance are the number of societies active during the 1850's, their location, and the work they did. Some of the first societies

EARLY AGRICULTURAL SOCIETIES AND FAIRS

naturally were organized in the counties that had the greatest population densities in the early 1850's—counties such as Benton, Ramsey, and Hennepin.

The Benton County society was incorporated by an act of the legislature approved on March 5, 1852. There were ten charter members of the society, among them Oliver H. Kelley. Most of the members were fur traders, but the formation of the society inspired the editor of an eastern farm journal to write: "Those who have not lately visited the far west, can hardly credit the statement, that in a region so recently a wilderness, there already exists a fully-organized and flourishing society of men, deeply interested in the growth and success of agricultural industry. But this is the fact."[8]

On March 6, 1852, the Ramsey County Agricultural Society received a legislative charter and it held its first meeting on April 10. Listed among its members were editors, a minister, politicians, a barber, and other urbanites who believed that the organization of agricultural societies was an excellent way to advertise the resources of Minnesota to the outside world.[9]

The Hennepin County Agricultural Society was chartered by the territorial legislature on March 5, 1853. The prime mover behind the organization was John H. Stevens, and the first meeting of the society was held at the courthouse in St. Anthony on September 7, 1853. A large audience heard addresses by various notables and decided to hold a fair in October, 1853. The fair of 1853 did not materialize, but in October, 1854, the society did hold a fair, the first such exhibition in the territory, and it proved a success. It was located at what was later known as Bridge Square in Minneapolis. Governor Gorman, ex-Governor Ramsey, and ex-Justice Bradley B. Meeker gave high-sounding addresses, typical of the day, and more than fifty exhibitors displayed their wares of grains, roots, vegetables, livestock, poultry, dairy products, fine arts, machinery, ladies' work, and miscellaneous materials. The premiums, amounting to several hundred dollars, were all paid—a real accomplishment. It was claimed that the exhibits would have done credit to one of the oldest and richest counties of New York. Some strangers were so impressed that they later became permanent residents of Minnesota.

All in all, this first agricultural fair was a valuable advertisement for the territory.[10]

As time went on other county organizations appeared. Some of the most prominent were the Dodge County Agricultural Society, formed in 1856; the Dakota County Agricultural Association and the Fillmore County Agricultural Society, both organized in 1858; and the Faribault County Agricultural Society and the McLeod County Agricultural Society, which dated from 1859. All these groups suffered early vicissitudes, which, however, they were able to weather, and they finally emerged in healthy conditions. The ideals for which they were established—to encourage the importation of blooded stock and the introduction of choice seeds, grains, and fruit trees—ultimately transcended difficulties such as inadequate finances and rivalries among towns concerning fair sites.[11]

In addition to the formation of county societies, the 1850's witnessed the organization of a society to represent the farming interests of all Minnesota. At the first meeting of the Hennepin County Agricultural Society in 1853, the following resolution was unanimously adopted: "Resolved, that this society deems it expedient that there should be a convention held at St. Paul on the first Wednesday of January next, to form a territorial agricultural society; and that other agricultural societies in the territory are respectfully requested to send delegates to said convention."[12]

From this resolution and the action taken in pursuance of it grew the Minnesota Territorial Agricultural Society. The organization meeting suggested in the resolution was held in the Capitol at St. Paul on January 4 and 5, 1854, and, in spite of inclement weather, the attendance was good. Delegates from Benton, Chisago, Dakota, Hennepin, Nicollet, Pembina, Ramsey, Scott, and Washington counties were present. Governor Gorman was elected president and Judge Andrew G. Chatfield made the main address. One of the newspapers said that many of the delegates were practical farmers, and added: "The organization of this Society should be hailed with pleasure, and it is hoped that our farmers and others will give it their unqualified support."[13]

The second annual meeting of the Territorial Agricultural society was held in the Capitol on January 10, 1855. This gathering was addressed by Henry H. Sibley, who made a plea for a federal bureau of agriculture. He pointed out that the whole subject of husbandry was then committed to the bureau of patents. His plea was answered in 1862, when the United States Department of Agriculture was created. The establishment of the department was in no little way the result of the work of various agricultural societies throughout the country. At the 1855 meeting of the society, Stevens was elected president and it was decided to hold a fair. It was impossible, however, for the society alone to raise the necessary funds, and so the fair held at Minneapolis on October 17 and 18 was sponsored jointly by the territorial and the Hennepin County societies.[14]

This first fair was truly a success. Newspapers stated that it drew the largest crowd of whites ever assembled in the territory and that many ladies were present. People from as far away as the James River, west of Big Stone Lake, attended. There were excellent exhibits of grain, vegetables, and livestock, and for the first time in the upper Mississippi region the dairy interest was represented. A good display of cheese, made by Mrs. Joel B. Bassett of Minneapolis, was among the entries. But only three counties exhibited products at the fair—Hennepin, Ramsey, and Washington. Among the horses entered, Morgans were the most popular, a stallion and a colt of this breed winning first premiums. The first premium for bulls went to E. L. Larpenteur for his three-year-old Durham, and J. G. Lennon won in the sheep class with a Leicestershire, the breed made famous in England by Robert Bakewell. The hog exhibit was mediocre, but there were chickens in abundance, mainly Shanghais, Chittagongs, and Brahmapootras. Yellow Dent corn that yielded eighty-five bushels to the acre was on display, and Stevens exhibited a stalk of corn seventeen feet high. The wheat, rye, and buckwheat shown were produced chiefly in Hennepin County. The vegetable display "astonished even the natives," with Ramsey County leading in cabbages, pumpkins, and squashes, and Hennepin in potatoes, turnips, beets, and onions. One radish that was shown weighed nearly eighteen pounds, and potatoes weighing nearly three pounds and yielding four hundred bushels to an acre were numerous.

Among the ladies' exhibits were house plants, butter, carpets, flowers, rugs, needlework, and fancy articles. A highlight and a harbinger of the future was the showing of three fine apples by the Reverend Gideon H. Pond. Another attraction drawing much attention from the two thousand spectators was a contest of horsemanship among the ladies. Later, however, the department of ladies' equestrianship was abolished, because great dissatisfaction, and even feuds, developed among the contestants' friends.[15]

In 1856 the society held a fair of its own in Minneapolis, and in 1857 it sponsored another, this time in St. Paul. The latter event coincided with the panic of 1857, which caused great financial loss to the society. Political rivalry also hurt the fair. Many Republicans refused to attend because they believed it was part of a Democratic machine. No fair was held in 1858 because of depressed economic conditions, but in 1859 the society joined with the Hennepin County society again and presented a "Union Fair" at Minneapolis, which was only partially successful.[16]

An act of the legislature approved on February 16, 1860, gave the society, henceforth known as the Minnesota State Agricultural Society, the powers of a corporate body and provided for the organization of county agricultural societies. Thus, although the act was not well drawn up, the state society was placed on a legal and permanent basis. An attempt at this time to get the legislature to appropriate money for the society's work failed.[17]

Having achieved a sounder basis, the society renewed its work with enthusiasm. A fair was held at Fort Snelling from September 26 to 28, 1860, which of all the fairs "from Donnybrook to Nijni-Novgorod" was not surpassed in the satisfaction it afforded those who attended. Among the notable exhibits was Manny's combined reaper and mower, the only machine of its kind on the ground. There were entries of cattle, horses, sheep, hogs, farm products, horticultural products, farm implements, articles of domestic manufacture, and miscellaneous materials. The largest hog in Minnesota, a 640-pound Chester White barrow, was shown by Wyman Elliot of Minneapolis. An address lasting two hours was given by Cassius Clay of Kentucky. Only perfunctory applause came at the end.[18]

The Civil War changed the plans of the state society, which did not attempt to arrange fairs in 1861 or 1862. In the former year the Anoka and Blue Earth county groups held fairs, but they were not successful. Economic conditions were disturbed, crops were poor, and people were greatly concerned over the war. At times even the weather conspired to defeat the well-laid plans of fair sponsors. In the words of the editor of one Minnesota newspaper: "The first Tuesday . . . of our second annual Fair was drizzly, mizzly, nasty, dirty, disagreeable, and generally otherwise uncomfortable, besides being somewhat moist." Still, some people wanted to see agricultural society work continued, and there were unsuccessful efforts during these years to get state aid for such bodies.[19] The leading state farm journal in 1861 commented as follows on the subject:

"Minnesota is one of few states that has done nothing to advance her great interests of agriculture. An effort was made last winter to have the Legislature make a small appropriation in aid of the various agricultural societies, but without avail. Money could be found for almost any other purpose, but when a few hundred dollars were asked to aid our State and county societies there was a general plea of poverty. Not a few seemed to think that appropriating money for such a purpose was entirely new and unheard of in the annals of modern legislation. The body was composed largely of farmers, but . . . most of them took little or no interest in the subject.

"We are now engaged in a war that is making a fearful show for heavy taxes, and it may be deemed altogether inexpedient to even talk of an appropriation for our agricultural societies at such a time. . . .

"The cultivation of the soil and raising stock of various kinds will always be the chief occupation of our people. It is highly proper then that these great interests should be encouraged by the government. Even a small appropriation would result in great good. It would help the now feeble societies to attain the object of their organizations. In one year . . . we should hear of many efficient societies and annual fairs worthy of the name.

"This has been the result in other States. . . . We hope, therefore, something will be done by the present Legislature, and that a small appropriation will be made, not only for the State Society, but for every county that shall conform to certain conditions, which shall be specified in the act. Without such encouragement our societies will eke out a miserable existence, and make but little, if any, real progress." [20]

In 1861 many county societies were not in working order. The three old counties of Washington, Ramsey, and Benton had no organizations, though some new and remote counties, such as Blue Earth, Freeborn, and Faribault, had groups full of life and activity. The *Farmer and Gardener* placed the blame for lifeless societies upon their officers. Finally, in the legislative session of 1861–62, the house passed a bill giving twenty-five dollars to county societies, but the senate killed it. At that time there were only two farmers in the senate, and some of those in the house were described as "old fogyish." Probably about ten societies would have been ready to use the money. This would have meant a total outlay of two hundred and fifty dollars, or about half the cost of a daily legislative session. [21]

Available evidence indicates that the 1860's were difficult years for the county societies. Speaking of the Ramsey County Fair of 1863, Mitchell Y. Jackson recorded in his diary on February 7: "Attend what is called a Ramsey County fair which is a meagre collection of Cattle & horses brought in by their owners & offered for sale at auction. Offered my bull under a limit of 100.$ no sale Reach home about 10 Oclock cold and tired." [22]

For the Faribault County Fair in 1868 even the weather was inclement, and the exhibition could not begin until the day after that announced for the opening. "Two beets and a harness looked askance at each other downstairs," reads the newspaper report of the fair, "while out of doors, two fine wooled bucks occupied the rear of a lumber wagon. All took the premium. . . . The department of Fine Arts upstairs," continues the report, "was ornamented with a variety of useful and ornamental articles, including babies." Even the track was in poor condition; nevertheless, the horse races came off. [23]

During the 1860's the state society was in financial straits. In 1863 the state fair was renewed, and it was held annually thereafter, though all the fairs were not successes, by any means. The fair of 1863, which was characterized by a St. Paul paper as "a ridiculous failure, a burlesque," was located again at Fort Snelling; that of 1864, at Red Wing; that of 1865, at Minneapolis; and those of 1866 and 1867, at Rochester. At the conclusion of the fair of 1866 some interested people formed the Minnesota Fruit Growers' Association and elected the well-known editor and fruit-fancier, Daniel A. Robertson, as president. None of these fairs was unusual, but an action of the state society at its meeting in 1867 deserves recognition. It adopted a resolution stating "that the continual cropping of wheat, year after year, in the same field, without even a change of seed, is bad farming and ought to be discouraged." [24] Few farmers heeded this admonition, but it illustrates the society's interest in promoting better farming.

The year 1868 was notable in the history of agricultural societies in the state in at least two ways. First, the legislature finally appropriated money to aid both the state and county societies. The act, approved on February 27, gave a thousand dollars to the state body and set aside two thousand dollars to be apportioned among the county organizations. Two restrictions were placed on the use of the money: It could not be used to pay officers' salaries, nor to pay premiums on horse racing. A second development of the year was the formation of the State Farmers' Club at Minneapolis on October 2. Its purpose was to aid in the organization of farmers' clubs in various towns and to co-operate with the Minnesota State Agricultural Society and the Minnesota Fruit Growers' Association. Charles Hoag was elected president and John H. Stevens was chosen secretary. During 1867 and 1868 many farmers' clubs were organized in the state, and it was only logical that this development should culminate in the formation of a state club. [25]

In the early 1870's county agricultural society work was stimulated by the law of 1868. At the meeting of the state society in 1874 the secretary reported that there were forty-three county societies in the state, of which thirty-eight had made reports and had drawn fifty dollars each from the standing state appropriation. Even some of the western counties had societies by the early 1870's. For example, the Lac qui Parle County Agricultural Society was organized and held its first exhibit in 1872. "Within ten years," according to a county history, the annual fairs "had come to be recognized as among the leading events of their kind in western Minnesota and were largely attended by persons from all over this part of the state." [26]

The state fairs of 1868, 1869, and 1870 were held in Minneapolis, Rochester, and Winona, respectively, and nothing unusual marked any of them. During the 1870's, however, a bitter rivalry developed between St. Paul and Minneapolis over the location of the state fair site. In earlier years it seemed best to follow an itinerant system of exhibitions; but, with the extension of railroad facilities and the need for better accommodations at the fairs, it appeared advisable to obtain permanent fair grounds. Bitter struggles between towns contending for fair sites had occurred in many states, and Minnesota was no exception.[27] It did not obtain a permanent location for its state fair until 1885.

Beginning in 1871 and continuing through 1876, the state fairs were held at St. Paul, where they encountered many obstacles. Just two weeks before the Minnesota State Fair of 1871, Hennepin County held its fair, with Horace Greeley as the chief speaker. Then Minneapolis people "knocked" the Minnesota fair, and William S. King, the well-known Minneapolis livestock breeder, sent his finest cattle to the Illinois State Fair rather than show them in St. Paul. The general economic depression following the panic of 1873 and losses resulting from the grasshopper plagues were other causes for distress on the part of the state agricultural society. Hence, at the annual meeting of 1877 the secretary had the unpleasant task of announcing that the society was over three thousand dollars in debt. At the same gathering the agricultural society consolidated with the Minnesota Stock Breeders' Association, despite the opposition of some who objected to the latter's alleged leaning toward horse racing. From the financial standpoint, however, the breeders' association had much to offer, for it was out of debt. A joint fair held under the auspices of the two groups at Minneapolis from September 3 to 8, 1877, was a great success. Beer stands were

WILLIAM S. KING'S FARM IN MEEKER COUNTY
[From Andreas, *Historical Atlas of Minnesota*, 81.]

plentiful, side shows were numerous, and a crowd of twenty thousand was present on the second day. As a result of this exhibition, all debts of the agricultural society were paid and surplus funds were divided between the two organizations, which then dissolved partnership. For the first time in the fair's history people rode to the grounds in horse- or mule-drawn streetcars.[28]

In 1878 two fairs again divided honors, the Minnesota State Fair at St. Paul and a fair at Minneapolis sponsored by the Minnesota Agricultural and Mechanical Association. Rutherford B. Hayes and James G. Blaine attended both exhibitions and helped to attract many people. At St. Paul "the 'Britishers,' in their red coats and top boots, flying amid clouds of blinding dust," put on a genuine English hurdle race such as they enjoyed at the English colony of Fairmont. Nevertheless most accounts admit that the Minneapolis fair outshone the one at St. Paul; and in 1879 the same was true, when two fairs again were held in the rival cities.[29]

When delegates to the meeting of the state agricultural society assembled in St. Paul in February, 1880, they were a discouraged group. Unpaid debts totaled four thousand dollars, and the Minneapolis society had announced its intention of holding another great fair of its own. Members of the state society in the southern part of the state, however, came to the rescue, and the state fairs of 1880, 1881, and 1882 were held at Rochester. Trends in agriculture were well manifested at these fairs. The Minnesota State Wool Growers' Association and the State Dairymen's Association co-operated with the state society in promoting the fair of 1881, and more cattle, hogs, and milch cows began to be displayed. Farmers in the southern part of the state were paying less attention to wheat and were beginning to diversify their farming. The fair of 1883 was held at Owatonna, and whether or not it was a success seems to be a controversial matter.[30]

The legislature of 1883 passed a bill, framed by officers and friends of the state society, providing for an annual appropriation of four thousand dollars to the society and creating a board of auditors to report to the legislature at each session. At its annual meeting in 1884 the society took definite action for obtaining a permanent fair location. Action toward the same end in 1877 and in 1883 had proved premature. Now a committee was appointed, in pursuance of a resolution, to negotiate with citizens of St. Paul and Minneapolis with a view to buying from eighty to a hundred acres of land as a site. No location was selected in 1884, however, and so the state fair was again held at Owatonna. A joint committee to consider the matter, made up of representatives of the Minneapolis Board of Trade and the St. Paul Chamber of Commerce, met in November and again in December, but it failed to take action. In the meantime, H. S. Fairchild suggested to the Ramsey County commissioners that it might be well to sell a hundred acres of the Ramsey County Poor Farm for a fair site. After many discussions, conferences, and expressions of rivalry, the state society accepted as a gift from Ramsey County two hundred acres of land formerly included in its poor farm. Finally, the legislature, by an act approved on March 2, 1885, provided for the acceptance of the gift, though not without much opposition. During the debates on the question, Hennepin County state legislators even proposed that two fair grounds be established. The first state fair on the new site was held from September 7 to 15, 1885. In preparation for this event buildings had been constructed at a cost of $150,000 in the short space of ninety days. Thus, after many vicissitudes, the great Minnesota State Fair found the home which it still occupies. At the conclusion of the 1885 fair the *St. Paul Dispatch* expressed the opinion that "the results have justified the wisdom of locating the fair grounds midway between the two great cities," but a Minneapolis newspaper still voiced the hope that a northwestern exposition would be held in 1886 to compete with the state fair.[31]

With the advent of the 1870's, new social and economic conditions arose in Minnesota which called for other types of rural organizations in addition to the society and the fair. This was true in other Midwestern states as well. As one writer has pointed out, the period from 1850 to 1870 was the golden age of the agricultural fair, but about 1870 other types of farm associations arose to supplement these expositions. This did not injure the fairs, but they became agencies "through which a hundred other associations make a popular appeal." They were forced to readjust themselves, and to define their "relationship to other agricultural organizations." [32] They reflected the work and interests of other rural groups, but they no longer remained the sole agency to which the farmer might look for inspiration, education, and co-operation.

Thus, agricultural societies and fairs were no longer the sole outlets for farmers' organizing tendencies. In addition to the Patrons of Husbandry, which had become important in Minnesota by the middle 1870's, farmers' clubs and groups of specialists in various branches of agriculture were in existence before 1885. Among them, as has been noted, were the Winona County Poultry Association and the Minnesota State Poultry Association.[33] The state association did much to induce farmers to devote attention to poultry and eggs.

The Minnesota Stock Breeders' Association was organized in 1877 with William S. King as its first president and R. C. Judson as secretary. This organization was composed of farmers of central Minnesota, while breeders in the southern part of the state belonged to the Southern Minnesota Stock Breeders' Association. One outstanding figure in the Minnesota livestock business, Leonard Johnson of East Castle Rock, in 1878 was elected a vice-president of the National Association of Importers and Breeders of Norman Horses at a meeting in Peoria, Illinois.[34]

In February, 1878, a meeting of some thirty-five dairymen in St. Paul resulted in the formation of the State Dairymen's Association. Articles of incorporation were adopted and officers were chosen. S. S. Gardner of Wadena was elected president, and William Fowler of Newport and C. F. Whittier of Northfield were named vice-presidents. Several essays on dairying were read, aid was asked from the state for the publication of the association's transactions, and the secretary was instructed to gather data about the state's dairy interests and to report his findings as soon as possible. This meeting reflected a growing interest in dairying and revealed the farmers' desire to learn more about this branch of agriculture. The second meeting of the group was held at St. Paul in February, 1879.

Butter and cheese were exhibited, and papers were read on various subjects connected with dairying.[35] Undoubtedly this body was not without some influence in transforming Minnesota from a wheat-growing to a dairying state.

With the exception of the five years from 1860 to 1865, sheep production was neglected in Minnesota during the early period, and, in order to advance this interest, several prominent owners of sheep met in St. Paul on February 20, 1879, and organized the Minnesota State Wool Growers' Association. A constitution was adopted and a report was read asking that dogs be subjected to legal restrictions and that all owners pay a dog license annually to build up a fund for the benefit of sheep owners who suffered losses because of dogs. For many years dogs were the bane of sheep owners in the state, and the newspapers were filled with condemnations of dogs by sheep raisers. The act of 1873, which made the owner of a dog who killed or wounded sheep liable for the value of such sheep, evidently did not satisfy the sheep owners.[36]

Another important agricultural organization was the Minnesota State Butter and Cheese Association. This body grew out of a meeting of over eighty people at Rochester on March 7, 1882. There a temporary chairman and secretary were elected, a committee on permanent organization was chosen, and the association's aim—to gain knowledge of dairying—was defined. The next morning a second session convened, at which permanent officers were elected and a constitution and bylaws were adopted. After the business session, various persons related their experiences in the dairy business. Some of the subjects discussed were the "History and progress of dairying"; "Pioneer dairying, the adaptability of our soil for dairy purposes, and our wants as a dairy state"; "Are stock and dairy conventions useful and beneficial to the agricultural industries of the state?"; "The best and most practical means of operating creameries"; "Which pays the farmer better, the full milk or gathered cream system?"; and "The best stock for a dairy farm and how it could be obtained." In addition, a letter was read from the freight agent of the Chicago and Northwestern Railroad, dated March 1,

1882, saying that the railroad was interested in promoting the dairy business in Minnesota. Finally, committees were appointed on dairy implements, on butter and cheese, and on resolutions.[37]

In March, 1883, the association met again in Rochester, W. L. Brackenridge of that city making the address of welcome. W. D. Hoard of Fort Atkinson, Wisconsin, president of the Northwest Dairymen's Association, responded, stating that it was difficult to get farmers to change their ways until they were brought "down to the last depths of despair." Charles E. Marvin, in his presidential address, listed some of the obstacles to a rapid development of dairy and stock interests. These were, he said, lack of co-operation, improper handling or feeding of stock, buying too many cows, and building too many creameries.[38]

The Butter and Cheese Association meetings proved attractive and helpful to those who attended, and the association did much to build up dairy interests in Minnesota. In its published *Proceedings* it made available many important items of information that were useful to the farmer of the day. These publications seem to indicate that the organization was more active than the State Dairymen's Association. During its first three years of existence the Butter and Cheese Association paid out over fourteen hundred dollars in premiums. Thus, it was able to qualify for state aid under a legislative act of 1883. According to this law, a society might receive at least three hundred dollars from the state for premiums if it had paid out that much in premiums itself a year before applying for state aid. Incidentally, in 1883 there were forty agricultural societies in the state that met these conditions.[39]

It is interesting to compare the organizational development of agrarian interests in Minnesota in 1885 with that of the 1850's. In the earlier period, when the region was a frontier, slight evidence can be found of the existence of specialized farming groups. General societies, farmers' clubs, and fairs served the farmers' needs. In the later period, however, this situation no longer existed. Parts of the state had passed out of the stage of specialized wheat farming; and some farmers were concentrating on dairying, others were mainly interested in wool production, and a third group was devoting itself to raising livestock. New economic and social conditions necessitated new types of organization, and these organizations in turn played a part in the transition of agriculture from wheat raising to diversified farming. Specialization in wheat is often associated with a pioneer agriculture; yet, by 1885, as has been seen, Minnesota had progressed so far from this stage that it was awarded the "grand sweepstakes" for the best butter and the "grand diploma of honor" for an exhibit at the World Industrial and Centennial Exposition in New Orleans. To no small degree was this dairy development due to the efforts of the dairymen's associations in the state.[40]

Footnotes

A BIRD'S-EYE VIEW

[1] William W. Folwell, *A History of Minnesota*, 1:105, 230–233 (St. Paul, 1921); Edward V. Robinson, *Early Economic Conditions and the Development of Agriculture in Minnesota*, 40 (University of Minnesota, *Studies in the Social Sciences*, no. 3— Minneapolis, 1915); Hiram A. Haskell, *Joseph Haskell of Afton* (Windsor, California, 1941); *Weekly Pioneer and Democrat* (St. Paul), December 7, 1860; William A. Benitt, "Introduction to the History of Agriculture in Southern Washington County," 1–4, a manuscript narrative owned by the Washington County Historical Society, Stillwater. Theodore C. Blegen, in his *Grass Roots History*, 184 (Minneapolis, 1947), tells of Haskell's interest in books and magazines as well as in farming.

[2] The Minnesota Historical Society has a film copy of Brown's diary. This diary and that of another pioneer farmer, Mitchell Y. Jackson, have been edited by Rodney C. Loehr and published under the title, *Minnesota Farmers' Diaries* (Minnesota Historical Society, *Narratives and Documents*, vol. 3—St. Paul, 1939).

[3] Folwell, *Minnesota*, 1:230; Robinson, *Agriculture in Minnesota*, 41. The *Minnesota Pioneer* (St. Paul), May 5, 19, August 30, 1849, praises the resources, farms, farmers, and crops of Minnesota. The organic act may be found in any issue of the Minnesota *Legislative Manual*.

[4] Robinson, *Agriculture in Minnesota*, 41, 43; Joseph A. Wheelock, *Minnesota: Its Progress and Capabilities*, 73 (Minnesota Bureau of Statistics, *Second Annual Report*—St. Paul, 1862); Theodore Christianson, *Minnesota: The Land of Sky-tinted Waters*, 1:198 (New York, 1935); Benitt, "Agriculture in Southern Washington County," 5.

[5] *Pioneer*, June 6, 20, May 23, 1850; R. W. Murchie and M. E. Jarchow, *Population Trends in Minnesota*, 6, 24 (University of Minnesota, Agricultural Experiment Station, *Bulletins*, no. 327—May, 1936); Robinson, *Agriculture in Minnesota*, 43; Hildegard Binder Johnson, "Factors Influencing the Distribution of the German Pioneer Population in Minnesota," in *Agricultural History*, 19:39–57 (January, 1945); Henry S. Lucas, ed., "Early Dutch Settlement in Minnesota," in *Minnesota History*, 28:120–131 (June, 1947); Carlton C. Qualey, "Pioneer Norwegian Settlement in Minnesota," in *Minnesota History*, 12:247–280 (September, 1931).

[6] *Autobiography of Mary Jane Hill Anderson, 1827–1924*, 21 (Minneapolis, 1934); T. R. Stewart, "Caledonia's First Days Revealed in Memoirs," in *Caledonia Journal*, May 29, 1929; Ben R. Brainerd, "Public Opinion on the Federal Land Policies in Minnesota, 1837–1860," p. 78 (manuscript master's thesis, 1935); Forest Henry, "Pioneer Days in Minnesota," 2, a manuscript account of Henry's life on a farm in Olmsted County; Harriet Griswold to her father, October 17, 1856, in the Griswold Papers. *"Oh I Wish I could pay my debts,"* Levi N. Countryman, who farmed near Hastings, declared in his diary on May 21, 1859. On December 17 he noted: "Debt has hung like an incubus upon me." Countryman's diary, as well as the other manuscripts mentioned above, are owned by the Minnesota Historical Society.

[7] *Pioneer*, June 10, 1852.

[8] J. W. McClung, *Minnesota as It Is in 1870*, 177 (St. Paul, 1870); *Autobiography of Mary Anderson*, 18; Bertha L. Heilbron, ed., "A New Yorker in the Great West, 1867," in *Minnesota History*, 12:55 (March, 1931); *Weekly Pioneer and Democrat*, August 21, 1856; *Minnesota Monthly and North-western Magazine*, 1:25 (January,

1869); Brainerd, "Federal Land Policies," 78; Henry, "Pioneer Days," 3; Jay T. Wakefield to William A. Grigsby, July 17, 1857, in the Wakefield Papers in the possession of the Minnesota Historical Society. In "Some Early History of This Vicinity," in the *Harmony News*, December 6, 1928, L. O. Larson tells of professional grub breakers using twenty-inch plows and eight oxen. Countryman noted in his dairy on July 9, 1860, that he had finished breaking prairie and that "it will be ready for a crop next year."

⁹ Stewart, in *Caledonia Journal*, August 14, 1929; Robert Watson, *Notes on the Early Settlement of Cottage Grove and Vicinity, Washington County*, 16, 19 (Northfield, 1924); *Minnesota Farmer and Gardener*, 1:166 (May, 1861); *Massachusetts Ploughman*, 17:1 (May 22, 1858). Files of agricultural periodicals cited in the present volume are owned by the Minnesota Historical Society unless otherwise indicated. "Was there ever a finer school for civic and political training than the old rail fence, that fertile generator of thought, that unsurpassed promoter of friendly converse and community of interests?" asks Edmund C. Burnett, in *Agricultural History*, 22:32 (January, 1948). An excellent article on fencing in the United States in the 1850's, by Clarence H. Danhof, is in the same periodical, 18:168–186 (October, 1944).

¹⁰ Christianson, *Minnesota*, 1:240, quoting Andrews.

¹¹ *Autobiography of Mary Anderson*, 21; A. H. Wilcox, *A Pioneer History of Becker County*, 571–573 (St. Paul, 1907); *Weekly Pioneer and Democrat*, July 15, September 16, 1858; Brainerd, "Federal Land Policies," 48. Larson, in the *Harmony News*, December 6, 1928, recalls that in the winter of 1857–58 his family, with no money to buy shoes, made them out of beef hide. E. Hodges of Marion, in *The Country Gentleman*, 11:179 (March 18, 1858), condemns the wasteful method of farming practiced in Minnesota. "Beta," in the *Massachusetts Ploughman*, 16:1 (August 1, 1857), tells of the darker side of Minnesota farming. J. A. Kiester, in *The History of Faribault County*, 68, 86 (Minneapolis, 1896), repeats a little doggerel that might appeal to contemporary Minnesotans: "The little wretch that closest clings, the thing that most our patience wrings, is the nasty little mosquito."

¹² "Beta," in *Massachusetts Ploughman*, 16:1 (July 18, 1857); A. M. Goodrich, *History of Anoka County*, 75–87 (Minneapolis, 1905); Mr. and Mrs. Bromley to John Aiton, July 7, 1858, in the Aiton Papers, in the possession of the Minnesota Historical Society; letters to C. H. McCormick from Timothy Chapman, December 24, 1857, May 30, 1858, and from L. Westergaard, May 24, 1858, in the McCormick Harvesting Company Papers, in the possession of the McCormick Historical Association, Chicago, film copies of which are owned by the Minnesota Historical Society. Westergaard indicated that hard times had not brought on the high interest rate of forwarding and commission agents, which had been fifteen per cent a month for two or three years past.

¹³ Joseph A. Wheelock, *Minnesota: Its Place among the States*, 147–151 (Minnesota Bureau of Statistics, *First Annual Report*—Hartford, 1860); Robinson, *Agriculture in Minnesota*, 45; Brainerd, "Federal Land Policies," 49. J. E. Child, in his *History of Waseca County, 1854–1904*, 100 (Owatonna, 1905), indicates that all the gloom did not pass with 1857. In the winter of 1858–59 many farmers lived for months on corn bread, milk, and butter. Some lived during the spring on wild roots, fish, and wild fowl. The haying season of 1858 was so wet that there was a scarcity of hay, and cattle died of starvation.

¹⁴ Robinson, *Agriculture in Minnesota*, 45, 55; Murchie and Jarchow, *Population Trends*, 7. Some incomplete figures are given in Wheelock, *Minnesota: Its Progress and Capabilities*, 73.

¹⁵ Stevens to Christopher C. Andrews, December 16, 1878, in the Andrews Papers, in the possession of the Minnesota Historical Society.

¹⁶ Everett E. Edwards, "Agricultural Periodicals," in *Minnesota History*, 18:407, 413 (December, 1937).

¹⁷ *Farmer and Gardener*, 1:249, 272 (August, September, 1861); Robinson, *Agriculture in Minnesota*, 60; Franklyn Curtiss-Wedge, ed., *History of Fillmore County*,

1:505 (Chicago, 1912); G. W. Allyn, *When Blue Earth County Was Young*, 5 (Madison Lake, 1919). Lester B. Shippee, in "Social and Economic Effects of the Civil War with Special Reference to Minnesota," in *Minnesota History Bulletin*, 2:395 (May, 1918), states that there "was no such dearth of labor as was experienced by . . . Wisconsin."

[18] Shippee, in *Minnesota History Bulletin*, 2:397 (May, 1918); Christianson, *Minnesota*, 1:393. "The tide of emigration to this State continues unabated. From twenty to thirty teams, with the usual accompaniments of men, women and children, together with large droves of cattle, sheep, etc., daily pass through our village headed for the west," said the *Weekly Pioneer and Democrat*, June 20, 1862, quoting the *Chatfield Democrat*. The *Pioneer*, June 12, 1863, quoted the *La Crosse Democrat* as saying: "We begin to think that the granaries of Minnesota will never give out." See also the *Pioneer*, May 30, 1862.

[19] Franklyn Curtiss-Wedge, ed., *History of McLeod County*, 112, 118 (Chicago, 1917); J. E. Townsend, "Commodity Prices of 75 Years Ago," in *Belle Plaine Herald*, February 21, 1935; *Farmer and Gardener*, 1:173; 2:1, 107 (June, 1861; January, April, 1862); manuscript diary of H. H. Spencer, March 18, 19, 1862, in the possession of the Minnesota Historical Society. Farmers were urged to raise large crops by the *Weekly Pioneer and Democrat*, June 21, 1861. On June 25, 1862, Countryman noted in his diary that wheat was fifty-four cents a bushel in Hastings, a discouraging situation.

[20] Kiester, *Faribault County*, 199, 142; *Farmer and Gardener*, 1:204 (July, 1861); Shippee, in *Minnesota History Bulletin*, 2:396 (May, 1918); Biscoe to his sister Ellen, November 6, 1862, in the Biscoe Papers, in the possession of the Minnesota Historical Society. On March 2, 1862, Biscoe wrote to his mother from Cottage Grove: "I will enclose in this letter $3.00. . . . It is a bill received from one of the banks here and the only eastern bill I have seen aside from those I brought out with me. Eastern bills pass here, but Minnesota money will not pass in Wisconsin, nor Wisconsin money in Minnesota."

[21] Darwin S. Hall and Return I. Holcombe, *History of the Minnesota State Agricultural Society, 1854–1910*, 67–79 (St. Paul, 1910); Fred A. Shannon, *America's Economic Growth*, 326 (New York, 1940); Goodrich, *Anoka County*, 107; *Weekly Pioneer and Democrat*, February 19, 1864; Eliza Biscoe to Ellen, July 13, 1864, January 16, March 14, 1865; Biscoe Papers; manuscript diary of Allen W. Dawley, May 19, 25, 1865, in the possession of the Minnesota Historical Society. Child, in his *Waseca County*, 166, writes that during the high prices most people made their table beverages of barley, carrot, beet, corn, wheat, rye, or pea coffee and pennyroot or sage tea, which they drank with but little sugar.

[22] Shippee, in *Minnesota History Bulletin*, 2:398 (May, 1918); *Weekly Pioneer and Democrat*, November 27, 1863.

[23] Henry V. Arnold, *Old Times on Portland Prairie, Houston County, Minnesota*, 29 (Larimore, North Dakota, 1911); Cummins Diary, January 17, April 20, 1861, April 9, 1862, June 27, 30, July 1, 12, 1864.

[24] *Weekly Pioneer and Democrat*, July 18, 1862, May 22, 1863; *St. Paul Weekly Pioneer*, August 24, 1866, February 8, 1867.

[25] *Weekly Pioneer and Democrat*, March 4, April 29, November 4, 1858, December 9, 1859; *Glencoe Register*, February 19, May 1, 1858, April 9, May 28, 1859. The *Pioneer*, February 23, 1866, noted that Hastings tried to obtain the college.

[26] *Weekly Pioneer and Democrat*, March 16, 1860, February 8, 1861, July 28, 1865, January 12, 1866; *Weekly Pioneer*, January 17, February 14, 1868; *Glencoe Register*, January 26, April 20, 1861, February 25, 1869; *McLeod County Register* (Glencoe), July 11, 1868; *Farmers' Union*, vol. 1, no. 9, p. 4 (April, 1868). The *Union*, June, 1868, p. 4, noted that farm boys were admitted free of tuition to all branches taught at the state university; and on June 20, 1874, p. 188, it reprinted a circular letter from the board of regents which admitted that only a very few students had applied "for extended and systematic instruction in Scientific Agriculture" and announced a "Special Winter Course of Lectures" to begin in November

and continue for a hundred working days. The *Union*, July 25, 1874, p. 228, tells of the erection of an agricultural college building. The college farm was then composed of 120 acres. Andrew Boss and others, *The Early History and Background of the School of Agriculture at University Farm, St. Paul*, 11–19 (Minneapolis, 1941).

[27] *Glencoe Register*, January 23, 30, 1868; Child, *Waseca County*, 209–211; Robinson, *Agriculture in Minnesota*, 60–62, 102; Murchie and Jarchow, *Population Trends*, 8. "The inflation of the currency continues to keep prices in an unsettled condition, and until we have less volume and more value to our money, no permanent relief need be expected," said the *Weekly Pioneer*, June 1, 1866. "The situation of foreign affairs complicates our financial difficulties," it added.

[28] Robinson, *Agriculture in Minnesota*, 62, 73, 75, 102–104.

[29] Shannon, *America's Economic Growth*, 391; Mildred Hartsough, *The Development of the Twin Cities as a Metropolitan Market*, 163 (Minneapolis, 1925).

[30] Letters to McCormick from Edgar, October 20, 29, 1873, and from Rhodes, May 5, September 26, 1873, McCormick Harvesting Company Papers; R. I. Holcombe, ed., *Compendium of History and Biography of Polk County*, 119 (Minneapolis, 1916); *Farmers' Union*, 7:324 (October 11, 1873).

[31] Robinson, *Agriculture in Minnesota*, 76–80; Arthur P. Rose, *An Illustrated History of the Counties of Rock and Pipestone*, 237 (Luverne, 1911). On October 29, 1873, John Edgar wrote to McCormick from Rochester: "A large part of this district has been swept by the grasshoppers this season, and now later, a considerable portion has been scorched by Prairie fires and the result is that we shall get but very small returns this Fall. . . . That whole frontier country is full of risks. . . . The settlers are poor to start with—many of them men who have been broken up elsewhere and who go to these new homes already impoverished and with debts following them." The letter is in the McCormick Harvesting Company Papers. Christianson, in his *Minnesota*, 1:469, tells of the heavy loss of livestock in the blizzard of 1873. On the darker aspects of the relationships between farmer and miller and between farmer and transportation companies, see below, pp. 168-174.

[32] Murchie and Jarchow, *Population Trends*, 7, 9–12.

[33] Murchie and Jarchow, *Population Trends*, 12; Folwell, *Minnesota*, 3:140; Robinson, *Agriculture in Minnesota*, 104. The *United States Census*, 1880, *Agriculture*, 3:64, lists 8,003 farms of from 20 to 50 acres; 25,530 of from 50 to 100; 56,375 of from 100 to 500; and 886 of over 500 acres.

[34] Robinson, *Agriculture in Minnesota*, 84, 102, 104–106; Folwell, *Minnesota*, 3:140. The first report of the federal census on tenure, in 1880, showed 90.85 per cent of Minnesota farms operated by their owners.

[35] Minnesota Commissioner of Statistics, *Reports*, 1877, pp. 9, 186–188; *Independent Farmer and Fireside Companion*, 1:7 (February 1, 1879). The latter, on January 1, 1879, pp. 12, 16, quotes the *Albert Lea Enterprise* to the effect that at least 2,500 chattel mortgages had been given in Freeborn County the previous fall. A farm-mortgage house was set up in Minneapolis in 1874 and another two years later, according to N. S. B. Gras, "The Significance of the Twin Cities for Minnesota History," in *Minnesota History*, 7:12 (March, 1926).

[36] Rasmus S. Saby, "Railroad Legislation in Minnesota, 1849–1875," in *Minnesota Historical Collections*, 15:156. In June, 1881, farmers of Blue Earth County organized a mutual insurance company, according to Thomas Hughes, *History of Blue Earth County*, 190 (Chicago, 1909). Andrew Peterson, a farmer who lived near Waconia, noted in his diary on July 7, 1864, that he had insured his property for $200 against fire, at a cost of $4.75, undoubtedly in an old-line company. On March 25, 1871, he indicated that he had insured his house for $600 and his household goods for $200. His original diary in Swedish and an English translation by Emma M. Alquist are owned by the Minnesota Historical Society. A list of lightning and fire losses on farms is given in the *Farmers' Union*, vol. 1, no. 12, pp. 2, 8 (July, 1868).

[37] The Young America Mutual Insurance Company, another German group, was organized in Norwood in 1869, according to the *Stillwater Post-Messenger*, August

20, 1942. The Wheeling Mutual Fire Insurance Company of Rice County was organized in May, 1876. The rate of premium was three mills on a dollar at first, but in 1881 it was raised to five mills. Only farmers' risks were taken, and in 1882 sixty-five policies were in force. *History of Rice County*, 457 (Minneapolis, 1882).

[38] In 1860 the state tax was reduced from four mills. Wheelock, *Minnesota: Its Place among the States*, 127–129, and *Minnesota: Its Progress and Capabilities*, 121–125.

[39] Kiester, *Faribault County*, 232, 253–255.

[40] Child, *Waseca County*, 166.

[41] *Farmers' Union*, 8:164 (May 30, 1874). A letter in the *Union*, 8:140 (May 9, 1874), signed "Delinquent," said taxes were light before 1866, but heavy after that. So much land was owned by the government that only about a quarter of it was left for taxation. In 1873 the board of Yellow Medicine County "assessed a tax of eight mills on taxable property for county purposes, one mill for support of the poor, one mill for roads and bridges, and one-half mill for school purposes. The valuation of property in 1872 was $295,447, and the tax was $7,835." George E. Warner and Charles M. Foote, eds., *History of the Minnesota Valley*, 883 (Minneapolis, 1882).

[42] *Farmers' Union*, 8:140 (May 9, 1874); *Winona Weekly Republican*, March 26, 1873; Peterson Diary, June 29, 1860, January 25, 1861, July 16, 1862, February 6, 1865, January 26, 1866, January 25, 1867, June 30, 1869 (taxes $33.90), September 27, 1870 (taxes $31.40), January 17, April 17, 1874, June 3, September 21, 1875. W. C. Rice said taxes on 160 acres in southern Minnesota averaged fifty dollars a year. See Minnesota Butter, Cheese, and Dairy Stock Association, *Third Annual Meeting, 1883*, 106 (Austin, 1884). In 1877 the general tax on an improved quarter section in Redwood County was about six dollars, according to the *Minnesota Farmer*, vol. 1, no. 8, p. 18 (Minneapolis, April, 1878).

[43] Cummins Diary, December 31, 1858; *Farmer and Gardener*, 1:65, 97, 129, 161, 193, 225, 257, 289, 321, 353 (January, February, May–December, 1861); *Weekly Pioneer and Democrat*, January 27, 1865. C. N. Brainerd, traveling near Winnebago City in 1867, wrote: "Have just seen the second field on which manure has been hauled, since I entered the State. . . . in this State these two cases are so widely at variance with the prevailing custom of the farmers here, that I could not avoid the temptation to make a note of it. Almost every large barn I have seen on my route, has a tremendous pile of good manure which the farmers do not seem to know what to do with." Heilbron, ed., in *Minnesota History*, 12:52 (March, 1931). Countryman covered two potato pits, banked up one side of the house and one end of the stable, hauled a load of rutabagas, and repaired the backs of two chairs and an ox yoke on November 2, 1858, according to his diary.

A POWERFUL DETERMINANT

[1] Cummins Diary.

[2] Baker, "Land Utilization," in *Encyclopedia of the Social Sciences*, 9:132–137 (New York, 1933).

[3] Oliver E. Baker, "Agricultural Regions in North America," in *Economic Geography*, 2:489 (October, 1926).

[4] Baker, in *Economic Geography*, 2:460, 465 (October, 1926).

[5] Minnesota Auditor, *Reports*, 1943–44, p. 32; Robinson, *Agriculture in Minnesota*, 3; Christopher W. Hall, *Physiographic Conditions of Minnesota Agriculture: A Study in Physical Geography*, 3 (a lecture delivered before the Minnesota State Horticultural Society at Minneapolis, January 17, 1884—n.p., n.d.).

[6] Chessley J. Posey, "The Influence of Geographic Factors in the Development of Minnesota," in *Minnesota History Bulletin*, 2:444 (August, 1918); Marshall Conant, *The Southern Minnesota Railroad and Its Land* (La Crosse, 1868), quoting the *La Crosse Republican;* Ralph H. Brown, "Fact and Fancy in Early Accounts of

Minnesota's Climate," in *Minnesota History*, 17:243-261 (September, 1936). "By general consent Minnesota has enjoyed a superior reputation for climate, soil, and scenery beyond that of any other State in the Union, with, perhaps, a single exception," writes Ledyard Bill in his *Minnesota: Its Character and Climate*, 5 (New York, 1871).

[7] Robinson, *Agriculture in Minnesota*, 11; Posey, in *Minnesota History Bulletin*, 2:445 (August, 1918); Minnesota Writers' Project, Works Projects Administration, *Kittson County, Minnesota: A History for School Use*, 1 (St. Paul, 1940).

[8] Robinson, *Agriculture in Minnesota*, 18.

[9] The winter of 1873 set in on November 1, and it was bitter from that time on. Edgar to McCormick, January 20, 1873, McCormick Harvesting Company Papers; George Biscoe to Ellen, January 20, 1866, Biscoe Papers.

[10] Robinson, *Agriculture in Minnesota*, 11.

[11] Posey, in *Minnesota History Bulletin*, 2:446 (August, 1918); Robinson, *Agriculture in Minnesota*, 19. January is usually the coldest month and July the hottest, while June is the wettest month and February the driest. Frank Leverett and Frederick W. Sardeson, *Surface Formations and Agricultural Conditions of the South Half of Minnesota*, 23-40 (Minnesota Geological Survey, *Bulletins*, no. 14—Minneapolis, 1919).

[12] Robinson, *Agriculture in Minnesota*, 19, 26; University of Minnesota, Department of Agriculture, *Agriculture in Minnesota*, 2 (*Special Circular*—February, 1929); Cummins Diary, July 10, 14, 1870. In 1864 Fort Ripley received only 12.06 inches of rain. Hall, *Physiographic Conditions of Minnesota Agriculture*, 11.

[13] Christianson, *Minnesota*, 1:18; Christopher W. Hall, *The Geography and Geology of Minnesota*, 59 (Minneapolis, 1903); Robinson, *Agriculture in Minnesota*, 3; George A. Thiel, *The Geology and Underground Waters of Southern Minnesota*, 223 (Minnesota Geological Survey, *Bulletins*, no. 31—Minneapolis, 1944); Louis H. Powell, "Around a Geologic Clock in Minnesota," in *Minnesota History*, 15:141-147 (June, 1934).

[14] Leverett and Sardeson, *Agricultural Conditions of the South Half of Minnesota*, 15; Christopher W. Hall, "Minnesota: A Sketch," in *Journal of Geography*, 1:244 (June, 1902); Christianson, *Minnesota*, 1:19; William H. Emmons and Frank F. Grout, eds., *Mineral Resources of Minnesota*, 10 (Minnesota Geological Survey, *Bulletins*, no. 30—Minneapolis, 1943); interview with Dr. Laurence M. Gould, geologist and president of Carleton College, July 7, 1948.

[15] Christianson, *Minnesota*, 1:20; Hall, in *Journal of Geography*, 1:244 (June, 1902).

[16] Christianson, *Minnesota*, 1:21, 23; Leverett and Sardeson, *Agricultural Conditions of the South Half of Minnesota*, 18; Warren Upham, *The Glacial Lake Agassiz*, 1-6 (United States Geological Survey, *Monographs*, vol. 25—Washington, 1895); William A. Marin, "Sod Houses and Prairie Schooners," in *Minnesota History*, 12:150 (June, 1931).

[17] Christianson, *Minnesota*, 1:20; Leverett and Sardeson, *Agricultural Conditions of the South Half of Minnesota*, 5; Thiel, *Geology and Underground Waters of Southern Minnesota*, 127, 146, 187, 205, 255, 355, 387, 402, 443. Stillwater is 675 feet above sea level, Fergus Falls is 1,062 feet, and Brainerd is 1,200 feet. See Hall, *Physiographic Conditions of Minnesota Agriculture*, 3-5. The Minnesota bottoms at the Iowa line are 615 feet and the Red River Valley at the Canadian line is 748 feet. Robinson, *Agriculture in Minnesota*, 8.

[18] Christianson, *Minnesota*, 1:24-27; Robinson, *Agriculture in Minnesota*, 10; Warren Upham, *Minnesota in Three Centuries*, 1:68, 72 (New York, 1908). Glanville Smith, in his "Minnesota, Mother of Lakes and Rivers," in the *National Geographic Magazine*, 67:273 (March, 1935), divides the state into two triangles by drawing an imaginary line from the southeast corner of the state to the northwest corner. The upper triangle is the forested area and the other the prairie region.

[19] Robinson, *Agriculture in Minnesota*, 10; Foster, in the *Pioneer*, May 23, 1850;

Girart Hewitt, *Minnesota: Its Advantages to Settlers*, 21 (St. Paul, 1867); Southern Minnesota Railroad Company, *Report of the Chief Engineer to the President and Directors*, 9 (Milwaukee, 1858).

[20] Fred A. Shannon, *The Farmer's Last Frontier: Agriculture, 1860–1897*, 3–10 (*The Economic History of the United States*, vol. 5—New York, 1945); James C. Malin, *Grassland of North America: Prolegomena to Its History*, 48–61 (Lawrence, Kansas, 1947).

[21] University of Minnesota, Department of Agriculture, *Agriculture in Minnesota*, 2; Robinson, *Agriculture in Minnesota*, 8, 10; Posey, in *Minnesota History Bulletin*, 446–449 (August, 1918); Frank Leverett and Frederick W. Sardeson, *Surface Formations and Agricultural Conditions of Northeastern Minnesota*, 45 (Minnesota Geological Survey, *Bulletins*, no. 13—Minneapolis, 1917), and *Surface Formations and Agricultural Conditions of Northwestern Minnesota*, 43–53 (Minnesota Geological Survey, *Bulletins*, no. 12—Minneapolis, 1915), by the same authors.

[22] United States Department of Agriculture, *Soils and Men: Yearbook of Agriculture 1938* (Washington, 1938).

[23] Robinson, *Agriculture in Minnesota*, 10.

SETTLERS AND SPECULATORS

[1] Schafer, *The Social History of American Agriculture*, 1 (New York, 1936).

[2] Schafer, *American Agriculture*, 16. For the ordinance of 1785, see John C. Fitzpatrick, ed., *Journals of the Continental Congress, 1744–1789*, 28:375–381 (Washington, 1933).

[3] United States, *Statutes at Large*, 3:566; 5:453–458; Schafer, *American Agriculture*, 22.

[4] Thomas Donaldson, *The Public Domain: Its History with Statistics*, 164 (Washington, 1884); Henry N. Copp, *The American Settler's Guide: A Brief Exposition of the Public Land System of the United States of America*, 13 (Washington, 1880).

[5] Donaldson, *Public Domain*, 178, 182. An interesting account of the day-by-day life of the surveyors is found in Dwight L. Agnew, "The Government Land Surveyor as a Pioneer," in the *Mississippi Valley Historical Review*, 28:369–382 (December, 1941).

[6] *Statutes at Large*, 7:536–540; Robinson, *Agriculture in Minnesota*, 39.

[7] Christianson, *Minnesota*, 1:189; Walter F. Horton, *Land Buyer's, Settler's and Explorer's Guide*, 32 (Minneapolis, 1894); Donaldson, *Public Domain*, 180; Thomas Simpson, "The Early Government Land Survey in Minnesota West of the Mississippi River," in *Minnesota Historical Collections*, 10 (part 1): 57–67. Verne E. Chatelain, in "The Public Land Officer on the Northwestern Frontier," in *Minnesota History*, 12:380 (December, 1931), tells of hardships endured by Henry A. Wiltse in surveying the fourth principal meridian.

[8] Horton, *Land Buyer's Guide*, 30. The following notice was used:

Land Office at_____18___. Township N.___ of range No.__P.M., has been filed in this office. On and after the _____day of_____ 18__ this office will be prepared to receive applications for entry of the public lands in said township.

_____, Register
_____, Receiver

[9] Donaldson, *Public Domain*, 556–558; Chatelain, in *Minnesota History*, 12:379–389 (December, 1931); Christopher C. Andrews, *Minnesota and Dacotah: Letters Descriptive of a Tour through the North-west, in the Autumn of 1856*, 92 (Washington, 1857).

[10] William Watts, "Polk County," in *History of the Red River Valley, Past and Present*, 2:875 (Chicago, 1909); Christianson, *Minnesota*, 1:190.

[11] Watts, in *History of the Red River Valley*, 2:875. Land officers exerted great

power. Many people distrusted them, as did one man who said: "Speaking of rattlesnakes, reminds me to speak of the land officers here. Some people stand in much greater fear of these creatures than the animals themselves, assigning as a reason, that while the one gives warning before he strikes, the other strikes without warning. Their method of warfare, however, is pretty generally understood." *St. Paul Daily Times*, August 31, 1855.

[12] Christianson, *Minnesota*, 1:189; Robinson, *Agriculture in Minnesota*, 39; *Weekly Pioneer and Democrat*, April 17, 1856. William H. C. Folsom, in his *Fifty Years in the Northwest*, 639, 641 (St. Paul, 1888), gives 1848 as the date of the establishment of the first land office, and Donaldson, in his *Public Domain*, 176, gives 1860. Both are in error.

[13] Christianson, *Minnesota*, 1:189; J. Fletcher Williams, *A History of the City of St. Paul and of the County of Ramsey*, 183–185 (St. Paul, 1876); *Weekly Pioneer and Democrat*, April 17, 1856.

[14] *Pioneer*, May 5, 12, 1849. The notice, dated March 20, 1849, and signed by President Taylor, reads: "I do hereby declare and make known, that from and after the thirtieth day of June next, (1849) the land office for the sale of public lands in the Chippewa Land District, shall be removed from the Falls of St. Croix (Wisconsin) to 'Stillwater' in St. Croix County, Minnesota Territory."

[15] Folsom, *Fifty Years in the Northwest*, 641; Donaldson, *Public Domain*, 175; *Weekly Pioneer and Democrat*, September 30, 1858. Harriet Griswold wrote to her brother Henry from Cambridge on April 29, 1859: "About 3 weeks ago our celebrated Land Office took fire . . . and burned down." Griswold Papers.

[16] The Senate refused to ratify the half-breed treaty. It was not until 1854 that the tract was opened to settlement. Folwell, *Minnesota*, 1:321–325.

[17] *Statutes at Large*, 5:456; Robinson, *Agriculture in Minnesota*, 39; Edward B. Drew, "Pioneer Days in Minnesota," 111–114. This manuscript account, written in October, 1899, is in the Drew Papers in the possession of the Minnesota Historical Society.

[18] *Glencoe Register*, February 12, 1859.

[19] *Pioneer*, September 13, 1855; Brainerd, "Federal Land Policies," 121–124. In the *Amboy Herald*, December 7, 1945, the Reverend Charles E. McColley tells how his aunt lost her farm when a land sale was held.

[20] Franklyn Curtiss-Wedge, ed., *History of Freeborn County*, 195 (Chicago, 1911).

[21] Andrews, *Minnesota and Dacotah*, 120-122; *Weekly Pioneer and Democrat*, December 27, 1855; *Glencoe Register*, November 7, 1857.

[22] Andrews, *Minnesota and Dacotah*, 119–122; *Weekly Pioneer and Democrat*, January 24, 1856; *Glencoe Register*, November 7, 1857.

[23] *Statutes at Large*, 10:576; Andrews, *Minnesota and Dacotah*, 119, 121; Donaldson, *Public Domain*, 121, 214; *St. Croix Union* (Stillwater), June 16, 1855; *Pioneer*, May 16, 1850.

[24] *St. Croix Union*, August 11, 1855.

[25] Goodrich, *Anoka County*, 66. Loren W. Collins recalled that his uncle lived in Collins' father's cabin at Eden Prairie during the winter of 1853–54 to hold the claim while the elder Collins returned East to get his family. *Old Rail Fence Corners: The A. B. C.'s of Minnesota History*, 276–278 (Austin, 1914).

[26] Atherton v. Fowler, 96 *United States*, 513; *Glencoe Register*, November 7, 1857; Addison E. Sheldon, "Land Systems and Land Policies in Nebraska," in *Publications of Nebraska State Historical Society*, 22:41 (Lincoln, 1936); Curtiss-Wedge, ed., *Fillmore County*, 1:116. In his *Goodhue County, Past and Present*, 64 (Red Wing, 1893), Joseph W. Hancock states that a large number of farmers who came in 1854 and 1855 were subjected to this practice.

[27] Kiester, *Faribault County*, 98.

[28] *Glencoe Register*, November 7, 1857; Sheldon, in *Publications of Nebraska Historical Society*, 22:57; Joseph A. Leonard, *History of Olmsted County*, 28 (Chicago, 1910).

[29] Leonard, *Olmsted County*, 28; Copp, *American Settler's Guide*, 9, 10; *St. Croix*

Union, May 12, 1855; Rudolph Freund, "Military Bounty Lands and the Origins of the Public Domain," in *Agricultural History,* 20:8–18 (January, 1946). Land warrants could be had at ninety cents an acre, according to the *Weekly Pioneer and Democrat,* December 31, 1857. Watson, in his *Early Settlement of Cottage Grove,* 9, writes: "We had four Mexican War land warrants each for 160 acres; we gave Mr. Emerson two of them to use in entering two quarter sections adjoining, one for him and one for us; we kept the other warrants to locate later." Henry L. Moss of Stillwater announced in the *Minnesota Pioneer,* August 30, 1849, that he had "just received a quantity of Land Warrants," which he would "sell cheap for cash."

[30] Donaldson, *Public Domain,* 289.
[31] Folwell, *Minnesota,* 1:321–325; Hancock, *Goodhue County,* 119–123.
[32] Donaldson, *Public Domain,* 233; Copp, *American Settler's Guide,* 11.
[33] *Glencoe Register,* November 7, 1857.
[34] *Pioneer,* March 13, 1850, March 22, 1855; Blegen, *Grass Roots History,* 169.
[35] John H. Stevens, *Personal Recollections of Minnesota and Its People,* 180 (Minneapolis, 1890); Brainerd, "Federal Land Policies," 8; Charles J. Ritchey, "Claim Associations and Pioneer Democracy in Early Minnesota," in *Minnesota History,* 9:85–95 (June, 1928). The Minnesota Historical Society has the manuscript minutes of this association.
[36] *History of Wabasha County [and] Winona County,* 176, 278 (Chicago, 1884).
[37] Anderson's account, "Early History of Nearby Vicinity," in the Chaska *Weekly Valley Herald,* February 16, 1933, is based on the memoirs of the Reverend O. Paulsen, written in Norwegian.
[38] *History of Wabasha [and] Winona Counties,* 289; McColley, in *Amboy Herald,* December 7, 1945.
[39] Child, *Waseca County,* 56.
[40] See also the *Weekly Pioneer and Democrat,* December 18, 1856. Benton, Anoka, Sherburne, and Washington counties were known as speculators' areas in the 1850's, according to Brainerd, "Federal Land Policies," 34.
[41] *Weekly Pioneer and Democrat,* March 6, 1856; Andrews, *Minnesota and Dacotah,* 130.
[42] *Weekly Pioneer and Democrat,* January 3, 1856.
[43] *Weekly Pioneer,* November 23, 1866; *Weekly Pioneer and Democrat,* January 3, 24, February 21, April 17, 1856; Watson, *Early Settlement of Cottage Grove,* 23; Andrews, *Minnesota and Dacotah,* 131.
[44] Curtiss-Wedge, ed., *Fillmore County,* 1:115.
[45] *Minnesota Monthly,* 1:334 (September, 1869).
[46] *Weekly Pioneer and Democrat,* January 3, 24, February 21, March 6, 1856.
[47] *Weekly Pioneer and Democrat,* April 28, 1859.

FREE LAND AND RAILROADS

[1] Lycurgus R. Moyer and Ole G. Dale, eds., *History of Chippewa and Lac qui Parle Counties,* 1:365 (Indianapolis, 1916); Donaldson, *Public Domain,* 217–230; Mitchell, *Dakota County,* 25; Horton, *Land Buyer's Guide,* 51; *Farmer and Gardener,* 1:355 (December, 1861); *Weekly Pioneer and Democrat,* April 28, 1859, March 16, April 6, 1860. The enabling act may be found in any issue of the Minnesota *Legislative Manual.*
[2] Donaldson, *Public Domain,* 217–231; Julius A. Schmahl, *The Trust Funds of Minnesota: A Heritage to Protect* (St. Paul, 1942); Commissioner of Statistics, *Reports,* 1878, p. 108.
[3] Horton, *Land Buyer's Guide,* 42; *Stillwater Messenger,* October 4, 1878. By the act of 1863 pine land could not be offered for sale until the timber on it had been sold. Schmahl, *Trust Funds of Minnesota.*
[4] Christianson, *Minnesota,* 2:44; Wilcox, *Becker County,* 209. An amendment to the state constitution, adopted on November 5, 1872, prohibited the disposition

of the 500,000 acres of internal improvement land, or their proceeds, except by an act of the legislature approved by a majority of the people. Commissioner of Statistics, *Reports,* 1878, p. 108; Schmahl, *Trust Funds of Minnesota.*

[5] *Weekly Pioneer and Democrat,* November 21, 1862; Watson, *Early Settlement of Cottage Grove,* 30. "The whole school law now on our statute books . . . is a tissue of contradictions," said the *Farmer and Gardener,* 1:355 (December, 1861). The government gave relief to settlers who had pre-empted on sections 16 and 36 before August 23, 1857. See R. Brown to Aiton, August 14, 1857, in the Aiton Papers. Countryman wrote in his diary on February 17, 1860: "Cut and drew two loads of wood across the slough today. Some of it I got on what is called 'Uncle Sam's Land.'"

[6] *Weekly Pioneer and Democrat,* July 13, 1860.

[7] Donaldson, *Public Domain,* 347–349; Brainerd, "Federal Land Policies," 68, 104–118; Folwell, *Minnesota,* 2:331; *Weekly Pioneer and Democrat,* March 23, July 27, 1860, June 27, 1862. Buchanan's veto of the act of 1860 was a big help to Republicans in Minnesota. For the part of the federal land policy in the defeat of the Democrats in 1860, see Verne E. Chatelain, "The Federal Land Policy and Minnesota Politics, 1854-1860," in *Minnesota History,* 22:227–248 (September, 1941).

[8] Donaldson, *Public Domain,* 347–349.

[9] Heilbron, ed., in *Minnesota History,* 12:56 (March, 1931).

[10] J. Oyen, *Watson Community Pioneers,* 14 (Watson, n.d.).

[11] Hewitt, *Minnesota: Its Advantages to Settlers,* inside front cover; Donaldson, *Public Domain,* 355; Christianson, *Minnesota,* 1:327; *Weekly Pioneer and Democrat,* June 17, 1864. Guri Endreson, in a letter of December 2, 1866, tells of her daughter's homesteading. The letter is printed in Blegen, *Grass Roots History,* 79. Folwell, in his *Minnesota,* 2:332, tells of frauds in connection with homesteading. "Holding homesteads,—How amusing to see men, who apparently live in Luverne, show their caution at election time by refusing to vote here and going out to vote where they have homesteads. They don't live here after all," said the *Rock County Herald,* November 7, 1873.

[12] Donaldson, *Public Domain,* 349; *Farmer and Gardener,* 3:192 (May, 1880).

[13] Letter from Horace Austin, United States Land Office, Fargo, April 17, 1880, in *Farmer and Gardener,* 3:193 (May, 1880).

[14] Austin, in *Farmer and Gardener,* 3:193 (May, 1880); *Weekly Pioneer and Democrat,* May 26, 1865, quoting the *St. Cloud Democrat.*

[15] Donaldson, *Public Domain,* 229, 1019; *Farmer and Gardener,* 1:12 (May, 1878); Schmahl, *Trust Funds of Minnesota.* One source notes that 1,033,908 acres had been located in Minnesota with agricultural college scrip, generally for reasons other than actual settlement. See Commissioner of Statistics, *Reports,* 1878, p. 106. An item on the selection of agricultural college lands in southern and southwestern Minnesota and the funds derived from the lands is found in the *Farmers' Union,* 8:228 (July 25, 1874).

[16] Shannon, *America's Economic Growth,* 370; Leonard, *Olmsted County,* 28; *Weekly Pioneer,* January 4, 1867.

[17] *Weekly Pioneer,* January 17, 1868.

[18] *The Sale of the Sioux Reservation: Letter from Hon. Ignatius Donnelly in Reply to . . . the "Winona Republican"* (Washington, n.d.).

[19] *Statutes at Large,* 17:605; Donaldson, *Public Domain,* 360; Christianson, *Minnesota,* 2:92; *A Century of Farming in Iowa, 1846–1946,* 201 (Ames, 1946); *Farmers' Union,* 7:108 (April 5, 1873).

[20] Donaldson, *Public Domain,* 361; Christianson, *Minnesota,* 2:92; General Land Office, *Circular,* May 18, 1876, p. 9; *Statutes at Large,* 18:21; *Farmers' Union,* 8:155 (May 23, 1874). In his account of early Lyon County, in the *Minnesota Mascot* for October 30, 1931, C. O. Anderson writes: "Father . . . homesteaded a quarter section of land. He also made entry on another 120 acres under the tree planting act then in force."

[21] George B. Winship, "Forty Years of Development of the Red River Valley,"

FREE LAND AND RAILROADS

in *History of the Red River Valley*, 1:94; *Farmers' Union*, 8:232, 240 (August 1, 8, 1874).

[22] *General Laws*, 1873, p. 136. Counties also gave bounties for planting, cultivating, and protecting trees. A State Forestry Association was organized in St. Paul in the winter of 1875–76. Kiester, *Faribault County*, 416.

[23] Commissioner of Statistics, *Reports*, 1880, pp. 40–42; Christianson, *Minnesota*, 2:92; *History of Mower County*, 153 (Mankato, 1884). In 1881 farmers of the prairie regions placed orders for 1,200,000 trees with L. B. Hodges of the Northern Pacific Railroad. Minnesota's first official Arbor Day was in 1876. Elizabeth Bachmann, "Early Arbor Days," in *The Conservation Volunteer*, 11:18 (March, April, 1948).

[24] *Statutes at Large*, 11:195–197; Shannon, *America's Economic Growth*, 165; Brainerd, "Federal Land Policies," 38; *Weekly Pioneer and Democrat*, April 28, 1859.

[25] Arthur J. Larsen, "Transportation in Minnesota before the Railroad," in *Minnesota Alumni Weekly*, 31:324 (March 12, 1932); Robinson, *Agriculture in Minnesota*, 36, 38; Commissioner of Statistics, *Reports*, 1878, p. 110; Harold F. Peterson, "Railroads and the Settlement of Minnesota, 1862–1880," pp. 7–19 (1927), a manuscript master's thesis, a copy of which is owned by the Minnesota Historical Society.

[26] Commissioner of Statistics, *Reports*, 1878, p. 110.

[27] Peterson, "Railroads and the Settlement of Minnesota," 19–21.

[28] Commissioner of Statistics, *Reports*, 1878, pp. 109, 110. The state railroad commissioner in his *Report* for 1882, p. 37, said that if railroad lands were valued at five dollars an acre, the land grants to Minnesota railroads were worth $21,295 a mile of right of way.

[29] *Weekly Pioneer and Democrat*, April 23, 1857; *Weekly Pioneer*, May 25, 1866; C. C. Andrews to E. Knowlton, in *Boston Daily Advertiser*, April 9, 1857. Much litigation occurred over grants and squatters. See Moyer and Dale, eds., *Chippewa and Lac qui Parle Counties*, 1:367–370.

[30] Conant, *Southern Minnesota Railroad;* Moyer and Dale, eds., *Chippewa and Lac qui Parle Counties*, 1:366.

[31] Moyer and Dale, eds., *Chippewa and Lac qui Parle Counties*, 1:370; Watts, in *History of the Red River Valley*, 2:871, 959; Peterson, "Railroads and the Settlement of Minnesota," 60; Warren Upham, "The Settlement and Development of the Red River Valley," in *Minnesota Historical Collections*, 8:18–20; "A Load of Wheat Saved Red River Valley," in *Erskine Echo*, February 25, 1927. Some companies, to encourage large-scale farming, told how, for an initial outlay of about two hundred dollars, a person could obtain over a thousand acres of railroad and government land by purchase, homesteading, tree planting, and pre-emption. The *Independent Farmer*, 1:165–167, 175 (November 1, 1879), said that about thirty farms in the state embraced between 2,000 and 3,000 acres each, and that several had from 5,000 to 7,000 acres. Most of these large farms were in the new counties where bonanza wheat farming was common. William F. Davidson had 20,000 acres in Redwood County, with between 3,000 and 4,000 acres cultivated; John H. Camp had 33,000 acres near Willmar, with 6,000 cultivated; and O. B. Turrell owned 16,000 acres in Redwood County, on which were twenty-three houses, one of them worth $15,000.

[32] Peterson, "Railroads and the Settlement of Minnesota," 31–56, 63–84.

[33] Conant, *Southern Minnesota Railroad*.

[34] Peterson, "Railroads and the Settlement of Minnesota," 58, 61. Railroad land could be purchased along any of the tracks for four or five dollars an acre, according to the *Weekly Pioneer*, August 17, 1866. An advertisement proclaimed that the St. Paul and Pacific was offering 800,000 acres between St. Paul and Watab, and from St. Anthony to Forest City and west, for sale in tracts of forty and eighty acres and up. Ten years' credit would be given. The credit price for eighty acres was $640, and the cash price, $560. *Minnesota Monthly*, 1:34 (January, 1869).

[35] Robinson, *Agriculture in Minnesota*, 62, 83; Murchie and Jarchow, *Population Trends*, 9–11; Commissioner of Statistics, *Reports*, 1878, p. 111.

[36] Commissioner of Statistics, *Reports*, 1875, p. 15; 1878, p. 111. The number of vacant acres in each land district in 1870 is given in McClung, *Minnesota as It Is in 1870*, 175.

[37] See below, pp. 185–187. In 1875 R. Barden purchased 2,100 acres in Lakeside Township, Cottonwood County, at seven dollars an acre. By late 1879 the land was worth twenty dollars an acre, giving Barden a profit of $27,300 on the rise of his land values alone. He engaged largely in livestock raising, and one of his Hamilton stallions was valued at $25,000, according to the *Independent Farmer*, 1:176 (November 1, 1879).

THE FARMER'S HOME

[1] Murchie and Jarchow, *Population Trends*, 9; Qualey, in *Minnesota History*, 12:272 (September, 1931); *Grass: The Yearbook of Agriculture*, 20 (Washington, 1948).

[2] Evadene Burris, "Building the Frontier Home," in *Minnesota History*, 15:44 (March, 1934); *Old Rail Fence Corners*, 169. Some frame houses were built early where a sawmill was near. For an example of one built in 1854, see the *Hastings Gazette*, December 26, 1947. Countryman noted in his diary on November 20, 1858, that he plastered some of his house, as light was visible through the cracks in many places.

[3] *Old Rail Fence Corners*, 99, 174; Jacob Hodnefield, ed., "A Danish Visitor of the Seventies," in *Minnesota History*, 10:315 (September, 1929); Theodore C. Blegen, *Norwegian Migration to America: The American Transition*, 38 (Northfield, 1940).

[4] Burris, in *Minnesota History*, 15:43–47 (March, 1934); Joseph A. A. Burnquist, ed., *Minnesota and Its People*, 1:183, 188 (Chicago, 1924); *Old Rail Fence Corners*, 194; Blegen, *Norwegian Migration: American Transition*, 40–45. Burris mentions the French-plan cabin, which was built with grooved corner posts, into which other logs were fitted. Another type was the "elm shack," in which the logs in the walls were placed upright. The average size of cabins was twelve by twelve or twelve by fourteen feet, and from seven to fourteen feet high. One inexperienced German settler of the 1850's built a log cabin without a chimney, and the roof burned off. *Winsted Journal*, February 12, 1942.

[5] Burnquist, *Minnesota*, 1:184, 187; Evadene Burris, "Furnishing the Frontier Home," in *Minnesota History*, 15:183 (June, 1934); Blegen, *Grass Roots History*, 168; Alice M. George, *The Story of My Childhood*, 23 (Whittier, 1923). Austin W. Farnsworth tells of making all the furniture for his cabin in Fillmore County in the early 1850's out of a few popple poles and a basswood log. *Old Rail Fence Corners*, 70.

[6] *Minneapolis Sunday Tribune*, June 13, 1948; Thomas P. Christensen, "Danish Settlement in Minnesota," in *Minnesota History*, 8:367, 372 (December, 1927); Marin, in *Minnesota History*, 12:136 (June, 1931); Blegen, *Norwegian Migration: American Transition*, 45; *Amboy Herald*, October 6, 1944, January 19, 1945; Minnesota Writers' Program, *Kittson County*, 49.

[7] *Old Rail Fence Corners*, 70, 100; Evadene Burris, "Keeping House on the Minnesota Frontier," in *Minnesota History*, 14:263–268 (September, 1933); *History of Rice County*, 481 (1882); Oscar Hallam, "A Midwest Farm Boy of the 1870's," in *Minnesota History*, 27:92 (June, 1946). Matches were rare and a little fire had to be kept around the premises "for seed." Flint, steel, and tinder also were used. Burnquist, *Minnesota*, 1:194.

[8] Burnquist, *Minnesota*, 1:187; Burris, in *Minnesota History*, 14:268; 15:47, 183 (September, 1933; March, 1934); *Amboy Herald*, October 6, 1944. Cups and bowls were carved out of wood.

[9] Burris, in *Minnesota History*, 14:270 (September, 1933); *Old Rail Fence Corners*, 262; Marin, in *Minnesota History*, 12:145 (June, 1931). "In the afternoon went down to the spring after a bbl of water," wrote Countryman in his dairy on April 9, 1860.

[10] Hodnefield, ed., in *Minnesota History*, 10:164, 312 (June, September, 1929); Evadene Burris, "Pioneer Food," in *Minnesota History*, 14:378-383 (December, 1933); Burnquist, *Minnesota*, 1:193; *Amboy Herald*, April 28, 1944; *Chatfield News*, September 10, 1942.

[11] Heilbron, ed., in *Minnesota History*, 12:57 (March, 1931); *Old Rail Fence Corners*, 71, 116, 171; letters from Einar Hoidale, January 29, 1930, and from J. H. Klovstad, January 3, 1930, in *Minnesota History*, 11:64, 67-71 (March, 1930); Thomas Rowley, "The Ordeal of Pioneering," in *Minnesota History*, 10:405 (December, 1929); Burris, in *Minnesota History*, 14:280 (September, 1933); Marin, in *Minnesota History*, 12:151-153 (June, 1931); *Amboy Herald*, April 28, 1944.

[12] Burris, in *Minnesota History*, 14:379 (December, 1933); Burnquist, *Minnesota*, 1:190. Yeast cakes were made of home-grown hops and corn meal. Salt-rising bread was delicious, but it smelled to high heaven while baking. Countryman noted in his diary on July 19, 1862, that he took "salt to Mr. Beswick to salt the steers." The family of Mrs. Martha Thorne, during their first winter near Lake Crystal, in 1854-55, lived on salt and potatoes for five weeks. Three pounds of sugar cost a dollar, and a barrel of musty flour was eighteen dollars. *Chatfield News*, September 3, 1942; *Old Rail Fence Corners*, 80, 166, 174.

[13] *Old Rail Fence Corners*, 143; Burnquist, *Minnesota*, 1:189; Burris, in *Minnesota History*, 14:386-389 (December, 1933); Blegen, *Norwegian Migration: American Transition*, 188-204; *Chatfield News*, September 10, 1942.

[14] Burris, in *Minnesota History*, 14:272; Peterson Diary, May 31, 1870; *Farmer and Gardener*, 1:87; 2:80 (January, 1861; March, 1862).

[15] Burris, in *Minnesota History*, 14:273 (September, 1933); *Old Rail Fence Corners*, 76, 94; *Chatfield News*, September 10, 1942. "We are told that the women in America have much leisure time, but I haven't yet met any women who thought so," said a pioneer Norwegian woman. See Blegen, *Grass Roots History*, 22. A brief description of flax hatchels used to process flax fibers on early Kandiyohi County farms is found in the *Montevideo American*, February 22, 1946. Countryman noted in his diary on March 7, 1860, that he had "run off a lot of lye for soap." See also the manuscript diary of Henry A. Smith, April 29, 1878, in the possession of the Minnesota Historical Society.

[16] Grace Lee Nute, "Wilderness Marthas," in *Minnesota History*, 8:247 (September, 1927); *History of Rice County*, 317 (1882); Countryman Diary, June 2, 8, 1859. "Paint the pioneer woman the great and splendid heroine that she really was. She has not received that full measure of credit which is her due," wrote Hoidale, in *Minnesota History*, 11:70 (March, 1930).

[17] Blegen, *Grass Roots History*, 78-80; Le Roy G. Davis, "The Study of Pioneer Life: A Communication," in *Minnesota History*, 10:435 (December, 1929); *Old Rail Fence Corners*, 78. Countryman wrote in his diary on August 22, 1858: "Alte was called away to Hugh Moores to assist Mrs. Moore in childbed." On March 27, 1861, he wrote: "In the night about midnight—Alte aroused me to go for Sister Lany, and in about twenty minutes after her arrival, my dear Alte was safely delivered of a little daughter."

[18] Le Roy G. Davis, "Frontier Home Remedies and Sanitation," in *Minnesota History*, 19:369-374 (December, 1938); *Old Rail Fence Corners*, 57. "When Grandmother was a pioneer settler in Minnesota, she found her knowledge of herbs 'came in handy' to help the other settlers when they were sick and there were no doctors to be had, and also to find food before the crops could be harvested," writes Orcella Rexford, in her *101 Useful Weeds and Wildlings*, 3 (Denver, 1942). If a doctor was available he was sometimes consulted, though probably not always in the following way: "Then we went to Dr. Lars and I made a bargain with him. If he could remove the growth that Anna has I will pay him $25.00 but if he was not successful he is to have nothing, not one cent." Peterson Diary, September 3, 1872.

[19] Davis, in *Minnesota History*, 19:371 (December, 1938); Countryman Diary, September 12, 13, 1858, February 23, 1859.

[20] Davis, in *Minnesota History*, 19:374-376 (December, 1938); Shannon, *Farm-*

er's Last Frontier, 371. Blegen, in his *Norwegian Migration: American Transition*, 57–68, tells of the prevalence of fever, ague, cholera, malaria, and typhoid fever among many of the early Norwegian immigrants, and of the miseries associated with childbirth. Two pioneer mothers arriving in St. Paul in 1854 became ill "with what was thought to have been the cholera." In eight days both were dead. See also the Chaska *Weekly Valley Herald*, March 7, 1946; the *Amboy Herald*, September 28, 1945; the *Winona Republican Herald*, March 24, 1941; and the *Chatfield News*, September 3, 1942. The following is quite typical: "We had lost on the day we received your letter our little babe about nine months old. It had taken a severe cold. . . . the little babe run in to a severe bowel complaint and simtoms of the croup it died on the fourth day." E. Porter to "Friends," September 20, 1852, in the H. R. Robertson Papers in the possession of the Minnesota Historical Society.

[21] Murchie and Jarchow, *Population Trends*, 57, 63; Klovstad, in *Minnesota History*, 11:73 (March, 1930); Heilbron, ed., in *Minnesota History*, 12:53 (March, 1931); Theodore C. Blegen, *Building Minnesota*, 183–185 (New York, 1938).

[22] *History of Rice County*, 462 (1882); Christensen, in *Minnesota History*, 8:372 (December, 1927). "We see more frame houses than sod," recorded Jane Grout in her diary in 1873, referring to the area around Jackson in southwestern Minnesota. Quotations from this diary are found in Blegen, *Grass Roots History*, 144.

[23] Christianson, *Minnesota*, 1:395; Burris, in *Minnesota History*, 15:48 (March, 1934); *Farmer and Gardener*, 1:6 (January 1, 1879); Shannon, *Farmer's Last Frontier*, 368–371; *Sleepy Eye Herald-Dispatch*, May 2, 1940; manuscript diary of Edwin H. Atwood, December 12, 1877, in the possession of the Minnesota Historical Society. Atwood farmed at Maine Prairie in Stearns County. The Roche house in Jackson County, built in 1879, was forty-four feet square and two stories high, and it contained twenty-six rooms. In 1930 Charles Johnson cut off the top story. See the *Worthington Daily Globe*, September 4, 1942. "I daubed the first layer on the foundation of the new house," noted Peterson in his diary on June 9, 1870. Two days later he bought sixty-eight feet of gutters at five cents a foot. On August 8 "J. Nilson began the finishing work in the house." On August 12 Peterson began to paint the window frames, and three days later he painted the eaves troughs. Between August 22 and 27 window frames and holes were made, material for door frames was cut out, and the walls were lathed. On September 9 plastering began; four days later the brick chimney was begun; on the seventeenth the eaves troughs were put up and Nilson worked on partitions. The windows were hung on the nineteenth and the attic floor was laid four days later. Doors were hung on October 8 and painted on the twelfth and thirteenth. The outside cellar door was made on October 15, and the stairs to the cellar on November 1 and 2. On November 14, 1870, the family moved into the new house.

[24] Marin, in *Minnesota History*, 12:141 (June, 1931); Hallam, in *Minnesota History*, 27:89, 92 (June, 1946).

[25] Hallam, in *Minnesota History*, 27:90 (June, 1946); Marin, in *Minnesota History*, 12:138 (June, 1931); Charles S. Cleland, *The Clelands*, 6 (Philadelphia, 1939).

[26] Hallam, in *Minnesota History*, 27:89, 91 (June, 1946); Marin, in *Minnesota History*, 12:138 (June, 1931); Burris, in *Minnesota History*, 15:184–190 (June, 1934); *Winona Republican Herald*, February 13, 1942. The prism candlesticks and the old clock on the mantel in the sitting room left lasting images in the mind of Charles S. Cleland, who removed to Wilton in 1864. See his *The Clelands*, 6. Mrs. George said that her mother's Wheeler and Wilson sewing machine, which she got in the 1860's, did not help much when ruffles came into fashion, and sewing still took a lot of time. See her *Story of My Childhood*, 53. A testimonial for the Franklin sewing machine in the *Farmer and Gardener*, 1:317 (October, 1861), read: "The machine you sent me works beautifully, as easily managed as a wheelbarrow."

[27] George, *Story of My Childhood*, 51; Thomas Kenny to H. V. Arnold, August 29, 1868, in the Arnold Papers in the possession of the Minnesota Historical Society. A library of 269 books opened in Northfield in 1858, according to Blegen, in his *Grass Roots History*, 182. Several farmers in Houston County united in 1869 to take

Harper's Weekly. The *Youth's Companion* was popular also. See Arnold, *Old Times on Portland Prairie,* 69, 91. "Father was a great reader, and took ten papers during the war. . . . I . . . held the candle every night while father read the war news to a crowd of neighbors," wrote G. W. Allyn, in his *When Blue Earth County Was Young,* 5.

[28] Blegen, *Grass Roots History,* 183; many entries in the Countryman Diary, 1858–62; Peterson Diary, December 4, 1872, January 6, 1873; *Sleepy Eye Herald-Dispatch,* April 4, 1940.

[29] Marin, in *Minnesota History,* 12:137 (June, 1931); William G. Gresham, *History of Nicollet and Le Sueur Counties,* 1:460 (Indianapolis, 1916); *Hayfield Herald,* March 22, 1934; Arnold, *Old Times on Portland Prairie,* 49, 63, 100; George Biscoe to Ellen, February 27, 1865, Biscoe Papers. "This forenoon Royal and I made a pen to stack the wheat and oats in," Countryman noted in his diary on July 26, 1858. On July 31, 1858, he wrote: "Commenced building a shed, for the cattle next winter." On October 27, 1858, he built a corncrib. On June 21, 1860, he laid the floor in his new granary and helped a neighbor raise a barn. On July 19, 1860, he laid the upper floor in the granary. See also the entries for April 9, 21, 26, September 1, 1860. Peterson noted in his diary for November 16, 1871: "Took off the old rotten straw on the cow barn roofs." From June 21 to 26, 1872, he worked on a wood shed. See also Hodnefield, ed., in *Minnesota History,* 10:316 (September, 1929); and Heilbron, ed., in *Minnesota History,* 12:50 (March, 1931).

[30] Rowley, in *Minnesota History,* 10:407 (December, 1929); *Amboy Herald,* October 13, 1944, February 23, 1945; Countryman Diary, April 22, 1862; Atwood Diary, May 7, 1877. The *Farmer and Gardener,* 1:240 (August, 1861), urged farmers to build barns. Barn dances were held frequently in the new barns, according to the *Sleepy Eye Herald-Dispatch,* April 18, 1940. In the early sixties W. L. Ames had a stone and brick barn, one hundred by fifty feet, in Ramsey County; and Owen Roche about 1880 built a barn in Jackson County about the same size, fastened together with wooden pegs. See the *Farmer and Gardener,* 1:210 (July, 1861), and the *Worthington Daily Globe,* September 4, 1942. A farm near Cannon City, with a lawn, flower gardens, and ornamental trees, is described in the *Minnesota Monthly,* 1:321 (September, 1869). Pictures contrasting a farm home of the 1850's and one of the late 1870's are found in the *Independent Farmer,* 1:5, 7 (February 1, 1879). See also pictures of farms in A. T. Andreas, *Illustrated Historical Atlas of the State of Minnesota* (Chicago, 1874).

RURAL SOCIAL LIFE

[1] *Old Rail Fence Corners,* 266.

[2] George, *Story of My Childhood,* 30; *Old Rail Fence Corners,* 77. Some settlers opposed visiting on the Sabbath. Said one: "I believe it a bad thing to run about among neighbors on the Lord's day." He also complained about the amount of work visitors made for his wife. Countryman Diary, September 12, 1858, May 25, 1860.

[3] Burnquist, *Minnesota,* 1:183, 188; *Old Rail Fence Corners,* 119; Christensen, in *Minnesota History,* 8:373 (December, 1927).

[4] *Glencoe Register,* November 6, 1858; *Amboy Herald,* September 8, 1944; *Mankato Free Press,* December 18, 1946; Francis Grierson, *The Valley of Shadows,* 108 (New York, 1948).

[5] *Old Rail Fence Corners,* 118, 141; Marin, in *Minnesota History,* 12:142–144 (June, 1931). "Quite a number of young people came in the evening and had a dance," noted Atwood in his diary on January 16, 1877. For the position of the Methodist church on dancing, card playing, and drinking, see Minnesota Annual Conference, Methodist Episcopal Church, *Minutes,* 36 (St. Paul, 1867), and the *St. Cloud Democrat,* March 7, 1861.

[6] Malcolm A. Shurtleff, "The Introduction of Methodism in Minnesota," 28 (1922), a manuscript master's thesis, a copy of which is owned by the Minnesota

Historical Society; S. T. Sterrett to C. Hobart, March 10, 1866; Noah Lathrop, "Methodist Preacher of the Olden Time," 48; William McKinley, "Sketch of Ministry," 12. The last three manuscripts are in the papers of the Methodist Historical Society in the possession of the Minnesota Historical Society. Before a Catholic church was built at Winsted, the sacraments were administered and babies were baptized by missionaries in the homes. *Winsted Journal*, February 12, 1942; Countryman Diary, July 29, December 12, 1858.

[7] *Statistics of the Population of the United States*, 543 (Washington, 1872); Blegen, *Norwegian Migration: American Transition*, 208; *Amboy Herald*, July 28, 1944; George, *Story of My Childhood*, 74; Countryman Diary, July 18, 1858.

[8] *Winona Argus*, May 14, 1857; *St. Cloud Democrat*, February 8, March 15, 1866; *Worthington Advance*, April 9, 1875; *Rochester Republican*, July 1, 1863; *Hastings Gazette*, July 17, 1875; Richard B. Eide, "Minnesota Pioneer Life as Reflected in the Press," in *Minnesota History*, 12:398 (December, 1931); Peterson Diary, September 16, 1871; Atwood Diary, January 24, 1876. "Took oxen & load of women to Donation Party," noted Countryman in his diary on December 24, 1858.

[9] *Old Rail Fence Corners*, 216; Peterson Diary, October 28, 1870.

[10] A. J. Nelson, "The Pioneer Church of Minnesota," 46–48, and T. M. Fullerton to C. Hobart, undated, in the Methodist Historical Society Papers; copy of a notice, dated August 22, 1855, for the *Northern Christian Advocate*, in James Peet's scrapbook, in the possession of the Minnesota Historical Society; Countryman Diary, September 17, 19, 1858; Grierson, *Valley of Shadows*, 133–152.

[11] Mrs. H. A. Hobart, *Memories and Incidents of Red Rock Park* (Red Wing, 1887); Register of Deeds, Washington County, "Mortgage Record, Book R," 452; *St. Paul Daily Pioneer*, July 2, 7, 1869, June 28, 29, July 1, 1879; *Hastings Gazette*, July 2, 9, 1870; *St. Paul Pioneer Press*, June 30, July 1, 1877, June 22, 25, July 2, 1883.

[12] Le Roy G. Davis, "Some Frontier Institutions," in *Minnesota History*, 20:19 (March, 1939); *Winona Republican Herald*, February 13, 1942. On fairs, see below, pp. 245–261.

[13] *Old Rail Fence Corners*, 160, 257; Blegen, *Grass Roots History*, 111, and his *Building Minnesota*, 179. Academies or church seminaries which charged tuition fees furnished schooling beyond the grades. Hamline University was founded at Red Wing in 1854. Countryman was graduated there in 1861. See his diary, June 20, 1861.

[14] Countryman Diary, November 5, 16, 17, 22, December 14, 1858, January 14, March 6, 1859, May 31, 1860; Blegen, *Grass Roots History*, 147. Minnesota from 1849 on furthered the cause of free elementary education for all. But as late as 1876 more than eight hundred school districts in the state had schools in session only three months a year. Local taxes supported the schools at first, but after 1862 state aid was added. Men teachers received an average of twenty-one dollars a month in 1863 and women received thirteen dollars. Thomas Kenny was elated to get forty dollars a month in a school near Northfield in 1870. Trustees who examined teachers were elected by the voters of a settlement. Blegen, *Building Minnesota*, 307; Kenny to Arnold, October 15, 1870, Arnold Papers; *Autobiography of Mary Anderson*, 34.

[15] Countryman Diary, November 26, December 3, 14, 1858, March 10, June 11, 1859, July 27, 1860, June 3, 6, 1862; Peterson Diary, March 25, 1871; Atwood Diary, November 19, 1877; Kenny to Arnold, January 30, 1869, Arnold Papers; *Old Rail Fence Corners*, 281; *Sleepy Eye Herald-Dispatch*, April 11, 1940; *Amboy Herald*, October 5, 1945; Gordon Wilson, *Passing Institutions*, 99–119 (Cynthiana, Kentucky, 1945); George, *Story of My Childhood*, 31, 49–51, 64–67; Shannon, *The Farmer's Last Frontier*, 372–376. At times the teacher's remuneration was mainly in satisfaction. Countryman, in the summer of 1859, sold his school order of $70.00 for $22.50 cash and $22.95 in lumber, "a ruinous discount but I could do no better." One woman bemoaned the primitive condition of the schools in St. Paul in the middle 1860's. Mrs. Joseph Ullman, "St. Paul Forty Years Ago: A Personal Remin-

RURAL SOCIAL LIFE

iscence," 75, a typewritten manuscript in the possession of the Minnesota Historical Society.

[16] Davis, in *Minnesota History*, 20:26 (March, 1939); *Sleepy Eye Herald-Dispatch*, April 18, 1940; *Old Rail Fence Corners*, 281. "Alte and Octavus and Lizzie went down to Hastings at noon to the picnic, of Mr. Traver's School," wrote Countryman in his diary on July 21, 1858. Politics interested many of the farmers. See Countryman Diary, October 11, 1859, March 26, September 19, November 6, 1860. "In the morning I went to the election. We Swedes voted for Grant for president," wrote Peterson in his diary on November 5, 1872. Atwood recorded in his diary on June 12, 1877, that he "went to election all day."

[17] *Sleepy Eye Herald-Dispatch*, April 4, July 4, 1940; Countryman Diary, April 19, 1860.

[18] Ralph H. Gabriel, *Toilers of Land and Sea*, 128 (*The Pageant of America*, vol. 3—New Haven, 1926); Burnquist, *Minnesota*, 1:195; Atwood Diary, June 25, 1877.

[19] George M. Stephenson, *American History since 1865*, 63 (New York, 1939); Blegen, *Grass Roots History*, 92, 100; *Amboy Herald*, December 8, 1944; *Winona Republican Herald*, February 13, 1942. In 1867 the "Young America" team of Faribault defeated the "Young Recruit" club of Northfield 91 to 42 in a four-hour baseball game. Faribault *Central Republican*, August 21, 1867.

[20] Marin, in *Minnesota History*, 12:149 (June, 1931); *Amboy Herald*, August 11, 1944, April 27, 1945; *Mankato Free Press*, December 18, 1946; Bertha M. Peterson, *The Three Branches*, 44 (Butterfield, [1941]).

[21] Marin, in *Minnesota History*, 12:149 (June, 1931); *Winona Republican Herald*, March 24, 1941; *Amboy Herald*, June 30, August 11, 1944, April 27, 1945. Slippery elm bark was a treat for children, according to the *Chatfield News*, September 3, 1942. "I suppose you will have good times playing ball this summer. . . . Do you play croquet much this summer? I have wished many times that I could be there to play that game," wrote H. Shumway to Henry V. Arnold on May 18, 1876. See also Kenny to Arnold, July 17, 1866, in the Arnold Papers, and the Atwood Diary, November 8, 1877.

[22] Ullman, "St. Paul Forty Years Ago," 68; *Sleepy Eye Herald-Dispatch*, July 4, 1940; Rowley, in *Minnesota History*, 10:406 (December, 1929); Blegen, *Grass Roots History*, 85. Mary W. Berthel, *Horns of Thunder: The Life and Times of James M. Goodhue*, 173–175 (St. Paul, 1948); Margaret Snyder, *The Chosen Valley: The Story of a Pioneer Town*, 198–200 (New York, 1948). St. Paul held a Fourth of July celebration as early as 1849. Eide, in *Minnesota History*, 12:392 (December, 1931).

[23] Countryman Diary, July 4, 1860, July 4, 1862; Peterson Diary, July 4, 1870; Smith Diary, July 4, 1878, July 4, 1879; Atwood Diary, July 4, 1877.

[24] Bertha L. Heilbron, "Christmas and New Year's on the Frontier," in *Minnesota History*, 16:378 (December, 1935); *Old Rail Fence Corners*, 195; *Farmer and Gardener*, 1:53 (December, 1860); Countryman Diary, November 25, 1858, November 28, 1861. Peterson went to religious services in 1870. Atwood killed hogs one year. Peterson Diary, November 24, 1870; Atwood Diary, November 29, 1877.

[25] Heilbron, in *Minnesota History*, 16:374–384 (December, 1935); Blegen, *Grass Roots History*, 86–88; *Old Rail Fence Corners*, 141, 198, 324; George, *Story of My Childhood*, 35; Hallam, in *Minnesota History*, 27:90, 94 (June, 1946); *Winona Republican Herald*, March 24, 1941; Countryman Diary, December 25, 1858, December 24, 25, 1860, December 24, 25, 1861; Atwood Diary, December 24, 25, 1875, December 25, 1877; Smith Diary, December 24, 25, 1870. Smith went to a church service Christmas Eve. The presents in his stocking the next morning were mostly homemade, but "they were none the less pleasant to receive." Mrs. George received a pink calico apron, a stick of striped candy, an apple, and a china doll in 1861. Countryman and his wife sat up quite late Christmas Eve in 1860 making "nic nacs for the little ones." The next morning the children were delighted "over the caps & bonnets full of nice things."

THE EARTH BROUGHT FORTH

²⁶ Eide, in *Minnesota History*, 12:402 (December, 1931); *Old Rail Fence Corners*, 226; Countryman Diary, December 31, 1859; Berthel, *Horns of Thunder*, 168.
²⁷ Blegen, *Grass Roots History*, 90; Hallie M. Gould, *Old Clitherall's Story Book: A History of the First Settlement in Otter Tail County, 1865–1919*, 14 (Battle Lake, [1919]); Grierson, *Valley of Shadows*, 110–112; Christensen, in *Minnesota History*, 8:369 (December, 1927); Burnquist, *Minnesota*, 1:196; *Winsted Journal*, February 12, 1942; Peterson Diary, November 14, 1870.
²⁸ Countryman Diary, June 17, 19, October 20, 1859, February 2, 3, 26, September 26, 27, 28, 1860; Peterson Diary, July 19, December 12, 1870, March 15, June 27, September 22, 1871; Atwood Diary, April 8, 1877; Smith Diary, May 1, 1878; Blegen, *Grass Roots History*, 93; *Winsted Journal*, February 12, 1942.
²⁹ Solon J. Buck, *The Granger Movement: A Study of Agricultural Organization and Its Political, Economic, and Social Manifestations, 1870–1880*, 280, chart (Cambridge, 1913); Shannon, *America's Economic Growth*, 393–397; *Farmers' Union*, 8:221 (July 18, 1874). "We all went to Fair Haven to the Grange Picnic had a good time," wrote Atwood in his diary, July 4, 1874. On January 20, February 17, and March 17, 1877, he mentioned going to the Grange in the evening, and on March 6, 1877, he noted: "Augusta & I went to Fair Haven to Co Grange got home at one o'clock at night."
³⁰ *Sleepy Eye Herald-Dispatch*, July 4, 18, 1940; *Hastings Gazette*, May 13, 1871, May 18, 1872, May 17, 1873; Countryman Diary, October 8, 1858; Atwood Diary, December 15, 1877.
³¹ Countryman Diary, September 27, 1859; *Worthington Daily Globe*, September 4, 1942.

TOWARD MECHANIZATION

¹ Loehr, ed., *Minnesota Farmers' Diaries*, 15, 78, 80, 81.
² Gould, *Old Clitherall's Story Book*, 18.
³ Gould, *Old Clitherall's Story Book*, 18, 19.
⁴ Loehr, ed., *Minnesota Farmers' Diaries*, 17; Drew, "Pioneer Days in Minnesota," 102. J. S. Minor used cattle to thresh his oats, according to the *Pioneer*, October 16, 1851.
⁵ Leo Rogin, *The Introduction of Farm Machinery*, 178 (University of California, *Publications in Economics*, vol. 9—Berkeley, 1931); *History of Mower County*, 213 (1884).
⁶ McColley, in the *Amboy Herald*, March 2, 1945, describes the husking pins his father made of hickory, five or six inches long, and big enough around to enable a man to get a good grip. Around the pin two grooves were cut two inches apart, in which a leather band could be fitted. The pin, sharpened to a fine point by scraping it with glass, was gripped by placing the two middle fingers through the band. "I was quite feeble all day but managed to cradle wheat," wrote Countryman in his diary on July 17, 1858. On August 5, 1858, he noted: "Royal and I cut and bound oats all day. It is exceedingly hard work." Again, on August 4, 1859: "Cradled and bound oats all day."
⁷ *Minneapolis Tribune*, May 17, 1925.
⁸ *Pioneer*, November 14, 1850; Drew, "Pioneer Days in Minnesota," 30.
⁹ Drew, "Pioneer Days in Minnesota," 41; Loehr, ed., *Minnesota Farmers' Diaries*, 11, 15; Benitt, "Agriculture in Southern Washington County," 9. "Our plows are wrought cast-steel. The number sold is very large and price high," wrote R. A. Mott in the *Faribault Herald* in 1858, quoted in *History of Rice County*, 283 (1882).
¹⁰ Rogin, *Farm Machinery*, 89–91; Farrington to McCormick, February 22, August 22, 1854, and J. C. Burbank and Company to Norton and Hempsted, April 15, 1854, McCormick Harvesting Company Papers.
¹¹ On May 31, 1856, for example, McCormick wrote to Farrington: "As we have now little time to look please advise us whether you will be able to sell machines

this season. Will it be safe for me to ship you any and if so how many?" And on December 15, 1856, he wrote to William Constance: "I . . . trust you can make large sales. Can't you make arrangements and canvass Minnesota or part of it thoroughly?" See also McCormick to Timothy Chapman, March 21, 1857, and to W. H. Harrington, April 17, 1858, McCormick Harvesting Company Papers.

[12] James J. Hill, "History of Agriculture in Minnesota," in *Minnesota Historical Collections*, 8:278; Rogin, *Farm Machinery*, 77, 103; W. H. Harrington to McCormick, August 26, 1858, McCormick Harvesting Company Papers. Two machines manufactured by John H. Manny were purchased in St. Paul and taken to McLeod County in 1859, according to Curtiss-Wedge, ed., *McLeod County*, 272.

[13] William Willford's narrative, in Curtiss-Wedge, ed., *Fillmore County*, 1:117, 118. The *St. Croix Union*, January 16, 1855, offered for sale "Salmon's Improved Patent Grain and Grass Seed Separator," which won the first premium at the New York World's Fair and the New York State Fair of 1852. In Minnesota it was sold by McCloud and Brothers of St. Paul.

[14] Rogin, *Farm Machinery*, 30, 33; Benitt, "Agriculture in Southern Washington County," 9; *Weekly Pioneer and Democrat*, May 29, 1856, November 4, 1858; Countryman Diary, October 8, 1858.

[15] Rogin, *Farm Machinery*, 164–166.

[16] Hill, in *Minnesota Historical Collections*, 8:278.

[17] Louis H. Powell, "Some Notes on Early Territorial Days from the Records of Nathaniel and Oliver Powell," 3–6, a typewritten manuscript in the possession of the Minnesota Historical Society.

[18] Curtiss-Wedge, ed., *Fillmore County*, 1:118; Rogin, *Farm Machinery*, 168–171; *Caledonia Journal*, October 2, 1929; *United States Census*, 1860, *Agriculture*, xxiii. Cummins wrote in his diary on August 20, 1858: "Threshing machine came today and threshed out 102 bus of winter wheat. This machine threshes and cleans at the same time, using 8 horses at a time."

[19] Loehr, ed., *Minnesota Farmers' Diaries*, 18; Rogin, *Farm Machinery*, 171, 174, 175. "My lot was to hand bundles to the band cutter," wrote Countryman in his diary on August 29, 1860.

[20] Gould, *Old Clitherall's Story Book*, 20.

[21] *Glencoe Register*, July 23, 1859.

[22] Curtiss-Wedge, ed., *Fillmore County*, 1:116, 117. On August 27, 1858, Countryman noted in his diary a near tragedy connected with well drilling: "Franklin Fitch was buried up in the well. He had gone down to dig some more as they had found water and wanted to take some more sand out of the way, when it caved in and buried him 2 feet under the sand, it was immediately opened and after hard labor for five hours he was got out alive, to the joy and rejoicing of the whole neighborhood present."

[23] Robinson, *Agriculture in Minnesota*, 45, 55, 56; Murchie and Jarchow, *Population Trends*, 7; *Farmer and Gardener*, 1:120, 267 (February, September, 1861) The latter notes that a plant in Winona manufactured threshing machines.

MECHANIZATION GAINS MOMENTUM

[1] *Weekly Pioneer and Democrat*, July 20, 27, 1860.

[2] *Pioneer and Democrat*, July 6, 1860.

[3] Rogin, *Farm Machinery*, 96, 98; *Pioneer and Democrat*, August 3, 10, October 5, 1860. According to the *Pioneer*, August 10, harvest hands were much in demand near Red Wing, where they were offered from $1.50 to $2.00 a day.

[4] Rogin, *Farm Machinery*, 100; *Autobiography of Mary Anderson*, 20.

[5] *Farmer and Gardener*, 1:196 (July, 1861); *Farmers' Union*, vol. 1, no. 2, p. 4 (September, 1867); John Edgar to McCormick, August 8, 1867, McCormick Harvesting Company Papers. Edgar notes that the Manny, New Yorker, Woods, Johnston, and Syracuse machines had good runs, and he complains that other manufacturers gave the farmers better terms than did McCormick.

[6] *Weekly Pioneer*, August 23, 1867. The Johnston machine took first prize in a trial held near Carver in 1868, with about 125 farmers present. *Farmers' Union*, vol. 2, no. 1, p. 2 (August, 1868); Hall and Holcombe, *State Agricultural Society*, 101.

[7] Rogin, *Farm Machinery*, 102–106; Oyen, *Watson Community Pioneers*, 25; E. W. Brooks to McCormick, October 3, 1867, McCormick Harvesting Company Papers. Some farmers liked the header, but it was going out of use, according to the *Independent Farmer*, 1:61 (March, 1879).

[8] Rogin, *Farm Machinery*, 108; Oyen, *Watson Community Pioneers*, 26.

[9] *Glencoe Register*, April 8, 1869; *Mankato Weekly Record*, May 28, 1870. H. C. Howard of Mankato had exclusive control of the sale of the Marsh machine in southwestern Minnesota. See Allyn, *When Blue Earth County Was Young*, 6. On August 14, 1861, Countryman noted in his diary: "5 of us follow the reaper and it is not half hard." But on August 16 he complained: "Oh, how racked in body I feel. Sore and lame all over my body; fingers cut up etc. It is absolutely hard work to follow a reaper."

[10] P. P. Quist, "Early Harvest Days Told by Pioneer," in *Winthrop News*, July 31, 1930; William T. Hutchinson, *Cyrus Hall McCormick*, 2:74 (Chicago, 1930). Peterson recorded in his diary on May 16, 1873: "I bought a Wood's reaper with the latest improvements . . . for $235.00 with the freight which is $25.00. The freight I am to pay at once, then $100.00 in June, 1874, and the rest $110.00 in June, 1875, also I am to pay 10% interest."

[11] Edgar to McCormick, October 14, 1866, McCormick Harvesting Company Papers.

[12] Edgar to McCormick, August 8, 1867, November 25, December 17, 1869; Brooks to McCormick, September 30, November 5, 1868, McCormick Harvesting Company Papers. Several McCormick agents complained of the difficulties involved in making collections, blaming poor roads, snow, and grain prices, among other causes. In a letter of 1869 Edgar complained that "at the present juncture your agents cannot live on the ten per cent com[mission]. The collecting last year, and especially this, is so *very, very* hard that no man can do justice to it at 5%. The labor and expenses of collecting is eating up everything there is in it." Two years earlier he had reported that the money market in Minnesota was nearly broken, that multitudes of farms were run entirely on credit, that interest rates ran as high as from twenty-five to forty per cent, and that some of the machines sold earlier had to be reclaimed.

[13] *Glencoe Register*, June 24, July 15, 22, 1869. The item from the *Leader* is reprinted in the *Minnesota Monthly*, 1:190, 439 (June, December, 1869).

[14] Marin, in *Minnesota History*, 12:141 (June, 1931).

[15] *Pioneer and Democrat*, October 5, 1860.

[16] *Farmer and Gardener*, 1:123, 203; 2:59 (February, July, 1861; February, 1862). One account tells of a huge load of plows from Woodley and Berry on the road to St. Paul.

[17] *Farmer and Gardener*, 1:175, 191 (June, 1861).

[18] Marion D. Shutter, ed., *History of Minneapolis*, 1:381 (Chicago, 1923); *Farmer and Gardener*, 2:59 (February, 1862).

[19] *Farmers' Union*, vol. 1, no. 1, pp. 5, 7; vol. 2, no. 8, p. 5 (August, 1867; March, 1869); Hall and Holcombe, *State Agricultural Society*, 100; *Pioneer*, December 20, 1867, August 21, 1868; *Glencoe Register*, June 24, 1869.

[20] Rogin, *Farm Machinery*, 35–37; *Pioneer*, October 12, 1866. According to the *Rochester Post*, August 19, 1871, the chief defects of the common two-horse plow were the lack of proper temper and polish; as a result it wore out quickly and would not scour. Some startling developments in plowing were suggested. J. W. McClung of St. Paul, for example, described a plan to build a "rotary steam plow, driven by *cogs*." *Farmer and Gardener*, 1:193 (July, 1861).

[21] *Farmer and Gardener*, 1:170 (June, 1861).

[22] *Farmer and Gardener*, 1:208 (July, 1861); Arnold, *Old Times on Portland Prairie*, 52; "Theshing in the Early Days of Murray County," in *Lake Wilson Pilot*,

August 22, 1935; Oyen, *Watson Community Pioneers*, 27. Threshing with flails, horses, and oxen in Rock County in 1869 is described in Rose, *Counties of Rock and Pipestone*, 53. Flails were used near Glencoe as late as 1866, when there was only one machine, old-fashioned and weather-beaten, in the vicinity, according to the *Glencoe Enterprise* of April 14, 1904. An accident near Eyota in which a man was caught by a tumbling rod is recorded in the *Rochester Post* of December 11, 1869.

[23] "Threshing in the Early Days," in *Lake Wilson Pilot*, August 22, 1935; *Farmer and Gardener*, 1:296 (October, 1861); *Pioneer*, September 4, 1868; Oyen, *Watson Community Pioneers*, 28; Peterson Diary, September 10, 1866. Peterson paid seven cents a bushel to have his wheat and rye threshed, six cents for his barley, and five cents for his oats.

[24] *Farmer and Gardener*, 1:183, 206, 221 (June, July, 1861); *Pioneer and Democrat*, October 5, 1860; *Pioneer*, July 20, October 12, 1866, December 20, 1867, August 21, 1868; *Farmers' Union*, vol. 2, no. 4, p. 3 (November, 1868). Among important centers of the implement trade were Mankato, St. Peter, New Ulm, Winnebago, and Blue Earth.

[25] Rogin, *Farm Machinery*, 175; *Farmers' Union*, vol. 1, no. 4, p. 4 (November, 1867); *Minnesota Monthly*, 1:357 (October, 1869). The excitement resulting from the use of a steam thresher at Hesper, Iowa, is described in the *Preston Republican* for September 8, 1869.

[26] *Pioneer*, May 24, 1867; *Farmer and Gardener*, 2:97 (April, 1862); George Gilbertson, "Pioneer Days in Vernon Township," in *Hayfield Herald*, July 19, 1934. Gilbertson recalls that cornfields were marked with wooden markers and that three or four kernels of corn were dropped at the points where they crossed. An individual followed the planter with a hoe and covered the seed. Hand planters and drills were later developments. As late as 1877 one farmer sowed seed by hand where land was rocky. Atwood Diary, April 16, 1877.

[27] Rogin, *Farm Machinery*, 196.

[28] *Pioneer and Democrat*, October 5, 1860, March 28, 1862; *Pioneer*, October 12, 1866, August 21, 1868; *Minnesota Monthly*, 1:31 (January, 1869). Gilbertson, in the *Hayfield Herald*, July 19, 1934, recalls that his father used a McSherry drill with ten holes, and that it was necessary to drive steadily, in order to drill in from eight to ten acres a day.

[29] *Pioneer and Democrat*, October 5, 1860; *Pioneer*, October 12, 1866. The *Pioneer*, August 21, 1868, reports that 174 revolving and sulky rakes were sold at Mankato in 1868 for a total of $3,723, an average price of $22. Some of them were manufactured in Mankato.

[30] Oyen, *Watson Community Pioneers*, 25.

[31] Robinson, *Agriculture in Minnesota*, 62, 73, 75, 103, 104; *United States Census*, 1870, *Agriculture*, 82, 86, 87. Countryman still used oxen in the early 1860's. On November 3-8, 1862, he wrote in his diary: "Within the past 8 days I have plowed 20 acres with a yoke of oxen. This is undoubtedly the quickest time on record, besides this work, I milk 3 cows night and morning, have been husking corn some nights, husk for 3 hogs regularly, besides many other chores."

MECHANIZATION TAKES ON MODERN ASPECTS

[1] *Weekly Pioneer*, October 12, 1866. In 1877 George A. Brackett of Minneapolis developed a paper band binder which was placed on the Dewey harvester, manufactured in Minneapolis. *Minnesota Farmer*, vol. 1, no. 5, p. 3; no. 6, p. 1 (January, February, 1878).

[2] Leonard, *Olmsted County*, 103; *Rochester Post*, April 17, 1869, August 13, 1870. Whitney's self-binder was exhibited at the state fair of 1869. Hall and Holcombe, *State Agricultural Society*, 101.

[3] Shannon, *America's Economic Growth*, 377; Quist, in *Winthrop News*, July 31,

1930; Allyn, *When Blue Earth County Was Young*, 6. Not until 1878 did the self-binding mechanism of the wire binder near perfection. By 1880 the "self-rake reaper was still by far the most prominent of the grain harvesting machines." Some farmers still used cradles in the 1870's. Rogin, *Farm Machinery*, 110–116; Peterson Diary, July 25, 1870, August 13, 1872.

[4] *Minnesota Farmer*, 2:89 (December, 1878). Wire sold for eleven cents a pound in the late 1870's, though many thought it should be only seven cents, according to the *Independent Farmer*, 1:53 (March 1, 1879). One settler said the wire had to be cut and was a nuisance at threshing time. Townsend, in *Belle Plaine Herald*, September 14, 1933.

[5] W. R. Baker to McCormick, Rochester, August 16, 1875, McCormick Harvesting Company Papers; Shannon, *America's Economic Growth*, 377; *Farmers' Union*, 7:142 (May 3, 1873); *Rochester Post*, April 24, 1869. Gordon's self-binder attached to the Harvester King appeared in 1876, according to the *Rock County Herald* of July 29, 1876. N. C. Thompson's string binder could be seen in the fields of Minnesota, Iowa, and Illinois in 1877; and the Deering binder, a combination of the Marsh style of harvester with Appleby twine-binding mechanism, was designed in 1878. Other leading harvester manufacturers applied the twine binder to their machines later. A Norwegian, John P. Johnson of Acton, Meeker County, invented a twine knotter for a harvester in 1877. *Minnesota Farmer*, vol. 1, no. 11, p. 22 (July, 1878); *Independent Farmer*, 1:60 (March, 1879); Rogin, *Farm Machinery*, 115; *Willmar Daily Tribune*, October 3, 1942.

[6] *Minneapolis Tribune*, August 16, 1882; Christopher C. Andrews, *The Condition and Needs of Spring Wheat Culture in the Northwest*, 28 (United States Department of Agriculture, *Special Reports*, no. 40—Washington, 1882).

[7] Letters to McCormick from Edgar, March 3, 1873; from John Rhodes, January 20, 27, 1874; and from Brooks, July 17, 1874, McCormick Harvesting Company Papers; Hughes, *Blue Earth County*, 178; *Farmers' Union*, 7:135; 8:204 (April 26, 1873; July 4, 1874).

[8] McCormick Harvesting Company Papers.

[9] Edgar to McCormick, February 14, 1873, June 5, 1874. "If we trust Homesteaders, we take our own risk," wrote Edgar on July 14, 1874. In a letter of November 3, 1873, Edgar tells of bidding in land sold by the sheriff on a judgment. Collections were extremely difficult in 1871, 1872, and 1873, he wrote from Rochester on October 29, 1873. McCormick Harvesting Company Papers.

[10] Townsend, in *Belle Plaine Herald*, September 14, 1933; John Hall and George H. Brewster to McCormick, July 17, 1873, McCormick Harvesting Company Papers.

[11] Brooks to McCormick, March 27, April 1, 1873, McCormick Harvesting Company Papers. J. Holt, in the *Winona Weekly Republican*, March 26, 1873, claimed that farmers paid far more for their machinery than it was worth. To prove his point he listed statistics obtained from McCormick's sworn testimony before a Congressional committee, and from a manufacturer. Monopolies and middlemen were condemned, and it was claimed that taxes on $104,000,000 worth of taxable property in Minnesota were paid mainly by farmers.

[12] Brooks to McCormick, April 1, 1873, January 17, 1874, McCormick Harvesting Company Papers. On April 5, 1873, Edgar wrote McCormick: "It will be worth while to make something of a study of the best way to deal with the Grangers. The farmers are combining to get prices down and they will make a strong effort." On July 13, 1874, he wrote that the Grangers had the Werner harvester and the Hubbard Meadow Lark made in the state.

[13] Brooks to McCormick, March 12, 1874, McCormick Harvesting Company Papers. J. S. Denman, Grange purchasing agent for Minnesota, made terms with Dowdall and Hughes of St. Louis for riding plows at a reasonable discount. Denman was elated at a trial of the Werner harvester in timothy and green rye on William S. King's farm. See the *Farmers' Union*, 7:233; 8:204 (July 26, 1873; July 4, 1874), and Shannon, *America's Economic Growth*, 396. The Minnesota agency never did business on a large scale, according to Buck, *Granger Movement*, 242. See

also Arthur H. Hirsch, "Efforts of the Grange in the Middle West to Control the Price of Farm Machinery, 1870–1880," in the *Mississippi Valley Historical Review*, 15:473–496 (March, 1929).

[14] Rogin, *Farm Machinery*, 175. Farmers disliked patent rights that prevented one machine from having all the best improvements, according to Andrews, in his *Spring Wheat Culture*, 31. William H. Brewer in 1879 wrote: "In all of the greatest grain-growing states most of the thrashing is done by steam; it is probable that not more than 20 per cent. of the entire crop of wheat is thrashed by horse-power, and a not much larger portion of the oats and barley." Brewer, "Report on the Cereal Production of the United States, in *United States Census*, 1880, *Agriculture*, 435.

[15] Brooks to McCormick, January 24, 1873, McCormick Harvesting Company Papers. A contest at the Washington County Fair between the Minnesota Chief thresher and a machine invented by William Leyde of Cottage Grove is reported in the *Stillwater Messenger*, September 29, 1876. Leyde's machine, raising 108 pounds of steam in 19 minutes, threshed 26 bushels of wheat; while the Chief took 26 minutes and 110 pounds of steam to perform the same task. An excellent account of threshing with a Case machine near Madelia in 1870 is found in the *Mankato Free Press*, December 12, 1946.

[16] Commissioner of Statistics, *Reports*, 1879, p. 79; "Montgomery Steam Engine Goes to Dearborn Exhibit," in *Mankato Free Press*, July 24, 1933.

[17] Rogin, *Farm Machinery*, 119; *Minnesota Monthly*, 1:235 (July, 1869).

[18] Plowing with a steam tractor did not come into practical use until the 1890's, and then only to a limited extent in restricted parts of the country. Major Tenny of Glyndon received a steam plow in 1874. Riding plows were introduced into the Red River Valley only after 1875, and the gang plow began to be used there about 1879. Elsewhere single plows were more common. Atwood tried out a sulky plow in 1877, but he did not like it, for it would not scour. He gave it up for a John Deere plow. Rogin, *Farm Machinery*, 36, 38, 41; *Farmers' Union*, 7:329; 8:177, 188 (October 18, 1873; June 13, 20, 1874); *Minnesota Farmer*, vol. 1, no. 11, p. 4 (July, 1878); *Independent Farmer*, 1:103 (April 1, 1879); Atwood Diary, August 30, September 12, 17, 22, 1877.

[19] *Minnesota Farmer*, vol. 1, no. 8, p. 7; vol. 1, no. 10, p. 10 (April, June, 1878).

[20] *Minnesota Farmer*, vol. 1, no. 12, p. 22; vol. 2, no. 2, p. 33 (August, October, 1878).

[21] Arnold, *Old Times on Portland Prairie*, 85; Horace B. Hudson, *A Half Century of Minnesota as Territory and State*, 46 (Minneapolis, 1900); *Farmers' Union*, vol. 1, no. 5, p. 5; vol. 8, no. 10, p. 66 (December, 1867; March 7, 1874); *Minnesota Farmer*, 2:96, 239 (December, 1878; May, 1879).

[22] Commissioner of Statistics, *Reports*, 1876, pp. 153–157. Probably no branch of manufacturing in the state had increased more in the preceding four years than that of farm machinery.

[23] Christianson, *Minnesota*, 2:90. "Paid 100.83 on last machine note," wrote Atwood in his diary on May 16, 1877.

[24] Commissioner of Statistics, *Reports*, 1876, p. 154; 1878, p. 220. An Elward harvester was displayed at the state fair of 1874. The buildings and machinery of the Elward plant cost $125,000, and there was great demand for the harvester. It won over the Marsh harvester in a trial near Marine in 1874. The St. Paul Harvester Works also introduced the Eureka mower, a machine new in principle to the West. Hall and Holcombe, *State Agricultural Society*, 119; *Farmers' Union*, 8:148 (May 16, 1874); *Stillwater Messenger*, August 7, 1874.

[25] The Monitor was the only big company in the West to keep out of the plow ring formed against the Grange in the fall of 1873. *Farmers' Union*, 7:84, 392; 8:172 (March 15, December 6, 1873; June 6, 1874).

[26] Commissioner of Statistics, *Reports*, 1876, p. 157; *Independent Farmer*, 1:101 (April 1, 1879).

[27] *Farmers' Union*, 7:308; 8:204 (September 27, 1873; July 4, 1874); *Minnesota Farmer*, vol. 1, no. 9, p. 22; no. 10, p. 2 (May, June, 1878).

[28] Commissioner of Statistics, *Reports*, 1878, p. 225; Hartsough, *Twin Cities as a Metropolitan Market*, 55; Andrew Morrison, ed., *The Flour City*, 52 (Minneapolis, 1887); *Minneapolis Tribune*, April 8, 1881.

[29] *Independent Farmer*, 1:106 (April 1, 1879).

[30] *Farmers' Union*, 7:111 (April 5, 1873).

[31] Commissioner of Statistics, *Reports*, 1876, p. 156; *Minnesota Farmer*, 2:46, 239 (October, 1878; May, 1879); *Independent Farmer*, 1:177 (November 1, 1879).

[32] Dwight M. Sabin, *Reply to Washburn Slanders*, 4 ([St. Paul], 1889). The *Stillwater Messenger*, October 4, 1879, claimed that Sabin used his influence to wipe out the state's claims against him for contract convict labor. On December 4, 1880, the *Messenger* noted that four carloads of threshers were being shipped to San Francisco via New York and Panama; on February 12, 1881, the paper claimed that the legislature had awarded convict labor to Sabin at forty-five cents a day each, although Sabin's was the second highest bid; and on May 17, 1884, it reported that the company showed assets of $4,000,000, half of which were farmers' notes.

[33] Robinson, *Agriculture in Minnesota*, 104, 106, 167, 232; *United States Census*, 1880, *Agriculture*, 4. In 1910 the average value of implements per farm was $335.14. New York in 1880 had farm implements and machinery worth $42,592,741, and Pennsylvania ranked second, with a valuation of $35,473,037.

WHEAT: KING OR TYRANT?

[1] *Farmer and Gardener*, 1:17 (November, 1860); Henrietta M. Larson, *The Wheat Market and the Farmer in Minnesota, 1858–1900*, 17 (New York, 1926).

[2] *Pioneer*, May 26, 1849, December 11, 1851; *Weekly Pioneer and Democrat*, September 9, November 18, December 2, 1859, April 6, 20, September 28, 1860; Robinson, *Agriculture in Minnesota*, 43, 60, 102. The *Chicago Journal* is quoted in the *Weekly Pioneer and Democrat*, September 9, 1859. Nine counties—Fillmore, Olmsted, Dakota, Winona, Goodhue, Hennepin, Rice, Wabasha, and Houston—produced more than 100,000 bushels each in 1860, according to C. W. Thompson, "The Movement of Wheat-growing: A Study of a Leading State," in *Quarterly Journal of Economics*, 18:570 (August, 1904).

[3] George B. Merrick, *Old Times on the Upper Mississippi*, 169 (Cleveland, 1909).

[4] *Weekly Pioneer and Democrat*, November 4, 1859, April 27, August 31, September 28, 1860. Rates were very changeable in the years following 1865, according to Andrews, *Spring Wheat Culture*, 49.

[5] Prices at the best interior markets were about seventy-five per cent of those paid at Winona and fifty per cent of Milwaukee prices. Larson, *The Wheat Market and the Farmer*, 22.

[6] *Lake Benton News*, August 16, 1935; Larson, *The Wheat Market and the Farmer*, 23. One observer wrote that when marketing wheat a settler wore a flannel undershirt and drawers, a linsey shirt, a vest, a coat, homemade lined woolen pantaloons, a cap of cloth, muskrat, or coonskin, woolen mittens faced with cloth or deerskin, woolen socks, and cowhide boots. See Curtiss-Wedge, ed., *Fillmore County*, 1:113. Frank Slocum, in *Old Rail Fence Corners*, 114, tells of farmers coming through Cannon Falls on their way to Hastings "with their grain on their ox drawn wagons. They had a journey of two hundred miles from Owatonna to Hastings and back. They would go in companies and camp out on the way."

[7] Robinson, *Agriculture in Minnesota*, 43, 107; *Weekly Pioneer and Democrat*, April 14, 1859; *Glencoe Register*, July 29, 1869.

[8] Larson, *The Wheat Market and the Farmer*, 28–34. Average wheat prices at Winona varied from $.60 in the winter of 1859 to $1.99 in the summer of 1867.

[9] George Biscoe to Ellen, May 18, 1866, Biscoe Papers.

[10] G. W. Schatzel, "Among the Wheat Fields of Minnesota," in *Harper's Monthly*, 36:190–201 (January, 1868); Folwell, *Minnesota*, 3:66; *Wabasha County Leader*, April 18, 1935.

[11] *Glencoe Register*, February 13, 20, 1868; C. H. Phinney, "Herman Was Center

of Early Wheat Shipping," in *Grant County Herald* (Elbow Lake), February 21, 1935.

[12] *Glencoe Register*, February 20, 1868; Larson, *The Wheat Market and the Farmer*, 35; *House Journal*, 1867, pp. 118, 180, 210.

[13] Larson, *The Wheat Market and the Farmer*, 36–39. The *Weekly Pioneer and Democrat*, July 27, 1860, quotes the *Chicago Times* on the Minnesota wheat trade.

[14] *Minnesota Executive Documents*, 1869, p. 7; Christianson, *Minnesota*, 2:18; Robinson, *Agriculture in Minnesota*, 61; *Mankato Record*, January 15, February 12, 1870; *Rochester Post*, January 29, March 12, April 2, December 3, 1870; Saby, in *Minnesota Historical Collections*, 15:86. Edward Harkness, a Fillmore County farmer, recorded in his diary on May 10, 1870, that wheat was selling for fifty-five cents at Houston. A partial copy of this diary is owned by the Minnesota Historical Society. Cummins noted in his diary on August 15, 1870, that he took wheat to Shakopee, but brought it home again as he could not sell it for what it was worth. See also Edgar to McCormick, November 17, 1870, for a remark from Rochester that many farmers were going down hopelessly; farmers' antirailroad meetings, he said, were common. The demands of one such meeting, for uniform freight rates, abolition of the prevailing system of grading wheat, and the prohibition of railroad ownership of elevators and of railroad consolidations, are given in the *Rochester Post*, December 3, 1870.

[15] *Weekly Pioneer*, October 5, 1866; Christianson, *Minnesota*, 2:15; John D. Hicks, "The Origin and Early History of the Farmers' Alliance in Minnesota," in *Mississippi Valley Historical Review*, 9:209–215 (December, 1922). The *Wabasha County Leader*, November 25, 1927, mentions a buyers' pool in Lake City in 1871.

[16] *General Laws*, 1871, pp. 56–59, 61–66; Christianson, *Minnesota*, 2:18–21, 23–25; Saby, in *Minnesota Historical Collections*, 15:95–111; *Stillwater Messenger*, May 1, 1874; *Farmers' Union*, 8:161 (May 30, 1874); Buck, *Granger Movement*, 161, 164, 165, 211. Thirty thousand bushels of wheat were sent from St. Paul to Glasgow by water in 1882 at a cost of twenty-nine cents a bushel, according to Andrews, *Spring Wheat Culture*, 55.

[17] Robinson, *Agriculture in Minnesota*, 76; Charles B. Kuhlmann, "The Influence of the Minneapolis Flour Mills upon the Economic Development of Minnesota and the Northwest," in *Minnesota History*, 6:153 (June, 1925); Cummins Diary, June 18, 1874.

[18] *Minnesota Farmer*, 2:41 (October, 1878); *Independent Farmer*, vol. 1, no. 1, pp. 4, 11; no. 2, pp. 6, 13; no. 3, p. 51 (January, February, March, 1879). The Minneapolis Millers' Association was organized perhaps as early as 1865. A law of 1869 was intended to help farmers in matters of weights and measures, but it was repealed. Charles B. Kuhlmann, *The Development of the Flour-milling Industry in the United States*, 260 (New York, 1929); *Rochester Post*, April 3, 1869.

[19] *Independent Farmer*, 1:47, 51, 109 (March, May, 1879).

[20] George N. Lamphere, "History of Wheat Raising in the Red River Valley," in *Minnesota Historical Collections*, 10:26; Hicks, in *Mississippi Valley Historical Review*, 9:216; *General Laws*, 1885, pp. 243–253.

[21] Lamphere, in *Minnesota Historical Collections*, 10:27, 28; Folwell, *Minnesota*, 3:68; *General Laws*, 1885, pp. 136–148.

[22] Biscoe to his sister, August 21, 1862, September 18, 1865, Biscoe Papers; Robinson, *Agriculture in Minnesota*, 60; *Wabasha County Leader*, November 11, 18, 1927; *Winona Republican Herald*, November 20, 1930; *Minnesota Monthly*, 1:326 (September, 1869); *Weekly Pioneer and Democrat*, January 25, 1866.

[23] Christianson, *Minnesota*, 2:14; *Weekly Pioneer*, November 27, 1868. The 1868 season was too hot, that of 1869 too cold and wet, and that of 1870 too dry and hot. Robinson, *Agriculture in Minnesota*, 75.

[24] Folwell, *Minnesota*, 3:60; Thompson, in *Journal of Economics*, 18:570; Robinson, *Agriculture in Minnesota*, 102.

[25] Robinson, *Agriculture in Minnesota*, 76; Peterson, "Railroads and the Settlement of Minnesota," 14–17.

[26] *History of the Red River Valley*, 1:199; Lamphere, in *Minnesota Historical Collections*, 10:4, 12–19. The early settlers had to learn how to farm in the Red River region through bitter experiences, writes Marin in *Minnesota History*, 12:147 (June, 1931). The *Weekly Pioneer and Democrat*, December 9, 1858, and the *Farmer and Gardener*, 1:164 (June, 1861), recognized the potential productivity of the Red River Valley.

[27] *History of the Red River Valley*, 1:201; *United States Census*, 1880, *Agriculture*, 454; Bertha L. Heilbron, ed., "A British Agricultural Expert in the Red River Valley, 1879," 97, in *North Dakota Historical Quarterly*, 7:95–113 (January, April, 1933). An account of Dalrymple's large-scale farming in Washington County is found in the *Farmers' Union*, vol. 2, no. 1, p. 5 (August, 1868).

[28] Robinson, *Agriculture in Minnesota*, 78, 260; *United States Census*, 1880, *Agriculture*, 177; Louis B. Schmidt and Earle D. Ross, eds., *Readings in the Economic History of American Agriculture*, 370–380 (New York, 1925). Minnesota's wheat production is given as 31,886,520 bushels in United States Commissioner of Agriculture, *Reports*, 1879, p. 135.

[29] Robinson, *Agriculture in Minnesota*, 77; Folwell, *Minnesota*, 3:68; Christianson, *Minnesota*, 1:461; *Minneapolis Journal*, November 11, 1928; *United States Census*, 1880, *Agriculture*, 561–579.

[30] Robinson, *Agriculture in Minnesota*, 77; Folwell, *Minnesota*, 3:70; Kuhlmann, *Flour-milling Industry*, 113–125; *Minneapolis Journal*, November 11, 1928; Hudson, *Half Century of Minnesota*, 59. "Hard spring wheat commands in the market six cents more per bushel than any other sort," wrote Andrews in 1882. See his *Spring Wheat Culture*, 3.

[31] *Independent Farmer*, vol. 1, no. 1, p. 7 (January 1, 1879); *Farmers' Union*, vol. 2, no. 12, p. 1; vol. 8, no. 22, p. 16 (July, 1869; May 30, 1874); *Minnesota Farmer*, 2:151 (February, 1879).

[32] *Weekly Pioneer and Democrat*, July 24, 1856, May 12, 1859; Kuhlmann, *Flour-milling Industry*, 77; *Farmer and Gardener*, 1:8 (November, 1860).

[33] *Farmers' Union*, vol. 2, no. 2, p. 4 (September, 1868); Kuhlmann, *Flour-milling Industry*, 77. In 1869 Minnesota produced 18,789,188 bushels of spring wheat and 76,885 bushels of winter wheat. Winona, Houston, and Wabasha counties produced most of the latter. *United States Census*, 1870, *Wealth and Industry*, 181; Peterson Diary, September 8, 1873, September 7, 1874.

[34] *Statistics of Minnesota*, 1869, p. 4; *Pioneer*, December 11, 1851; *Weekly Pioneer and Democrat*, November 18, 1859, August 31, 1860; *Farmer and Gardener*, 1:263 (September, 1861). For discussions of Fife, Black Sea, and Tea or Java wheat, see J. Allen Clark and B. B. Bayles, *Classification of Wheat Varieties Grown in the United States*, 58, 71, 100 (United States Department of Agriculture, *Technical Bulletins*, no. 459—Washington, 1935).

[35] *Farmer and Gardener*, 1:209, 239, 269, 293, 329 (July–November, 1861); *Farmers' Union*, vol. 1, no. 4, p. 4; vol. 1, no. 6, p. 4 (November, 1867; January, 1868); *Minnesota Monthly*, 1:128 (April, 1869); Kiester, *Faribault County*, 352, 367, 386. Among other varieties introduced and tried by Minnesota farmers were Arnautka, Lost Nation, Defiance, and Champlain. See the *Rochester Post*, December 4, 1869; *Minnesota Farmer*, 1:5; 2:154 (February, 1878; February, 1879); Andrews, *Spring Wheat Culture*, 7; Clark and Bayles, *Wheat Varieties*, 140.

[36] *Farmer and Gardener*, 1:134 (May, 1861); *Weekly Pioneer and Democrat*, August 10, 1860; Frederick D. Heald, *Manual of Plant Diseases*, 718 (New York, 1933).

[37] Frank R. Holmes, *Minnesota in Three Centuries*, 4:107–114 (New York, 1908); "Beta," in *Massachusetts Ploughman*, September 12, 1857, January 9, 1858; *Weekly Pioneer and Democrat*, July 15, 1858, June 23, July 14, 1865; Folwell, *Minnesota*, 3:93–111; Edgar to McCormick, June 10, 1873, June 5, 1874, McCormick Harvesting Company Papers; *Stillwater Messenger*, January 9, 1874, June 18, 1875. "Ed Corliss said he came home after the grasshoppers had eaten everything

in his onion patch and they were all sitting up on the fence in a row and he could smell their breath as he approached and knew what had happened," wrote Gould, in his *Old Citherall's Story Book*, 15. A Minnesota farmer recorded that the air was so full of grasshoppers "that when you looked at the sun it looked as if it was snowing." See Peterson Diary, August 26, 1876, April 26, June 6, 1877. The crop failure of 1876 was caused not only by grasshoppers, but also by hot weather, drought, and the chinch bug—a new foe, according to Commissioner of Statistics, *Reports*, 1877, p. 17.

[38] *Glencoe Register*, January 30, February 6, 1868; *Winthrop News*, July 31, 1930; *Farmers' Union*, vol. 2, no. 1, p. 5 (August, 1868). A hired man who worked the year round usually received fifteen dollars a month in addition to board, room, and washing, according to Andrews, *Spring Wheat Culture*, 42. The Chicago *Advance* of September 5, 1878, noted that four hundred harvest hands went to Winona from Davenport by steamer.

[39] Andrews, *Spring Wheat Culture*, 32–35; *Rochester Post*, November 20, 1869; *Farmer and Gardener*, 2:100 (April, 1862). With wheat at a dollar a bushel, a farmer made a profit of $175 on forty acres, according to the *Minnesota Monthly*, 1:75 (March, 1869). "The farmer would make three dollars per acre," wrote Biscoe to his sister on July 3, 1862, "but he does not make that if the labor of carrying it to market is counted anything." Biscoe Papers.

[40] *Weekly Pioneer*, July 14, 1867. Somewhat similar cases are described in the *Weekly Pioneer and Democrat*, September 22, 1865, and the *Minnesota Monthly*, 1:90, 118, 119 (March, April, 1869).

[41] *Independent Farmer*, 1:8 (January, 1879); *Farmers' Union*, 8:228 (July 25, 1874); *Glencoe Register*, October 14, 21, 28, December 16, 1869; Cummins Diary, November 27, 1880; Arnold, *Old Times on Portland Prairie*, 100. "I know several men who in their ambition to have large farms bought more than they could pay for and after struggling along several years lost the whole," wrote Biscoe to his sister on July 3, 1862. Biscoe Papers.

[42] *Farmers' Union*, vol. 1, no. 8, p. 3; vol. 2, no. 5, p. 4 (March, 1868; January, 1869); *Minnesota Monthly*, 1:216 (July, 1869). The farmer was constantly being urged to diversify his crops. *Farmer and Gardener*, 2:13 (January, 1862); *Weekly Pioneer*, May 10, 17, December 27, 1867, February 14, 1868; *Glencoe Register*, February 24, 1870; *Mankato Record*, April 30, 1870; Commissioner of Statistics, *Reports*, 1870, p. 41; *History of Mower County*, 151, 156 (1884).

[43] Robinson, *Agriculture in Minnesota*, 79; Christianson, *Minnesota*, 1:458. According to Christianson, there was a slow but steady decline in wheat prices from 1872 to 1875.

[44] Laura M. Hamilton, "Stem Rust in the Spring Wheat Area in 1878," in *Minnesota History*, 20:156–164 (June, 1939); Robinson, *Agriculture in Minnesota*, 79; Leonard, *Olmsted County*, 107; *Winona Republican*, November 20, 1930.

[45] Thompson, in *Journal of Economics*, 18:572; Robinson, *Agriculture in Minnesota*, 260; Shannon, *America's Economic Growth*, 379; Commissioner of Statistics, *Reports*, 1883, p. 9. The *Report* shows that wheat occupied 68.98 per cent of the total cultivated area of Minnesota in 1878, and 53.35 per cent in 1882.

[46] Thompson, in *Journal of Economics*, 18:573–584; Commissioner of Statistics, *Reports*, 1883, p. 9. C. W. Lyman of Northfield, in C. C. Andrews, *Some Minnesota Farmers Who Are Making Money*, 9 (St. Paul, 1893), tells of going through the transition from wheat production to stock raising and dairying. In the *Spring Valley Tribune* of August 23, 1924, J. C. Mills tells of farmers in Fillmore County who lost their farms about 1880 and removed to Dakota. Marin, in *Minnesota History*, 12:153–156 (June, 1931), tells of seeing prairie schooners filled with migrants to Dakota from southeastern Minnesota during the early 1880's. The *Caledonia Journal*, March 13, 1941, prints the following interesting record of one farmer's yearly experience with wheat in Houston County. The year 1878 stands out particularly clearly:

Year	Acres	Bushels	Bushels per acre	Price
1863	40	702	17.5	$ .86
1864	60	960	16.5	1.04
1865	58	1358	23.5	1.24
1866	68	1185	17.25	1.40
1867	76	1335	17.75	1.51
1868	78	1556	20	.98
1869	110	2060	18	.70
1870	110	1660	15	1.05
1871	110	1450	13	1.10
1872	120	2060	17	1.07
1873	130	2582	20	1.06
1874	110	1997	19	.85
1875	130	2186	17	.96
1876	120	540	4.5	1.19
1877	90	1353	15	.91
1878	120	600	5	.56
1879	115	900	7.5	.89
1880	110	540	5	.90
1881	60	495	8	1.05

[47] Schmidt and Ross, eds., *Readings in American Agriculture*, 379.

LIVESTOCK

[1] Frank E. Balmer, "The Farmer and Minnesota History," in *Minnesota History*, 7:205–207 (September, 1926); Robinson, *Agriculture in Minnesota*, 40.

[2] *Minnesota Democrat*, October 25, 1854; Hartsough, *Twin Cities as a Metropolitan Market*, 66.

[3] Loehr, ed., *Minnesota Farmers' Diaries*, 49, 50, 52. An interesting article by Edmund C. Burnett on hog raising in Tennessee and hog driving from there to South Carolina during the mid-nineteenth century appears in *Agricultural History*, 20:86–103 (April, 1946).

[4] *Pioneer*, May 19, 26, 1849.

[5] Gresham, ed., *Nicollet and Le Sueur Counties*, 1:460; Robinson, *Agriculture in Minnesota*, 41. H. C. Howard wrote that, following the prairie schooner of the early pioneer, "would be found one or two cows, poor, ill-fed creatures, oftentimes minus their caudal appendage, that useful member having been left in possession of the dog back in Wisconsin. The pioneer gave but little thought to his cow." See Minnesota Butter, Cheese, and Dairy Stock Association, *Annual Convention*, 1885, p. 27 (Red Wing, 1886). In his "Federal Land Policies," 26, Brainerd states that many new settlers in the prairie region engaged in stock raising in the middle 1850's, but that, since few brought cattle with them, they had to buy from drovers who demanded cash. In 1855 at St. Peter, milch cows cost from $35 to $70; year-old heifers, from $15 to $25; work oxen, from $130 to $175 a yoke; and three-year-old steers, from $75 to $120.

[6] *Pioneer*, February 6, 1851, January 1, 1852.

[7] *Pioneer*, July 15, 1852; weekly edition, May 4, 1854.

[8] Andrews, *Minnesota and Dacotah*, 158.

[9] *Weekly Pioneer*, April 19, 1855.

[10] Hall and Holcombe, *State Agricultural Society*, 16; *St. Anthony Express*, May 27, 1853. One year Haskell attended the Illinois State Fair and bought a Durham bull, which he named "Sangamon." Haskell, *Joseph Haskell*, 8.

[11] Hall and Holcombe, *State Agricultural Society*, 31; Ulysses P. Hedrick, *A History of Agriculture in the State of New York*, 358 (Albany, 1933). Devon and Dur-

ham cattle were becoming numerous in Freeborn County. *Farmer and Gardener,* 1:72 (January, 1861).

[12] Larson, *The Wheat Market and the Farmer,* 17; *Weekly Pioneer and Democrat,* November 18, 1859.

[13] *Weekly Pioneer and Democrat,* April 27, May 25, 1860.

[14] Robinson, *Agriculture in Minnesota,* 62; Willard, *Blue Earth County,* 6.

[15] *Pioneer,* September 29, 1853; *Weekly Pioneer and Democrat,* July 14, 1859 (quoting the *St. Peter Statesman*), February 3, 1860. For an interesting account of sheep washing and shearing, see the *Amboy Herald,* July 6, 1945.

[16] *Weekly Pioneer and Democrat,* June 8, August 31, October 12, 1860, July 17, 1863; *Weekly Pioneer,* September 7, 1866; *Farmer and Gardener,* 1:194 (July, 1861). Wool exports from St. Paul amounted to 3,000 pounds in 1861, to 36,105 in 1862, to 114,698 in 1863, and to 175,000 in 1864.

[17] *Weekly Pioneer,* May 18, 1866, January 25, 1867. The figures for livestock are undoubtedly far too low. The 1860 census reported 16,879 horses, 106,009 cattle, 384 mules, 12,595 sheep, and 104,479 hogs.

[18] *Weekly Pioneer,* May 18, 1866; *Farmer and Gardener,* 2:15 (January, 1862). Andrew Peterson bought three pounds of wool at eighty cents a pound, according to his diary, July 2, 1864.

[19] *Farmer and Gardener,* 2:11, 75 (January, March, 1862); *Weekly Pioneer and Democrat,* February 5, 1864; *General Laws,* 1873, p. 140. On April 1, 1864, Peterson recorded in his diary that he collected $5.50 for a sheep killed by a dog.

[20] *United States Census,* 1880, *Agriculture,* 4; *Farmers' Union,* 8:216 (July 18, 1874); *Minnesota Farmer,* 2:184; 3:128 (March, 1879; February, 1880); Commissioner of Statistics, *Reports,* 1876, p. 139; Robinson, *Agriculture in Minnesota,* 62, 105. For information on a slightly later period, see D. E. Salmon, *Special Report on the History and Present Condition of the Sheep Industry of the United States* (52 Congress, 2 session, *House Miscellaneous Documents,* no. 105—serial 3124).

[21] Robinson, *Agriculture in Minnesota,* 103, 105, 244; *United States Census,* 1860, *Agriculture,* cviii; 1870, *Wealth and Industry,* 82; 1880, *Agriculture,* 4.

[22] *Minnesota Monthly,* 1:31 (January, 1869); letter written by George Biscoe from Cottage Grove, July 24, 1863, Biscoe Papers.

[23] *Farmer and Gardener,* 1:120 (February, 1861); *Belle Plaine Enquirer,* February 9, 1861; *St. Cloud Democrat,* April 4, 1861.

[24] Townsend, in *Belle Plaine Enquirer,* September 7, 1933. See also a letter to Mrs. Nancy Aiton from her brother Andrew, December 4, 1851, in the Aiton Papers. Details of killing and processing are given by Burnett, in *Agricultural History,* 20:96 (January, 1948). "Busy all day Killing and dressing hogs," wrote Countryman in his diary on November 22, 1860. See also Atwood Diary, November 29, 30, 1877.

[25] *Farmer and Gardener,* 1:264 (September, 1861); Hedrick, *Agriculture in New York,* 375.

[26] Commissioner of Statistics, *Reports,* 1876, pp. 135–137. The average price for hogs in several western states in 1874 was as follows: Iowa, $6.78; Missouri, $3.13; Wisconsin, $5.17; Michigan, $6.80; Illinois, $6.31; Kansas, $3.69; California, $5.77; and Minnesota, $5.08.

[27] *Winona Weekly Republican,* February 12, 1873.

[28] *Minnesota Farmer,* vol. 1, no. 8, p. 7; vol. 2, p. 182 (April, 1878; March, 1879). "I made Sausage (75 lbs)," wrote Atwood in his diary on December 22, 1876.

[29] Robinson, *Agriculture in Minnesota,* 103, 105, 244; *United States Census,* 1860, *Agriculture,* cviii; 1870, *Wealth and Industry,* 82; 1880, *Agriculture,* 4.

[30] *Minnesota Monthly,* 1:155 (May, 1869); *Farmer and Gardener,* 1:72, 154 (January, May, 1861).

[31] Hall and Holcombe, *State Agricultural Society,* 75, 104, 121–123, 140. On his farm near Lake City, Willis Baker had eighteen brood mares and sixty-three horses and colts, as well as a driving park. The average price of horses in 1874 was $72.80

in Minnesota and $89.82 in New York. Commissioner of Statistics, *Reports*, 1876, pp. 121–124.

³² Child, *Waseca County*, 256; Kiester, *Faribault County*, 356. Various remedies for horses' ailments are given by Countryman in his diary, January 4, 1860.

³³ John W. Mason, ed., *History of Otter Tail County*, 1:605 (Indianapolis, 1916); Gladys H. Du Priest, "The Waseca County Horse Thief Detectives," in *Minnesota History*, 13:153 (June, 1932). The Waseca County organization held its eighty-first annual meeting on March 31, 1945. *Waseca Journal*, April 4, 1945; *Amboy Herald*, September 14, 1945; Faribault *Central Republican*, September 4, 1867.

³⁴ Robinson, *Agriculture in Minnesota*, 103, 105, 244; *United States Census*, 1860, *Agriculture*, cviii; 1870, *Wealth and Industry*, 82; 1880, *Agriculture*, 4.

³⁵ Commissioner of Statistics, *Reports*, 1876, pp. 124–126, 132–135; *Minnesota Farmer*, 2:12 (September, 1878); *Farmers' Union*, vol. 2, p. 1 (September, 1869); *Minnesota Monthly*, 1:242, 250 (July, 1869); *Independent Farmer*, 1:180 (November 1, 1879); *Weekly Pioneer*, October 23, 1868.

³⁶ *Farmers' Union*, 3:148, 164 (May 16, 30, 1874).

³⁷ Commissioner of Statistics, *Reports*, 1876, pp. 130–132. The state press tried to stimulate cattle production. See, for example, the *Weekly Pioneer and Democrat*, February 22, 1861. Farmers in Freeborn County received $6,000 for beef cattle in the fall of 1860, according to the *Farmer and Gardener*, 1:72 (January, 1861). "Thos Spaulding came over and killed two Steers for me. . . . I took 7 quarters of beef to St. Cloud got $32.70. . . . cut up and salted down the beef," wrote Atwood in his diary, December 15, 19, 21, 1876.

³⁸ Hall and Holcombe, *State Agricultural Society*, 117, 119, 140; Commissioner of Statistics, *Reports*, 1883, p. 220; Minnesota Butter, Cheese, and Dairy Stock Association, *Third Annual Meeting*, 1883, p. 120. Owen H. Roche, who bought two thousand acres of land in western Jackson County in 1879, developed a fine Angus herd there. *Worthington Daily Globe*, September 4, 1942.

³⁹ Watson, *Early Settlement of Cottage Grove*, 19; Child, *Waseca County*, 203; *Weekly Pioneer*, March 22 1867; letter written by Biscoe, July 7, 1863, Biscoe Papers. "When we drove from St. Paul to Cannon Falls in '56 we only saw one small piece of fence on the way," wrote Frank Slocum, in *Old Rail Fence Corners*, 114.

⁴⁰ Christianson, *Minnesota*, 1:459; Moyer and Dale, eds., *Chippewa and Lac qui Parle Counties*, 1:484; *General Laws*, 1874, p. 191–193; 1879, p. 82; H. P. McLellan, "History of the Early Settlement and Development of Polk County, Minnesota," 84. The last item is a master's thesis prepared at Northwestern University in 1928; the Minnesota Historical Society has a copy. The manufacture of barbed wire was displayed at the state fair of 1879. See Commissioner of Statistics, *Reports*, 1879, p. 79. Marin, in *Minnesota History*, 12:159 (June, 1931), tells of herding stock in the early eighties near Crookston.

⁴¹ Willard, *Blue Earth County*, 6; Hartsough, *Twin Cities as a Metropolitan Market*, 66; *Independent Farmer*, 1:7 (January 1, 1879).

THE BEGINNINGS OF DAIRYING

¹ Detailed figures on livestock, and on milk, butter, and cheese production in Minnesota from 1850 to 1880 are given by Robinson in his *Agriculture in Minnesota*, 103, 105, 244. Butter production was as follows: 1850, 1,100 pounds; 1860, 2,957,673 pounds; 1870, 9,522,010 pounds; and 1880, 19,161,385 pounds. The amount of milk sold was not reported in 1850 nor in 1860, but in 1870 it was 208,130 gallons, and in 1880 it was 1,504,407 gallons. Cheese production in 1860 was 199,314 pounds; in 1870 it was 233,977 pounds of farm made and 37,500 pounds of factory made; and in 1880 it was 523,138 pounds of farm made and 462,191 pounds of factory made. New York, Pennsylvania, Ohio, and Iowa led in butter production in 1880; New York, Ohio, Illinois, and Pennsylvania led in the amount of milk sold; and California, New York, Wisconsin, Ohio, and Vermont led in farm cheese production. *United States Census*, 1880, *Agriculture*, 4.

THE BEGINNINGS OF DAIRYING

² Gresham, *Nicollet and Le Sueur Counties*, 1:461; Curtiss-Wedge, ed., *Fillmore County*, 1:518. On March 14, 1861, Countryman wrote in his diary: "When people do without milk and butter for some time, they hail with joy the time when they can have them in abundance again. Our good old cow gave us a fine devon calf, and from henceforth we shall have what belong to good living."

³ Minnesota Butter, Cheese, and Dairy Stock Association, *Third Annual Meeting*, 1883, p. 49; Kenneth D. Ruble, *Men to Remember: How 100,000 Neighbors Made History*, 5 (Chicago, 1947).

⁴ *Farmer and Gardener*, 1:199, 241, 367 (July, August, December, 1861). A correspondent complained of the great amount of unpalatable butter which reached the St. Paul market. Cream should not stand more than eight hours after skimming before it was churned, it was claimed, and "Butter should *never be washed*."

⁵ Gresham, *Nicollet and Le Sueur Counties*, 1:461; Townsend, in *Belle Plaine Herald*, September 7, 1933; Shannon, *The Farmers' Last Frontier*, 257; Henry E. Alvord, "Dairy Development in the United States," in *Agricultural Yearbook*, 1899, p. 400 (Washington, 1900).

⁶ *Minnesota Monthly*, 1:56 (February, 1869).

⁷ *Farmer and Gardener*, 1:131 (May, 1861).

⁸ *Glencoe Register*, June 10, 1869; *Minnesota Monthly*, 1:217 (July, 1869).

⁹ Gilbertson, in *Hayfield Herald*, March 23, 1934. One writer asserted that private dairying meant doubtful profits, slavery for women, and annoyance and waste of time to the farmer and his help; another told of losing livestock from disease. See Curtiss-Wedge, ed., *Fillmore County*, 1:519, and *Glencoe Register*, July 8, 1869. Countryman noted in his diary on December 29, 1860, that he melted ice for his cattle in preference to taking them to the well.

¹⁰ The *St. Peter Statesman* is quoted in the *Farmer and Gardener*, 1:265 (September, 1861). See also the *Farmers' Union*, vol. 3, no. 1, p. 5 (August, 1869), and Martin J. Anderson, *The Development of the Dairy Products Industry in Minnesota*, 1 (Minnesota Dairy and Food Department, *Bulletins*, no. 52—Minneapolis, 1913). A shipment of dairy products from the Wells creamery to St. Louis is noted, with the prophecy that it might be the beginning of wonderful things for Minnesota, in the *Minnesota Farmer*, 2:93 (December, 1878). An important development in the dairy industry was the successful employment of refrigerator railroad cars for the first time in 1871 or 1872. Schmidt and Ross, eds., *Readings in American Agriculture*, 418.

¹¹ *Pioneer*, July 29, 1852; *Weekly Pioneer and Democrat*, August 26, 1859.

¹² Alvord, in *Agricultural Yearbook*, 1899, p. 385; *Minnesota Monthly*, 1:233 (July, 1869); Anderson, *Dairy Products Industry*, 51; Minnesota Butter and Cheese Association, *Second Annual Meeting*, 1883, p. 28 (Rochester, 1883); Robinson, *Agriculture in Minnesota*, 81. Cheese factories were opened at Wells and Lake Crystal in the spring of 1872, according to Kiester, *Faribault County*, 344, and Hughes, *Blue Earth County*, 174. Atwood noted in his diary on May 12, 1877, that he attended a cheese factory meeting.

¹³ The articles of incorporation of the Langdon Butter and Cheese Association are printed in the *Stillwater Messenger*, November 12, 1875. See also Commissioner of Statistics, *Reports*, 1876, p. 151; 1877, p. 55, and Alvord, in *Agricultural Yearbook*, 1899, p. 386.

¹⁴ *Minnesota Farmer*, 2:5 (September, 1878); Commissioner of Statistics, *Reports*, 1882, p. 26; Robinson, *Agriculture in Minnesota*, 83.

¹⁵ *Minnesota Farmer*, 2:153, 226 (February, May, 1879).

¹⁶ Butter, Cheese, and Dairy Stock Association, *Third Annual Meeting*, 1883, p. 60; Commissioner of Statistics, *Reports*, 1880, p. 40; John A. Brown, *History of Cottonwood and Watonwan Counties*, 1:197 (Indianapolis, 1916).

¹⁷ *Minnesota Farmer*, vol. 1, no. 7, p. 4 (March, 1878); Butter and Cheese Association, *First Annual Convention*, 1882, pp. 3-9, 12 (Rochester, 1882); Alvord, in *Agricultural Yearbook*, 1899, p. 391.

¹⁸ Butter and Cheese Association, *Third Annual Meeting*, 1883, p. 22; *Illustrated Album of Biography of Southwestern Minnesota*, 685 (Chicago, 1889).

¹⁹ *History of Mower County*, 154 (1884); Hughes, *Blue Earth County*, 193; Butter and Cheese Association, *Third Annual Meeting*, 1883, p. 20; *Preston Republican*, November 1, 1934.

²⁰ "Farmers of Locality Operated Skimming Station Years Ago," in *Independent* (Parkers Prairie), February 8, 1934; *History of Mower County*, 154 (1884); Gresham, *Nicollet and Le Sueur Counties*, 1:463.

²¹ Butter and Cheese Association, *First Annual Convention*, 1882, p. 94. Cooley's Portable Creamery, which was manufactured at Northfield, is described and advertised in the *Minnesota Farmer*, vol. 1, no. 9, pp. 2, 20 (May, 1878), where it is claimed to be economical and a labor saver. See also Iowa State College of Agriculture and Mechanic Arts, *A Century of Farming in Iowa*, 219 (Ames, 1946).

²² Anderson, *Dairy Products Industry*, 2; Butter, Cheese, and Dairy Stock Association, *Third Annual Meeting*, 1883, pp. 52–54, 85; "The Danielson Creamery and Its Fortieth Anniversary," in *Willmar Daily Tribune*, July 29, 1930.

²³ Commissioner of Statistics, *Reports*, 1876, p. 149; 1882, p. 26; *Minnesota Farmer*, 2:231 (May, 1879); Butter and Cheese Association, *Second Annual Meeting*, 1883, pp. 15, 19, and *Annual Convention*, 1885, pp. 30, 34. It was estimated that the average yield in Minnesota was eighty pounds of butter annually for each cow owned in the state. From 1939 to 1941 the herd average at Mount Hope Farm in Massachusetts was 13,398 pounds of milk and 552 pounds of butterfat. The Mount Hope ideas on breeding contrast with earlier theories. See E. Parmalee Prentice, "Mount Hope and Its Dairy Cattle," in *Agricultural History*, 20:193–209 (October, 1946).

²⁴ Floyd Sorenson, "The Development of a Co-operative Community—Clark's Grove," in *Evening Tribune* (Albert Lea), July 7, 9, 1934; Christensen, in *Minnesota History*, 8:368 (December, 1927); Everett E. Edwards, "T. L. Haecker, the Father of Dairying in Minnesota," in *Minnesota History*, 19:155–157 (June, 1938): *Minneapolis Tribune*, July 18, 1915; Mary C. Swain, "Early Cooperative Creameries in Minnesota," 9. The last item is a term paper prepared at the University of Minnesota in 1930; the Minnesota Historical Society has a copy.

²⁵ Anderson, *Dairy Products Industry*, 18; *Independent Farmer*, 1:164 (November 1, 1879); Butter and Cheese Association, *First Annual Convention*, 1882, pp. 3, 15–19; Commissioner of Statistics, *Reports*, 1876, p. 150.

²⁶ Minnesota State Dairy Commissioner, *First Biennial Report*, 5, 8, 13, 15, 20, 43, 56 (St. Paul, 1887); Christianson, *Minnesota*, 2:134.

²⁷ Butter, Cheese, and Dairy Stock Association, *Annual Convention*, 1885, p. 13; Christianson, *Minnesota*, 2:133.

²⁸ Christianson, *Minnesota*, 2:134; Anderson, *Dairy Products Industry*, 16.

²⁹ Commissioner of Statistics, *Reports*, 1878, p. 38; "Dairying in Minnesota," in *Northwest Illustrated Monthly Magazine*, vol. 14, no. 11, p. 26 (November, 1896). By 1890 Minnesota ranked ninth among the states in milch cows. *United States Census*, 1890, *Agriculture*, 75.

BIZARRE EXPERIMENTS AND SOUND AGRICULTURE

¹ *Weekly Pioneer and Democrat*, June 2, 9, 1859; Countryman Diary, May 25, 1859; Commissioner of Statistics, *Reports*, 1860, p. 110; Franklyn Curtiss-Wedge, ed., *History of Wright County*, 1:211 (Chicago, 1915); Goodrich, *Anoka County*, 87; "Early Settlers Saved Homes with Ginseng," in *Wright County Journal Press* (Buffalo), August 13, 1931. "It [ginseng] was a Godsend to some of us as it brought ready money and enabled me to buy my first stock," wrote one settler. *Le Center Leader*, October 31, 1940.

² Robinson, *Agriculture in Minnesota*, 55; *Weekly Pioneer and Democrat*, June 2, 1859. Tobacco was raised in some places. *Pioneer*, October 9, 1851; Curtiss-Wedge, ed., *McLeod County*, 270.

BIZARRE EXPERIMENTS AND SOUND AGRICULTURE

[3] Robinson, *Agriculture in Minnesota*, 43.
[4] See above, p. 4.
[5] *Pioneer*, August 2, December 12, 1849. During the winter of 1848–49 corn sold for a dollar a bushel.
[6] *Pioneer*, November 14, 1850, January 5, 1854.
[7] *New England Farmer* (Boston), 10:128 (March, 1858); *Massachusetts Ploughman*, 17:1 (December 26, 1857).
[8] Dent corn was not safe in Minnesota, and Canada and New England corn were not profitable because of low yield, said the *St. Peter Tribune* of August 29, 1860. One man bought, fenced, broke, and planted six acres to a Canadian corn at a cost of $150. The first crop of four hundred bushels brought him $200, a clear profit of $50 plus fodder. Evergreen sweet corn also was grown in the state. *Weekly Pioneer and Democrat*, May 9, 1860.
[9] Robinson, *Agriculture in Minnesota*, 44, 55, 102.
[10] Henry W. Hamilton, *Rural Sketches of Minnesota, the El Dorado of the Northwest*, 10 (Milan, Ohio, 1850); *Boston Daily Advertiser*, May 22, 1850.
[11] *St. Peter's Courier*, May 17, 1855; *Pioneer*, May 13, 1852; Andrews, *Minnesota and Dacotah*, 140; Robinson, *Agriculture in Minnesota*, 44.
[12] *Pioneer*, October 25, 1855; *Glencoe Register*, August 22, 1857; Curtiss-Wedge, ed., *McLeod County*, 269; Cummins Diary, October 15, 22, 23, 27, 1858. Hundreds of bushels of sweet potatoes raised in Minnesota were sold at the St. Paul market, according to the *Weekly Pioneer and Democrat*, November 8, 1855.
[13] *Glencoe Register*, August 22, 1857; Cummins Diary, April 17, June 4, September 15, 1858; *Farmer and Gardener*, 1:59 (December, 1860). On September 15, 1858, Countryman sold eleven bushels of potatoes at forty cents a bushel, according to his diary.
[14] Robinson, *Agriculture in Minnesota*, 55, 102, 267.
[15] *Pioneer*, January 5, 1854; Robinson, *Agriculture in Minnesota*, 45, 55, 102. S. B. Olmsted of Fort Gaines sold his oats at a dollar a bushel and straw at the fort at six dollars a ton. See the *Pioneer*, November 14, 1850. J. S. Minor of Point Douglas got sixty-seven bushels of oats to the acre, said the *Pioneer*, October 16, 1851. "We learn that a large quantity of oats is now being shipped from Hastings, Dakota County, for St. Louis, and that several large dealers are purchasing from the farmers in that neighborhood, and in the valley of the Cannon River, between Hastings and Faribault," wrote the *Weekly Pioneer and Democrat*, September 9, 1858.
[16] Robinson, *Agriculture in Minnesota*, 102, 244. "Took some rye to the mill, but it ground slowly, only about six bushels an hour. The toll charge was ⅛ of the amount ground," Cummins noted in his diary on September 10, 1858. "Not much rye grown yet," reported the *Pioneer*, January 5, 1854.
[17] See above, p. 175.
[18] Robinson, *Agriculture in Minnesota*, 62, 102; Cummins Diary, July 19, 1861; *Minnesota Monthly*, 1:327 (September, 1869). "Take load of barley to the brewery, 2168 lbs," Drew wrote in his diary on February 6, 1867.
[19] Cummins Diary, November 2, 1861, May 10, 1862, January 12, February 27, June 6, November 23, 1863, February 20, April 23, October 3, 1864, November 19, 1867, November 13, 1868, March 11, September 21, 1870. The *McLeod County Register*, May 14, 1868, reported corn at $1.00, oats at $.60, and potatoes at from $.50 to $.60. Peterson noted the following prices in his diary: February 2, 1864, barley $.85; February 4, 1865, barley $1.00; February 7, 1866, barley $.40; November 23, 1867, barley $1.28; October 3, 1868, barley $1.45; October 11, 1869, barley $1.00; June 13, 1870, oats $.40; August 30, 1870, barley $.59.
[20] *Weekly Pioneer and Democrat*, September 16, 1858; *Farmer and Gardener*, 1:315, 321, 330 (October, November, 1861). Charles Snyder soaked his seed corn in boiling water twelve hours, then poured the water off and put in a little tar to prevent birds from eating it. Birds were usually a menace, as were gophers, said the *Weekly Pioneer and Democrat*, February 19, 1864. Horace Greeley at the Minneapolis

fair said, "You don't raise as good corn in Minnesota as you might." There were too many weeds in the corn. The editor of the *Rochester Post*, February 24, 1872, said that the corn crop of the last two or three years had demonstrated that corn should not be considered as a secondary feature of Minnesota farming. See also the *Glencoe Register*, May 1, 1858, and the *Rochester Post*, September 23, 1871.

[21] *Farmer and Gardener*, 1:330 (November, 1861). Barley was the best crop after wheat and corn. It found a ready market in the breweries at $1.25 a bushel, and it was a good food for stock. Buckwheat was not raised as much as it should be, stated the *Weekly Pioneer* of April 5, 1867. Members of the Viola Farmers' Club were divided in their opinion of barley. *Rochester Post*, March 30, 1872.

[22] Goodrich, *Anoka County*, 107; Kiester, *Faribault County*, 301; *Weekly Pioneer*, July 26, 1867; Robinson, *Agriculture in Minnesota*, 267; Child, *Waseca County*, 199. The contraction of potato tillage was due partly to ravages of bugs, according to the *Minnesota Monthly*, 1:327 (September, 1869).

[23] *Minnesota Monthly*, 1:117 (April, 1869).

[24] Robinson, *Agriculture in Minnesota*, 104. Illinois and Iowa were the leading corn producing states in 1880 and Minnesota ranked twenty-second among the states. California and New York were the leaders in barley production and Minnesota ranked fifth. In oat production Iowa led, and Minnesota was seventh. New York and Pennsylvania led in Irish potato production, Minnesota ranking tenth. *United States Census*, 1880, *Agriculture*, 6, 9.

[25] *Minnesota Farmer*, 2:62 (November, 1878); Cummins Diary, many entries during the 1870's. Peterson recorded the following prices in his diary: November 21, 1872, barley $.45; July 11, 1873, corn $.45; October 10, 1874, barley $1.00. On November 11, 1874, he wrote, "took a few bushels of barley to the brewery."

[26] Potato raising near a market was very profitable. Potatoes should be planted before May 10, advised the *Minnesota Monthly*, 1:159 (May, 1869).

[27] *Rochester Post*, March 23, 1872.

[28] Goodrich, *Anoka County*, 108–110.

[29] *Minnesota Farmer*, vol. 1, no. 5, p. 3; vol. 1, no. 6, p. 5 (January, February, 1878); *Minnesota Monthly*, 1:118 (April, 1869); Cummins Diary, September 13, 1870, September 16, 19, 1871.

[30] Canadian, Probsteir, and Black Norway were considered the best oats in 1875 and 1876, according to the *Minnesota Farmer*, vol. 1, no. 5, p. 2; vol. 1, no. 6, p. 5 (January, February, 1878). The *Rochester Post*, March 13, 1869, claimed that Brunswick oats would yield a hundred bushels per acre.

[31] Holmes, *Minnesota in Three Centuries*, 4:112, 114; Folwell, *Minnesota*, 3:101.

[32] "These figures," wrote the commissioner of statistics in his *Report*, 1883, p. 9, "record the revolution which is taking place in the direction of the agricultural industry of this state. . . . Minnesota farmers have been gradually resorting to a diversification of their labor, and particularly to cattle-growing and dairying." C. C. Andrews wrote that corn raising was coming into its own as a basis for hog and stock raising. Yellow Dent, he said, was most common. A two-horse corn planter operated by two men cost $35, and a sheller, $33. Andrews, *Spring Wheat Culture*, 37.

[33] Robinson, *Agriculture in Minnesota*, 243, 284; Gilbertson, in *Hayfield Herald*, May 24, 1934. Mrs. Georgiana M. Way, who settled on a farm south of Blue Earth in the middle 1850's, wrote: "It was hard to keep chickens for the country was so full of foxes." *Old Rail Fence Corners*, 118.

[34] Townsend, in *Belle Plaine Herald*, September 7, 1933; Cummins Diary, June 6, 1863, February 20, 1864.

[35] *Minnesota Monthly*, 1:206 (June, 1869); *Farmers' Union*, vol. 1, no. 6, p. 3; vol. 3, no. 10, p. 4 (January, 1868; May, 1870); Butter, Cheese, and Dairy Stock Association, *Third Annual Meeting*, 1883, p. 46.

[36] *Farmers' Union*, vol. 1, no. 6, p. 3; vol. 2, no. 3, p. 5 (January, October, 1868); *Rochester Post*, August 28, 1869; Commissioner of Statistics, *Reports*, 1876, p. 143; *Minnesota Monthly*, 2:27 (January, 1870). Peter Gideon contended that the Dominick was the best hen, though he praised Brahma, Black Spanish, and Gray Dorking chickens also.

BIZARRE EXPERIMENTS AND SOUND AGRICULTURE

[37] *Winona Weekly Republican*, January 1, March 19, 1873.

[38] *Minnesota Farmer*, vol. 1, no. 8, p. 2 (April, 1878); *Farmers' Union*, 8:188 (June 20, 1874); Butter, Cheese, and Dairy Stock Association, *Third Annual Meeting*, 1883, p. 46.

[39] Butter, Cheese, and Dairy Stock Association, *Third Annual Meeting*, 1883, p. 69, and *Annual Convention*, 1885, p. 29; *Weekly Pioneer*, May 10, 1867. "This afternoon set Royal to plowing some more land for Hungarian grass," wrote Countryman in his diary on July 19, 1858.

[40] Goodrich, *Anoka County*, 35; Curtiss-Wedge, ed., *McLeod County*, 273; Atwood Diary, August 15, 1877. According to the *Massachusetts Ploughman*, 16:1 (August 22, 1857), the price of hay was very high in the spring of 1857, because much of it had been left uncut or burned during the previous season, and some cattle died for want of it. The government paid fifteen dollars a ton in 1864, according to the *Weekly Pioneer and Democrat*, August 4, 1865. Cummins noted in his diary on May 25, 1875, that there was much hay in town; and on June 8, 1875 he said that hay at sixteen dollars a ton was down somewhat.

[41] Stevens, *Personal Recollections*, 98; *Pioneer*, January 5, 1854; *Weekly Pioneer and Democrat*, May 8, 1856; Cummins Diary, July 3, September 17, 1858, April 30 1859. The *Farmer and Gardener*, 1:162, 170 (June, 1861), recommended Hungarian grass and said that the day was coming when farmers could not make their hay where they pleased. W. L. Ames grew timothy and clover, according to the same periodical, 1:209 (July, 1861). F. M. Libby wrote to the author from Boston on April 19, 1948, that if hay was slow on the market, he took it to Ingersoll's Field's, or Lamprey's and put it in with the waybill.

[42] *Minnesota Monthly*, 1:165 (May, 1869). Cummins recorded in his diary on January 5, 1880, that he sold thirteen bushels of clover seed at $4.75 a bushel.

[43] *Rochester Post*, August 26, 1871; Butter, Cheese, and Dairy Stock Association, *Annual Convention*, 1885, p. 29. Robinson, in his *Agriculture in Minnesota*, 103, 105, 244, notes that 126 bushels of clover seed were produced in 1870 and 18,003 in 1880, an increase of 14,188.2 per cent. The price of timothy hay in the winter of 1861–62 was given as ten dollars a ton by the *Farmer and Gardener*, 2:106 (April, 1862). New York, Iowa, and Illinois were the leading hay-producing states. *United States Census*, 1880, *Agriculture*, 8.

[44] *Rochester Post*, June 29, 1872; *Minnesota Monthly*, 1:156 (May, 1869).

[45] Everett E. Edwards and Horace H. Russell, "Wendelin Grimm and Alfalfa," in *Minnesota History*, 19:21–23 (March, 1938).

[46] Robinson, *Agriculture in Minnesota*, 73, 84, 102–105; *Minnesota Monthly*, 1:25 (January, 1869); *Stillwater Messenger*, April 24, 1874; *Rochester Post*, March 25, 1871. In the *Post*, March 16, 1872, a correspondent advocated fall plowing as best for flax and advised sowing from eighteen to twenty-four quarts of seed per acre. In the March 23, 1872, issue, "J. A." urged the establishment of a paper mill to make paper from flax lint.

[47] Robinson, *Agriculture in Minnesota*, 73, 84, 103, 105.

[48] Robinson, *Agriculture in Minnesota*, 103, 105; Peterson Diary, April 1, 1856, April 24, 1865, October 23, 1877; Cummins Diary, August 15, September 23, 1858, March 25, 1861. Allyn, in his *When Blue Earth County Was Young*, 6, tells of making maple sugar. Maple sugar in 1865 brought twenty-five cents a pound and syrup, two dollars a gallon, according to the *Weekly Pioneer*, April 12, 1867. "Octavus and I stripped sugar cane in the forenoon, and in the after noon I took a load of it to mill to be crushed into juice," wrote Countryman in his diary on October 11, 1858.

[49] Robinson, *Agriculture in Minnesota*, 55, 73, 84, 102, 105, 244; Benitt, "Agriculture in Southern Washington County," 5; *Independent Farmer*, 1:9 (January 1, 1879); *Pioneer*, October 20, 1853. A certain Robertson raised seed leaf tobacco in 1851, according to the *Pioneer*, October 9, 1851. Cummins complained in his diary on May 10, 1858, that cut worms were destroying his cabbage plants. "Beta," in the *Massachusetts Ploughman* (September, 1859), told of a farmer living five miles south of St. Paul who turned to market gardening in 1852. By 1859 he had paid

for his farm, had rebuilt his house, and had saved $5,000, besides supporting his family of four.
⁵⁰ *Independent Farmer*, 1:94 (April 1, 1879); *Weekly Pioneer and Democrat*, July 29, 1858.
⁵¹ Blegen, *Building Minnesota*, 240; *Minnesota Monthly*, 1:319–324, 346 (September, October, 1869); *Farmers' Union*, 7:331 (October 18, 1873); Robinson, *Agriculture in Minnesota*, 73, 79, 103, 105; Countryman Diary, April 22, 1862; Peterson Diary, September 30, October 11, 1871, March 6, 7, 8, 1872. Peterson made his own wine press and pressed his own grapes. The State Horticultural Society was organized in 1866, with Daniel A. Robertson as president. For a comprehensive account of fruit raising in the early days, see *History of the Minnesota Horticultural Society* (St. Paul, 1873). An account of the Wealthy apple may be found in the *Farmers' Union*, vol. 2, no. 5, p. 4; vol. 2, no. 6, p. 2 (December, 1868; January, 1869).

EARLY AGRICULTURAL SOCIETIES AND FAIRS

¹ See H. J. Carman and R. G. Tugwell's foreword in Wayne C. Neely, *The Agricultural Fair*, 2 (New York, 1935).
² Loehr, ed., *Minnesota Farmers' Diaries*, 24; Neely, *Agricultural Fair*, 82.
³ Earle D. Ross, "The Evolution of the Agricultural Fair in the Northwest," in *Iowa Journal of History and Politics*, 24:454 (July, 1926).
⁴ Ross, in *Iowa Journal of History and Politics*, 24:453–458; Child, *Waseca County*, 233. William Brisbane delivered the address at the Waseca County Fair of 1870, dwelling upon the wholesome and honorable calling of the farmer.
⁵ Louis L. Snyder, *A Survey of European Civilization*, 1:483 (Harrisburg, Pennsylvania, 1941); *Stillwater Messenger*, October 1, 1875.
⁶ Hall and Holcombe, *State Agricultural Society*, 7; *Pioneer*, November 10, 1853.
⁷ *Pioneer*, November 15, 1849.
⁸ Hall and Holcombe, *State Agricultural Society*, 7; *American Agriculturist* (New York), 12:201 (June 7, 1854). The latter item is among transcripts, made for the Minnesota Historical Society, of material of Minnesota interest in eastern periodicals.
⁹ Hall and Holcombe, *State Agricultural Society*, 7; *Pioneer*, April 8, 22, 1852.
¹⁰ Hall and Holcombe, *State Agricultural Society*, 17–19, 27; Stevens, *Personal Recollections*, 208, 242; *Pioneer*, April 28, September 8, 1853; *St. Anthony Express*, September 17, 1853.
¹¹ *History of Winona, Olmsted, and Dodge Counties*, 1256 (Chicago, 1884); Kiester, *Faribault County*, 102–110; *Glencoe Register*, March 26, July 23, October 22, 1859; *Dakota County Tribune* (Farmington), March 9, 1934; *Spring Valley Tribune*, August 16, 23, 1934. In 1859 members of the state legislature and others organized at the Capitol the Agricultural and Mechanics' Club of the Legislature of Minnesota, with John H. Stevens as president. Farm problems and agricultural methods were discussed at its meetings. See the *Weekly Pioneer and Democrat*, December 30, 1859, January 13, 1860. Countryman wrote in his diary on August 13, 1858: "After noon I went down to Nininger to attend a meeting of the Executive Com of the Agril Society   no one there but myself. Fear that no one has an interest."
¹² Stevens, *Personal Recollections*, 208; Hall and Holcombe, *State Agricultural Society*, 19.
¹³ Hall and Holcombe, *State Agricultural Society*, 19; Folwell, *Minnesota*, 1:361; *Pioneer*, November 10, 1853, January 5, 12, 1854.
¹⁴ *Pioneer*, January 18, March 29, 1855; Hall and Holcombe, *State Agricultural Society*, 28–31.
¹⁵ *Pioneer*, October 18, 25, 1855; Loehr, ed., *Minnesota Farmers' Diaries*, 24, 25; Hall and Holcombe, *State Agricultural Society*, 31–34.

EARLY AGRICULTURAL SOCIETIES AND FAIRS

[16] *Pioneer,* October 16, 1856; Hall and Holcombe, *State Agricultural Society,* 35-47.
[17] *Laws,* 1860, pp. 143-145; *Farmer and Gardener,* 1:44 (December, 1860); Hall and Holcombe, *State Agricultural Society,* 48-53.
[18] Hall and Holcombe, *State Agricultural Society,* 55-64.
[19] *St. Peter Tribune,* September 26, 1860; Hall and Holcombe, *State Agricultural Society,* 65-70; Countryman Diary, September 16, 1859, September 21, 1860. Countryman called the fair of 1860 at Hastings a humbug.
[20] *Farmer and Gardener,* 1:362 (December, 1861).
[21] *Farmer and Gardener,* 1:258; 2:73 (September, 1861; March, 1862).
[22] Loehr, ed., *Minnesota Farmers' Diaries,* 217.
[23] Kiester, *Faribault County,* 264.
[24] Hall and Holcombe, *State Agricultural Society,* 73-96; *Pioneer,* October 4, 1863.
[25] *Laws,* 1868, pp. 33-35; *Farmers' Union,* vol. 1, no. 6, p. 4; vol. 2, no. 4, p. 8 (January, November, 1868); *Glencoe Register,* March 25, April 29, 1869; *Rochester Post,* November 13, 1869, March 12, 19, 1870; *Farmer and Gardener,* 1:37 (December, 1860); *Minnesota Farmer,* 2:269 (June, 1879); Kiester, *Faribault County,* 264; Hall and Holcombe, *State Agricultural Society,* 97.
[26] Hall and Holcombe, *State Agricultural Society,* 118; Moyer and Dale, eds., *Chippewa and Lac qui Parle Counties,* 1:592; *Western Guard* (Madison), August 15, 1947; *Pope County Tribune* (Glenwood), September 11, 1941.
[27] *Weekly Pioneer,* October 2, 1868; *Rochester Post,* October 2, 1869, February 19, 26, 1870; Hall and Holcombe, *State Agricultural Society,* 96-104; Ross, in *Iowa Journal of History and Politics,* 24:462-465.
[28] Hall and Holcombe, *State Agricultural Society,* 107-133; Ross, in *Iowa Journal of History and Politics,* 24:470. The *Stillwater Messenger,* September 20, 1878, urged farmers to turn out and make the county fair a fair and not an "agricultural hoss trot."
[29] Hall and Holcombe, *State Agricultural Society,* 130, 135-139; Maurice Farrar, *Five Years in Minnesota,* 84 (London, 1880); Cummins Diary, September 5, 1878.
[30] Hall and Holcombe, *State Agricultural Society,* 141-157; David M. Fyffe, "Reminiscences," 55-58. The latter is a manuscript in the possession of the Minnesota Historical Society. The writer, who settled in Pipestone County as the manager of a colonization company in 1882, describes the Owatonna fair. There were sheds about the outside of the grounds for the horses and some beef cattle, and cheap sheds on the grounds for sheep, hogs, and cattle. The judging was accompanied by numerous quarrels.
[31] *Laws,* 1883, p. 198; 1885, pp. 214-216; *St. Paul Dispatch,* September 15, 1885; Hall and Holcombe, *State Agricultural Society,* 158-191, 194.
[32] Neely, *Agricultural Fair,* 99-109.
[33] *Winona Weekly Republican,* January 1, March 19, 1873; *Minnesota Farmer,* vol. 1, no. 8, p. 2 (April, 1878). The Minnesota State Poultry Association filed its articles of incorporation with the secretary of state on March 16, 1885. These and the association's bylaws are owned by the Minnesota Historical Society.
[34] *Minnesota Farmer,* vol. 1, no. 6, p. 3; no. 7, p. 7; no. 8, p. 9 (February, March, April, 1878).
[35] *Minnesota Farmer,* vol. 1, no. 7, p. 4; vol. 2, p. 153 (February, March, 1879).
[36] *Minnesota Farmer,* 2:184; 3:128 (March, 1879; February, 1880); *Laws,* 1873, p. 140.
[37] Anderson, *Dairy Products Industry,* 8; Butter and Cheese Association, *First Annual Convention,* 1882, pp. 3-9, 15-79.
[38] Butter and Cheese Association, *Second Annual Meeting,* 1883, pp. 6-11.
[39] Butter and Cheese Association, *Second Annual Meeting,* 1883, p. 117.
[40] Butter, Cheese, and Dairy Stock Association, *Annual Convention,* 1885, p. 13; Christianson, *Minnesota,* 2:133.

Index

Afton, early farming, 3
Agricultural college, efforts to establish, 16, 17
Agricultural college lands, 62, 78
Agricultural periodicals, 11, 12. *See also* individual periodicals
Agricultural societies, 16, 126, 224, 229, 245–261. *See also* individual societies
Agriculture, development, 3–26; economic aspects, 5–11, 13–15, 17–25, *see also* various commodities, prices; effects of war on, 12, 13, 14, 195, 228, 265; growth of mechanized, 21, 27, 120–164, *see also* Implements and machines; diversified, 22, 185–187, 223, 231, 296; influenced by physical environment, 27–40, by social, political, and economic factors, 27, 28; experiments, 222, 223; produce, *see* various products; specialized, *see* Wheat, Bonanza farms, Red River Valley; statistics, *see* Dairying, Livestock, various crops. *See also* Crops; Farmers; Farms
Albert Lea, 203; land sale meeting, 48; railroad, 72
Alexandria, land office, 78
Alfalfa, Grimm, 239
Allyn, G. W., 12
American Dairymen's Association, 215
Anderson, A. G. W., 55
Anderson, Hogan, wheat farmer, 176
Anderson, Jens, wheat farmer, 176
Anderson, Mrs. Mary Jane Hill, 5, 8
Andrews, Christopher C., 8, 190, 226
Anoka, starch factory, 233
Anoka County, ginseng, 223; potatoes, 230, 233; fair, 251; speculation, 271
Anti-brass kettle meetings, 173
Anti-Horse Thief Association, 202
Antirailroad meetings, 287
Apgar, Mrs. Anna S., 80
Appleby, John, invents twine binder, 149
Atwood, Edwin H., 114, 277; Grange activities, 280; machine debt, 285; makes sausage, 291; sells beef, 292
Austin, Gov. Horace, criticizes railroads, 171; urges diversified farming, 175
Austin, 72, 85
Averill, John T., contest with King, 45

Babcock cream tester, 217, 221
Bailly, Alexis, 165
Baker, Oliver E., 28
Baker, Willis, horse raiser, 291
Ballard, Dr. Charles W., stock raiser, 203, 204, 205
Bank failures, 9, 13
Baptist church, 3, 105
Barden, R., stock raiser, 274
Barley, production: 4, 229, statistics, 227, 228, 231; prices, 231, 295, 296; grasshopper losses, 233
Barnes, John S., railroad bonds, 75
Barns, 83, 98, 277
Bassett, Mrs. Joel B., 249
Beans, 186; production statistics, 223, 241, 242
Beatty, Mrs. J. R., 86
Becker, George L., railroad mortgage, 74
Becker County, swamp lands, 63
Beef, prices, 189, 190
Belle Plaine, blacksmith shop, 123; plow factory, 138, 139
Bennett, R. H., raises sheep, 194
Benson, land office, 78; reaper exhibit, 150
Benton County, farms, 4; soldiers' homesteads, 67; speculation, 271
Benton County Agricultural Society, 224, 247
Berthiaume, Louis, factory superintendent, 160
Big Woods, 35, 222, 223
Bigflow, Murdock, and Co., machine agents, 142
Biscoe, Rev. George, 13, 31, 97, 175, 195, 265, 289
Blacksmith shops, social aspects, 111; importance to farmer, 123, 126
Blaine, James G., at fairs, 256
Blaine, Robert, promotes ginseng, 222
Blake, John D., and Co., sues railroad, 171
Blegen, Theodore C., 82
"Blight," wheat, 17
Blizzards, 19, 31, 86, 266
Bloomington, school, 108
Blue Earth, implement trade, 283
Blue Earth County, labor shortage, 12;

301

livestock, 194, 206; fair, 251; agricultural society, 252; farmers' insurance company, 266
Bogert, Ed, poultry raiser, 235
Bonanza farms, 176, 273
Boomhower, ———, farmer, 141, 142
Boutwell, Rev. William T., 188
Brackenridge, W. L., 260
Brackett, George A., invents binder, 283
Brainard, H. J., dairyman, 209, 210
Brainerd, C. N., 92, 267
Brainerd, altitude, 268
Breckenridge, railroad, 72, 176
Brimhall, William E., gardener, 243
Brissette, E., farmer, 188
British settlers, 5
Broadcasting machines, 144, 146
Brooks, E. W., machine agent, 153
Brockway Brothers, stock raisers, 197, 203
Brown, H. F., stock raiser, 203
Brown, Joseph R., raises wheat, 165, 237; timothy, 237
Brown, William R., farmer, 3, 120, 188
Brownsville, land office, 47
Bruns, Henry A., wheat farmer, 176
Bryant, Dr. ———, poultry raiser, 235
Buchanan, land office, 60
Buckwheat, production, 227, 228; grasshopper losses, 233
Budd, William A., farmer, 5
Buffalo, ginseng agency, 222
Burbank, J. C., and Co., machine agents, 124
Burchard, H. M., dairyman, 220
Butter, prices, 9, 13, 14, 190, 213-216; methods of making, 208, 209, 214; quality, 208, 214-216, 293; markets, 211; exported, 211, 216; factories, 213, *see also* creameries; coloring, 215; Danes in industry, 219; award to Minnesota, 220, 261; lead over cheese, 221; production statistics, 292. *See also* Dairying

Cambridge, 5; land office, 46, 60, 270
Camp, John H., landowner, 75, 273
Camp meetings, 105-107
Cannon City, plow factory, 126, 138
Cannon Falls, school, 109
Cannon River Improvement Association, swamp land grant, 63
Carlton County, cattle, 203
Carson, P. W., sheep raiser, 192
Carver, railroad, 72
Carver County, claim club, 55; livestock, 194; alfalfa, 239
Cass County, railroad lands, 75
Castle Rock, 104; horses, 200
Catholic church, 103

Cattle, prices, 190, 192, 204, 205, 292; exported, 191; breeds and breeding, 191, 203-205, for dairying, 216, 219; numbers, 193, 291; production statistics, 202, 203; marketing problems, 206; summer herding, 206. *See also* Livestock
Chadbourn, C. H., implement factory, 148; dairyman, 220
Chaffee, E. W., land agent, 75
Chandler, Clayborne, 101
Chapman, Edward, invents self-binder, 148
Chapman, Timothy, 9
Chaska, 72, 116
Chatfield, Judge Andrew G., 248
Chatfield, 5; land office, 60, 167; market, 167
Cheese, 207; markets, 211; factories, 211-213, 214, 221, 293; prices, 213; Swiss in industry, 219; decline, 220, 221; exhibited, 258; production statistics, 292. *See also* Dairying
Chicago (Ill.), Minnesota wheat market, 170
Chicago and Milwaukee Railroad, 13, 171
Chicago and Northwestern Railroad, interest in dairying, 260
Chicago, Clinton, Dubuque, and Minnesota Railroad, 73
Children, role on frontier, 92; recreation, 112
Chinch bugs, 19, 187, 289
Chippewa County, railroad lands, 65
Christmas, observance, 113-116, 279
Churches, in frontier life, 102-107
Circuit riders, 102. *See also* Preachers
Civil War, 108, 251; immigration, 12; effects on agriculture, 12, 13, 15, 131, 146; prices, 13, 14, 175, 228, 265; deflation following, 17, 135; sheep raising, 192
Claim associations, 54-56
Claim jumping, 51, 55, 56, 65
Claims, under Homestead Act, 12, 65, 68; disputes over, 53, 55-57. *See also* Homestead Act; Pre-emption
Clark, N. P., cattle raiser, 203
Clarks Grove, creamery, 219
Clay, Cassius, at fair, 250
Clay County, wheat, 176
Clitherall, early farming, 121, 122
Clothing, farm families', 87, 88, 100, 264
Clover, 236-239, 297
Cobb, M. G., 87
Collins, Loren W., schoolteacher, 109
Colorado beetle, damage to potatoes, 229, 230, 296

INDEX

Conolly, Col. A. P., 105
Cooke, Jay, and Co., failure, 18, 75
Co-operatives, cheese factories, 213; creameries, 218, 219
Cormack, John, 127
Corn, production: 3, 4, 15, 224–225, statistics, 223, 225, 227, 228, 231, costs, 229; planting, 6, 126, 145, 229, 283; yields, 8, 9, 14, 224, 228, 231; prices, 8, 9, 14, 224, 228, 231, 295, 296; in frontier diet, 87; grinding, 87; harvesting, 126; breeding, 224; varieties, 224, 225, 228, 229, 295; exports, 225; grasshopper losses, 233; damaged by birds and gophers, 295; profits, 295; Minnesota's rank, 296
Corn brushers, 146
Corn planters, price, 296
Corn shellers, 146, 296
Corncribs, 99, 277
Cottage Grove, early farming, 93, 97, 124; Gournsey farm, 133; wheat, 175; sheep, 194; butter and cheese factory, 213; tow mill, 240
Cottonwood County, dugouts, 83; Barden farm, 274
Countryman, Levi, farmer, 108, 117, 119, 275, 280–283, 298; reading, 96; schoolteacher, 109, 110, 118, 278; social life, 113, 114, 277; crops, 243, 295, 297; debts, 263; house, 274; livestock, 291, 293
Cradles and cradling, 121, 123, 280, 284
Cranberries, 8
Cray, Judge Loren, 100
Cream, prices, 217; testing, 217, 218, 221
Creameries, 216, 221; farmers' complaints, 218; co-operative, 218, 219
Crookston, land office, 44, 78; railroad, 73
Crops, production, *1850's*, 4, 130; hazards, 8, 18, 69, 86, 295, *see also* Blizzards, Chinch bugs, Colorado beetle, Grasshoppers, Plant diseases, Prairie fires; on new land, 16; economic factors determining, 28. *See also* various crops
Crosby, John, miller, 149
Crosby, Thomas, horse raiser, 200
Cross, Dr. C. E., speaker, 215
Crow River Agricultural Society, 229
Cultivators, 122, 162
Cummins, John R., 26; drafted, 15; criticizes millers, 172; crops, 226, 228, 231, 232, 238; maple sugar, 241; threshing, 281
Currency, inflation, 9, 13, 265, 266

Dairying, development, 207–221; profits, 210; stock feeding, 210; co-operatives, 213, 218, 219; cattle breeds, 216, 219; equipment, 216, 294; leading dairymen, 220; malpractices, 220; laws, 220; products exhibited, 249, 250; products exported, 293. *See also* Butter; Cheese
Dakota County, 20; Jenkins farm, 144; wheat, 175, 186, 286; livestock, 194; hay, 238; nurseries, 243
Dakota County Agricultural Association, 16, 126, 248
Dalrymple, Oliver, wheat farmer, 176, 288
Danish settlers, 93; in butter industry, 219
Davidson, William F., farm, 273
Davis, Le Roy G., 97, 110
Davison and Connelly, plow factory, 139
De Graff, Charles, stock raiser, 199, 203
De Laval cream separator, 217, 221
Dean, William B., plow factory head, 160
Deering, Samuel, dairyman, 220
Denman, J. S., Grange agent, 284
Detroit Lakes (Detroit), land office, 14
Diaries, farmers', 103
Dickson, J., raises clover, 238
Dodd, William B., breeds corn, 224
Dodge County, cheese factories, 214
Dodge County Agricultural Society, 248
Donnelly, Ignatius, aids settlers, 68, 69; denounces speculators, 69; criticized, 154
Douglas County, farming, 18
Drew, Edward B., describes early threshing, 122; plows city lots, 124
Drills, 144–146, 163, 283
Droughts, 12, 289
Duluth, railroad, 73, 76; land office, 78; wheat market, 176, 179
Duluth and Iron Range Railroad, swamp land grant, 73
Dundas, sugar factory, 241
Dunwoody, William H., miller, 149

Eastman, W. W., and Co., reaper factory, 134
Easton, J. C., stock raiser, 205
Eden Prairie, 15, 127
Edgar, John, machine agent, 18, 266, 281, 282, 284
Edwards, Everett, 12
Eggs, prices, 3, 13, 14, 234; imported, 235
Elevators, grain, built by railroads, 169; act regulating, 174; Red River Valley, 176; Minneapolis, 179
Elliot, Wyman, stock raiser, 250
Ellis, A. V., stock raiser, 205

303

Elward, John H., harvester, 151, 158, 285; thresher, 163
Ely, Rev. Edward, speaker, 236
Endreson, Guri, experiences in Sioux war, 89
Episcopal church, 3
Esterley, George, reaper, 125
Ether, Vere, wheat farmer, 176
Evans, Dr. O. O., horse raiser, 200
Excursions, boat and train, 104
Eyota, livestock, 197, 203; wages, 183

Fairchild, H. S., 257
Fairmont, English colony, 256
Fairs, role in social life, 107; territorial, 191, 248–250; judging, 245; addresses, 245, 247, 250, 254, 256; plowing matches and reaper trials, 246; county, 246, 247, 249, 251, 252, 254, 258, 298; amusement features, 246, 250, 254, 255, 299; political rivalry, 250; exhibits, *see* Crops, Dairying, Implements and machines, Livestock; state, *see* Minnesota State Fair
Fanning mills, 122, 126, 128, 130, 146
Faribault, Jean Baptiste, raises wheat, 165
Faribault, plow factory, 140; railroad, 72; baseball, 279
Faribault County, early farming, 8; windmill company, 157; fair, 252
Faribault County Agricultural Society, 248, 252
Farm journals, 11, 12. *See also* individual journals
Farmers, work routine, 6; economic conditions, 9, 10, 15, 52, 135, 137, 158, 168, 263, 266, 282, 287, *see also* Agriculture, economic aspects; interest in war, 15, in politics, 279, *see also* Grange, Farmers' Alliance; relation to environment, 27–40, 86; living conditions, 80-89, *see also* Farmhouses, Foods, Sanitation; clothing, 87, 88, 100, 264; reading, 95–97, 263, 276, 277; democracy, 100; recreation, 100–119, *see also* Social life; education, 108; relations with machine makers and agents, 130, with millers, 172, 173, with creamerymen, 218; complaints against wheat weighing and grading, 170, 171, 287, against railroads, 171, 172, 287. *See also* Farms
Farmers' Alliance, influence on legislation, 173, 174
Farmers' Board of Trade, 173
Farmers' clubs, 149, 192, 210, 229, 253, 258, 296
Farmers' Union, 11, 22, 71, 154, 185, 235, 243

Farmhouses, log cabins and shanties, 80–83; furnishings, 80, 82, 93, 95, 274, 276; construction, 81, 93, 274, 276; sod, 83; dugouts, 83; lighting and heating, 84, 94; water, 85, 94; sanitation, 91, 94; of later period, 92–96; frame and brick, 92, 93, 274; cellars, 94
Farming. *See* Agriculture
Farms, values, 4, 10, 11, 18, 21, 130; acres in, 4, 10, 18, 21, 78, 164; numbers, 4, 10, 18, 21, 130; average sizes, 4, 10, 18, 21, 266; pioneer, described, 6–8; increase in large, 21, 75, 144, 273, *see also* Bonanza farms; insurance, 22, 23, 266, 267; taxes, 23–25, 267, 278; trees, 70, 71, 273; landscaping, 99, 277; areas in various crops, 223, 227; owner operated, 266; buildings, 276, 277, *see also* Barns, Farmhouses, Stables
Farnsworth, Austin W., 274
Farrington, George W., machine agent, 124, 125; raises horses, 200
Fences and fencing, 7, 97, 98, 205, 206, 264, 292
Fergus Falls, land office, 78; Anti-Horse Thief Association, 202; altitude, 268
Ferguson and Clark, plow factory, 140
Fertilizing, 25, 267
Fillmore County, labor shortage, 12; implements, 126; wheat, 175, 286; sheep, 194
Fillmore County Agricultural Society, 248
Flails and flailing, 121, 122, 141, 283
Flax, 186, 240, 297
Floods, 86
Flour, prices, 9, 14, 178, 275
Flour milling, new processes, 19, 178, 179; St. Paul, 162; Minneapolis, 179
Folsom, Simeon S. P., sells hay, 237
Folwell, William W., 4
Fond du Lac, livestock, 188
Foods, cooking methods, 83, 84; native, 85; in frontier diet, 86, 87, 264, 265, 275; preserving methods, 87
Ford, Charles H., 181
Ford, L. M., editor, 11
Forest City, land office, 60
Fort Ridgely, 242; hay market, 237
Fort Snelling, 103, 114; market, 3, 237; settlers on reservation, 55; horses, 200; state fairs, 250, 253
Foster, Dr. Thomas S., 37
Fourth of July, celebrations, 101, 111, 113, 114, 279
Fowler, William, dairyman, 190, 258
Freeborn County, settlers protest land sales, 48; horses, 200; agricultural

INDEX

society, 252; chattel mortgages, 266; cattle, 291
Freight rates, 17; affect prices, 13; protests against, 171, 172, 287; regulations, 171, 174. *See also* various commodities
French settlers, 5, 45, 115
Fruit raising, 243, 244
Fuel, on frontier, 18, 84
Funk, Mrs. Margaret R., 108
Furber, S. W., tow mill, 240

Gardner, S. S., heads dairy group, 258
General Land Office, commissioner, 42; administers public lands, 42, 43; allows pre-emption on half-breed tract, 54
George, Mrs. Alice, 96
German Farmers' Mutual Fire Insurance Co., 23
German settlers, 5; insurance company, 23, 266; at camp meeting, 106; social life, 111, 115; Winsted, 116; raise rye, 222
Getty, J. G., imports sheep, 193
Gideon, Peter, raises poultry, 235, 296; develops Wealthy apple, 243
Gilman, N. F., invents twine binder, 149
Gilpatrick, Martha, 87
Ginseng, dug and sold, 222, 223, 294
Gleaners, wheat, 146
Glencoe, 129, 168; proposed agricultural college, 16, academy, 17; tax delinquency, 25; farmers' club, 210
Glencoe Register, 59, 137
Gold, scarcity, 13; value, 14
Golden Gate, farmers' meeting place, 111
Good Templars, 118
Goodhue, James M., urges raising wheat, 165, corn, 224
Goodhue, W. S., 163
Goodhue, dairying, 220
Goodhue County, settlers fight speculators, 53; school lands, 63; Grange, 154; wheat, 175, 286; livestock, 194
Gorman, Gov. Willis A., 72, 224, 227; speaker, 247
Gotteborg, claim club, 55
Grain, act providing for inspection and weighing, 174. *See also* various grains
Granaries, 98, 99, 277
Grange, 11, 258, 280; social aspects, 117; Minnesota lodges, 118; condemns machine makers, agents, and prices, 130, 153, 154, 184; produces machines, 154, 160, 184; plow ring formed against, 285. *See also* Grange laws; Minnesota State Grange
Grange Advance, editors criticized, 154

Grange laws, 173, 174, 179
Grasshoppers, 86, 176, 288; plagues, 8, 9, 19, 69, 151, 181, 233, 254, 266
Greeley, Horace, speaker, 254, 295
Gregg, Oren C., dairyman, 220, 236
Grimm, John, 71
Grimm, Wendelin, develops alfalfa, 239
Gristmills, 167, 168; social aspects, 111. *See also* Flour mills and milling
Griswold, Harriet, 5, 270
Grote, Henry, 93
Grout, Jane, 276

Hallam, Oscar, 95
Hamilton, Henry W., 225
Hamline University, 278
Haney, D., horse raiser, 200
Harrington, Lewis, builds cabin, 81
Harris, starch factory, 233
Harrison and Co., plow factory, 140
Harrows, 146
Harvesters. *See* Reapers
Harvesting, early methods, 121, 123, 280, 284. *See also* Reapers; Threshers; Threshing; various crops
Haskell, Joseph, farmer, 3, 124; reading, 96, 263; cattle, 191, 290
Hastings, railroad, 72, 265; excursion, 104; Fourth celebration, 113; market, 165, 227, 286, 295; shipping, 223, 227; fair, 299
Hastings and Dakota Railroad, 72, 73
Hatch and Roberts, plow factory, 140
Hay, prices, 9, 13, 237, 297; cultivated, 186, 236–240; wild, 236; production statistics, 238; scarcity, 264. *See also* Alfalfa; Clover; Hungarian grass; Redtop; Timothy
Hayes, Rutherford B., at fairs, 256
Heating, farmhouses, 84, 94
Hedman, Ole, dugout, 83
Heidelberg, traction engine, 155
Helberg, Freidrich, builds house, 93
Henderson, land office, 54, 60
Hennepin County, livestock, 190, 194; potatoes, 227; flax, 240; market gardening, 242; fairs, 247, 249, 254; wheat, 286
Hennepin County Agricultural Society, 247, 248
Henry, Forest, early settler, 5
Hersey and Staples, landowners, 58
Hewitt, Girart, 37
Hews, Robert, wheat profits, 184
Hilgard, E. W., 37
Hill, James J., sells threshers, 127; stock raiser, 205
Hineline, George, miller, 149

305

Hoag, Charles, raises flax, 240; club officer, 253
Hoard, W. D., heads dairy group, 260
Hodges, Leonard B., 184
Hodges, S. P. and P. F., machine agents, 142
Hoes, 121, 146
Hogs, prices, 13, 291; numbers, 193, 291. *See also* Livestock; Swine
Holbrook and Co., packers, 199
Holcombe, William, land officer, 58; horse raiser, 191
Holmes, E. G., buys swamp lands, 63
Hollister, Castle, and Co., seed farm, 243
Home Department. *See* U. S. Department of Interior
Homestead Act, 16; claims under, 12, 65, 68; raises tax problem, 23; Minnesotans' attitude toward, 64; procedure under, 64, 65; provisions, 64, 67, 173; amendments, 66; irregularities under, 67, 272; land distributed under, 78
Honeyman and Andyke, plow factory, 126
Hopkins, Daniel, horse raiser, 191
Hops, 186, 241
Horses, scarcity, 6; used for threshing, 122, 127–129, 141, 142; numbers, 147, 193, 199, 200, 291; breeds and breeding, 200; diseases, 202, remedies, 291; stealing, 202; prices, 291. *See also* Plows
Horton and Case, cheese factory, 211
Housekeeping, on frontier, 83–92
Houston, wheat prices, 287
Houston County, driftless area, 32; wheat, 286, 289
Howard, H. C., machine agent, 236, 282
Hoyt, A. S., invents twine binder, 149
Hubbard Harvester Co., 161
Hungarian grass, 297
Hurlburt, Joseph, Methodist preacher, 103
Husking pins, 280
Hutchinson, Moses, dairyman, 220

Iberia, farmers' meeting place, 111
Immigration, 265; promotion by newspapers, 5, 29, by railroads, 75, 76; during war, 12; following Homestead Act, 64; literature, 76
Immigrant reception houses, 76
Implements and machines, values, 18, 21, 130, 146, 147, 163, 164, 286; effects on agriculture, 21, 27, 120, 130; early, 120–123, 126; imported, 123, 124, 130, 131; Minnesota agents: 124, 125, 135, 161, 163, 236, competition, 125, 132, 150, complaints against, 130,

collection difficulties, 135, 151–153, 282, 284, repair machines, 153; freight charges, 125, 149; Minnesota factories, 130, 139, 140, 146, 148, 158–163, 283, 285; use increased by labor shortages, 131; exhibited, 133, 134, 140, 144–146, 247, 250, 283; credit buying, 135, 137; care, 137. *See also* various implements and machines
Independent Farmer and Fireside Companion, 12
Indian treaties, Chippewa: *1837*, 43, *1854*, 53; Sioux: *1837*, 43, 47, *1851*, 47; Sioux half-breed, *1849*, 270
Insurance, agents, 22; fire, 22, 23; farmers' companies, 23, 266
Interest rates, 22, 52, 137, 153, 264, 282
Internal improvement lands, 61; distributed to *1878*, 78; act regulating disposal, 271
Irish settlers, 5

Jackson, Mitchell Y., farmer, 252
Jackson, land office, 78
Jackson County, Roche estate, 119, 276, 277, 292
Janesville, cattle, 203
Jenkins, Sylvanus, raises wheat, 144
Jensen, Hans Peter, in co-operative movement, 219, 220
Johnson, Leonard, horse raiser, 200, 258
Johnston, L. H., invents self-rake, 134
Jones, D. C., machine agent, 145
Jones, John A., farmer, 80, 81, 86
Jones, William Ashley, surveyor, 47
Jones, W. H., machine agent, 161
Jordan, Thomas, machine agent, 153
Judson, R. C., stock raiser, 258

Kandiyohi County, flax, 275
Kaposia, corn growing, 224
Kelley, Oliver H., 247; on labor shortage, 12, on implements, 140, 148
Kemp, Rev. B. A., 104
Kennedy, Mrs. Duncan, 101
Kennedy, John S., railroad bonds, 75
Kerosene lamps, 84, 93
King, William S., in political contest, 45; stock raiser, 197, 203, 204, 235, 254, 258
Kingston, ginseng agency, 222
Kuhlmann, Charles B., 172

La Crescent, railroad, 72
La Crosse (Wis.), railroad, 72
Labor, shortages, 12, 101, 131, 132, 182, 265; wages, 12, 127, 183, 281, 289; imported, 182
Lac qui Parle, livestock, 188

INDEX

Lac qui Parle County, fairs, 254
Lac qui Parle County Agricultural Society, 254
Lake City, wheat buyers' pool, 287
Lake City Leader, 137
Lake Crystal, cheese factory, 293
Lake Superior and Mississippi (Northern Pacific) Railroad, construction, 73, 176; land sales, 75, prices, 77; issues land exploration tickets, 76; freight rates, 179
Lamb, Thomas, pork dealer, 195
Land claims. *See* Claims
Land Grant College Act, 16
Land grants, railroad, 63, 65, 72–74, 78, 273
Land offices and officers, 43; Minnesota, 14, 43, 45, 46, 47, 49, 54, 58, 60, 66, 67, 78, 167, 173, 220, 270; importance, 44, 45, 269; move with settlement, 77
Land warrants and scrip, Indian and half-breed, 42, 53, 54; soldiers', 42, 53, 54, 60, 66, 68, 271; agricultural college, 42, 57, 67, 68, 272; prices, 46, 52, 53, 63; speculation, 42, 53, 54, 57, 67, 68; Virginia commutation, 54; land distributed through, 78, 272
Lands, prices, 9, 59, 60, 63, 135, 272. *See also* Farms; Public lands; Speculation; State lands
Langdon, butter and cheese factory, 213, 214
Laraway, Perrine, and Co., plow factory, 140
Larpenteur, Auguste L., farmer, 6
Larpenteur, Charles N., farmer, 237
Larpenteur, Eugene N., farmer, 232
Larpenteur, E. L., stock raiser, 249
Larsen, Gilbert I., 167
Larson, Nels, wheat farmer, 176
Larssen, Edward, legislator, 173
Le Sueur County, traction engine, 155
Leaming, Alonzo, plow factory, 138, 139
Leavenworth, farmers' meeting place, 111
Leech, Samuel, land officer, 45
Leland, C. F., and R. L. Hall, starch factory, 233
Lennon, J. G., stock raiser, 249
Leyde, William, invents thresher, 285
Libby, Mark F., raises hay, 238
Lighting, farmhouses, 84, 94, 274
Lightning rods, salesmen, 22
Lincoln County, wheat prices, 167
Litchfield, land office, 78; farmers' meeting, 173
Little Canada, dairying, 209
Livestock, runs at large, 7, 206; values, 11, 18, 193; production, 15, 21; shelters, 97, 188, *see also* Barns, Stables;

development, 188–206; imported, 188, 190, 191, 290; breeding, 190; transportation costs, 190; prices, 190, 290; exhibited, 197, 200, 205, 245, 247, 249, 250, 256; herd laws, 206; wolf menace, 210. *See also* Cattle; Fences and fencing; Horses; Oxen; Poultry; Sheep; Swine
Long Prairie, dairying, 210
Lowth and Howe, machine factory, 162
Lumber, price, 97
Lutheran church, 3; attitude toward social diversions, 102, 111
Lyon County, dairying, 220

McCloud and Brothers, machine agents, 281
McClung, J. W., 6, 282
McColley, Charles E., 98
McCormick, Cyrus H., reaper, 120, 124
McCormick Harvesting Co., Minnesota agents, 125, 135, 151, 153, 154, 155, 280, 282
McGregors Landing, implement trade, 142
McKenty, Henry, landowner and speculator, 58, 59
McKinley, Rev. William, 103
McKinstry, Azro P., creameryman, 216, 220
McLean, N. C., dairyman, 219, 220
McLeod, Martin, grows potatoes, 226
McLeod County, land claimed under tree act, 71; potato prices, 226; farm machinery, 281
McLeod County Agricultural Society, 248
Man, Albon P., land deed, 74
Mankato, court, 56; implement factories, 140, 283; implement trade, 146, 283
Mankato Record, 229
Mann, T. T., potato grower, 233
Maple sugar and syrup, 241
Marin, William A., 95
Marion, implement trade, 131
Market gardening, 241–243, 297
Markets and marketing, facilities, 3, 6, 8, 19, 166, 229. *See also* various commodities and market towns
Marshall, Gov. William R., denounces speculators, 68; protests reservation sale, 69
Martin County, Christmas observance, 115
Martindale, L., farmer, 142
Marvin, Charles E., dairyman, 216, 220, 260
Masonic lodges, 118
Mechanization. *See* Implements and machinery

307

Meeker, Judge Bradley B., speaker, 247
Meeker County, cattle, 204
Mendota, treaty, 47; railroad, 72
Merrick, George B., 166
Methodist church, attitude toward social diversions, 102, 277; preachers, 103; revivals and camp meetings, 105, 106
Mihin, J. J., farmer, 141, 142
Milk, production statistics, 292
Milk cows, statistics, 207, 294
Milking machines, 156
Miller, John P., imports cattle, 191
Miller, Gov. Stephen, on agricultural college, 17
Millers, influence on wheat development, 172; farmers' complaints against, 172, 173
Millet, 238
Mills, J. C., 12
Milwaukee (Wis.), Minnesota wheat market, 170
Minneapolis, population, *1860*, 10; land office, 58, 60; implement trade, 134, 161, factories, 139, 140, 156, 160, 161, 283, agencies, 161; meat packing, 199; market, 179, 215, 232, 242; flour mills, 179; elevators, 179; shipping, 225; cordage factory, 240; linseed oil factory, 240; fairs, 250, 254, 256, 257; state, 253, 254
Minneapolis and Duluth Railroad, 73
Minneapolis and St. Louis Railroad, 73
Minneapolis Board of Trade, 257
Minneapolis Chamber of Commerce, 179
Minneapolis City Market, 233
Minneapolis Harvester Works, 160
Minneapolis Millers' Association, 287; protests use of wire binders, 149; criticized, 173, 179
Minneapolis Tribune, 161
Minnesota, location, 29; waterways, 29; area, 29, 78; climate, 29–32, 268; growing season, 30, 31; glaciation, 32–35; soils, 32–40; topography, 34; altitudes, 34, 268; vegetation, 35; geographical divisions, 39; admission to Union, 61; area surveyed to *1878*, 78
Minnesota Agricultural and Mechanical Association, 256
Minnesota and Pacific Railroad. *See* St. Paul and Pacific Railroad
Minnesota attorney general, opinions on homestead taxation, 24
Minnesota auditor, orders homesteads assessed, 24; land office commissioner, 62
Minnesota Butter, Cheese, and Dairy Stock Association, meetings, 215, 217, 236, 259, 260

Minnesota Central Railroad, 72
Minnesota City, lots plowed, 124
Minnesota Dairymen's Association, 214, 215
Minnesota Farmer, 11, 173, 214
Minnesota Farmer and Gardener, 11, 12, 13, 133, 141, 243, 252
Minnesota Farmers' Mutual Fire Insurance Association, 22
Minnesota Fruit Growers' Association, 253
Minnesota Historical Society, farmers' diaries, 15
Minnesota Horticultural Society, 243
Minnesota legislature, agricultural college acts, 16, 17; creates equalization boards, 23; homestead taxation and exemption act, 23; reforms tax law, 24; prescribes maximum railroad rates, 171; agricultural and mechanics' club, 298
Minnesota Linseed Oil Co., 240
Minnesota Monthly, farm journal, 11, 156, 195, 213, 234, 243
Minnesota Pioneer (St. Paul), 5, 47, 165, 225
Minnesota Railroad Commissioner, office established, 171
Minnesota River, settlement, 10, 80; wheat farming in valley, 178
Minnesota State Agricultural Society, 11, 148, 194; efforts for agricultural college, 16; fair grounds, 133, 256, 257; incorporated, 250; fairs, 250, 253–256; finances, 252, 254–256; legislative appropriation, 253, 256
Minnesota State Dairymen's Association, 256, 258
Minnesota State Fair, early fairs, 250, 253, 254, 256, 257; Twin City rivalry, 254, 257; obtains permanent location, 254, 257; buildings, 257
Minnesota State Grange, 22, 23. *See also* Grange
Minnesota State Poultry Association, 235, 258
Minnesota State Wool Growers' Association, 194, 256, 259
Minnesota Stock Breeders' Association, 254, 258
Minnesota Territorial Agricultural Society, fairs, 191, 248–250
Minnesota Valley Railroad. *See* St. Paul and Sioux City Railroad
Minnetonka, Lake, orchards, 243
Mission stations, farming, 3; livestock, 188
Mississippi River, settlement, 10, 80
Mohr and Danber, plow factory, 140

INDEX

Monitor Plow Manufacturing Co., 139, 160
Monk, George Henry, 188
Monticello, ginseng agency, 222; starch factory, 233
Moorhead, railroad, 73, 176
Morrill Land Grant College Act, 17, 62
Morrison, D., landowner, 58
Morrison, George, dairyman, 214
Morristown, syrup factory, 241
Mosquitoes, 8, 86, 264
Moss, Henry L., land agent, 59; sells land warrants, 271
Mower County, 20; early farming, 123; stem rust, 186; creameries, 216; seed nurseries, 243
Mules, numbers, 291

National, The, poultry journal, 235
National Banking Act, *1863*, 14
Neche, wheat farming, 176
Nelson and Gunderson, plow factory, 140
New England, settlers from, 111; observe Christmas, 115
New Prague, traction engine, 155
New Ulm, 146; railroad, 72; land office, 78; implement trade, 183
New Year's, observance, 113, 116
Newspapers, promote immigration, 5, 29; interest in pre-emption law, 46; on speculators, 57, 58; on Homestead Act, 64; denounce machine makers and agents, 130; on diversified farming, 175, 215. *See also* individual newspapers
Newton, Isaac, U. S. commissioner of agriculture, 16
Niemann, Mrs. W. L., 115
Nimocks, W. A., editor, 22
Nininger, agricultural association meeting, 16, 126
Norman County, wheat farming, 176
Norris, James S., pioneer farmer, 3, 124
North Branch, starch factory, 233
Northern Pacific Railroad. *See* Lake Superior and Pacific Railroad
Northfield, railroad, 72; pork trade, 196; library, 276; baseball, 279; portable creamery factory, 294
Northwest Dairymen's Association, 260
Northwestern, The, poultry journal, 235
Norton, Senator Daniel, requests reservation sale, 68
Norwegian settlers, churches, 103; school, 108
Nute, Grace Lee, 88

Oats, prices, 3, 9, 14, 224, 228, 231, 232, 295; production: 4, 229, statistics, 223, 227, 228, 231, 296; exported, 227; varieties, 230, 233; grasshopper losses, 233
Odd Fellows, 118
Odegard, Peter, builds house, 93
Oleomargarine, laws regulating, 220
Olin, Salathiel, exports cattle, 191
Oliver, James, riding plow, 140
Olmsted, S. B., pioneer farmer, 295
Olmsted County, school lands, 63; farming, 175, 178, 184, 186, 286; livestock, 193, 194, 197; cheese factories, 214; hay, 239
Ordinance of *1785*, 41
Osmundson, Osmund, builds house, 93
Osseo, plow factory, 160
Otter Tail County, early threshing, 129; wheat, 186; corn, 231
Owatonna, claim dispute, 56; railroad, 72; implement factories, 146, 162; market, 211, 215; dairying, 220; state fairs, 256, 257, 299
Oxen, scarcity, 6; used for plowing, 121, 264, 283, for threshing, 122, 141, 283; numbers, 147, 200; haul wheat, 167, 286

Paist, William, Grange officer, 154
Panic of *1857*, 9, 11, 58, 59, 63, 165, 250; of *1873*, 18, 73, 178, 250
Patrons of Husbandry. *See* Grange
Peas, production, 4, 186; statistics, 223, 241, 242; varieties, 243
Pembina County, livestock, 189, 202
Pepin, Lake, half-breed tract. *See* Wabasha Reservation
Peterson, Andrew, 214, 289; taxes, 25; reading, 97; makes maple sugar, 241; raises fruit, 243; insurance, 266; farm buildings, 276, 277; threshing costs, 283; makes wine, 298
Pierce, E. W., poultry raiser, 235
Pike, Zebulon M., 188
Pillsbury, Gov. John S., on farmers' machine debts, 158
Pioneer and Democrat (St. Paul), 16, 196, 223
Piper, G. W., exports cattle, 191
Plant diseases, 8, 17, 19, *see also* Blight, Stem rust
Planting, methods, 144, 145. *See also* Implements and machines; various crops
Plowing, methods, 120-122, 141; matches, 246. *See also* Implements and machines; Plows; various crops
Plows, 140, 146; breaking, 121, 124, 126; early, 123, 124, 126; Minnesota fac-

309

tories, 126, 130, 138–140, 160; steam, 126, 156, 285; buggy, 140; gang, 140, 156, 285; prairie and brush breakers, 156; wooden and iron-beam, 156; sulky, 156, 285; prices, 157; cast steel, 280; defects of two-horse, 282; riding, 285. *See also* Implements and machines

Pond, Rev. Gideon H., exhibits apples, 250

Pond, Mrs. Gideon, teaches school, 108

Population, Minnesota, total: *1849*, 4, *1850*, 4, 10, *1860*, 10, *1870*, 17, *1875*, *1880*, 19; distribution, 4, 5, 10, 18, 20, 78, 80; urban, 4, 10, 17, 19, 20, 21; rural, 10, 17, 18, 20, 21, 130. *See also* Minneapolis; St. Anthony; St. Paul; Stillwater

Pork, 9; packing, 15, 162; in frontier diet, 87; prices, 189, 190, 199; transportation costs, 196

Potatoes, production: 3, 4, 225–227, statistics, 223, 227, 228, 231, 296; sown on new land, 6; prices, 8, 9, 14, 224–226, 228, 231, 232, 295; in frontier diet, 87; exported, 225, 226; varieties, 226, 230, 233; yields, 226, 231, 232; damaged by Colorado beetle, 229, 230, 296, by grasshoppers, 233

Poultry, prices, 13, 14, 235; raising, 234–236; production statistics, 234; care, 234; markets, 234; breeds and breeding, 235, 236, 296; exhibited, 235; leading raisers, associations, and journals, 235; fox menace, 296

Powell, Louis H., 127

Powell, Newell, threshing machine, 127

Prairie du Chien (Wis.), wheat seed from, 165

Prairie fires, 9, 19, 86, 216, 266

Prairies, breaking, 6, 124; early misconceptions, 80

Preachers, frontier, 102, 103, 117; salaries and gifts, 104

Pre-emption, of public lands, legal requirements, 44, 46–50; in Minnesota, 50–60; irregularities, 51, 52, 75

Pre-emption acts, *1841*, 41, 46–49; *1854*, 49, 50

Presbyterian church, 103

Price, James T., raises clover, 239

Prices. *See* various commodities

Prince, John S., agricultural society officer, 16

Public buildings lands, 62; distributed to *1878*, 78

Public lands, administration, 41–44; legislation, 41, 42, 46, 49, 64, 66, 67, 69; squatters, 41, 50, 55; surveys, 42, 43, 47, 78; ceded by Indians, 43, 47, 53, 270, *see also* Indian treaties; sales, 45, 60, 78. *See also* General Land Office; Homestead Act; Land offices and officers; Land warrants and scrip; Preemption acts; Speculation; State lands; Timber Culture Act

Pumps, 85

Quist, P. P., reaper, 135

Ruddock, Rev. Charles A., patents harvester attachment, 150

Railroad and Warehouse Commissioners, Board of, 173

Railroads, 5; land grants, 63, 65, 72–74, 78, 273; construction, 72, 73, 176, 178; finances, 74, 75; promote immigration, 75, 76; encourage large farms, 75, 273; land prices, 77, 273; excursions, 104, 106; build elevators, 169; farmers' complaints, 171, 172, 287; act regulating, 173; influence on wheat production, 175; squatters on lands, 273; refrigerator cars, 293. *See also* Elevators; Freight rates; individual railroads

Rakes, hand, 122; revolving, 146; sulky, 146, 156

Ramsdell, D. W., and Co., seed dealers, 230

Ramsey, Alexander, governor, 17; senator, 68; requests reservation sale, 68; speaker, 247

Ramsey County, number of farms, *1850*, 4; improved land, *1880*, 20; early threshing, 127; livestock, 191, 192, 200, 203; hay, 237; market gardening, 242, 249; fairs, 252

Ramsey County Agricultural Society, 247

Reading materials, farmers', 95–97, 276, 277

Reapers, makes used in Minnesota, 123–125, 131–135, 151, 156, 160, 161; Minnesota factories, 130, 133, 134, 151, 158–160, 285; imported, 131; handrake, 131, 132, 133; self-rake, 131, 132, 133, 284; combined with mowers, 132, 133; trials, 133, 150, 246, 282, 284, 285; headers and droppers, 134; prices, 135, 149, 151, 157, 282; self-binding, 148–151, 283, 284; exhibited, 150. *See also* Implements and machines

Recreation. *See* Social life

Red River Valley, 288; soils, 39; wheat farming, 39, 176–178; railroad lands, 75; water problem, 85; social life, 102;

INDEX

threshers, 163; bonanza farms, 176; elevator and flour mill, 176; land values, 178; grasshoppers, 181; altitude, 268; gang plows, 285

Red Rock, 103; camp meetings, 106; early farming, 120

Red Wing, land office, 53, 56, 57, 60; camp meeting, 106; state fair, 253; Hamline University, 278; wages, 281

Redtop, 238

Redwood County, taxes, 267; bonanza farms, 273

Redwood Falls, land office, 78; dairying, 220

Reeves, Charles M., swine raiser, 197

Religion, rivalry between sects, 103. *See also* Churches; individual churches

Remedies, home, 90–92

Renville, livestock, 188

Revivals, 105

Reynolds, Judge Reuben, land officer, 45

Rhodes, John, 18

Rice, production, 223

Rice, Edmund, railroad mortgage, 74

Rice, W. C., dairyman, 220

Rice County, school lands, 63; church meeting, 103; gristmill, 168; livestock, 192; nurseries, 243; insurance company, 267; wheat, 286

Richardson, C. W., cheese factory superintendent, 211

Richardson, F. A., speaker, 208

Robertson, Daniel A., editor, 11, 243; heads horticultural group, 253, 298

Robinson, Edward V., 10, 34, 37, 39

Roche, Owen H., estate, 119, 276, 277; herd, 292

Rochester, 18, 24; railroad, 72; social life, 104; plow factory, 140; wages, 183; livestock, 191, 200; dairy meetings, 215, 259, 260; dairying, 220; state fairs, 254, 256

Rock County, threshing, 283

Rockford, ginseng agency, 222

Rockwood, B. L., pioneer farmer, 121

Rohrer, Daniel, hay contract, 237

Roosevelt, James A., railroad bonds, 75

Ruble, George S., horse raiser, 200

Ruble Brothers, machine agents, 142

Ruggles, Samuel B., railroad deed, 74

Rutabagas, 4; on new land, 6; in frontier diet, 87

Rye, production statistics, 227, 228, 231, 297; prices, 228, 231; raised by German settlers, 229; grasshopper losses, 233

Sabin, Dwight M., heads machine company, 163

St. Anthony, road, 5; population: *1850*, 4, *1860*, 10; sale of site, 45; railroad, 72; plow factory, 138, 140; corn shipped, 225; agricultural society meeting, 247

St. Anthony Agricultural Association, 246

St. Cloud, land office, 60, 67, 78; social life, 104; cattle, 203

St. Cloud Democrat, 67

St. Croix County (Wis.), livestock, 189

St. Croix Falls (Wis.), 103; land office, 45, 270

St. Croix, Lake, settlement, 4

St. Croix River, settlement, 10, 80

St. Croix Union, 50

St. James, railroad, 73

St. Louis (Mo.), Minnesota wheat market, 166, 170

St. Paul, market, 3, 166, 192, 211, 213, 215, 242; population: *1850*, 4, *1860*, 10; road, 5; farm journal, 11; sale of site, 45; claim association meeting, 54; railroads, 72, 73, 176; revival meeting, 105; steamboats, 106; implement trade, 124, 131, 132, 138, 142, 145, 158–162; factories, 139, 160, 162; wholesale trade, 162; flour mill, 162; livestock and meat business, 195, 196; shipping, 223, 227; agricultural society meeting, 248; fairs, 250, state, 254–257; dairy meetings, 258; schools, 278; Fourth celebration, 279

St. Paul and Chicago Railroad, construction, 72; swamp land grant, 73

St. Paul and Duluth Railroad, swamp land grant, 73

St. Paul and Pacific Railroad, 176; construction, 72, 73; mortgages lands, 74; mortgages foreclosed, 74, 75; value of bonds, 75; land prices, 77, 273

St. Paul and St. Croix Steamboat Co., 106

St. Paul and Sioux City Railroad, construction, 72, 73; land prices, 77

St. Paul Chamber of Commerce, 173, 257

St. Paul Dispatch, 257

St. Paul Fire and Marine Insurance Co., 22

St. Paul Harvester Works, 158–160, 285

St. Paul Market, 238

St. Paul, Minneapolis, and Manitoba Railroad, buys St. Paul and Pacific property, 74

St. Paul Plow Works, 160

St. Paul Weekly Pioneer, 57

St. Peter, land office, 60, officers, 68; railroad, 72; livestock, 191; pork trade, 196; butter market, 211; ginseng depot, 223; farmers' club, 229; implement trade, 283

311

St. Peter Statesman, 192
Saline lands, 61, 62; distributed to *1878*, 78
Saloons, in frontier life, 110
Sandy Lake, livestock at post, 188
Sanitation, frontier, 91; later improvements, 94
Sargeant, M. Wheeler, 55
Sauk Centre, social life, 104
Sauk Rapids, land office, 49
Sauk River Valley, settlers on unsurveyed lands, 49
Sausage manufacturing, 199
Scandia, Fourth celebration, 114
Scandinavian settlers, 5; attitude toward social diversions, 111; observe Christmas, 115
Schafer, Joseph, 41
Scherffius, P., poultry raiser, 235
Schiedlen, Bell, and Siedle, cordage factory, 240
School lands, 61, 272; sales, 63, 78
Schools, 108–110, 278; taxes, 23; social aspects, 107, 110, 115; teachers, 108, 109
Scotch settlers, 5
Scott County, soil, 138
Scrip. *See* Land warrants and scrip
Seed dealers, malpractices, 230
Seed farms, 243
Seeders, 146, 162
Separators, made in Minnesota, 163
Settlement, distribution, 4, 5, 10, 18, 20, 78, 80. *See also* population
Settlers' and land buyers' guides, 46
Sewing machines, 276
Seymour, C. M., machine company officer, 163
Seymour, Sabin, and Co., machine factory, 162, 163, 286
Shakopee, 15; wheat market, 166
Sheep, production during war, 15; wool yields, 192; imported, 192, 193; numbers, 192, 193, 194, 291; breeds and breeding, 193; diseases, 194; dog menace, 194, 259, 291. *See also* Wool
Sherburne County, speculation, 271
Sherwin, C. A., farmer, 224
Shingles, prices, 97, 98
Sibley, Henry H., speaker, 16, 126, 176, 249; bids for claimants of St. Paul site, 45
Sibley County, soil, 138
Silver, scarcity during war, 13
Sioux Falls (S. D.), railroad, 73
Sioux Indian Reservation, opened to preemption, 68; sale: 68, settlers protest, 69
Sioux Indians, removed from state, 68.

See also Indian treaties; Sioux Indian Reservation; Wabasha Reservation
Sioux Outbreak, *1862*, 12, 68, 89, 176
Skinner, G. W., acts for settlers, 48
Sleepy Eye, sod houses, 83, 93; Fourth celebration, 101
Sletten, Paul C., land officer, 44
Slotte, O. E., farmer, 146
Smith, B. M., farmer, 131
Smith, Mrs. C. A., early settler, 102
Smith, David, blacksmith, 123
Smith, George H., cattle raiser, 203
Smith, Henry A., farmer, 114
Smith, Truman, gardener, 243
Snyder, C. L., plow factory, 140
Soapmaking, 87, 275
Social life, house raisings, 81, 101; visiting, 100, 277; husking bees and logrollings, 101; dancing, 101, 102, 111, 112; holidays, 101, 111, 113–116, 279; singing, 102; role of church, 102–107, fair, 107, store, 107, 108, school, 107, 110, 115, saloon, 110, blacksmith shop, 111, mill, 111, Grange, 117, 118, fraternal orders, 118; games, 102, 111, 112, 279; sleigh rides, 104, 111; picnics, 104, 111, 114; revivals and camp meetings, 105, 107; skating, 111; baseball, 111, 279; weddings and funerals, 113, 116, 117
Songs, early popular, 102
Sorghum, 186; production, 15, 240, 241
Southern Minnesota Railroad, construction, 72, 73; land grants, 73, 74; deeds lands, 74; land prices, 77
Southern Minnesota Stock Breeders' Association, 258
Spearin, S. B., horse raiser, 200
Speculation, land, 9, 42, 53–59, 67–69, 271; railroad securities, 18; land warrants, 42, 53, 54, 57, 67, 68; meetings opposing, 54, 57
Squatters, on public lands, 41, 50, 55
Squires, Thomas, market gardener, 242
Stables, straw, 97
Starch factories, 232
State lands, 61–63. *See also* Agricultural college lands; Internal improvement lands; Public buildings lands; Saline lands; School lands; Swamp lands; University lands
Steamboats, excursions, 104, 106; commodities shipped by, 127, 166, 226
Stearns County, 20; farming, 18; soldiers' homesteads, 67; corn, 225
Steele County, butter, 208
Stem rust, 18, 186, 187
Stenbakken, Hans O., house, 93

INDEX

Stevens, John H., editor, 11; president proposed agricultural college, 16; imports cattle, 190, 191; activities in agricultural groups, 229, 247, 249, 253
"Stevens' Academy," proposed school at Glencoe, 17
Stewart, T. R., farmer, 5, 7
Stillwater, population: *1850*, 4, *1860*, 10; sale of site, 45; land office, 45, 46, 58, 60; implement factory, 162, 163; pork trade, 196; altitude, 268
Stillwater and St. Paul Railroad, 73
Stinson, James, landowner, 58
Stores, country, social aspects, 107, 108; described, 108, 209
Strong and Miller, packers, 196
Sugar, prices, 14, 275
Sunrise, land office, 46
Superior, Lake, origin, 33; altitude, 34
Surveys, of public lands, 42, 43, 47, 78
Swamp lands, 61, 62; granted to railroads, 73; distributed to *1878*, 78
Swedish settlers, 102, 103
Swine, production: during war, 15, statistics, 195; killing and marketing, 196, 197; exported, 197; breeds and breeding, 197-199; prices, 197, 199. *See also* Hogs; Livestock
Swiss settlers, 5; in cheese industry, 219

Taylor's Falls, land office, 46, 78
Taxes, 23-25, 267, 278
Tea, prices, 14; in frontier diet, 87
Teachers, salaries, 278
Teeter, Michael, farmer, 114
Temple and Beaupre, machine agents, 132
Thanksgiving, observance, 113, 114
Theater, attitude toward, 111, 112
Thompson, Horace, railroad mortgage, 74
Thompson, Ole, wheat farmer, 176
Thompson, Peder, claim jumped, 55
Thompson, T. A., Grange grand lecturer, 154
Thorne, Mrs. Martha, early settler, 89, 275
Threshing, early methods, 121-122, 127-129; charges, 127, 142, 155, 184, 283; later methods, *see* Threshers
Threshers, steam, 23, 141, 144, 155; horsepower, 127-129, 141, 142, 155; makes used in Minnesota, 127, 128, 142-144, 155, 162, 163; prices, 127, 144, 155, 157, 163, 238; imported, 131; exhibited, 144; Minnesota factories, 162, 163. *See also* Implements and machines

Thurston, J. M., dairyman, 220
Tilden, Samuel J., railroad mortgage, 74
Timber Culture Act, 69-71; land distributed under, 78
Timothy, 236, 237, 239, 297
Tobacco, production, 15, 186, 241, 294, 297
Townships, taxes, 23; plats, 43
Tractors, steam, 155, 156, 285
Transportation, early lack, 18, 166; development in *1870's*, 19; charges, *see* Freight rates. *See also* Railroads; Steamboats
Traverse des Sioux, treaty, 47
Traverse, Lake, wheat raised, 165
Trees, planted under Timber Culture Act, 70; under state act, 71; county bounties, 273
Turrell, O. B., farmer, 273
Twin Cities, cattle market and slaughtering center, 206; rivalry over state fair, 254, 257
Twine binders, 148, 149-151, 284

Ullman, Mrs. Joseph, 113
U. S. Department of Agriculture, established, 16, 249
U. S. Department of the Interior (Home Department), land office under, 42
U. S. Treasury Department, land office under, 42
University lands, 62; distributed to *1878*, 78
University of Minnesota, potato experiments, 233; agricultural school, 265, 266
Upham, Warren, geologist, 35

Vaccination, 90
Van Cleve, H. P., dairyman, 210
Van Dusen, G. W., dairyman, 220
Van Styke, W. A., butter dealer, 214
Van Voorhes, Abraham, land officer, 45
Veal, prices, 9
Vegetables, 4. *See also* Beans; Market gardening; Peas
Viola Farmers' Club, 296

Wabasha County, wheat, 175, 286; livestock, 192, 195, 202
Wabasha Reservation, treaty for cession, 46; surveyed, 53
Wages. *See* labor
Wagons, 121, 146, 157
Wakefield, Warren, early settler, 88
Waseca, railroad, 72; cattle ordinance, 205, 206
Waseca County, taxes, 24; claim dispute, 56; fair, 298

Waseca County Horse Thief Detectives, 202, 292
Washington County, early farming, 3, 4; number of farms, *1850*, 4; improved land, *1880*, 20; insurance company, 23; school lands, 63; threshing, 127; livestock, 189, 195, 202; market gardening, 241; fairs, 246, 285; speculation, 271; Dalrymple farm, 288
Wasioja, wheat profits, 184
Watab, 246; railroad, 72
Water, on farms, 85, 94, 274
Watertown, Swedish settlers, 102; ginseng agency, 228
Watson, Robert, buys school lands, 63
Watson and Eastman, butter dealers, 208
Way, Mrs. G. M., early settler, 86
Weeks, Mrs. Mary, early settler, 88
Wells and Smith, plow factory, 138, 139
Wells (Minn.), creamery, 214, 293; cheese factory, 293
Wells, drilling, 129, 146, 281
Western Farm and Village Association, 124
Wheat and wheat farming, early, 12, 13, 165, 166; during war, 12–15; prices, 13, 14, 17, 135, 166, 167, 169, 175, 178, 184, 265, 286–290; diseases and pests, 17, 18, 186, 187; production statistics, 21, 166, 175, 178, 186, 288; threshing, 122, 127–129, *see also* Threshers; planting, 145; seed, 165; rise and decline of specialized, 165–187, 227; spring, 165, 166, 178, 288; exported, 165, 166, 287; winter, 165, 180, 288; freight charges, 166, 167; markets and marketing, 166–170, 175, 176, 179, *see also* individual towns; weighing, grading, and inspecting, 170, 171, 173, 174, 287; buyers' pools, 171, 287; factors influencing, 172, 175, 185; land in, 175, 178, 289; bonanza farms, 176, 273; yields, 178, 180, 186, 290; varieties, 180, 181, 288; equipment, 183, *see also* Cradles, Implements and machines, Reapers, Threshers; profits and losses, 183–185, 289; movement north and west, 187. *See also* Elevators; Farms; Red River Valley
White, Edward, contractor, 17
White, Milo, wheat buyer, 167
Whiting, Lewis, farmer, 129
Whiting, Lurett, farmer, 121, 129
Whitney, Charles S., land officer, 45
Whitney, John H., invents wire binder, 148
Whittier, C. F., dairy group officer, 258
Wilcox, A. H., buys swamp lands, 63

Wilcox, N. Green, land officer, 45
Williams, Alan K., binder factory, 148
Williams, J. M., binder factory, 148
Willoughby, John, farmer, 6
Wilson, George P., poultry raiser, 235
Wiltse, Henry A., surveyor, 269
Windmills, 157
Windom, William, aids reservation settlers, 68
Wine, production, 223, 298
Winnebago (Winnebago City), land office, 66; railroad, 72; creamery, 216; implement trade, 283
Winnebago City Homestead, 66
Winnebago Indians, 237
Winnowers, 128
Winona, lyceum, 55; land office, 58, 60; social life, 104; early farming, 122; fanning mill, 122; implement trade, 131; plow factory, 140, 281; market, 165, 170, 172; pork trade, 196; fairs, 200, state, 253, 254; oats shipped, 227; wheat prices, 286
Winona and St. Peter Railroad, construction, 72; land prices, 77; sued, 171, 172
Winona Carriage Works, 146
Winona County, school lands, 63; wheat, 175, 286
Winona County Poultry Association, 235, 258
Winona, Mankato, and New Ulm Railroad, 73
Winona Republican, 229
Winsted, German settlers, 116; Catholic church, 278
Wire, prices, 284
Wire binders, 148, 149
Wisconsin, interest rates, 22
Withington, Charles B., invents self-binder, 149
Wollgate, ———, horse raiser, 200
Women, role on frontier, 85, 87–92, 275; exhibits at fair, 250
Wood, Walter A., machine agent, 149
Woodley and Berry, plow factory, 138
Wool, prices, 15, 192, 194, 291; production, 193; exported, 193, 291
Worthington, railroad, 73; land office, 78; social life, 104
Worthington Methodist Church, 104
Wright County, market gardening, 242

Yellow Medicine County, taxes, 267
Young, William B., and Co., plow factory, 140
Young America Mutual Insurance Co., 266

www.ingramcontent.com/pod-product-compliance
Lightning Source LLC
Chambersburg PA
CBHW032017230426
43671CB00005B/119